MW01252905

COCAINE TRAFFICKING IN LATIN AMERICA

Global Security in a Changing World

Series Editor: *Professor Nana K. Poku, John Ferguson Professor, Department of Peace Studies, University of Bradford, UK*

Globalisation is changing the world dramatically, and a very public debate is taking place about the form, extent and significance of these changes. At the centre of this debate lie conflicting claims about the forces and processes shaping security. As a result, notions of inequality, poverty and the cultural realm of identity politics have all surfaced alongside terrorism, environmental changes and bio-medical weapons as essential features of the contemporary global political landscape. In this sense, the debate on globalisation calls for a fundamental shift from a status quo political reality to one that dislodges states as the primary referent, and instead sees states as a means and not the end to various security issues, ranging from individual security to international terrorism. More importantly, centred at the cognitive stage of thought, it is also a move towards conceiving the concept of insecurity in terms of change.

The series attempts to address this imbalance by encouraging a robust and multi-disciplinary assessment of the asymmetrical nature of globalisation. Scholarship is sought from areas such as: global governance, poverty and insecurity, development, civil society, religion, terrorism and globalisation.

Other titles in this series:

A Decade of Human Security
Global Governance and New Multilateralisms
Edited by Sandra J. MacLean, David R. Black and Timothy M. Shaw
978-0-7546-4773-7

Non-Traditional Security in Asia
Dilemmas in Securitization
Edited by Mely Caballero-Anthony, Ralf Emmers and Amitav Acharya
978-0-7546-4701-0

Cocaine Trafficking in Latin America
EU and US Policy Responses

SAYAKA FUKUMI

ASHGATE

Published by
Ashgate Publishing Limited
Gower House
Croft Road
Aldershot
Hampshire GU11 3HR
England

Ashgate Publishing Company
Suite 420
101 Cherry Street
Burlington, VT 05401-4405
USA

Ashgate website: http://www.ashgate.com

British Library Cataloguing in Publication Data
Fukumi, Sayaka
   Cocaine trafficking in Latin America : EU and US policy
   responses. - (Global security in a changing world)
   1. Cocaine industry - South America 2. Drug control - South
   America 3. Drug control - European Union countries 4. Drug
   control - United States 5. Drug control - International
   cooperation
   I. Title
   363.4'5'098

Library of Congress Cataloging-in-Publication Data
Fukumi, Sayaka, 1973-
   Cocaine trafficking in Latin America : EU and US policy responses / by Sayaka Fukumi.
      p. cm.
   Includes bibliographical references and index.
   ISBN 978-0-7546-7043-8 (alk. paper)
 1. Drug control--European Union countries. 2. Drug control--United States. 3. Transnational crime--Government policy--European Union countries. 4. Transnational crime--Government policy--United States. 5. National security--European Union countries. 6. National security--United States. 7. Cocaine industry--Latin America. 8. Drug traffic--Latin America. I. Title.

   HV5840.E85F85 2007
   363.45098--dc22

2007023685

ISBN 978-0-7546-7043-8

Printed and bound in Great Britain by TJ International Ltd, Padstow, Cornwall.

Contents

Acknowledgements

I would like to thank my colleagues and friends for their unwavering support and trust in me while completing this project. Honest opinions and suggestions have been invaluable. My particular gratitude to Dr Wyn Rees and Dr Sue Pryce for their invaluable advice and encouragement whilst preparing the manuscript for publication.

I am also very grateful to those who agreed to conduct interviews with me and who spared their precious time for my research: K.H. Vogel of the European Commission, J. Vos of the European Council, E.H. Moguel Flores of the Mexican Ministry of Foreign Affairs, and officials at the Embassy of Bolivia (Brussels), the Embassies of Colombia (Brussels, London, and Washington DC), the Embassies of Mexico (Brussels and Washington DC), the European Commission, the EU Delegation to the United States, the Latin America Working Group, the Organization of American States, the United States Department of State, the United States Agency for International Development, the United States Office of National Drug Control Policy, and the United States Mission to the European Union. The information they gathered has provided great insights and was an inspiration for me to pursue my research. I treasure every interview that I have conducted. I would also like to acknowledge special thanks to Dr Joseph Vorbach and Captain Michael Chaplain whose assistance enabled me to conduct fruitful interviews at the ONDCP.

In addition to people above, I am very grateful to the editors at Ashgate Publishing who gave me this opportunity and are patient with my slow progress.

Last but not least, I am much obliged to my family who supported me all the way through this project. I hope that this will make them proud and will be a comfort to the sacrifice they made.

Introduction

Transnational organised crimes (TOCs), particularly drug trafficking, began to be recognised as serious security threats as globalisation expanded in the post-Cold War era. Furthermore, the linkage between terrorist groups and TOCs is considered to have the potential to be a greater threat to the people, states and the international community after the terrorist attacks on 11 September 2001. This alliance between terrorist groups and criminal organisations is, to some extent, the link between violence and financial power. TOCs can be lucrative businesses due to their illicit nature. One such business is drug trafficking.

Over a decade after the collapse of the communist bloc, the expansion of market economies and the process of globalisation technology in the spheres of transport systems and the Internet have rapidly progressed. Globalisation in various areas has led to the increase in cross-border transactions in business, combined with the movement of people this has brought new opportunities to the world for the pursuit of wealth through international trade. As legal economic activities flourish in the international markets, illegal economic activities have also expanded at the global level.

Following such international trends, transnational organised crime began to be recognised as a new security issue after the dissolution of the communist threat. Large illegal industries developed in international markets. Organised crime and drug trafficking per se are not new phenomena, but what is striking about transnational organised crime since the 1990s is that criminal organisations have developed vast networks connecting different parts of the world.[1] The international networks created by criminal organisations make it possible to distribute illicit commodities on a world-wide basis. The development of transnational organised crime is closely associated with the growth of these international markets.[2] The globalisation of markets expands the opportunities for illicit business, particularly for narcotics, because the demand for drugs is far greater now than it was in the early twentieth century when the League of Nations adopted drug prohibition.[3] Most important of

---

1   Strange, S., *The Retreat of the State: The Diffusion of Power in the World Economy*, 1996, Cambridge: Cambridge University Press, p. 111.

2   Findley, M., *The Globalisation of Crime: Understanding Transitional Relationships in Context*, 1999, Cambridge: Cambridge University Press, p. 76.

3   The European states in particular have experienced a sharp increase of drug abuse, according to a report from the European Monitoring Centre for Drugs and Drug Addiction in 2001. The EU estimates the number of cocaine addicts as over 2 million. The 1985 report from the US government estimated that there are a few million cocaine addicts in Latin American States. Strange, *The Retreat of the State*, p. 113; EMCDDA, *Annual Report on the State of the Drugs Problem in the European Union 2001*, Luxembourg: Office for Official Publications of the European Communities; EMCDDA, *Annual Report on the State of the Drugs Problem in the European Union 2000*, Luxembourg: Office for Official Publications of the European

all, the drug problem represents a complex interplay between developed northern hemisphere states and the producer and transit states of the developing south. Economically, drugs are one of the commodities that reflect the very nature of the capitalist economic system – the mechanism of the markets: if there were no demand, there would be no supply. In drug trades, the developing countries are the suppliers of the lucrative finished products to the developed North. Politically, drug trades are believed to be the major financial source to terrorist groups. The incidents on 11 September 2001, and the indication that the Al Qaeda was involved in opium poppy cultivation struck fear into the international community by showing the potential financial power residing in TOCs. Consequently, the development of transnational organised crime generated international attention, and posed new concerns to states. The debate about controlling drugs takes place in the post-Cold War environment of globalisation.

This book will investigate the drug control policies conducted by the United States and the European Union in the Andes, the major cocaine-producing region in Latin America. These two actors are chosen because they possess significant political and economic influence on international politics. This is not to say that their influences are equal; the United States, as a unitary actor, has been the dominant player since 1990. The European Union has been rising as not only an economic actor, but also a political one, through recent integration and enlargement. The amount of resources the United States spends on drug control is enormous. No other state spends a similar amount in an attempt to reduce their country's supply of drugs. Therefore, the European Union, a body for pursuing the collective interests of member states, could only be a comparative actor in drug control.

The aim of the book is to explain why the United States and the European Union take fundamentally different approaches to controlling drugs, although they are aiming at the same goal of reducing cocaine production in, and flow from, the Andes. The United States perceived cocaine trafficking as a national security threat that needed to be eliminated to defend the homeland by the 1980s. On the other hand, in 2005 the European Union perceived cocaine trafficking as a societal security threat that should be curbed through economic and social policies. This EU understanding of cocaine trafficking is formed through its experience of the rapid increase of drug abusers in the 1990s,[4] and was an initial reaction to handle the situation by using social policies. Because of these differing views on cocaine trafficking, the European Union and the United States do not agree about the most effective approach to drug control.

Communities, pp. 19–20; Carneiro, L., *Report: Transnational Organised Crime*, PE 301.417, RRI435185EN.doc, 15 March 2001, Luxembourg: Office for Official Publications of the European Communities , p. 3; and US Department of State, *International Narcotics Control Strategy Report*, 1985, Washington DC: US Department of State.

4   According to the report, the UK, Greece and Belgium registered 50–60% increase in drug use in less than 5 years. In addition, "Of Europe's two million cocaine consumers, Spain and Germany account for some 500,000 and Italy 300,000". The amount of drug abuse in the EU member states has been increasing and has reached about 20–25% of the European adult population by 2001. (The number of addicts includes heroin and cocaine as well as other drugs.) Carneiro, op cit.

There are two approaches to drug control under the current drug prohibition regime. One is demand reduction and the other is supply reduction. It is arguable which approach is more effective in reducing the size of the drug industry. The European Union emphasises the importance of demand reduction. It is attempting to reduce the amount of drugs consumed by the domestic population. In theory, a capitalist market requires both demand and supply of the commodity to function, and demand has particular significance if the market is to exist. An EU official acknowledges that demand control though rehabilitation, prevention and deterrence is the most effective way to control the drug market but it is almost impossible to stop all drug abusers.[5]

Supply reduction, on the other hand, is a measure the United States strongly supports. It intends to reduce the flow of drugs from producer states. To intercept and destroy cocaine before it reaches Europe and the United States is the main aim of this policy. Moreover, supply reduction is easier to measure through seizures of drugs and crackdowns on trafficking organisations.

The differences between these two actors' policies come from their perception of cocaine trafficking and their understanding of its nature. The different perceptions to cocaine trafficking in the European Union and the United States are constructed on their geographical, historical and cultural backgrounds and their experiences with cocaine problems. The impact of drug problems is unique to each actor as cocaine trafficking may affect various fields to varying degrees, for example economic, political and social fields. The degree of impact depends on each actor's weakness in their political, economic and social integrity. This differentiates non-traditional security threats from traditional security threats (namely wars), which affect all victims in a similarly destructive manner. Cocaine trafficking is a feature of transnational organised crimes that is regarded as a non-traditional security threat. 'Different impacts on different actors' is one of the major characteristics of a non-traditional security threat.

The following sections will provide a background on Latin American cocaine trafficking and an overview of this book. Firstly, it will concern itself with existing literature regarding this field of research, namely cocaine trafficking and EU and US drug control policy. Secondly, the nature of Andean cocaine trafficking, including a historical background of coca cultivation, will be explained. Thirdly, it will deliver an overview of the framework of the book.

Literature on US and European Drug Trafficking

This book builds upon an existing literature in the field of drug trafficking. There is a body of work by international scholars on the subject of transnational organised crime and cocaine trafficking. This includes the work of Lupsha, Williams, and Dziedzic, who argue that the threat posed by the activities of transnational criminal organisations are of a political-economic nature, but their analysis focuses on

---

5   Interview with an official at the European Commission in Brussels on 15 January 2003.

the impact of TOCs on regional and international security.[6] Others, such as Toro, examine the internal disturbances caused by the US counter-narcotics policy from the socio-economic and political point of view.[7] Tullis examines the consequences of drugs trafficking in nine major 'drug-producing countries' in different parts of the world from a socio-economic perspective.[8] As for the specific studies on cocaine trafficking in Latin America, Lee III and Clawson investigate the power of drug cartels in the Andean countries, focusing on their economic power and influence over society.[9] In addition, Painter provides a well-researched study of the Bolivian coca industry.[10] What makes this book different is that it is comparing and accounting for the different policies of the United States and the European Union towards cocaine trafficking. This book will consider the securitisation of cocaine trafficking and its implications for EU and US drug control policies.

Another body of work explains the European approach to drug control. Estievenart gives a good overview of both internal and external European Union drug control policies, as well as those of some of its member states.[11] Also, the work of Bigo examines the rationale of the European Union's drug control efforts from the perspective of internal security and policing within its member states.[12] As for the drug control efforts of new EU member states, Bogusz and King investigate the impact of the Union's drug control policies on Central European states, particularly the Czech Republic, Hungary and Lithuania.[13] Other literature investigates the development of European drug markets. For example, Zaitch examines the business

---

6   Williams, P., and Savona, E.U., *The United Nations and Transnational Organized Crime*, 1996, Frank Cass: London; Dziedzic, M.J., 'The transnational drug trade and regional security', *Survival*, Vol. XXXI, No. 6, November/December 1989; Lee III, R.W., 'Global Reach: The Threat of International Drug Trafficking', *Current History*, Vol. 94, No. 592, May 1995; Lupsha, P.A., 'Transnational Organized Crime versus the Nation-State', in *Transnational Organized Crime*, Vol. 2, No. 1, Spring 1996; Williams, P., and Black, S., 'Transnational Threat: Drug Trafficking and Weapons Proliferation', *Contemporary Security Policy*, Vol. 15, No. 1, April, 1994; Williams, P., 'Transnational Criminal Organisations and International Security', *Survival*, Vol. 36, No. 1, 1994.

7   Toro, M.C., *Mexico's 'War' on drugs*, 1995, London: Lynne Rienner.

8   Tullis, L. *Unintended Consequences: illegal drugs & drug policies in nine countries*, 1995, Colorado: Lynne Rienner.

9   Clawson, P.L. and Lee III, R.W., *The Andean Cocaine Industry*, 1998, New York: St Martin's Griffin; and Lee III, R.W., *The White Labyrinth: Cocaine & Political Power*, 1989, New Jersey: Transaction Publishers.

10   Painter, J., *Bolivia and Coca: A Study in Dependency*, 1994, London: Lynne Rienner.

11   Estievenart, G. (ed.), *Policies and Strategies to Combat Drugs in Europe*, 1995, London: Martinus Nijhoff Publishers.

12   Bigo, D., 'The European Internal Security Field: States and Rivalries in a Newly Developing Area of Police Intervention', in Anderson, M. and den Boer, M. (eds), *Policing Across National Boundaries*, 1994, London: Pinter.

13   Bogusz, B. and King, M., 'Controlling Drug Trafficking in Central Europe: The Impact of EU Policies in the Czech Republic, Hungary and Lithuania', in Edwards, A. and Gill, P. (eds), *Transnational Organised Crime: Perspectives on Global Security*, 2003, Oxon: Routledge.

networks of Colombian drug traffickers in the Netherlands.[14] On drug control policies against developing drug markets, Dorn, Jepsen and Savona provide case studies of individual European states and the European Union;[15] and Ruggiero and South offer studies of London and Turin.[16] These books are excellent in describing drug problems within the European Union. However, there is little attention to drug control outside the Eurasian continent. Green, who examined British drug control policy, questions the lack of European interest in Africa and Latin America.[17]

There are several interesting pieces of work on American drug policies. For example, US policies and the DEA agents' activities in Latin America are examined by Riley, Menzel, and Malamud-Goti.[18] Menzel, an ex-DEA agent, investigates the US narcotics policies in the Andes based on his experiences and expertise, and Malamud-Goti provides Latin American perspectives on US drug policies. Also, Léons and Sanabria explore Bolivian views on US narco-diplomacy, and Bagley and Walker III examine US narcotic policies in Latin America on a bilateral basis.[19] Carpenter focuses on the negative aspects of US foreign narcotics policy; namely the pursuit of US profits regardless of the consequences in Latin American states.[20] US involvement in Colombian drug control is examined by Crandall through a comparison of the policies of the Clinton and G.W. Bush administrations to support Plan Colombia.[21] This literature provides high quality information and analysis on American policy from Latin American as well as American angles. There is, however, little analysis on alternative approaches to US drug control despite the criticisms, partly because there is not much publicity for the European drug control policy in the United States.

---

14 Zaitch, D., *Trafficking Cocaine: Colombian Drug Entrepreneurs in the Netherlands*, 2002, The Hague: Kluwer Law International.

15 Dorn, N., Jepsen, J., and Savona, E. (eds), *European Drug Policies and Enforcement*, 1996, London: Macmillan.

16 Ruggiero, V. and South, N., *Eurodrugs: drug use, markets and trafficking in Europe*, 1995, London: Routledge.

17 Green, P., *Drugs, Trafficking and Criminal Policy*, 1998, Winchester: Waterside Press.

18 Malamud-Goti, J., *Smoke and Mirrors: The Paradox of the Drug Wars*, 1992, Oxford: Westview Press; Menzel, S.H., *Fire in the Andes: US Foreign Policy and Cocaine Politics in Bolivia and Peru*, 1996, New York: University Press of America; Menzel, S.H., *Cocaine Quagmire: implementing the US anti-drug policy in the north Andes - Colombia*, 1997, Maryland: University Press of America; and Riley, K.J., *Snow Job? The War Against International Cocaine Trafficking*, 1996, New Jersey: Transaction Publishers.

19 Bagley, B.M., and Walker III, W.O. (eds), *Drug trafficking in the Americas*, 1996, Miami: North South Center Press; Léons, M.B. and Sanabria, H. (eds), *Coca, Cocaine, and the Bolivian Reality*, 1997, New York: State University of New York Press.

20 Carpenter, T.G., *Bad Neighbor Policy: Washington's futile war on drugs in Latin America*, 2003, New York: Palgrave.

21 Crandall, R., *Driven by Drugs: U.S. Policy Toward Colombia*, 2002, Boulder: Lynne Rienner.

Cocaine Trafficking as a Manifestation of Transnational Organised Crime

Transnational organised crime includes various illicit businesses, such as money laundering, international human trafficking and drug smuggling. Drug smuggling is the most lucrative business among the illicit economic activities, and it attracts not only criminal organisations but also insurgency groups and terrorist groups.[22] This section will explore the characteristics and operations of cocaine trafficking and the variety of actors involved. This section will also focus on Latin American cocaine trafficking to explain the emergence of cocaine business in the nineteenth century and the development of illicit cocaine trafficking in the twentieth century.

Transnational Organised Crime and Transnational Criminal Organisations

Transnational organised crime is a feature of the international capitalist market economy where the motive is to pursue maximum wealth with minimum risk.[23] It emerged as criminal organisations seized the opportunity to expand their business to the international level using networks established with other criminal organisation in the world. The term 'organised crime', however, has been used since the 1920s. It started as a term to describe problems experienced by the US prohibition of alcohol.[24] The addition of 'transnational' emphasises the internationalised business nature of organised crime.[25] Transnational organised crime can operate as an industry involving the production and distribution of goods and services, such as in the drug industry. It also stretches to include commodities such as the illicit trades in human body parts, arms and toxic waste.[26] In sum, transnational organised crime is any form of illicit international trade.[27]

Transnational criminal organisations are diverse in structure, size, scale, outlook and memberships: there is no single model to describe them, as each is unique in its own way. Even the way in which these organisations operate differs, for example,

22 Matthew, R.A. and Shanbaugh, G.E., 'Sex, Drugs, and Heavy Metal: Transnational Threats and National Vulnerabilities', *Security Dialogue*, Vol. 29, No. 2, June 1998, p. 170.

23 Lupsha, op cit., p. 34; Naylor, 'Mafia, Myths, and Markets', in *Wages of Crime: Black Markets, Illegal Finance, and the Underworld Economy*, 2002, Ithaca: Cornell University Press, p. 3; and Schmid, A.P., The Links between Transnational Organized Crime and Terrorist Crimes', *Transnational Organized Crime*, Vol. 2, No. 4, Winter 1996, p. 43.

24 Woodiwiss, M., 'Crime's Global Reach', in Pearce, F. and Woodiwiss, M. (eds), *Global Crime Connections: Dynamics and Control*, 1993, London: Macmillan, pp. 8–9.

25 Lupsha, op cit., p. 21; and Williams, and Savona, op cit., pp. 4–5.

26 The activities listed by Williams and Savona are: the theft of cultural property; trafficking in arms; illegal gambling; smuggling of illegal migrants; trafficking in women and children for sexual slavery; extortion; violence against the judiciary and journalists; corruption of government and public officials; trafficking in radioactive material; illicit infiltration of licit business; trafficking in body parts; trafficking in endangered species; transnational auto-theft; money laundering; computer-related crimes; and international fraud. Williams, and Savona, op cit., p. 154; and Committee for a Safe Society, *Defining Organized Crime*, 6 April 1996, http://www.alternatives.com/crime2.html (Accessed 6 May 1999).

27 Schmid, op cit., p. 47.

some may be specialised in one operation, such as the Colombian cartels that focus on drug trafficking, and others may be involved in various activities, such as gambling, or the smuggling of several commodities.[28]

Despite the differences among criminal organisations, they share certain characteristics. TOCs often consist of networks of small criminal groups with a division of labour in their business. They rely on co-operation amongst groups to function. These small groups tend to be rooted in a particular community or area and be formed with criminals from the same region or with blood ties, for instance, the Sicilian Mafia and the Russian Mafiya.[29] The level of organisation within and among the criminal groups can vary from a strict hierarchical structure known as a patron-client relationship (partito) to a fluid and dynamic network based one.[30] Firm hierarchical structure provides a solid command system and discipline under the leaders. The loose connections of criminal groups enable the entire business network to function without too much dependence on one group and, thereby, allow the business operation to continue even after crackdowns by law enforcement agencies.[31] Such structures allow transnational criminal organisations to be flexible and highly adaptable to the changes of situation in which they operate.[32]

Criminal organisations are motivated by and operated for economic gain,[33] they will find a business opportunity anywhere as long as it will bring profit, and this is a reason why several transnational criminal organisations operate various businesses.[34] Unlike insurgency groups, transnational criminal organisations do not consider religion, political beliefs and ideology important for their business. They ally with any organisation, such as governments, guerrilla groups, and other criminal organisations. Global illicit markets are functioning on the networks of these governmental and 'non-governmental' connections that transnational criminal organisations have established internationally. For example, Latin American drug traffickers cultivate relationships with Asian criminal organisations to learn know-how from heroin production in Asia for the development of a heroin industry in Latin America.[35] What are important for transnational criminal organisations is business opportunities within the markets. They are willing to make contacts in both legal and illegal foreign organisations and to support the government if it does not

---

28 Williams, and Savona, op cit., p. 12; Williams, op cit., p. 101; and Moore, M.H., 'Organized Crime as a Business Enterprise', in Edelhertz, H. (ed.), *Major Issue in Organized Crime Control*, Symposium Proceedings, 25–26 September 1986, Washington: US Government Printing Office, p. 54.

29 Lupsha, op cit, pp. 22 and 31.

30 Kelly, R.J., 'The Nature of Organized Crime and Its Operations', in Edelhertz, H. (ed.), *Major Issue in Organized Crime Control*, Symposium Proceedings, 25–26 September 1986, Washington: US Government Printing Office, p. 23.

31 Naylor, 'Mafia, Myths, and Markets', p. 38.

32 Williams, op cit., p. 105; and Williams, and Savona, op cit., p. 4.

33 Williams, op cit., p. 108; and Williams, and Savona, op cit., p. 6.

34 Naylor, 'Mafia, Myths, and Markets', p. 3; and Lupsha, op cit., p. 28.

35 Van de Velde, J.R., 'The Growth of Criminal Organizations and Insurgent Groups Abroad due to International Drug Trafficking', *Low Intensity Conflict & Law Enforcement*, Vol. 5, No. 3, Winter 1996, p. 469.

interfere with their business. This is because transnational criminal organisations are underground business corporations, and they require a certain stability[36] to operate their economic activities. Illicit businesses require a permissive environment in which there are minimal law enforcement restrictions. In some cases, transnational criminal organisations support certain regimes and political parties, and even support coups d'état in order to secure non-intervention from the government in their businesses.[37] In other cases, they will 'buy' customs and judicial officials. Corruption is a feature always associated with the operation of transnational organised crime.[38]

Bribery is less acceptable in modern democratic states due to the established law enforcement culture and the norms of the society.[39] Therefore, criminal groups prefer to conduct their business in a state with weak economic and political integration but with a relatively stable social environment.[40] They are seeking opportunities and profits in grey areas of the economy where laws do not restrict their activities. Criminal organisations may operate both illicit and legitimate businesses made possible with money obtained from illicit trades. The tendency of transnational criminal organisations to dominate the markets in which they operate could cause a problem for legitimate corporations because some market strategies criminal organisations employ are impossible for legitimate corporations to operate.[41]

Corruption usually comes hand-in-hand with intimidation.[42] The use of violence by criminal organisations usually does not target ordinary people, but has the specific aim to eliminate rivals. Intimidation and bribery ensure that the operation of criminal groups continues with impunity.[43] Violence for criminal organisations is a tool for

---

36 Criminal organisations are also favourable to law and public order, although this does not imply they respect the laws and public order themselves. The environment in which legal corporations can flourish is the same environment in which illegal businesses can flourish.

37 See below for the example of Latin American cocaine trafficking.

38 Ruggiero, V., 'The *Camorra*: 'Clean' Capital and Organised Crime', in Pearce, F. and Woodiwiss, M. (eds), *Global Crime Connection*, 1993, London: MacMillan, p. 143; and Smith Jr., D. C., 'Some Things That May Be More Important to Understand About Organized Crime Than Cosa Nostra', *University of Florida Law Review*, Vol. 24, No. 1, Fall 1971, p. 22.

39 Godson, R. and Williams, P., 'Strengthening Cooperation Against Transnational Crime', *Survival*, Vol. 40, No. 3, 1998, p. 67; Lupsha, op cit., p. 24; and Williams, op cit, p. 109.

40 Naylor, 'Mafia, Myths, and Markets', p. 4.

41 TCOs can set prices that are too low to make profits by drawing on their resources, so that the legitimate corporations cannot survive in the market. Also, TCOs use market strategies that are often used by legitimate corporations, such as a fancy name for their products and the creation of brand name. Lupsha, op cit., p. 23.

42 Marlts, M.D., 'On Defining "Organized Crime": The Development of a Definition and a Typology', *Crime and Delinquency*, Vol. 22, No. 3, July 1976, p. 341; Blickman, T., 'The Rothschilds of the Mafia on Aruba', *Transnational Organized Crime*, Vol. 3, No. 2, Summer 1997; and 'All this and Drugs', *The Economist*, 13 June 1998, p. 66.

43 For example, two magistrates in Italy, Falcone and Borsellino, were fighting against the Mafia and their lives were under threat by assassination. They were both killed by the Mafiosi. For details, see, for example: Marelli, F., 'Falcone, Borsellino and the Difficult Antimafia Struggle', *OC Newsletter*, May issue 2002, http://members.lycos.co.uk/ocnewsletter/

internal discipline, protection of business and elimination of competition.[44] In addition, due to the vast financial resources at their disposal, transnational criminal organisations are capable of purchasing weapons, hiring assassins and acquiring protection from insurgency groups.[45] Criminal organisations and insurgency groups co-operate only when their interests[46] are compatible. The linkage between criminal organisations and insurgency groups is usually only a 'marriage of convenience'.[47]

The Nature of Latin American Cocaine Trafficking

Although cocaine is classified as an illegal narcotic[48] substance, it was used in various ways in the past, and coca leaves, the raw material for cocaine, have for centuries been associated with social, medical and religious purposes in the Andes. The demand for this prohibited substance has made the Andean cocaine industry grow into the largest industry in Latin America. This section will elucidate the history of coca and cocaine consumption, trace its prohibition in the early 20th century and analyse the nature of the cocaine industry in the Andes.

Coca leaves come from coca bushes, a shrub that lives for about 25 years, and have been chewed in the Andes for over 4,000 years.[49] Coca chewing was limited to those with a prestigious status such as priests until the Inca period. It came to be available more widely among indigenous people because of severe environmental conditions and tenuous food supply.[50] Another way to consume coca leaves is to drink it as tea, which brings a similar physical effect to coca chewing. Coca chewing and drinking mate de coca (coca tea) have the effect of reducing hunger and fatigue, and this has been a necessary means of survival in such harsh conditions. The inhabitants of the altiplano chew and take coca leaves as tea in order to help them live at high

---

SGOC0502/Francesco.html (Accessed 23 June 2002); Siebert, R., 'Living Under Siege: In Memory of Francesca Morvillo', *OC Newsletter*, May issue 2002, http://members.lycos. co.uk/ocnewsletter/SGOC0502/Renate.html (Accessed 23 June 2002).

44 Committee for a Safe Society, op cit.

45 Dziedzic, op cit., p. 534.

46 Criminal groups need public order for their economic and political activities, but the insurgency groups often want to overturn the government and create a new regime that will destabilise the economic and political order.

47 Williams, op cit.

48 In this book, the term 'narcotic' is used as a general term for 'Class A' drugs, cocaine and heroin, although in strict terms, cocaine is not a narcotic in the medical sense. The term narcotic refers to a substance that: 'induces drowsiness, stupor or insensibility. Narcotics include opium and synthesized compounds with morphine-like properties.' Ashton, R., *This is Heroin*, 2002, London: Sanctuary.

49 See Morales, E., *Cocaine: White Gold Rush in Peru*, 1989, Tucson: The University of Arizona Press; and Streatfield, D., *Cocaine: An Unauthorised Biography*, 2001, London: Virgin Publisher.

50 Spedding, A.L., 'The Coca Field as a Total Social Fact', in Léons, M.B. and Sanabria, H. (eds), *Coca, Cocaine and the Bolivian Reality*, 1997, New York: State University of New York Press, pp. 48–51; and Morales, op cit., chapter 1.

altitude. During the colonial era, coca leaves were consumed particularly among heavy-duty workers, such as miners, for both practical and religious reasons.[51]

Coca was (and is) considered to be a valuable commodity and is used as an equivalent of a mechanism of exchange money. Denial of coca culture and destruction of coca fields would affect the economy and the way of life in the altiplano severely. During the Spanish colonisation, workers of the silver mines were paid with coca leaves, although Spanish priests disapproved of the payment by coca because of its linkage to pagan ceremonies.[52] This is partly because indigenous people used for mining demanded leaves as payment and it was essential that the Spanish operated mines with little expense.[53] The significance of coca has not changed. In remote rural areas in which currency does not function, coca has commercial value and can be exchanged as the equivalent of money.

Cocaine was extracted from coca leaves in the mid-1880s by a German scientist, and tested for medical and commercial purposes.[54] At the beginning, cocaine was used for a tropical anaesthetic, therapeutic remedy, cure for catarrh, asthma, hay fever and addiction.[55] It was also widely used in commercial products, such as wine, Coca-Cola, and cigarettes.[56] Coca and cocaine in the late 19th century were profitable legal commodities, and traded internationally.[57] According to Gootenberg, in the early 1900s, Peru was the largest legal coca producer to meet international demand, particularly that from the Untied States.[58] Coca and cocaine were expensive commodities and, hence, involvement in this trade meant an advantageous business position.

---

51 Sanabria, H., *The Coca Boom and Rural Social Change in Bolivia*, 1993, Michigan: The University of Michigan Press, p. 40.

52 Coca's connection to paganism was regarded by the Spanish Church as something against Christian values and morality. Streatfield, op cit., p. 29.

53 Ibid.

54 Spillane, J.F., 'Making modern drugs: the manufacture, sale, and control of cocaine in the United States, 1880-1920', in Gootenberg, P. (ed), *Cocaine: Global Histories*, 1999, London: Routledge, pp. 22–32; Streatfield, op cit.; and Musto, D.F., *The American Disease: Origins of Narcotics Control*, 1987, Oxford: Oxford University Press, p. 7.

55 It was believed that cocaine could be a remedy to cure opiate, alcohol, and tobacco dependency.

56 Musto, op cit.

57 Dutch, Japanese, and German businessmen were competing with those of the Andes in the legal coca/cocaine market. De Kort, M., 'Doctors, diplomats, and businessmen: conflicting interests in the Netherlands and Dutch East Indies, 1860-1950', in Gootenberg, P. (ed.), *Cocaine: Global Histories*, 1999, London: Routledge; Karch, S.B., 'Japan and the cocaine industry of Southeast Asia, 1864-1944', in Gootenberg, P. (ed.), *Cocaine: Global Histories*, 1999, London: Routledge; and Friman, H.R., 'Germany and the transformations of cocaine, 1880-1920', in Gootenberg, P. (ed.), *Cocaine: Global Histories*, 1999, London: Routledge.

58 At the turn of the century, the United States was importing about 8 tonnes of coca/cocaine. Gootenberg, P., 'Reluctance or resistance? Constructing cocaine (prohibitions) in Peru, 1910-1950', in Gootenberg, P. (ed.), *Cocaine: Global Histories*, 1999, London: Routledge.

Coca is a profitable crop for farmers to grow. Coca cultivation does not require advanced agricultural knowledge or high skills, and can bring an average of three harvests annually. Furthermore, coca can grow almost anywhere because it can survive in severe environments unlike other commercial crops, such as in areas with poor soil. Prohibition of coca and cocaine made its cultivation even more lucrative. There were continuous demands, and buyers came to pick up coca rather than the producers carrying them to the markets. For those in the Andes, coca cultivation, therefore, was a way to escape from poverty and misery.[59]

The control of cocaine was not an international issue for the majority of countries in the early 20th century.[60] It was in 1961, under US hegemony, that international society adopted the United Nations Single Convention on Narcotics Drugs, with a US-oriented 'prohibitionist approach' to drug control.[61] The United States considered the adopted convention was insufficient for effective drug control, although it allowed the United States to influence drug control operation internationally.[62] It was the Reagan administration that extended a War on Drugs to combat Latin American cocaine in the 1980s in order to consolidate international drug prohibition.[63]

During the 1970s, the United States experienced the coca boom from Latin America. Cocaine returned as a drug for recreation in the 1960s and the number of users rapidly increased.[64] This trend was stronger in the United States than European

---

59 Manwaring, M.G., 'National Security Implications of Drug Trafficking for the USA and Colombia', *Small Wars and Insurgencies*, Vol. 5, No. 3, Winter 1994, p. 391.

60 Great Britain and the Netherlands in particular were making profits out of the drug trade. The US influence was not sufficient to persuade them to stop. The US, however, swiftly appealed for an international ban on cocaine, since modern medical research found that it was a source of harm. For the harm that cocaine causes in the human body see: Erickson, P.G., Adlaf, E.M., Murray, G.F., and Smart, R.G., *The Steel Drug: Cocaine in Perspective*, 1987, Lexington, Mass: Heath; Fagan, J., 'Intoxication and Aggression', in Tonry, M., and Wilson, J.Q. (ed.), *Drugs and Crime: Crime and Justice: A Review of Research*, 1990, Chicago: The University of Chicago Press; and Bewley-Taylor, D.R., *The United States and International Drug Control, 1909-1997*, 1999, London: Pinter, chapter 1.

61 The United States was keen to take a prohibitionist approach due to the problems that stemmed from the earlier drug ban. For the 1961 Single Convention, Great Britain, the Netherlands, Switzerland, Italy, Japan, Latin American states, and the Soviet bloc resisted the US proposed draft for the convention. Bewley-Taylor, op cit., p. 85; and McAllister, W.B., *Drug Diplomacy in the Twentieth Century: An International History*, 2000, London: Routledge, p. 200.

62 In fact, the United States voted against the 1961 Single Convention at the UN General Assembly.

63 The United States used economic aid and assistance, on which developing countries depended, as incentives for developing countries to comply with the US style drug control. McAllister, op cit., pp. 235–239.

64 Astorga, L., 'Cocaine in Mexico: a prelude to "los Narcos"', in Gootenberg, P. (ed.), *Cocaine: Global Histories*, 1999, London: Routledge; and Roldán, M., 'Colombia: cocaine and the "miracle" of modernity in Medellín', in Gootenberg, P. (ed.), *Cocaine: Global Histories*, 1999, London: Routledge.

countries, where heroin was more popular.[65] The countries of the Andes were the largest suppliers and the United States became the largest consumer of coca/cocaine in the world. By the time the 1971 UN Convention of Psychotropic Drugs was adopted, other western states came to regard their own expanding drug problems as something caused by the lack of control outside their territories.[66]

Latin American cocaine trafficking currently is mostly controlled by Colombian drug organisations. Colombian drug trafficking organisations were not the main operators of illicit cocaine trafficking during the 1950s and 1960s, although Medellín in Colombia was functioning as a large cocaine production centre. Before the Colombians gained control of cocaine trafficking, Cuban and Chilean drug trafficking organisations dominated the trade: shipping was controlled by Cubans and the production of coca/cocaine was under the control of the Chileans.[67] The cocaine shipment routes, therefore, go through the Caribbean islands as transit points to the United States.

The change occurred when both Cuban and Chilean organisations sought direct trade with Colombian trafficking organisations in order to be competitive. As a result, Colombian trafficking organisations came to establish their own shipping routes as well as producing cocaine to supply Cuban and Chilean trafficking organisations. By the 1970s, Colombians were challenging the business of the Cubans, and the direct connection of Carlos Lehder, one of the drug traffickers of Medellín, to American markets made the position of Medellín drug traffickers, such as Pablo Escobar, dominant.[68]

The Medellín cartel with Lehder's American connection came to dominate the trade quickly during the 1970s and 1980s. The cartel used Mexican routes rather than the usual Caribbean routes, which were monitored by law enforcement officers, to ship the cocaine loads to the United States.[69] The establishment of Mexico as a

---

65 It was the Reagan and Bush administrations that escalated the war on drugs into an operation by military forces with huge budgets. Since then, the US expenditure on the war on drugs increased until the 11 September terrorist attacks. See chapters 3, 5, and 6 for the details. Interview with US government officials at ONDCP on 28 May 2003; Clinton, W.J., *A National Security Strategy for a New Century*, Washington DC: The White House, October 1998, p. 5; and United Nations Office for Drugs and Crime, *Global Illicit Drug Trends 2003*, 2003, Vienna: UNODC, p. 63.

66 McAllister, op cit.

67 Streatfield, op cit, chapter 9.

68 Ibid.

69 Constantine, T.A., *DEA Congressional Testimony Regarding Drug Trafficking in Mexico*, before the Senate Committee on Banking, Housing, and urban Affairs, 26 March 1996, http://www.usdoj.gov/dea/pubs/cngrtest/ct960328.htm (Accessed 6 June 1999); Constantine, T.A., *DEA Congressional Testimony Regarding Cooperation with Mexico*, before the National Security, International Affairs and Criminal Justice Subcommittee of House Government Reform and Oversight Committee, 25 February 1997, http://www.usdoj. gov/dea/pubs/cngrtest/ct970225.htm (Accessed 8 June 1999); Drug Enforcement Agency, *The South American Cocaine Trade: An "Industry" in Transition*, June 1996, http://www. usdoj.gov/dea/pubs/intel/cocaine.htm (Accessed 20 February 2002); Builta, J., 'Mexico faces corruption, crime, drug trafficking and political intrigue', *Criminal Organizations*, Vol. 10, No. 4, Summer 1997, http://www.acsp.uic.edu/iasoc.crime_org/vol10_4/art_4v.htm (Accessed 21

transit point ensured the safer shipment of Andean coca and cocaine to the North American market.[70] This change of shipping route has enabled Mexican drug trafficking organisations to expand their influence in cocaine trafficking as well as their financial power.

International cocaine trafficking is operated by a division of labour through networks of criminal organisations in various states. The basic structure is that coca leaves and coca paste are produced in Bolivia and Peru and transported to Colombia where they are manufactured into cocaine, as a white powder. Due to continuous drug control efforts, coca cultivation sites and cocaine production sites were moved across borders, and Colombia became the major producer. Cocaine is then shipped to the United States via Mexico and the Caribbean. Inside each country associated with the cocaine industry, there are several criminal organisations co-ordinating and co-operating over the operations.

The size of the cocaine industry in Latin America can be estimated through the financial power of the criminal organisations involved. The Cali cartel,[71] the largest Colombian drug trafficking organisation in the mid-1990s, was estimated to have an annual income of US$7 billion,[72] and Williams referred to it not only as 'the developing world's most successful' transnational criminal organisation, but also as 'its most successful transnational corporation'.[73] Bolivian drug trafficking organisations were the least wealthy groups involved withLatin American cocaine. Nevertheless, in the late 1980s, at the height of their business operations, they earned about US$1.5 billion annually in total.[74] As Mexican drug cartels came to play a major role in the 1980s, they rapidly established their wealth through cocaine trafficking.

September 1998); and Reuters, 'Mexico finds cocaine in joint operation with U.S.', *ABC News*, 7 December 1999, http://abcnews.go.com/wire/World/reuters19991207_201.html (Accessed 8 December 1999).

70 Drug trafficking organisations from different nationalities play different roles in cocaine trafficking, Colombia is referred to as the headquarters of cocaine trafficking, Bolivia and Peru are producer states, and Mexico and the Caribbean states are transit states.

71 The definition of the term 'cartel' differs from the one used in economics and simply means a drug trafficking organisation.

72 Constantine, T.A., *Congressional Testimony, National Drug Control Strategy and Drug Interdiction*, Before the Senate Caucus on International Narcotics Control, and The House Subcommittee on Coast Guard and Maritime Transportation, 12 September 1996, http://www.usdoj.gov/dea/pubs/cngrtest/ct960912.htm (Accessed 13 December 1998).

73 Williams, op cit.

74 In the 1990s, because of the decline of Bolivian drug trafficking organisations in the cocaine industry as a consequence of law enforcement operations, the total earnings from the industry reduced. Andreas, P., *Free Market Reform and Drug Market Prohibition: US Policies at Cross-Purposes in Latin America*, 1995, http://www.lindesmith.org/news/news.html (Accessed 7 July 1999); Lee III, R., 'Dimensions of the South American Cocaine Industry', *Journal of Interamerican Studies and World Affairs*, Vol. 30, Nos 2&3, 1988, p. 89; Spedding, A.L., 'Cocataki, Taki-Coca: Trade, Traffic, and Organized Peasant resistance in the Yungas of La Paz', in Léons, M.B. and Sanabria, H. (eds), *Coca, Cocaine and the Bolivian Reality*, 1997, New York: State University of New York Press, p. 120; Sanabria, op cit., p. 61; United Nations Office for Drugs and Crime Control Policy, *Global Illicit Trends*, 1999, New York: UNODCCP, p. 42.

By the early 1990s, the Tijuana cartel, one of the biggest trafficking organisations, was operating routine shipments of 'approximately 7 tons of cocaine and returned $90 million to Mexico within a 90-day time frame'.[75]

Drug traffickers invest in the legitimate economy because they need to 'launder' the money they have acquired. Money laundering, in short, is a mechanism to 'legalise' the narco-dollars. The drug traffickers deposit narco-dollars to the banks, and transfer them to different domestic and international banks several times to erase the sources of income.[76] For effective money laundering, drug trafficking organisations tend to have various legal 'front companies' that are owned by drug traffickers, or under the names of different persons. Wealthy drug traffickers, such as Colombians, tend to possess the majority of local businesses and service industries.[77] The jobs created by the needs of criminal organisations were enough for rural populations to migrate to the cities and increased the employment rate.[78] The

---

75 Constantine, T. A., *DEA Congressional Testimony* before the Senate Drug Caucus, 24 February 1999, http://www.usdoj.gov/dea/pubs/cngrtest/ct022499.htm.

76 Latin American drug traffickers have several international bank accounts and businesses for money laundering purposes, and this was revealed through international drug control operations executed by law enforcers from various states. United Nations Drug Control Policy, *World Drug Report*, 1997, Oxford: Oxford University Press, p. 236; Westrate, D., *Remarks* in Caucus on International Narcotics Control of the United States Senate, The Congressional Research Service, 8 May 1987, Washington DC: GPO, p. 4; and Wankel, H. D., *DEA Congressional Testimony*, Money Laundering by Drug Trafficking Organizations, before the House Banking and Financial Committee, 20 February, 1996, http://www.usdoj.gov/ dea/pubs/cngrtest/ct960228.htm (Accessed 20 February 2003); Andreas, P., 'When Policies Collide', in Friman, H.R. and Andreas, P., *The Illicit Global Economy & State Power*, 1999, New York: Rowman & Littlefield Publishers, Inc., p. 131; Menzel, S.H., *Cocaine Quagmire*, p. 25; Jiménez, J.B., 'Cocaine, Informality, and the Urban Economy in La Paz, Bolivia', in Partes, A., Castells, M., and Benton, L.A. (eds), *The Informal Economy: Studies in Advanced and Less Developed Countries*, 1989, Baltimore: The Johns Hopkins University Press, p. 145; and Painter, *Bolivia and Coca*, p. 61.

77 Domestically, drug traffickers own many businesses and facilities, for example: banks, construction companies, pharmaceutical companies, sports clubs, private security companies, automobile dealerships, radio stations, higher educational institutions, newspaper companies, cattle ranches, residential properties, restaurants, five star hotels, and football teams. *Corruption and Drugs in Colombia: Democracy at risk*, A Staff Report to the Committee of Foreign Relations United States Senate, February 1996, Washington DC: GPO, pp. 10–11; Lee III, *The White Labyrinth*, p. 5; Lee, R.W., 'Why the US Cannot Stop South American Cocaine', *Orbis*, Vol. 32, No. 4, Fall 1988, p. 505; Lazare, D., 'Drugs & Money', *NACLA: Report on the Americas*, Vol. XXX, No. 6, May/June 1997, p. 37; Wankel, op cit., 1996; Tuckman, J., 'Mexican town falls victim to its own drug trade', *The Guardian*, 30 March 2000, http://www.newsunlimited.co.uk/international/story/0,3604,153554,00.html (Accessed 20 February 2003); and Reuter, 'Mexico Drug money-laundering operation had U.S., Russian ties', *CNN News*, 20 February 2000, http://www.cnn.com/2000/WORLD/americas/02/28/ mexico.drugs.reut/index.html (Accessed 20 February 2000).

78 Tullis, op cit., p. 167; Abruzzerse, R., 'Coca-leaf production in the countries of the Andean subregion', *Bulletin on Narcotics*, 1989, Issue 1, http://www.undcp.org/adhoc/ bulletin/1989/bulletin_1989-01-01_page008.html (Accessed 10 September 1998); Menzel, *Cocaine Quagmire*, p. 42; 'Exactly what impact do drug exports have on the Colombian

penetration of drug trafficking organisations in the legitimate national economy has created a situation of dependency.[79] For example, Bolivia registered that 8% of its workforce was engaged in occupations related to the cocaine industry in the 1980s.[80] In Medellín, the cocaine industry and related businesses provided jobs when its main industry, textiles, collapsed in the mid-1980s, and it employed about 30% of the city's population.[81]

In order to establish an environment suitable for illicit economic activities, drug cartels use corruption and intimidation (plomo o plata – death or money) targeting specific individuals in charge of key sectors for cocaine trafficking, such as customs, law enforcement and policy-making. As one of the Cali cartel's leaders, Gilberto Rodriguez Orejuela allegedly said: 'We don't kill judges or ministers, we buy them.'[82] Drug traffickers are believed to spend millions of dollars in bribery.[83] For

economy?', Latin American Regional Report: Andean groups report, 29 June 1995, p. 1; and Lee III, 'Global Reach', p. 208.

79 The cocaine traffickers also contributed to the establishment of social infrastructures and housing projects for slums. Clawson, and Lee III, op cit., p. 167; Lupsha, op cit., p. 42; Kendall, S., 'Bogota counts cost of crackdown', *Financial Times*, 30 August 1999; Menzel, *Cocaine Quagmire*, p. 42; and Lee, 'Why the US Cannot Stop South American Cocaine', p. 503.

80 Clawson, and Lee III, op cit., chapter 1.

81 When the textile industry collapsed, the Medellín cartel and its drug industry provided jobs to the workforce and, therefore, the city economy could still earn $313 million by 1987, as: 'About 28,000 new jobs were created and … the unemployment rate dropped by about 30%.' Also, the crackdown on the Cali cartel brought the shut down of 210 businesses, leading to a 20% decline in the construction industry, and an increase in Cali's unemployment by 33%. In addition, over 2500 coca farmers lost their means of earning an income. Menzel, *Cocaine Quagmire*, p. 41; Youngers, C., 'Coca Eradication Efforts in Colombia', *WOLA Briefing Series: Issues in International Drug Policy*, 2 June 1997, http://www.worldcom.nl/tni/drugs/links/guaiare.htm (Accessed 23 October 1998); Clawson, and Lee III, op cit., p. 168.

82 The Mexican cartels spend an estimated $500 million per year on bribes, and the Colombian cartels spend more than $100 million. Lee, 'Global Reach', p. 208; and Gelbard, R., *Press Briefing by Robert Gelbard, Assistant Secretary of State for International Narcotics Matters; Richard Newcombe, Assistant Secretary of the Treasury, Office of Foreign Assets Control; George Ward, Acting Assistant Secretary of State for International Organizations; and Richard Clarke, Senior Director, Global and Multinational Affairs, NSC*, The White House: Washington, DC, October 22, 1995, http://www.pub.whiltehouse.gov/uri-res/I2R?urn: pdi://oma.eop.gov.us/1995/10/23/6.text.1 (Accessed 20 February 2004); and Robinson, L., 'An inferno next door', *Newsweek*, 24 February 1997, pp. 37–38.

83 Gilberto Rodriguez Orejuela, one of the Cali cartel's leaders, had a payroll that listed the names of 2,800 Colombian citizens from pop stars to politicians. In Bolivia, about 14,000 police officers were sacked because of corruption between 1990 and 1998. The largest sum offered as a bribe could be one from the Tijuana cartel, Mexico's biggest drug cartel. It offered 'the amount of $1.5 million per month – or $18 million per year' to the Delegado for Tijuana. Gelbard, op cit.; *Corruption and Drugs in Colombia*, p. 19; Bagley, B.M., 'Dateline Drug Wars: Colombia: The Wrong Strategy', *Foreign Policy*, No. 77 Winter 1989–90, p. 160; Constantine, T.A., DEA *Congressional Testimony, International Organized Crime Syndicates and their impact on the United States*, Before the Senate Foreign Relations Committee, Subcommittee on the Western Hemisphere, Peace Crops, Narcotics, and Terrorism, 26 February 1998, http://

example, the presidential election campaign of Ernsto Samper was supported by a US$6 million donation from the Cali cartel.[84] The involvement of drug traffickers in political affairs created the term 'narcocracy' to describe governments under the influence of drug trafficking groups.[85] Not only elections, but also coup d'état have been financed by drug traffickers. The Maza regime of Bolivia established in the early 1980s was a result of a 'coca coup' that was supported by the drug trafficking organisations in exchange for impunity from prosecutors.[86]

Refusal of bribery is not welcomed by the drug traffickers. As the police chief of Tijuana, the city with the largest drug cartel in Mexico, maintained: 'First [drug traffickers] send you a briefcase full of money. Then, if you reject [that], they send you a briefcase with a gun.'[87] The majority of violent attacks target professionals and government officials in order to intimidate, not only the individuals, but also to challenge the government.[88] Those who work against the drug cartels and their

www.usdoj.gov/dea/pubs/cngrtest/ct980226.htm; Ledwith, W., *Counter-narcotics in Mexico*, Testimony before the Subcommittee on Criminal Justice, Drug Policy, and Human Resources, 29 February 2000, http://www.usdoj.gov/dea/pubs/cngrtest/ct022900.html; The Bureau of International Narcotics and Law Enforcement Affairs, *International Narcotics Control Strategy Report 1998*, http://www.state.gov/www/global.narcotics_law/1998_narc_report/ samer98.html; Robinson, op cit., pp. 37–38; Tullis, op cit., p. 169.

84 Also in Bolivia, it is reported that 10% of the 1989 Bolivian Parliamentary election candidates had some connections to drug cartels, as had an estimated US$15 million to $20 million spent on campaigning in the 1989 elections, equivalent to $10 a vote. Painter, *Bolivia and Coca*, p. 74; Painter, J., 'Drugs may fund Bolivian campaign', *Independent*, 6 May 1989; 'Colombian poll win 'bought' by drug cartel', *Daily Telegraph*, 15 March 1994; Menzel, *Fire in the Andes*, p. 90; *Corruption and Drugs in Colombia*, p. vi; and Ross, T., 'Blow to Colombia as tape links parties to Cali drug cartel', *The Guardian*, 28 June 1994.

85 Isikoff, M., 'Colombia's Drug King Becoming Entrenched', *The Washington Post*, 8 January 1989; Moore, M., 'Mexican Seeks Ex-Governor on Drug Charges', *The Washington Post*, 8 April 1999, http://www.washingtonpost.com/wp-srv/inatl/longterm/mexico/mexico. htm (Accessed 8 April 1999) Dillon, S., 'In Letter From Hiding, Mexican Governor Charges Political Plot', *The New York Times*, 7 April 1999, http://www.nytimes.com/library/world/ americas/040799mexico-governor.html (Accessed 8 April 1999); and Associated Press, 'Former Mexican governor said negotiating surrender in drug case', *CNN News*, 20 February 2000, http://www.cnn.com/2000/WORLD/americas/02/20/bc.mexico.fugativegov.ap/index. html (Accessed 20 February 2000).

86 After the collapse of the Meza regime, Bolivian drug trafficker Roberto Suárez made an offer in 1983 to the President that he would pay off the foreign debt of $2 billion to ensure that drug traffickers in Bolivia remain untouchable. Tullis, op cit., p. 128; Painter, *Bolivia and Coca*, p. 27; and Henman, A., 'Cocaine Futures', in Henman, A. et al., *Big Deal: The Politics of the Illicit Drug Business*, 1985, London: Pluto Press, p. 140; Chepesiuk, R., 'The Colombian Drug Connection: its source, distribution and impact', *Journal of Defense & Diplomacy*, April 1998, p. 27.

87 Moore, M., 'Mexican Stunned by Killing of Police Chief', *The Washington Post*, 29 February 2000, http://www.washintonpost.com/wp-srv/WPlate/2000-02/29/0791-022900- idx.html (Accessed 29 February 2000).

88 Those hired assassins are known as *sicarios* in Colombia, and there are about 6,000 of them in Medellín working for over 500 criminal organisations. Also, it is reported that the Medellín cartel ordered over 600 assassinations between 1989 and 1991. Bagley, B.M.,

interests are often assassinated.[89] For example, Colombian judicial officials have become reluctant to take drug-related cases. The only special attorney who survived assassination attempts after convicting Pablo Escobar and Jorge Ochoa, claimed that more than 1,000 members of the Colombian judicial system were 'in serious danger'.[90] The situation is the same in Mexico. Builta maintains: 'it seems that any law enforcement official who can't be corrupted is killed'.[91]

The challenge to government autonomy occurs when it adopts particular policies that target drug traffickers. Some drug cartels demonstrate their sentiment through attacking cities and high-ranking officials. In Mexico, the Tijuana police chief was killed two days after an anti-drug trafficking speech by President Zedillo in Baja, California.[92] Considering the timing of the assassination, it was argued that the assassination was ordered by the Tijuana cartel to challenge the government decision on re-enforcement in drug control operations. During the 1980s, the Medellín cartel also challenged the government decision on the extradition treaty of criminals with the United States. The cartel was involved in the bombings of several cities in Colombia, such as Bogotá and Medellín: there were over 200 bombs in Bogotá alone during a six-month period in 1990.[93]

'Colombia and the War on Drugs', *Foreign Affairs*, Vol. 67, No. 1, Fall 1988, p. 73; Menzel, *Cocaine Quagmire*, p. 91; Skol, M., *Cocaine Production in the Andes*, Hearing before the Select Committee on Narcotics Abuse and Control , House of Representatives 101st Congress, 1st session, 7 June 1989, GPO: Washington, p. 67; and Nordland, R. and Contreras, J., 'Where Cocaine Is King', *Newsweek*, 29 February 1988, pp. 37–38.

89 In Tijuana, it is believed that a journalist was killed by a member of Arellano Felix's organisation (known as the Tijuana cartel) on 25 June 2004. Those whose jobs conflict with drug traffickers' interests are, for example, politicians with anti-drug policies, journalists reporting and investigating on drug trafficking and drug cartels, police officers and customs officers who refuse to accept bribes, legal entrepreneurs who are competing in the same markets as drug traffickers invests, and insurgents who kidnap drug traffickers' families. Sullivan, K., 'Tijuana Gang Figure Held After Slaying of Journalist', *The Washington Post*, 26 June 2004, http://www.washingtonpost.com/wp-dyn/articles/A6989-2004Jun25.html (Accessed 28 June 2004).

90 Ross, T., 'Colombian judges court death', *Independent*, 18 November 1991.

91 Builta, op cit.

92 Dillon, S., 'Tijuana Official Says Slaying Shows Traffickers' Power', *The New York Times*, 29 February 2000, http://www.nytimes.com/yr/mo/day/news/world/tijuana-slaying. html (Accessed 1 March 2000); Moore, M., 'Mexican Stunned by Killing of Police Chief'; and Golden, T., 'Mexican Tale of Absolute Drug Corruption', *The New York Times*, 9 January 2000, http://www.nytimes.com/library/world/americas/010900mexico-us-drugs.html (Accessed 10 January 2000); for other examples, Moore, M., 'Hostility Violence Threaten Rights Defenders in Mexico', *The Washington Post*, 26 December 1999, http://www.washingtonpost.com/wp-srv/Wplate/1999-12/26/1411-122699-idx.html (Accessed 20 February 2004).

93 It is believed that the cartel paid US$1 million to the M-19 to carry out bombings at the Supreme Court, government institutions, Police headquarters, and politicians' accommodation. Claudio, A., 'United States-Colombia Extradition Treaty: Failure of a Security Strategy', *Military Review*, December 1991, p. 71; Chomsky, N., *The Drug War*, http://www.mega. nu:8080/ampp/drugtext/ial5.html (Accessed 18 February 2004); and Salias, C.M., 'Colombia and the Kaleidoscope of Violence', *US Foreign Policy in Focus*, Vol. 1 No. 18, 27 October

There are documented cases where drug cartels work in conjunction with insurgency movements.[94] Through such an alliance with drug cartels, the Revolutionary Armed Force of Colombia (FARC), the largest leftist guerrilla group in Colombia, has expanded in size and financial power.[95] Resources obtained through cocaine trafficking have allowed FARC to be more visible and active.[96] Consequently, FARC came to possess influence over the government, and obtained a territory the size of Switzerland as a 'demilitarised zone' within Colombia.[97] Currently, according to a US report, FARC controls 30% of the Colombian cocaine market through the establishment of a monopoly, particularly in southern Colombia, and operates business independently from Mexican drug cartels.[98]

To sum up, Latin American cocaine trafficking is the biggest industry in Latin America. The financial resources cocaine traffickers generate allow them to exercise economic and political influence over local and national governments in order to

1997, http://www.igc.apc.org (Accessed 20 February 2000); Tullis, op cit., p. 95; Menzel, *Cocaine Quagmire*, p. 80; and Lee, R.W., 'Policy Brief: Making the Most of Colombia's Drug Negotiations', *Orbis*, Vol. 35, No. 2, Spring 1991, p. 242.

94 Zackrison, J.L. and Bradley, E., 'Colombian Sovereignty Under Siege', *Strategic Forum*, No. 112, May 1997, Institution for National Strategic Studies, p. 2.

95 FARC allegedly earns 50% of its annual income (estimated US$5–1.5 billion) from cocaine trafficking, and the rest from kidnapping, taxation and extortion. The wealth generated from cocaine trafficking increased the number of FARC members to 18,000, several times more than in the early 1980s. Rohter, L., 'Colombia Agree to Turn Over Territory to Another Rebel Group', *The New York Times*, 26 April 2000, http://www.nytimes.com/library/world/americas/042600colombia-rebels.html (Accessed 26 April 2000); Dudley, S., 'Colombia sets negotiations with a second rebel group', *The Washington Post*, 26 April 2000, http://www.washingtonpost.com/wp-dyn/articles/A14228-2000Apr25.html (Accessed 28 April 2000).

96 Colombian election campaigns are frequently associated with violence, such as kidnappings, bombings, and killings. These acts used to be conducted by guerrilla groups, but since the 1980s, when the Medellín cartel started violent protests against the government, the drug cartels have also begun to be involved in these acts. Bureau of International Narcotics and Law Enforcement Affairs, *Drug Control Fact Sheet – Colombia*, 3 March 1998, http://www.state.gov/www/global/narcotics_law/1997_narc_report/fs_colombia.html (Accessed 5 June 1998); Lee III, *The White Labyrinth*, p. 101; Ross, T., 'Colombian rebels launch pre-election attacks', *The Guardian*, 23 February 1994; Kendall, S., 'Violence mars road to Colombia elections', *Financial Times*, 9 March 1994; Hodgson, M., 'Colombian rebels pose as soldiers to kidnap state MPs', *The Guardian*, 12 April 2002, http://www.guardian.co.uk/international/story/0,3604,683118,00.html (Accessed 11 July 2004); and Taylor, R., 'Rebels Kidnap Colombian Presidential Candidate', *The Guardian*, 25 February 2002, http://www.guardian.co.uk/informer/story/0,1191,657897,00.html (Accessed 11 July 2004).

97 Hodgson, M., 'Troops close in on Colombia's rebel heaven', *The Guardian*, 12 January 2002, http://www.guardian.co.uk/international/story/0,3604,631544,00.html (Accessed 11 July 2004); Guardian Staffs and Agencies, Colombian President vows to retake rebel land, *The Guardian*, 21 February 2002, http://www.guardian.co.uk/colombia/story/0,11502,653729,00.html (Accessed 11 July 2004).

98 Boucher, R., 'Colombian Rebel Connection to Mexican drug Cartel', *US Department of State Office of the Spokesman Press Statement*, 29 November 2000, http://secretary.state.gov/www/briefings/statements/2000/ps001129.html (Accessed 12 January 2001); Lee, R., 'Why the US Cannot Stop South American Cocaine', pp. 501–502.

ensure their business operations. Also, they buy protection for their businesses from government officials and insurgency groups. In other words, they ally with anyone useful for the cocaine trade. At the same time, cocaine traffickers do not hesitate to use violence against those who try to disrupt cocaine trafficking. Therefore, in the Andean states, the governments have lost part of their sovereignty, and state functions are paralysed in drug related issues.

The Approach of This Book

This book will compare US and European approaches towards combating cocaine trafficking from the Andes. Chapter 1 will explain how drug trafficking has come to be conceptualised as a security threat. It will investigate how a phenomenon comes to be recognised as a security issue (securitisation), and how state policy is formed within a domestic and international environment. To analyse the nexus between the domestic and international influences, two aspects will be taken into consideration. First, the domestic cocaine situation, which measures the impact of cocaine trafficking in the EU member states[99] and the United States, and the effect of international drug prohibition on state behaviour, will be explained. International drug prohibition functions as a legal and moral framework to control cross-border and cross-jurisdictional actions with a direct and indirect impact on members of the international community through facilitating co-operation.[100] Compliance with drug prohibition will affect each state's policies because it will shape the policy in the direction of international norms to control drugs. For the analysis on the conceptualisation of threat, the implications of cocaine trafficking will be investigated through a multidimensional approach to take various aspects of state functions into consideration. In order to simplify the analysis but still to cover the major impacts of cocaine trafficking on a state, the assessment of the threat posed by the cocaine business will be examined from four aspects of the state functions: economic, political, public order and violence, and diplomatic. This is because the impact of cocaine trafficking may need to be studied as a combined effect on all four aspects of state functions. Cocaine trafficking might create various degrees of damage to a state, depending on the strength of its systems. Each state affected by cocaine trafficking, therefore, could see the threat differently.

In chapters 2 and 3, the problems triggered by cocaine trafficking and consumption in the EU member states and the United States will be investigated using the framework presented in chapter 1. Chapter 2 will examine the extent to which EU member states are affected by cocaine trafficking. EU member states registered cocaine trafficking as a social problem rather than a security issue until recently.[101]

---

99 In this book, the term 'the European Union' and 'the EU member states' refer to the European Union with 12 member states before its expansion in 2004.

100 Young, O.R., 'Regime Dynamics: The Rise and Fall of International Regime', *International Organisation*, Vol. 36, No. 2, Spring 1982, p. 277; and see chapter 1 for other details.

101 The European Commission, *A Secure Europe in a Better World: European Security Strategy*, 12 December 2003, Brussels: The European Community.

Although the member states of the European Union maintain their sovereignty and jurisdiction over fundamental issues, market integration and the single currency have made illegal businesses easier to operate in the European economic bloc. Through the examination of the impact of cocaine trafficking, this chapter will investigate how Europeans have securitised cocaine trafficking.

Chapter 3 will focus on cocaine trafficking in the United States and its impact on state functions. Geographical proximity to Latin America and a wealthy population have made the United States a desirable cocaine market. The large size of the American cocaine market causes various problems at the state level, as well as at the societal level. The United States has declared cocaine trafficking is a 'national security threat'. The thirty-year effort to control drugs indicates the seriousness of the drug problem in the United States. This chapter will focus on the four aspects referred to in chapter 1 (economic, political, public order and violence, and diplomatic), and investigate the implications of cocaine trafficking for American security.

As for drug control policy, chapters 4 and 5 will be dedicated to the examination of EU and US policies to control drugs in the Andes in the 1990s. In chapter 4, EU drug control policy toward the Andes will be examined. Bilateral co-operation with the Andean states reflects the securitisation by the European Union that will be analysed in chapter 2. The EU drug control policy emphasises economic, political and social development to curb cocaine production indirectly by improving living conditions in the region. These differences in EU and US drug control policies reflect their different conceptualisations of the threat from cocaine.

Chapter 5 will concern itself with US drug control policy toward the Andes on the basis of bilateral co-operation. US drug control is often associated with a military oriented law enforcement operation to attack drug trafficking organisations and eradicate coca fields – the cultivation areas of the raw ingredient for cocaine.[102] The military oriented approach of the United States, known as the 'war on drugs', is underpinned by the understanding of cocaine trafficking as a national security threat. Through the investigation of the EU and US drug control operations, chapters 4 and 5 will establish the characteristics of EU and US approaches to drug control and the nexus of their policies with the securitisation of cocaine trafficking.

In chapter 6, the EU and US policy under the framework of Plan Colombia (Phase I), a large-scale multidimensional drug control project will be analysed. This chapter will elaborate the differences in EU and US approaches more clearly by examining their actions and reactions under the multinational co-operation scheme. Plan Colombia will provide a comparison of EU and US policy. The focus of this chapter will be to analyse the differences in EU and US approaches further, as well as analysing their attitudes to drug control through the way in which they contributed to Plan Colombia, reflecting the arguments on drug prohibition and state policy-making discussed in chapter 1.

---

102 See chapters 5 and 6 of this book for details.

Chapter 1

Securitisation and Drug Control Policy: Theoretical Frameworks

Introduction

This chapter will examine the conceptualisation of security and threat. It will also look at the influence of the drug prohibition regime on state policy in order to analyse the link between recognising and understanding a phenomenon and policy making around it. The notion of transnational organised crime as a security threat is a relatively new concept in the field of security studies. States are traditionally believed to respond to security threats by military means. Since the end of the Cold War, however, new threats have emerged, which require a broader range of responses. State responses to transnational organised crime vary. Through the investigation of theories related to security and policy making, this chapter will attempt to provide a framework to analyse why the United States and the European Union are pursuing drug control in the Andes in such different manners.

The chapter will be divided into three sections to provide a framework for analysis: firstly, the concept of security and the 'securitisation' of a phenomenon will be investigated. Through this section, the difference between traditional security threats and non-traditional security threats will be illustrated. Also the way in which states conceptualise a security threat from a phenomenon will be analysed. Secondly, the implication of transnational organised crime as a non-traditional security threat and state policy on drug control will be investigated. Since drugs only have an indirect impact on state existence, unlike invasion by other states, the impact of a non-traditional security threat needs to be analysed from a different angle from that of a traditional security threat. This section will focus on four state functions to analyse the threat posed to the state by transnational organised crime. These four functions are related to economic, political, public order and diplomatic relations. Drug trafficking organisations may affect economic activities through their financial power, and this financial power may enable them to corrupt government officials in order to ensure their activities are not interdicted. The development of drug markets can lead to competition among drug traffickers. Such competition tends to result in violent disputes. In order to look at public order and community safety, violence related to drug trafficking will be examined as well as infectious diseases spread through the unhygienic use of drugs. Then, international pressures on a state to control drugs and limitations on their sovereignty stemming from international drug prohibition will be examined. Compliance with international rules and peer pressures would affect state decision making on drug related issues. Following the analysis on the threat posed by a non-traditional security threat, this chapter will discuss international influences on the policy making of an actor. In addition to the understanding of drug control, actors might take some other issues in international relations into consideration. The motivation for drug related policy making in the international community will be analysed from the perspective of national interests (Realist perspective) and social identity and of moral values (Social Constructivist perspectives).

Security Threat and 'Securitisation'

A new set of arguments that emerged from the collapse of the communist bloc was those related to the concepts of security and 'enemies'. As communism as a threat disappeared from political and security spheres, there have been movements to include unconventional issues into the security sphere, such as the environment, organised crime, and migration.[1] The non-traditional security threats that came to attention in the post-1989 era were not considered as security issues under the pre-1989 definition of security. The rapid progress of globalisation, however, raised alarm about the potential threat posed by transnational phenomena and increased the need to reconceptualise security, as Wæver advocates, to embrace broader issues as security concerns.[2] This section will examine the concept of security from both Realist and Social Constructivist perspectives. These may offer explanations of how states recognise threats from other phenomena.

According to Desch, Realism provides a model for studying security in which states are concerned with state survival in an anarchic world.[3] This is because the state is the actor in international relations, and in order to be recognised as a state, it is necessary to possess territories and sovereignty to control the territories. States are also required to protect citizens to ensure their safety. Since states are struggling for power, according to the Realist perspective,[4] they may attempt to obtain more

---

1   For example, Mathews, J.T., 'Redefining Security', *Foreign Affairs*, Vol. 68, No. 2, Spring 1989.

2   Wæver, O., 'Securitization and Desecuritization', in Lipschutz, R.D. (ed.), *On Security*, 1995, New York: Columbia University Press, p. 67.

3   Desch, M.C., 'Culture Crash: Assessing the Importance of Ideas in Security Studies', *International Security*, Vol. 23, No. 1 Summer 1998, p. 166.

4   Morgenthau, H., *Politics Among Nations: The Struggle for Power and Peace*, 1972, New York: Knopf; Bull, H., *The Anarchical Society*, 1977, Basingstoke: Macmillan; Terriff *et al.*, *Security Studies Today*, 1999, Cambridge: Polity Press; Wight, M., *Power Politics*, 1995, Leicester: Leicester University Press; Mearsheimer, J., 'Back to the Future: Instability After the Cold War', *International Security*, Vol. 15, No. 1, 1990; Carr, E.H., *Twenty Year's Crisis 1919-1939: An Introduction to the Study of International Relations*, 2001, Basingstoke: Palgrave Macmillan; Kissinger, H., *A World Restored: From Castlereagh, Metternich and the Restoration of Peace, 1812-1822*, 1957, Boston: Houghton Mifflin; Herz, J.H., 'Idealist Internationalism and the Security Dilemma', *World Politics*, 1950, Vol. 2, No. 2; Jervis, R., *Perception and Misperception in International Relations*, 1976, Princeton: Princeton University Press; Walfers, A., *Discord and Collaboration: Essays on International Politics*, 1962, Baltimore: Johns Hopkins University Press; Machiavelli, N., *The Prince*, in Skinner, Q. (ed.), 1988, Cambridge: Cambridge University Press; Holsti, K., *The State, War, and the State*

power through material gain, such as more land or resources. Security, therefore, is closely related to the physical damage to a state and state survival based on the sustainability of its territories. The principal security threats are war and invasion by other states.[5] Strange argues that for a state, territories and resources are directly related to state strength, which is perceived as power.[6] In this sense, state interest is to obtain power, and to maintain its power – power is the goal for national interests. In order to maintain its territory and to ensure survival in the anarchic world, states can ally with those who share the same interests to preserve their status quo through the mechanism known as 'balance of power'.[7] Balance of power has functioned as a mechanism to prevent 'cheating' from allied states and to ensure maintenance of the relationships through complex connections between and among states inside the mechanism.

Neo-Realists differ from Realists in seeing the structure of the international system as the principal determinant of state action.[8] The concept of balance of power was taken further to develop the concept of the international system. Gilpin studied the world equilibrium during the Cold War and describes it as a bipolar system between the Soviet Union and the United States, unlike the traditional Realist concept requiring several states to keep the balance.[9] The changes within the international system can be analysed through mutual interaction between and among three levels – international, state and individual – following the change in the distribution of power in the international system.[10] In respect to the concept of power, neo-Realists, such as Waltz, argue that state power is a means to pursue an influential position in the international system, and hence not necessarily military force but also the combination of economic and political resources.[11] In other words, power consists of several elements rather than a simple military factor.

---

of War, 1996, Cambridge: Cambridge University Press; Gilpin, R., *War and Change in World Politics*, 1981, Cambridge: Cambridge University Press; Kaldor, M., *New and Old Wars: Organized Violence in a Global Era*, 2002, London: Polity Press; Doyle, M., *Ways of War and Peace*, 1997, New York: MIT Press; Booth, K., 'Security in anarchy: Utopian Realism in theory and practice', *International Affairs*, Vol. 67, No. 3, July 1991; Spanier, J., *Games Nations Play: Analyzing International Politics*, 1972, London: Nelson; Keohane, R. (ed.), *Neorealism and its Critics*, 1986, New York: Columbia University Press.

5   Krasner, S.D., *Structural Conflict: The Third World Against Global Liberalism*, 1985, Los Angeles: University of California Press.

6   Strange, S., *States and Markets*, 1988, London: Pinter.

7   Morgenthau, op cit.

8   Waltz, K., *Theory of International Politics*, 1979, New York: McGraw-Hill; Gilpin, R., *The Political Economy of International Relations*, Princeton: Princeton University Press; Keohane, op cit.; Walt, S.M., 'The Renaissance of Security Studies', *International Studies Quarterly*, 1991, Vol. 35, No. 2; Mann, M., *The Source of Social Power: A History of Power from the Beginning to AD 1760*, 1986, Cambridge: Cambridge University Press; Gray, C., 'Global Security and Economic Wellbeing: A Strategic Perspective', *Political Studies*, 1994, Vol. 42, No. 1.

9   Gilpin, op cit.

10 Waltz, K., *Man, the State and War*, 1959, New York: Columbia University Press.

11 Waltz, op cit.; Gilpin, op cit.

Both Realists and neo-Realists conceptualise security in terms of the survival of states in an anarchic world through a struggle for power, and threats to national security emerge from another state's desires to expand its power through obtaining more resources available outside its own territories.[12] This is because what matters to a state is its relative power, that it is stronger than other states in the system. In short, from the Realist and the neo-Realist points of view, threats to a state are mostly posed by state(s), and what is at stake is material: a national security threat for a state is another state's desire to increase its power by obtaining more territories and other resources. In order to ensure security, states seek alliances. States, however, ally (co-operate) only when the alliance (co-operation) is advantageous to their national interests and relative gain.

The end of the Cold War, however, has brought an expansion of the interpretation of security and referent objects. During the 1980s, there was a movement to expand the security agenda from the security of a state to the security of people 'either as individuals or as a global or international collectivity' – an approach known as critical security studies.[13] For example, Booth and Strange, from their Liberal perspectives, eschew the state as the focal point for the analysis of security, arguing instead for a people-centred view, which is related to freeing humans through emancipation and preventing individual insecurity such as unemployment.[14] From the perspective of 'human security', the life and quality of life of individuals should be the central concern (the referent object) for security and the goal should be the sustainability and improvement of quality life.

The meaning of national security also departed from classic Realist views, and is more concerned about the governance of the state, for instance, the governing regime and state structure as a security concern. Ayoob and Ball consider that the state is the referent object for security analysis, although the concern is not the land but the security of the existing governing body and state structure, particularly for developing states.[15] Ayoob maintains the internal and external 'vulnerabilities' that

---

12 See footnote 4.

13 Wæver, 'Securitization and Desecuritization', p. 47; Krause, K. and Williams, M. (eds), *Critical Security Studies: Concept and Cases*, 1997, London: UCL Press; Klein, B, *Strategic Studies and World Order: The Global Politics of Deterrence*, 1994, Cambridge: Cambridge University Press; Adler, E., 'The Emergence of Cooperation: National Epistemic Communities and the International Evolution of the Idea of Nuclear Arms Control', *International Organization*, 1992, Vol. 46, No. 2; Booth, K., 'Human Wrongs and International Relations', *International Affairs*, 1995, Vol. 71, No. 1; Dalby, S., *Creating the Second Cold War: The Discourse of Politics*, 1990, New York: Guilford; Katzenstein, P.J., *Cultural Norms and National Security: Police and Military in Postwar Japan*, 1996, Ithaca, NY: Cornell University Press.

14 Booth, K., 'Security and Emancipation', *Review of International Studies*, Vol. 17, No. 4, October 1991, p. 319; Strange, *States and Markets*, ch. 3, 'The Security Structure', pp. 45–61.

15 Ayoob, M., *The Third World Security Predicament: State-Making, Regional Conflict, and the International System*, 1995, Boulder, OC: Lynne Reinner, p. 9; and Ball, N., *Security and Economy in the Third World*, 1988, Princeton: Princeton University Press.

have potential to, or threaten to, weaken state structures and governing regimes.[16] For example, weak economic and political structures of developing states facing continuous challenge by guerrilla groups could be weakened further by international interference, such as economic sanctions. Another sub-state referent object for security concern is discussed by Buzan who argues that sectoral security should be included – such as societal security,[17] that is, the sustainability of a society. A societal security threat is a threat to affect traditional moral values and culture in a society. It could lead to a collapse of trust among a community due to differences in morals and disciplines among the society members. According to this new term, non-traditional security threats, such as drugs, may harm society through undermining and discrediting morals and values.[18] These arguments indicate that national security can encompass internal aspects of a state rather than being limited to its physical existence.

Clark observes the trend that international security comes into focus as globalisation progresses because those new security concerns of states tend to share a transnational character, and the separation of national and international issues became ambiguous.[19] For example, illegal human trafficking is a national problem for the recipient states of the illegal immigrants, but simultaneously it is a problem of other states that can potentially be involved as recipient/transit/origin of trafficking. This blurring of borders between national and international security issues, Kolodziej argues, has led to international security being a reflection of domestic security concerns.[20] International affairs and domestic affairs are partially merging as globalisation progresses, and it has expanded national security toward a more transnational nature in order to cope with transnational phenomena.

Although the referent object for security varies from individual human beings to international society, this thesis focuses on national security, and concerns itself with the analysis of threats posed by international drug trafficking. Realists maintain that states are the main actors and units to determine international relations either individually or collectively. The significance of national security as the referent object for security arguments is also emphasised by Wæver. He argues that:

---

16 Ayoob, op cit., p. 9.

17 Threats to societal security are posed by 'situations in which significant groups within a society feel threatened, feel their identity is endangered by immigration, integration, or cultural imperialism, and try to defend themselves'. Wæver, 'Securitization and Desecuritization', p. 67.

18 See, for example, Buzan, B., Wæver, O., and de Wilde, J., *Security: A New Framework For Analysis*, 1998, London: Lynne Rienner.

19 Clark, I., *Globalisation and International Relations Theory*, 1999, Oxford: Oxford University Press, p. 111.

20 Kolodziej, E.A., 'What is Security and Security Studies?', *Arms Control*, Vol. 13, No. 1, April 1992, p. 12.

the only meaningful way to speak about 'security' is to relate [it] to the classic meaning (national security) and broaden the understanding of relevant dynamics … the issue of 'security' has to be read through the lens of 'national security'.[21]

Hence, international drug trafficking is non-governmental and non-militaristic in nature; the classic Realist state-centred approach may be appropriate for the analysis of the securitisation of a phenomenon and execution of state policies against the threat.

Setting a state and national security as the referent objects for analysis may be justified from the implication of ensured national security to security at other levels. The state's efforts to maintain national security may result in providing international, societal or individual security. This, according to Wæver, is because national security is 'fundamentally dependent on international dynamics (especially regional ones)'.[22] This tendency may increase as borders between domestic and international concerns become blurred through globalisation and interdependence. Under such circumstances, states share problems with other states, such as drug problems. Such a shared concern becomes one of the components of international society because international society forms its characteristics over the reflection of the characteristics of the individual states.[23] The existence of common enemies (problems), according to Haftendorn, forms the concept of international security that is 'based on a mutual interest in survival'.[24] International security, hence, implies the close linkage between 'the security of one state' and 'that of other states, at least one other state'.[25] In brief, the concept of international security emerged from the shared national security concerns among members of the international society.

Considering the connection between societal/individual security and national security, threats posed to individual and societal security could trigger national insecurity concerns through affecting state stability.[26] The insecurity of individuals and society may also result from the inability of the state to provide necessary services to the people. To some extent, as Wæver maintains, the relationship between national security and societal/individual security are two sides of the same coin.[27]

This may suggest that security issues on different levels could coalesce into a form of national security from a broader perspective: to some extent, international security is the globalisation of national security issues, and societal and individual security issues could be micro elements of national security. Including supra-state and sub-state elements in national security as 'dynamics of national security' makes the traditional understanding of national security more flexible, allowing it to contain wider issue areas that have come to be recognised as non-traditional security threats.

21 Wæver, quoted in Buzan, B., *People, States and Fear: An Agenda For International Security Studies In The Post-Cold War Era*, 1991, London: Harvester Wheatsheaf, p. 329.

22 Emphasis in original; Wæver, 'Securitization and Desecuritization', p. 49.

23 Buzan *et al.*, *Security*, p. 144.

24 Haftendorn, H., 'The Security Puzzle: Theory-building and Discipline-building in International Security', *International Security Quarterly*, Vol. 35, No. 1, 1991, p. 9.

25 Ibid.

26 Strange, S., *States and Markets*.

27 Wæver, 'Securitization and Desecuritization', p. 67.

It may, however, require redefining as to what is to be 'secured' under the concept of national security.

From the Realist perspective, transnational organised crime and drug trafficking are not recognised as security issues since they do not pose a physical threat to the state. The threat posed by non-traditional security threats is not directly to the physical survival of the state, but more a threat to the function of the state. Hurrell argues that non-traditional threats originated from the weakness of the state.[28] Williams maintains that: 'if one defines security as not just external military threats, but as a challenge to the effective functioning of society, then drug trafficking is much more serious than many issues that have traditionally been seen as a threat to security.'[29] The threats posed by drug trafficking affect the idea and identity of the state through disruption of its societal functions, and the rise of public disorder.

The protection of the idea and the identity of the state, as well as its functions, could be regarded as the preservation of the status quo.[30] This leads to a wider definition of national interests, not just material concern but values, qualities and ideas about the state. Therefore, phenomena that, Jordan and Taylor have argued, could 'threaten fundamental values and the vitality of the state' are regarded as national security threats.[31] For example, widespread criminal activities undermine public respect for laws and public order. The government becomes unable to control the political, economic and social affairs within its territory and this undermines its sovereignty.[32]

This kind of weakness in a state also influences the representation of the state within the international arena. This is because these state functions and structures, as well as political beliefs about the governing of a state, are seen as a demonstration of the quality of the state, which creates the institutional expression of the state.[33] Jackson argues that the recognition of a state in the international political arena depends on recognition of its sovereignty by other states.[34] Thereby, defending identity may secure quality and representation of states and allow a state 'to live as itself' – the preservation of the status quo.[35] In this respect, national security in a modern sense is still about defending the state and preserving the status quo as in classic national security, but its concern has broadened to the internal aspects of

---

28 Hurrell, A., 'Security in Latin America', *International Affairs*, Vol. 74, No 3, July 1998, p. 541.

29 Williams, P., 'Transnational Criminal Organisation and International Security,' *Survival*, Vol. 36, No.1, Spring 1994, p. 107.

30 Buzan, *People, States and Fear*, p. 65.

31 Jordan, A., and Taylor Jr., W., *American National Security*, 1981, Baltimore: Johns Hopkins University Press, p. 3.

32 Ullman, R., 'Redefining Security', *International Security*, Vol. 8, Summer 1983, p. 133.

33 Buzan, *People, States and Fear*, p. 65.

34 Jackson, R. (ed.), *Sovereignty at the Millennium*, 1999, Oxford: Blackwell.

35 Wæver, 'Securitization and Desecuritization', p. 67 (emphasis in original).

statehood, such as state identity and quality, from its physical existence and relative power in international relationships.[36]

According to the post-positivists, there is no 'objective truth'.[37] Threats do not exist until a phenomenon is recognised as a danger to individuals, society, states and the international community. Although Realists focus on threats and the defence of the state, they take the existence of 'threats' and 'enemies' for granted. From a Realist perspective the 'enemy' exists and it does not explain how it came to be recognised as such.[38] The arguments by post-positivists claim that threats do not exist unless a thing is interpreted and recognised as a threat. According to Ewald, 'Nothing is a risk in itself; there is no objective risk. But, anything can be a risk; it all depends on how one analyses the danger.'[39] The existence of an alleged threat is dependent on its interpretation. Campbell concludes that: 'Danger bears no essential, necessary, or unproblematic relation to the action or event from which it is said to derive.'[40] Danger (or threat) is created from understanding and from a focus on the factor of a phenomenon: in other words, 'an effect of interpretation.'[41] In other words, according to Mitsilegas et al., fear is created from exaggerated perception of a phenomenon.[42] Bigo has taken this concept further and concluded that the perception of threats is constructed and directed for political purposes.[43]

The conceptualisation of threats is, therefore, crucial because it could be influenced by the state's interests and cultural elements in addition to the actual impact of the phenomenon.[44] Neufeld maintains that 'there is a fundamental link between epistemology – the question of what counts as reliable knowledge – and politics – the problems, needs, and interests deemed important and legitimate by a given community.'[45] Social knowledge gives legitimacy and existence to a threat, and strengthens a collective identity based on that knowledge. This is because, as critical theorists claim, 'social knowledge requires a purpose', such as social exclusion of a

---

36 Wæver, O., Buzan, B., Kelstrup, M., and Lemaite, P., with Carlton, D., *Identity, Migration and the New Security Agenda in Europe*, 1993, London: Pinter, p. 21; Wæver, 'Securitization and Desecuritization', p. 47; and Fukumi, S., *National Security Threat in the Changing World: the Case of Andean Cocaine Trafficking*, MPhil Thesis at the University of Birmingham, UK, 2001.

37 Terriff *et al.*, *Security Studies Today*, pp. 100–101.

38 Desch, 'Culture Crash'.

39 Ewald, F., 'Insurance and Risk', in Burchell, G., Gordin, C., and Miller, P. (eds), *The Foucault Effect: Studies in Governmental Rationality*, 1991, Chicago: University of Chicago Press, p. 199 (emphasis in original).

40 Campbell, D., *Writing Security: United States Foreign Policy and the Politics of Identity*, 1998, Manchester: Manchester University Press, p. 2.

41 Ibid.

42 Mitsilegas, V., Rees, W., and Monar, J., *The European Union and Internal Security: Guardian of People?*, 2003, Basingstoke: Palgrave Macmillan, chapter 2.

43 Bigo, D., 'Security and Immigration: Toward a Critique of the Governability of Unease', *Alternatives*, Vol. 27, Special Issue, February 2002, p. 85.

44 Wæver, 'Securitization and Desecuritization', p. 65.

45 Neufeld, M., 'Reflexibility and International Relations Theory', in *Beyond Positivism: Critical Reflections on International Relations*, 1994, Boulder, CO: Lynne Rienner, p, 15.

particular group and alienisation of a phenomenon.[46] Heidensohn, who studied the conceptualisation of crime, concluded that the concept of social evil is 'not merely socially constructed' but also 'in part socially concernedly constructed'.[47] Hence, it can be understood that a security threat is created and institutionalised by an elite, and the created threats need to be recognised and accepted by the society.[48] In other words, threats can be 'produced' for political purposes.

For example, a state may choose a phenomenon as a threat because it serves as a convenient political tool. According to Christie and Bruun, illicit drugs are 'good' and 'useful' enemies because they do not jeopardise 'the interest of power groups'.[49] Illicit drugs are not related to profits for those in legal economic activities, such as corporations or lobby groups. The government, therefore, can be free from ties to these interest groups, and retains flexibility in decision-making on drug related issues. As Bullington et al. and Carpenter argue, the flexibility in decision-making and the nature of drugs[50] allow a government to use the threat of drugs at different times in its policy making according to the international circumstances.[51]

The US president has the responsibility of determining and prioritising national security threats.[52] Consequently, the priorities in US security concerns can differ from time to time. It was communism in the Cold War era, and has become drugs and terrorism in the post-Cold War era. During the Cold War era, the United States did not prioritise drug control as much as communist threats despite Reagan's 'war on drugs'; Treaster explained that the lack of drug control efforts in the Caribbean in 1984 was because communism appeared to be the more serious concern for the US government.[53] The Clinton administration in the post-Cold War era, however, continuously increased the budget on drug control in Latin America as well as other parts of the world during its eight years in office.[54] The Clinton administration's

---

46 See Linklater, A., 'The Achievement of Critical Theory', in Smith, S., Booth, K., and Zalewski, M. (eds), *International Theory: Positivism and Beyond*, 1996, Cambridge: Cambridge University Press, pp. 279–298.

47 Heidensohn, F., *Crime and Society*, 1989, London: Macmillan Education, p. 5.

48 Wæver, 'Securitization and Desecuritization', p. 57.

49 Christie, N., and Bruun, K., *Der Nuetzliche Feind: Die Drogenpolitik und ihre Nutzniesser*, 1991, Bielefeld: AJZ Verlag, pp. 53–54, translated in Gerber, J., and Jensen, E.L., 'The Internationalization of US Policy on Illicit Drug Control', in Gerber, J., and Jensen, E. L. (eds), *Drug War American Style: The Internationalization of Failed Policy and Its Alternatives*, 2001, New York: Garland Publishing, p. 8.

50 As above, drugs and drug trafficking organisations do not pose an immediate threat to the existence of a state or state boundaries, and the damage posed by them is not highly visible.

51 Bullington, B. and Block, A.A., 'A Trojan horse: Anti-communism and the war on drugs', *Contemporary Crises*, No. 14, 1990, p. 52; Carpenter, T.G., *Bad Neighbor Policy: Washington's futile war on drugs in Latin America*, 2003, New York: Palgrave Macmillan, p. 49; and Treaster, J., 'Jamaica, Close US Ally, Does Little to Halt Drugs', *New York Times*, 10 September 1984.

52 Sarkesian, S.C., Williams, J.A., and Cimbala, S.J., *U.S. National Security: Policymakers, Processes, and Politics*, Third Edition, 2002, London: Lynne Rienner, p. 297.

53 Treaster, op cit.

54 See later chapters on US drug control in the Andes and Plan Colombia.

policy had more emphasis on reducing demand by treating the addicts. This led to a relative increase in the drug control budget of the Clinton administration, although their supply reduction policy was not as active as that of the former administrations. For the Clinton administration, drugs were a serious security threat within the United States. The G.W. Bush administration did not downgrade the significance of drugs in its national security until 11 September 2001. Since the terrorist attacks on this day, drugs are no longer the priority in national security, and instead the war on terror has become the most significant national security issue for the United States.[55] The changes in security priority will lead to changes of identity.

The formation of a threat, as Hopf argues, can be analysed through the identity of a state and its perception of a phenomenon.[56] Claims about security 'emerge' with the formation of societal identity because social identity is easier to define through the differentiation of 'others' from 'self'.[57] For example, citizens of a state recognise 'self' against the recognition of 'foreigners' (or 'others'). It provides separation of 'self' from 'others' and creates relationships between 'self' and 'others', such as friends and enemies. Referring to the relationship between 'self' and 'others', Wendt argues that the creation of an 'enemy' and a 'threat' are necessary for states to justify what they are and their reason to exist.[58] McSweeney maintains that the insecurity of 'our' world will be registered when the: 'order is disrupted and ontological insecurity engendered insofar as we sense a cleavage or dissonance in the patterns of mutual knowledge, common norms and standards binding us in a condition of solidarity with others.'[59]

A similar notion has been studied in the field of social discipline and behaviour in the manner of crime.[60] In a society, crime represents immorality, and through the filter of immorality the members of a community distance themselves from undesirable behaviours. In international relationships, 'threat is an escapable feature of politics' and the cognition of relationships in quality and stability between 'us' and 'others'

---

55 The US National Security Council, *The National Security Strategy of the United States of America*, September 2002, Washington DC: The White House, http://www.whitehouse.gov/nsc/nss.html (Accessed on 25 May 2004); *The US National Security Council, U.S. National Security Strategy: Prevent Our Enemies From Threatening Us, Our Allies, and Our Friends with Weapons of Mass Destruction*, June 2001, http://www.state.gov/r/pa/ei/wh/15425.htm (Accessed on 25 May 2004); and US Commission on National Security, *Seeking a National Strategy: A Concert for Preserving Security and Promoting Freedom*, 2000, www.nssg.gov/PhaseII.pdf (Accessed on 25 May 2004).

56 Hopf, T., 'The Promise of Constructivism in International Relations Theory', *International Security*, Vol. 23, No. 1, Summer 1998, p. 187.

57 Wæver *et al.*, *Identity, Migration and the New Security Agenda in Europe*, p. 21; and Hopf, op cit., p. 199.

58 Wendt, A., *Social Theory of International Politics*, 1999, Cambridge: Cambridge University Press, pp. 272–278.

59 McSweeney, B., *Security, Identity and Interests: A Sociology of International Relations*, 1999, Cambridge: Cambridge University Press, p. 157.

60 Durkheim regards it as 'an escapable feature of society'. Durkheim, E., *The Rules of Sociological Method*, 1964, New York: Free Press, p. 69.

define security and insecurity of 'our' world.[61] A security threat is about 'others' that include not only 'other states' but also 'other things' that are incompatible with both state social identity and collective identity.

To summarise, then, a non-traditional security threat needs to be conceptualised in a broader sense than traditional security threats to include dangers to intrinsic aspects of state activities. A non-traditional security threat may be defined as a phenomenon that threatens a state's identity and undermines the quality of a state. The identity of a state is expressed in the form of governance and policies that reflect the ideology and beliefs of the state (or government) and are perceived as the international representation of the state by other states. Turning to the quality of a state, it is judged through its ability to perform state functions (political, economic and judicial) and its stability. A state's identity and quality may be interchangeable, in the sense that the malfunction of the state could affect its identity, for example, a destabilised state and an inability to maintain public order would undermine its status in international society. The impact of non-traditional security threats to a state is complex and abstract. Furthermore, the threat posed by non-traditional threats to a state can vary because the impact of the threat may be influenced by the strength of a state.[62]

Non-Traditional Security Threats and State Policy

This section will focus on one of the non-traditional security threats, cocaine trafficking, in order to examine the nature of the threat and to investigate the implications of the conceptualisation of cocaine trafficking as a threat to state policy. The securitisation of cocaine trafficking is to prioritise cocaine trafficking in political agendas because it is (or it will be) affecting the status quo of a state and other political actors, such as the European Union, significantly.[63] At the international level, according to Buzan et al., securitisation involves presenting an issue as urgent and significant and that needs to be dealt with by the international society.[64] The referent object at stake here is not only material, such as financial resources, but also a state's identity, including morals and values in the society.[65]

Examining the Impact of Cocaine Trafficking

In this section, the impact of cocaine trafficking on states will be examined. The nature of non-traditional security threats is complex and touches upon wide issue areas. Buzan et al. describe them as 'multidimensional security threats'.[66] In other

---

61 McSweeney, *Security, Identity and Interests*, pp. 101 and 143.

62 Strength here refers to the maturity of state systems, such as well-established state decision-making processes, rules and regulations for legal economic activities, and the justice system.

63 Buzan *et al.*, *Security*, p. 22.

64 Buzan *et al.*, *Security*, p. 29.

65 See section above for referent object.

66 Buzan *et al.*, *Security*, chapter 6.

words, the referent object for security needs to be perceived through a holistic approach recognising that the referent object for a state consists of multiple elements, not a single element. This is because the identity of a state is based on the complex functions that a state performs domestically and internationally.[67] Drug trafficking is a business with widespread networks, and trafficking organisations can be powerful with substantial amounts of wealth at their disposal.[68] Therefore, the greatest threat posed by drug trafficking organisations comes from their financial ability and their efforts to protect their business from law enforcers and rival organisations. Regarding the drug industry, Chalk argues that the threats posed by the narcotics trade affect various aspects of society, including crime rates, the spread of disease, loss of economic resources and the weakening of state structures through corruption.[69] He concludes: 'they have negatively affected nearly every dimension of viable human and state existence in a geographic area that spans virtually the entire international system.'[70]

The impact of cocaine trafficking on states will be analysed in relation to various state activities. The approach is derived from the work of Lupsha, which investigates four aspects of state affairs: economic, political, violence and public order, and diplomatic relations.[71] These aspects are chosen in order to analyse various state functions affected by the activities of criminal organisations. In other words, this approach intends to simplify the complexity and variety of state affairs for analysis, but still to ensure that sufficient coverage of the significant features is undertaken. Lupsha, in his argument, focuses on three of the four aspects: economic, political and the private use of violence by criminal organisations. His emphasis for analysis is on the impact within the state's domain, and exclusively as a domestic concern. In this thesis, however, the fourth aspect (the diplomatic aspect) has been added from the work of Fukumi to bring an international dimension to the analysis.[72]

The economic aspect is investigated because transnational organised crime seeks to profit from illicit economic activities. Also, business activities, both legal and illegal, and the national economy are significant issues for any state from a Neo-Realist point of view (see below). The political aspect and violence and public order are two sides of the same coin for criminal organisations. It is represented in the Spanish phrase 'Plomo o Plata',[73] offered by criminals, which means 'death or money'. For a state, it means bribery and coercion by the criminal organisations to manipulate government systems for their activities. These two aspects are closely linked to the legitimacy and sovereignty of the state. The diplomatic aspect concerns

67 Ibid., pp. 22–23.

68 Van de Velde, J.R., 'The Growth of Criminal Organizations and Insurgent Groups Abroad due to International Drug Trafficking', *Low Intensity Conflict & Law Enforcement*, Vol. 5, No 3, Winter 1996, p. 466.

69 Chalk, P., *Non-Military Security and Global Order: The Impact of Extremism, Violence and Chaos on National and International Security*, 2000, London: Macmillan, pp. 46–48.

70 Ibid., p. 56.

71 Lupsha, P.A., 'Transnational Organized Crime versus the Nation-State', *Transnational Organized Crime*, Vol. 2, No 1, Spring 1996; and Fukumi, op cit.

72 Fukumi, op cit.

73 Literally, this means 'lead or silver'.

the recognition and sovereignty of the state in international society. This may be an indirect impact from transnational organised crime as international reputations are formed by other states not by the criminal organisations. However, criminal activities that take place in the state may damage the state's position in the international community. Hence, it is also an impact of transnational organised crime. In the following sections, each aspect will be explored and argued.

Economic Impact   Transnational criminal organisations (TCOs) generate more wealth than many of the world's biggest multinational corporations.[74] The wealth at their disposal flows into the legal economic system with positive and negative implications, and influences both national and international markets. The penetration of TCOs into the legal economic and financial systems can affect legitimate economic activities.

The illicit gains need to be 'cleaned' before the criminals can use them in the legal economic system. The process of legalising this illicitly gained money is called 'money laundering,' and TCOs purchase legal companies and other legal investments as part of this scheme. Money laundering per se does not have any immediate negative effects for banks, since it will bring them business. In addition, a policy of transparency that some governments are encouraging does not promote the bank's business because not only illegal enterprises but also most legal corporations are reluctant to reveal their financial circumstances.[75]

Money laundering brings enormous sums of foreign currencies (mostly US dollars) into the national and international financial system.[76] The large sums[77] of narco-dollars flowing into the national economy can be an advantage as well as a disadvantage to a state, particularly to weak states. The inflow of US dollars to the national financial markets generated by illegal activities can create fictitious economic strength and lead to state currency appreciation against other major currencies.[78] Bolivia in the late 1980s, for example, experienced a lower exchange rate due to narco-dollars, and its legal industries lost competitiveness in domestic and international markets.[79]

---

74 See Introduction for the details of Latin American cocaine trafficking.

75 Strange, S., *Mad Money*, 1998, Manchester: Manchester University Press, pp. 129–133.

76 Transactions for money-laundering usually start with a transfer from local banks to the criminals, but the money will then be transferred to international banks with secrecy rules, such as Swiss Banks, or to off-shore banking. This disguises the origin of the cash by transferring it several times through different banks.

77 According to the UN estimate, illicit earnings worth £400 billion enter into the international financial system annually. UNDCP, *World Drug Report 1997*, 1997, Oxford: Oxford University Press.

78 Van de Velde, 'The Growth of Criminal Organizations and Insurgent Groups Abroad due to International Drug Trafficking', *Low Intensity Conflict & Law Enforcement*, Vol. 5, No. 3, Winter 1996, p. 480.

79 De Franco, M., and Godoy, R., 'The Economic Consequences of Cocaine Production in Bolivia: Historical, Local and Macroeconomic Perspectives', *Journal of Latin American Studies*, Vol. 24, 1992, p. 392.

Criminals seek to obtain access to and profits from the legal economic system. The criminal organisations, therefore, invest in and purchase some legitimate corporations and factories. Supported by illicit earnings, TCOs often trade in contraband goods and can supply commodities at cheaper prices than legitimate firms. The contraband businesses increase the flow of untaxed goods[80] and decrease the competitiveness of legal corporations in the markets.[81] Consequently, the government loses large amounts of revenue and the healthy growth of the national economy may be prevented.

The poor financial situation of a state or corporation will also give suitable opportunity to TCOs to 'colonise' the state or industries.[82] The weakness of legitimate corporations in the markets makes it difficult for some developing countries to reduce their narco-dependency since corporations operated by criminals are often the leading companies. In respect of the employment of the locals by TCO related industries, Findlay agues it is possible that such dependency brings local resistance against a crackdown on TCOs.[83]

Furthermore, efforts to combat transnational organised crime tend to be long-term and large projects, and are costly to governments.[84] In the case of drug related crimes, the government may need to operate both demand and supply reduction programmes for effective drug control.[85] The cost of the projects includes not only

---

80 According to Salomon Kalmanovitz of the Colombian central bank, there are estimated to be US$3.5 billion earnings from 'money-laundered contraband' entering Colombia untaxed. Weisman, A., 'The Cocaine Conundrum', *Los Angeles Times Magazine*, 24 September 1995, http://www.worldcom.nl/tni/drugs/links/lt950924.htm (Accessed 15 May 1998).

81 The wealth at a criminal organisation's disposal enables criminals to undermine market competition, for example by selling goods below profit levels, to eliminate competitors from the market. In the case of agricultural industries, the monopoly of land by criminal organisations is commonly seen. Interview with an official at the Colombian Embassy in Brussels, 10 July 2002; *Corruption and Drugs in Colombia: Democracy at Risk*, A Staff Report to the Committee of Foreign Relations US Senate, February 1996, Washington DC: GPO, p. 12; and Lee III, R., *Cocaine Production in the Andes*, Hearing before the Select Committee on Narcotics Abuse and Control, House of Representatives, 101st Congress, 1st Session, 7 June 1989, Washington DC: GPO, p. 13.

82 Findlay, M., *The Globalisation of Crime: Understanding Transitional Relationships in Context*, 1999, Cambridge: Cambridge University Press, p. 129.

83 Ibid., p. 128.

84 For example, Plan Colombia is a US$ 7.5 billion project and the Colombian government is relying on international support for most of the resources necessary for the project. For the details, see Chapter 6.

85 It has been argued that drug control requires a 'balanced approach' between demand and supply reduction for solid results. See for example, Hak-Su, K., *A drug-free Asia is an essential condition for sustainable economic and social development*, the paper presented at the International Congress in Pursuit of a Drug-free ASEAN 2015: Sharing the vision, leading the change, 11 October 2000, http://www.unescap.org/esid/hds/drug/drugfree.htm (Accessed 31 May 2004); Thomas, G.B., *Balance in Theory But Not in Practice: Exploring the Continued Emphasis on Supply Reduction in Canada's National Drug Control Policy*, http://www.johnhoward.ca/document/drugs/forum/1.htm (Accessed 31 May 2004); The US Office of National Drug Control Policy, *President's National Drug Control Strategy*, March 2004, http://www.whitehousedrugpolicy.gov/publications/policy/ndcs04/message.html   (Accessed

the expenditures on the project per se, but also the losses caused by the crackdown on criminal organisations. The states with heavy dependence on transnational organised crime related industries, particularly developing states, could face huge annual economic losses, and unemployment.[86] Also, in order to carry out law enforcement operations, it is necessary to have adequate equipment, such as helicopters and arms. Military equipment is expensive, particularly for developing states, and according to Ball, these military expenditures have a negative effect on economic growth.[87]

From the economic perspective, TCOs can harm a state through penetration and control of the national economic and financial systems. Although the impact of underground economic activities might be unclear, TCOs can have a strong impact on the international economy as well as the national economy simply through their power to control markets. Therefore, as Strange argues, organised crime can be 'the major threat to the world system in the 1990s and beyond' because of its potential to equalise the financial power of the criminal organisations to that of a state.[88]

Political Impact   Political impact refers to the influence of TCOs on government and the private sector through bribery. Corruption and intimidation allow TCOs to enjoy protection from government institutions and ensures their position in markets.[89] The risk of corruption is particularly high in the judicial sector, and also in the financial and banking sectors for money-laundering operations.[90] The effects of corruption are regarded, according to Williams, as 'the HIV or AIDS of the modern state'.[91]

Corruption undermines the legitimacy of the state; in other words, a state may endanger its identity as the de jure government. Being recognised as 'legitimate' is to be regarded as 'appropriate' and 'morally proper'.[92] A legitimate state can expect people to be obedient towards the law because of 'the rightfulness of a state' and people's belief in 'moral authority'.[93] The government should maintain and engender the belief that 'the existing political institutions are the most appropriate ones for

---

31 May 2004); US Drug Enforcement Agency, *Fact 2: A balanced approach of prevention, enforcement, and treatment is the key in the fight against drugs*, http://www.usdoj.gov/dea/demand/speakout/02so.htm (Accessed 31 May 2004); and UN Office on Drugs and Crime, 'Is the international community meeting its drug control targets?' in *Update 2003*, http://www.unodc.org/unodc/en/newsletter_2003-03-31_1_page004.html (Accessed 31 May 2004).

86   Bolivia is allegedly facing losses of US$ 500 million annually due to a crackdown on illicit coca cultivation.

87   Ball, op cit., pp. 163–167.

88   Strange, S., *The Retreat of the State: the Diffusion of Power in the World Economy*, 1996, Cambridge: Cambridge University Press, p. 121 (emphasis in original).

89   For intimidation, see the section titled 'Violence and Public Order'.

90   Richards, J.R., *Transnational Criminal Organization, Cybercrime, and Money Laundering*, 1999, Boca Raton: CRC Press, p. 45.

91   Williams, P., 'Transnational Crime and Corruption', in White, B., Little, R. and Smith, M. (eds) *Issues in World Politics* (Second Edition), 2001, Basingstoke: Palgrave Macmillan, p. 238.

92   Schaar, J.H., 'Legitimacy in the Modern State', in Connolly, W. (ed.), *Legitimacy and the State*, 1984, Oxford: Basil Blackwell, p. 108.

93   Barker, R., *Political Legitimacy and the State*, 1990, Oxford: Clarendon Press, p. 11.

the society.[94] A corrupt government loses its legitimacy. For example, criminals walking down the street with impunity undermine state authority.[95] The TCOs may become a 'state within a state' – a land controlled by the rules set by the criminals not the government.[96] Even worse it is possible that the corrupt military, loose from governmental control, can pose the threat of a coup d'état if the interests of the military and TCOs coincide. This happened in Bolivia.[97] When governments fail to maintain legitimacy, according to Beetham, they will face either 'illegitimacy'[98] or 'delegitimacy'.[99] The difference between the two is that an illegitimate state has a government that has obtained power illegally, a delegitimate state, on the other hand, has a government that has limited authority and power to control the territory and to

---

94 Lipset, S. M., 'Social Conflict, Legitimacy, and Democracy', in Connolly, William (ed.), *Legitimacy and the State*, 1984, Oxford: Basil Blackwell, p. 88.

95 Although the implications of corruption on state decision-making may not always be obvious to the public, according to Newell, it is possible to examine it through the laws passed (or not passed) to restrict illegal businesses. Newell, J.L., *Corruption mitigating policies in Italy*, paper presented at PSA Annual Conference, 15–17 April 2003, http://www.psa.ac.uk/cps/2003/James%20Newell.pdf (Accessed 31 May 2004).

96 St. Vincent, a Caribbean island, has been controlled by the drug traffickers because they are in a stronger financial position than the government. Smaller states can face bigger risks from TCOs than stronger states. 'All this and drugs', *The Economist*, 13 June 1998, p. 66.

97 In 1980, Bolivian cocaine cartels supported a coup known as the 'coca coup' to establish a military regime that would be supportive to drug trafficking. Painter, J., *Bolivia and Coca: A Study in Dependency*, 1994, London: Lynne Rienner, p. 59; Lee III, R.W., *The White Labyrinth: Cocaine & Political Power*, 1989, London: Transaction Publishers, p. 119; and Spedding, A.L., 'Cocataki, Taki-Coca: Trade, Traffic, and Organized Peasant Resistance in the Yungas of La Paz', in Léons, M.B. and Sanabria, H. (eds), *Coca, Cocaine, and the Bolivian Reality*, 1997, New York: State University of New York Press, p. 119.

98 Illegitimacy occurs when the power is: 'either acquired in contravention of the rules (expropriation, usurpation, coup d'état), or exercised in a manner that contravenes or exceeds them.' Illegitimacy, however, needs to be differentiated from 'legitimacy deficit' or 'weakness'. A legitimacy deficit related to 'the source of political authority' is described as: 'a *divergence* or *discrepancy* between the constitutional rules and the beliefs that should provide their justification, whether the divergence exists because the rules have been established or altered in a manner that is incompatible with established beliefs about the rightful source of authority, or because the beliefs of a society have themselves evolved over time in a way that weakens support for the constitutional order.' On the contrary, a legitimacy deficit relates to 'the ends or purpose of the government', and is described as: 'an *inadequacy* or *incapacity* of the constitutional rules to facilitate successful government performance, or to provide resolution in the event of failure, whether the failure is one of ineffectiveness or of partiality in respect of the ends that government exists to attain.' (Emphasis in original) Beetham, D., *The Legitimation of Power*, 1991, London: MacMillan, pp. 16, 207–208.

99 This inappropriateness and inadequacy bring 'delegitimacy' of a state that is explained as: 'to expose, not so much the government's lack of a valid source of authority, as its inability to secure the general interest.' Delegitimacy is caused by the withdrawal of consent by those 'whose consent is necessary to the legitimisation of government' through 'mass demonstrations, strikes, acts of civil disobedience'. Ibid., pp. 209–212.

secure general interests. Under such circumstances, the government will lose: 'moral standing ... [and] ... its capacity to rule.'[100]

A state that has lost its capacity to rule has lost its sovereignty. Although TCOs seek to control the government in order to create a comfortable environment for their business operations, the loss of control over the decision-making process and the judicial process may be crucial for its legitimacy. As Buzan, et al. argue, the maintenance of sovereignty is a matter of survival for a state, and hence, 'Anything that can be portrayed as a violation of sovereignty (an intervention) can be presented as a security problem.'[101]

Moreover, state identity is founded on the legitimacy of the government and the loss of it has significant implications for both the domestic and international representation of the state. This is because, as Buzan maintains: 'The government is both an important symbol and a major manifestation of the state. The fate of particular governments may not be of much account to the state as a whole, but congenital weakness of government brings into question the integrity, and even the existence of the state, and therefore has to be regarded as a national security issue.'[102] The challenge to the sovereignty and legitimacy of a state and the loss of them may detract from the idea of the state and the dignity of the nation. As a result of this, the government might lose the integrity of the state from the lack of mass support, as well as losing international recognition as a 'proper' state.[103]

Violence and Public Order   Transnational organised crime is often associated with violence in different forms. It can lead to an increase in the use of violence by other non-state actors, such as revolutionary groups, and occasionally by legitimate organisations, such as workers' unions. TCOs use violence, not to overthrow the government, but to intimidate and to manipulate it for their interests.[104] The use of violence by TCOs, nevertheless, challenges state sovereignty, that is to say, the monopoly of the use of violence. The private use of violence may affect individuals and the state both physically and psychologically as the government lacks the ability to provide the sense of security to the majority of the nation. The use of violence by non-state actors may be categorised in three forms in relation to drug trafficking: narco-terrorism, assassination and intimidation, and demonstrations by political groups.

Narco-terrorism, according to Schmid, can be defined in two ways. In the narrow sense, it refers to the terrorist style use of violence by drug trafficking organisations, frequently witnessed in Colombia in the 1980s.[105] In this sense, Sullivan argues: 'A blend of traditional terrorism and quasi-terrorism finds its form in narco-

---

100 Ibid., p. 209.

101 Buzan *et al.*, *Security*, p. 150.

102 Buzan, B., *People, States and Fear*, p. 105.

103 Ibid., p. 87.

104 Steve, 'Drug Wars: Interview Steve', *Frontline*, http://www.pbs.org/wgbh/pages/frontline/shows/drugs/interviews/steve.html.

105 Schmid defines narco-terrorism in the narrow sense as: 'activities initiated by drug traffickers using violence or the threat of violence against individuals, property, state, or its agents, to intimidate and coerce people into modifying their actions in ways advantageous to

terrorism.'[106] TCOs' use of planned, sophisticated, high-threat violence is an expression of disapproval of government decisions and a means to achieve goals and interests – larger profits from illegal activities.[107] The escalation of conflicts between the government and armed TCOs registers the resemblance to a civil war without political ideology. The use of violence by TCOs is a crime, since war in a traditional sense occurs when a state fights against other states employing the military. The aggressive challenge of TCOs, however, is regarded as internal warfare due to its military capability and the damages posed to the state. As van Creveld maintains in his analysis on the changing nature of warfare, the distinctions between war and crime became ambiguous and the concept of war has been expanded.[108]

Narco-terrorism, in its broad sense, is known as a 'marriage of convenience'.[109] This refers to the connection between the drug trafficking trade and the revolutionary groups that already pose a danger to states. Their alliance is for their own self-interest. Williams and Savona point out the factors of convergence between TCOs and terrorist groups as: 'the willingness of transnational criminal organizations to develop direct links with groups that engage in widespread use of violence for political purposes'; and the needs of terrorist groups to ensure sponsorship of their activities due to 'the changed political context' after the end of the Cold War.[110] This marriage of convenience makes government counter-measures difficult to operate because, in many cases, the units that deal with crime differ from those dealing with terrorism, that is to say the police and army respectively.[111] Also, the marriage of convenience can strengthen the operations of both TCOs and insurgency groups through the mutual support of financial resources and military skills.

This type of alliance and the resources it generates allows TCOs to intimidate and even to assassinate government officials, politicians and those who are against transnational organised crimes.[112] Among those targeted by the TCOs, the most vulnerable are those in the judicial sector, such as judges, prosecutors, lawyers and

---

the drug traffickers.' Schmid, A.P., 'The Links between Transnational Organized Crime and Terrorist Crimes', *Transnational Organized Crime*, Vol. 2, No. 4, Winter 1996, p. 66.

106 Sullivan, J.P., 'Third Generation Street Gangs: Turf, Cartel, and Net Warriors', *Transnational Organized Crime*, Vol. 3, No. 3, Autumn 1997, p. 97.

107 Taylor, C., Testimony at Joint hearing before Congress, *International Terrorism, Insurgency, and Drug Trafficking: Narcotic Trafficking, Terrorism, and Political Insurgency*, 14 May 1985, United States Senate, Committee on the Judiciary and Committee on Foreign Relations, p. 114.

108 Van Creveld, M., *The Transformation of War*, 1991, New York: Free Press, p. 204.

109 Westrate, D., 'Remarks', in *Caucus on International Narcotics Control of The United States Senate*, The Congressional Research Service, 8 May 1987, the Government Printing Office, p. 2.

110 Williams, P. and Savona, E.U., *The United Nations and Transnational Organized Crime*, 1996, London: Frank Cass, pp. 25–26.

111 For example, in the United States, terrorist groups in foreign states are dealt with by the Federal Bureau of Investigation, and drug related issues are dealt with by the Drug Enforcement Agency.

112 For the details, see the section on Latin American cocaine trafficking in the Introduction.

police because they face the criminals directly when enforcing the law. The fear of retaliation by criminals among the law enforcers poses a dilemma in bringing justice to the society.[113] Consequently, the judicial system does not function in cases related to TCOs, and some criminals have escaped with impunity.

The use of violence and intimidation by TCOs undermines public order, the security of individuals and the community environment due to the lack of ability of the government to ensure peoples' safety. Challenging the monopoly of violence and supremacy (or internal sovereignty) of the government may result in the lack of a state's ability and capability to control internal security. The impression created domestically and internationally of such a state may change the recognition of the state's identity, and affect its quality as a state. For example, the lack of the government's capability of enforcing laws against criminal organisations could be taken as neglect to control crimes, which could jeopardise the safety of its citizens.

Diplomatic Impact   This section concerns itself with the external relationship and issues of state sovereignty. Co-operation and interaction between states are inescapable features of international crime control due to the nature of transnational organised crime. Crime control and punishment, however, are sensitive issues for state sovereignty. The authority to punish citizens of a state is the power of violence and coercion at the government's disposal. In the case of transnational organised crime, criminals operate regardless of jurisdiction and national borders. Those states whose territories are penetrated by the TCOs therefore find themselves in a complex situation with other states,[114] and recognise the necessity for tighter regulations and laws.[115]

The essence of statehood is sovereignty, and therefore states need to protect it in order to survive.[116] Sovereignty in world politics is regarded as an essential element for a member of international society and is required in order to establish formal relationships with other members. The sovereignty of a state, therefore, needs to be

---

113 In some cities in Latin America, there are no judges who will try drug related cases because of death threats from drug trafficking organisations. See, for example, McCaughan, M., 'Cartel profits fuel a corrupt Colombian boom', *The Guardian*, 26 February 1992; and United States General Accounting Office, *Drug Control: US-Supported Efforts in Colombia and Bolivia*, Report to the Congress, November 1988, Washington DC: GAO, p. 26.

114 For example, foreign criminals operating in one (or more) state(s) are the concern of both the state(s) where the criminals operated and the state where the criminals hold their nationalities. In the case of human trafficking, the problem will be more complicated because it will involve the state where the victims hold their nationalities.

115 International laws and treaties between/among states are means to restrict state sovereignty and in general, states are reluctant to increase such restrictions over their sovereignty. Although modern states cannot enjoy their sovereignty in full (like the states in the 16th century) due to interdependence, there are core elements in sovereignty that are still largely at the disposal of individual states, such as law enforcement. James, A., *Sovereign Statehood*, 1986, London: Allen & Unwin, p. 154.

116 See the part regarding 'Security Threats and Securitisation'.

recognised by other sovereign states.[117] Mutual respect for each other's sovereignty works to bring order to international society.[118] Jackson notes that: 'Sovereignty is a judicial idea and [an] institution,'[119] he concludes that sovereignty is 'a distinctive way of arranging the contacts and relations of political communities, or states, such that their political independence is mutually recognised and they co-exist and interact on a foundation of formal equality and a corresponding right of non-intervention.'[120]

In relation to sovereignty and international agreements, there are increasing numbers of international conventions and treaties regarding transnational organised crime.[121] Although international laws do not have coercive power to enforce compliance, there are international pressures that can make it difficult for states not to comply. The modern state enjoys limited sovereignty due to interdependence, but developing states may experience more restrictions on their sovereignty than developed states.[122] This is because, as Evans and Strange argue, foreign assistance and aid as well as trade relationships can be used as incentives as well as coercive power, for encouraging states to accept and comply with international laws and norms.[123]

---

117 Philpott, D., 'Westphalia, Authority, and International Society', in Jackson, R. (ed.), *Sovereignty at the Millennium*, 1999, Oxford: Blackwell, p. 149.

118 Wight, M., *Systems of State*, in Bull, H. (ed.), Leicester: Leicester University Press; and the *United Nations Charter* article 2(4) and 2(7) for the exact sentences. Tabata, S., *Kokusai-hou shin-kou (Jou)*, 1990, Tokyo: Toushin-do, pp. 106–107.

119 Jackson, R., 'Sovereignty in World Politics: a Glance at the Conceptual and Historical Landscape', in Jackson, R. (ed.), *Sovereignty at the Millennium*, 1999, Oxford: Blackwell, pp. 10–31.

120 Ibid., p. 12.

121 See for example, UN Office for Drug Control and Crime Prevention, *The United Nations Convention against Transnational Organized Crime*, 2000, http://www.unodc.org/palermo/convmain.html (Accessed 1 June 2004); *The United Nations Convention against Transnational Organized Crime and its Protocols*, 2000, http://www.unodc.org/unodc/en/crime_cicp_convention.html (Accessed 1 June 2004); and UN Office on Drugs and Crime, *An Overview of the UN Conventions and the International Standards Concerning Anti-Money Laundering Legislation*, February 2004, http://www.imolin.org/Overview.pdf (Accessed 1 June 2004).

122 James, *Sovereign Statehood.*

123 For example, under the Saddam Hussein regime, Iraq did not comply with the UN resolution to disclose information regarding weapons of mass destruction from the end of the first Gulf War, and as a result it was under pressure from international society. In the case of drug control co-operation, Latin American states must comply with the European Union and the United States in certain areas, such as human rights, in order to receive aid and assistance. Interviews with officials at European Commission in Brussels between 2001 and 2002, and officials at US Office for National Drug Control Policy on 28 May 2003; Evans, P.B., 'Transnational Linkages and the Economic Role of the States: An Analysis of Developing and Industrialized Nations the Post-World War II Period' in Evans, P.B., Rueschemeyer, D. and Skocpol, T. (eds), *Bringing the State Back In*, 1985, Cambridge: Cambridge University Press, pp. 197–206; and Strange, S., *The Retreat of the State: the Diffusion of Power in the World Economy*, 1996, Cambridge: Cambridge University Press, p. 192.

According to the concept of sovereignty, acceptance of and compliance with the rules of international society depends on an individual state's will. In reality, however, the decision of a state is also influenced by international pressures and a states' wish to be accepted as a member of the international community. According to Strange, there is a risk for states that disassociate themselves from some international rules. They risk being isolated and being 'largely left alone and cut off from international trade, investment and corporation planning'.[124] This will affect state decision-making, and may force some states to follow international norms in order to secure economic gains from trade relationships and benefits received from other states.

The degree of enthusiasm and the way in which states comply with the rules can create tensions and constraints between states, particularly in the case of crime control. For instance, some states may be keen to punish drug traffickers with severe punishments, and hence are dissatisfied by other states' lighter sentences.[125] This gives rise to frustration in the former states, which may lead to extreme measures in order to bring criminals to justice through their own judicial system. For example, the United States accepts to try suspects brought into its jurisdiction forcibly from foreign states, which Herrera refers to as 'state sponsored abduction'.[126] In other cases, an approach to achieve common goals can cause tension and constraints. Law enforcement operations supported by the army have been an internationally argued issue in crime control from both efficiency and sovereignty perspectives. For a state at the receiving end of such intervention, the fact that a foreign military is operating in its territory may be a sensitive and serious issue for its sovereignty. Although if it is a joint operation with the foreign military, it is not considered a violation of sovereignty in the modern understanding of the word.[127]

It is widely acknowledged that state sovereignty in an interdependent world is limited. Transnational organised crime, however, has brought about further erosion of state sovereignty in order to cope with cross-jurisdiction and cross-border illicit activities. The real issue for a state may be that acceptance and compliance with the rules could be linked to the maintenance of economic and political relationships with others. States could face situations in which they need to accept and comply with the rules due to international pressures, and thereby lose authority to determine their own policy. In other words, it is possible that transnational organised crime can lead to an erosion of state sovereignty as a result of the conventions and pressures from international society and strong states.

The overall implications of transnational organised crime on states are not clearly visible. In addition, the degree of impact of transnational organised crime can vary from state to state because political and economic structures of the state can

---

124 Strange, S., *The Retreat of the State*, p. 191.

125 For example, some Europeans consider that drug users are 'sick', but to Americans they are criminals. Cf. Ruggiero, V. and South, N., *Eurodrugs*, 1995, London: Routledge.

126 The United States has abducted foreign criminals in foreign countries (mostly Latin Americans) in order to try them under the US judicial system. Herrera, H.A., 'Kidnapping Policy during the Drug War Era: Ethical and Legal Implications', *Low Intensity Conflict & Law Enforcement*, Vol. 5, No. 3, Winter 1996.

127 Camiller, J.A. and Falk, J., *The End of Sovereignty?* 1992, Aldershot: Edward Elgar, p. 154.

make a difference in the outcome. The use of violence by the criminals, however, may have the more visible effect of increasing the uncertainty about public safety in the community, and malfunction of the justice system may lead to clear injustice stemming from a state's inability to control the criminals. Consequently, state identity could be affected by declining state quality, which might also change the international impression of a state to a negative one. The international recognition of a state has significance in international relationships since state identity in the international arena plays an influential role for other states' understanding and decision-making in international affairs. In brief, concerning the threat posed by international drug trafficking, the referent object for security may need to be considered in a holistic manner. The combined impact of international drug trafficking to several referent objects can realise a threat to a state although these impacts might be minor in some of the four spheres (economic, political, public order and diplomatic). The spheres that international drug trafficking affects the most, therefore, influence the nature of the threat posed to the particular state.

Drug Prohibition and State Policy

Considering the various impacts of transnational organised crime, it becomes clear why international drug trafficking has been securitised by states.[128] The extent to which states securitise the issue of international drug trafficking depends upon how states perceive it. This section will investigate the implications of international drug trends from a Realist and a Social Constructivist perspective.

Realism and Neo-Realism may view the success of international drug prohibition as dependent upon the power and interests of a dominant state. Drug control is determined by the coercion, co-operation, and manipulation of incentives by dominant actors.[129] This is proved by the history of drug prohibition.[130] Although the convention adopted for international narcotic prohibition was not a law with enforcement power, it came to be recognised as a rule to which a state had to comply.[131] This is because the United States, as a hegemon, has formed and imposed drug prohibition. Compliance with drug prohibition by states does not necessarily come from the threat posed by drug trafficking *per se*. In accordance with Realist theory, it reflects the power to influence international relationships.[132] According to Gilpin, a dominant actor is able to promote institutional arrangements favourable

---

128 The European Union published a European Security Strategy in 2003 for the first time, and recognised organised crime as a security threat with 'an important external dimension'. The European Union, *A Secure Europe in a Better World: European Security Strategy*, 12 December 2003, Brussels, p. 4.

129 Harsanyi, J., 'Measurement of social power, opportunity costs and the theory of two-person bargaining games', *Behavioral Science*, Vol. 7, No. 1, 1962, pp. 67–80.

130 See Introduction.

131 Onuf, N., 'Constructivism: A User's Manual', in Kubálková, V., Onuf, N. and Kowert, P. (eds), *International Relations in a Constructed World*, 1998, London: M.E. Sharpe, p. 67.

132 Puchala, D.J., and Hopkins, R.F., 'International regimes: Lesson from inductive analysis', in Krasner, S.D. (ed.), *International Regimes*, 1983, London: Cornell University Press, p. 90.

to itself through various forms of leadership and the manipulation of incentives.[133] In other words, as Young claims, it stems from the power of a hegemon, and its capability to 'openly and explicitly [articulate] institutional arrangements and compel subordinate actors to conform [to] them'.[134]

Regarding the way in which drug prohibition was introduced to the international community, it may be considered as a 'metanorm'. A metanorm, according to Axelrod, is a norm established in coercive manner.[135] He claims that one way to enforce a norm is to take coercive measures and apply punishment 'not only against the violators of the norm, but also against anyone who refuses to punish the defectors'.[136] The way the US uses its economic and political power to lead drug-producing countries to control drugs[137] makes drug prohibition a metanorm. As Strange maintained, the United States can exercise authority over the world economy and society and can exclude others from international affairs.[138] According to Waltz's argument, a state's domestic policy can influence international outcomes, and thereby form an international trend (or incident).[139]

For weaker states, particularly drug-producing countries, non-compliance with drug prohibition and subsequent punishment would be costly because it could result in the cessation of US aid and trade benefits. In this respect, drug control becomes a policy by which a drug-producing state can protect its economic interests. This is because a positive commitment to drug control would secure US support. However, this dependency on the US will prevent drug-producing states from deciding their own policies, and forces them to follow the dominant state's policies.[140] It means that these states' policies are determined by the hegemon in order to be eligible for international assistance.[141] The hegemon may only support drug control when it is considered to be in its interests. It possesses the capability to disregard some norms,

---

133 Gilpin, R., 'Politics of International Economic Relations', *International Organizations*, Vol. 25, 1971, pp. 398–419.

134 Young, O.R., 'Regime dynamics: the rise and fall of international regimes', in Krasner, S. D. (ed.), *International Regimes*, 1983, London: Cornell University Press, p. 100.

135 Axelrod, R., *The Complexity of Cooperation: Agent-Based Model of Competition and Collaboration*, 1997, Princeton: Princeton University Press, p. 54.

136 Ibid., p. 54.

137 See Introduction and chapters 5 and 6 for further information.

138 Strange, *The Retreat of the State*, p. 193.

139 Waltz, *Man, the State and War.*

140 Wallerstein, I., *The Politics of World Economy: The States, the movements and the civilizations*, 1984, Cambridge: Cambridge University Press; Cox, R., *Production, Power, and World Order: Social forces in the making of history*, 1987, New York: Columbia University Press; Munch, R., *Politics and Dependency in the Third World: The Case of Latin America*, 1984, London: Zed; Linklater, A., *Beyond Realism and Marxism: Critical Theory and International Relations*, 1990, Basingstoke: Macmillan; and Gould, K., Weinberg, A., and Schnaiberg, A., 'Natural Resource Use in a Transnational Treadmill: International Agreements, National Citizenship Practices, and Sustainable Development', *Humboldt Journal of Social Relations*, Vol. 21, No. 1, 1995; for the details, see chapters 4–6.

141 Ruggie, J.G., 'International Response to Technology: Concepts and trends', *International Organization*, Vol. 29, No. 3, Summer 1975.

according to Deutsch – 'the ability to afford not to learn'.[142] Nadelmann is critical that international drug prohibition tends to protect the interests of dominant powers, to provide for order, and to enforce a particular sense of values.[143]

Drug-producing states have also tried to re-establish influence in international drug control rather than be dominated by a hegemon. During the 1990s, drug-producing states began to advocate the responsibility of consumers, and initiate a new agenda of 'shared responsibility'.[144] Drug-producing states took initiatives in large-scale drug control operations that were assisted by dominant states.[145] The influence of international trends on domestic policy, as Gourevitch argues, is called 'second image reversed'.[146] This claim of shared responsibility emerged from criticism of the neglect of control on cocaine consumption. According to a Colombian government official, the concept of shared responsibility has allowed drug-producing states to argue for greater support for international drug control at both the supply side and the consumer side.[147] This shift of power is what Haas refers to as 'the *acquisition of a capability* to act in a specific domain'.[148]

Social Constructivists argue that co-operative policies against drug trafficking emerge because states identify with other states, and feel an obligation and legitimacy to help others.[149] This means, as Wendt argues, that states make decisions in accordance with their collective and social identities formed through membership of a group.[150] States will also act on 'loyalty and obligations to the group'.[151] This is because norms and rules in a society, according to Social Constructivists, are instruments to form state identity and preserve moral values and order.[152] This is what Wendt regards as 'practico-ethical motivation' for states in policy-making.[153] In

142 Deutsch, K., *The Analysis of International Relations*, 1968, Englewood Cliffs, N.J.: Prentice Hall, Inc., p. 111.

143 Nadelmann, E.A., 'Global prohibition regimes: the evolution of norms in international society', *International Organisations*, Vol. 44, No. 4, 1990, pp. 480–481.

144 Interview with an official at the Colombian Embassy in Brussels on 10 July 2002.

145 For example, Bolivia's Plan Dignity was one of them. For other information, see Introduction.

146 Second image means state representation of policy decision making, which comes from K. Waltz's three level analysis in *Man, the State and war*, Gourevitch, P., 'The Second Image reversed: The International Sources of Domestic Politics', *International Organization*, Vol. 32, No. 4, Autumn, 1978, pp. 881–912.

147 Interview with an official at the Colombian Embassy in Brussels on 10 July 2002.

148 Haas, E.B., 'Why Collaborate?: Issue-Linkage and International Regime', *World Politics*, Vol. 32, No. 3, April 1980, p. 397 (Emphasis in original); see also, Krasner, S., *Structural Conflict: The Third World Against Global Liberalism*, 1985, Los Angeles: University of California Press, p. 309.

149 Powell, R., 'Anarchy in international relations theory: The neorealist-neoliberal debate', *International Organization*, Vol. 48, 1994, p. 318.

150 Wendt, A., *Social Theory of International Politics*, 1999, Cambridge: Cambridge University Press, pp. 293–294.

151 Ibid., pp. 293–294.

152 Russett, B.M., *Power and Community in World Politics*, 1974, San Francisco: W.H. Freeman & Co., pp. 255–281.

153 Wendt, *Social Theory of International Politics*, pp. 21–22.

other words, a state may be identified in the international community by its policies and characteristics.[154]

Identity for a state is the set of characteristics reflecting its political beliefs and culture, by which it is recognised as a member of a group.[155] This identity will be reflected in its policies, and functions as an indicator of the state's particular preferences towards other states. Identity shows whether the state is one of 'us' or 'other' to states in the international community. This will create an image of the state, which others may recognise and thus expect certain policies from the state. This is because, as Jepperson discusses, it: 'establish[es] expectation[s] about who the actors will be in a particular environment and about how these particular actors will behave.'[156] To some extent, as Boulding maintains, 'behaviour *is dependent upon image.*'[157] According to Social Constructivists, however, identity is not fixed; rather it needs to be redefined through interaction. State identity and interests are formed, as Onuf and Krasner argue, through the institutionalisation of behaviours and decisions by norms and rules.[158]

Participation in drug control will create an identity and policies to be considered as a 'proper' state by the international community.[159] In other words, states develop the understanding of what is a 'proper' attitude to drugs and drug control. This is what Mercer claims as the rightfulness of 'self' in a society.[160] In this sense, the exclusion from international relationships as a consequence of non-compliance with the drug prohibition means to a state the loss of its own identity and international reputation.[161] In order to maintain its rightfulness in the community, a state may adopt policies to pursue the goal of international drug prohibition. This international influence on individual states will push participating states' policy towards 'a common quality of

---

154 The arguments on international regimes can be examined in a similar way to the issue of forming policies in accordance with an international regime. Wendt, *Social Theory of International Politics*; Haas, E.B., 'Why Collaborate?'; Ruggie, J.G., 'International Regimes, Transactions, and Change: Embedded Liberalism in the Postwar Economic Order', *International Organization*, Vol. 36, No. 2, Spring 1982; Foucault, M., *The Archaeology of Knowledge and Discourse on Language*, 1972, New York: Pantheon Books; Hasenclever, A., Mayer, P., and Rittberger, V., 'Interests, Power, Knowledge: The Study of International Regimes, *Merschon International Studies Review*, Vol. 40, No. 2, October 1996; and Keeley, J.H., 'Toward a Foucaldian Analysis of International Regimes, *International Organization*, Vol. 44, No. 1, Autumn 1992.

155 *Dictionary of English Language*, 4th edition, 2000, Boston: Houghton Mifflin.

156 Jepperson, R.L., Wendt, A., and Katzenstein, P.J., 'Norms, Identity, and Culture in National Security', in Katzenstein, P.J. (ed), *The Culture of National Security: Norms and Identity in World Politics*, 1996, New York: Columbia University Press, p. 54.

157 Boulding, K.E., *The Image*, 1956, Ann Arbour: University of Michigan Press, p. 6, Emphasis in original.

158 Onuf, N., 'Constructivism: A User's Manual', in Kubálková et al., *International Relations in a Constructed World*, p. 62; and Krasner, *Structural Conflict*, p. 60.

159 Axelrod, op cit., p. 59.

160 Mercer, J., 'Anarchy and Identity', *International Organization*, Vol. 49, No. 2, Spring 1995, p. 247.

161 Cf., Cornes, R. and Sandler, T., *The Theory of Externalities, Public Goods, and Club Goods*, 1996, Cambridge: Cambridge University Press, Chapters 10–12.

outcomes'.[162] In such policies, as Wendt argues, states will reflect collective identity with its national identity, and act for mutual benefit and collective interests not only for national interests.[163] Campbell, however, argues that this creates 'a boundary [between states] rather than acting as a bridge' because it will draw clear distinctions between those who comply ('self') and those do not ('others').[164]

When a state is considering compliance with a rule, it is calculating the moral benefit and the moral cost arising from its action.[165] Under drug prohibition, complying (or not complying) with this international norm provides states with a particular identity. This process can also create interests for the state in the international arena.[166] McSweeney argues that identity and interests are 'mutually constituted'.[167] This is because incentives created by the dominant actors may shape and reshape international agendas following 'the constraints of economics and technology'.[168] Gellner observes, 'national identities are fluid and change for convenience' because they shift as a state's interests change, and as international environments change.[169] For example, those complying may receive international support for drug control, such as development support and trade relations. By contrast, those that do not comply may suffer the punishment of exclusion from some co-operation.[170] This is because, as Hopf maintains, 'identities strongly imply a particular set of interests or preferences with respect to choices of action in particular domains, and with respect to particular actors.'[171] As states negotiate co-operation, they may form their identity through the negotiation process as a 'learning process'.[172] It may also imply that a state with a strong identity provides a clear image that other countries may seek to emulate.

To sum up, from Realist and Neo-Realist perspectives, drug prohibition policy is a way for governments to pursue maximum benefits and obtain power within the international community. For some states, it is a means to impose their own interests

162 Waltz, *Theory of International Politics*, p. 74; and Weale, A., *The New Politics of Pollution*, 1992, Manchester: Manchester University Press, p. 207.

163 Wendt, *Social Theory of International Politics*, p. 337.

164 Campbell, *Writing Security*, p. 77.

165 Puchala and Hopkins, 'International Regimes', p. 274.

166 Onuf, 'Constructivism: A User's Manual', p. 70.

167 McSweeney, *Security, Identity and Interests*, p. 215; and Katzenstein, *The Culture of National Security*, p. 41.

168 Milner, H. and Keohane, R., 'Internationalization and Domestic Politics: Introduction', in Keohane, R.D. and Milner, H.V. (eds), *Internationalization and Domestic Politics*, 1996, Cambridge: Cambridge University Press, p. 24 and p. 256.

169 Gellner, E., *Nations and Nationalism*, 1983, Oxford: Blackwell; Anderson, B., *Imagined Communities: Reflections on the Origins and Spread of Nationalism*, 1989, London: Verso Press.

170 For example, Peru under the Fujimori administration experienced the halt of aid from the United States for two years because the administration refused to accept military oriented drug control.

171 Hopf, T., 'The Promise of Constructivism in International Relations Theory', *International Security*, Vol. 23, No. 1, Summer 1998, p. 187.

172 Haas, E.B., 'Why Collaborate?'

on the wider international community. They use their influential position in the international community, and employ economic and political power to achieve their goals. For other states, drug prohibition offers a way to receive economic and political benefits by following the policies of stronger states. Therefore, the motivation for states to become involved in drug control may be based on the rational choice of calculated gains.[173]

However, according to social constructivists, state policy is based on identity and image of self. A state forms its policy based on multi-faceted interests including material interests, a sense of moral obligation, and its own identity. Identity and interests are closely related and, hence, defining interests through its policy also means defining its identity through the policy. State policies will be standardised by the state to mimic the policy of dominant actors in order to associate it closely with the majority of the international community. This is because compliance to international norms may generate benefit and reputation, particularly for the weaker states. On the other hand, hegemons could influence collective identity through their domestic policies.

Conclusion

A non-traditional security threat is a threat that affects the internal mechanisms and functions of a state. Its impact is not always visible, but it may nevertheless affect various aspects of the state through complex connections and networks. This type of threat does not threaten the physical survival of the state, but it will impact on the quality and identity of the state. This is because the damage posed by a non-traditional security threat varies according to the strength of the political and economic integration of the states concerned.

In order to examine the wide-ranging impacts of non-traditional security threats, this chapter focused on four state functions and the impact of cocaine trafficking on them. The influence of cocaine trafficking organisations results from the wealth at their disposal. Violence related to cocaine trafficking may increase as the market expands, and become a concern for safety in a community. At the same time, the increase of drug addicts can grow to a point where it threatens moral values and the social identity of the community. Internationally, the state could be under pressure to comply with international drug prohibition in order to be recognised as a member with an 'adequate' policy against drug trafficking. The peer pressures and international influences can limit state sovereignty and affect its status in the international community. The impact of cocaine trafficking on these four spheres may vary. However, the combined impact on these four spheres could affect state identity in a serious way.

As non-traditional security threats affect states to various degrees, not all states will take the same approach to drug control. Some actors may treat it as a national security threat that affects their vital interests, and deal with it in a militarised

---

173 Axelrod, R., *The Evolution of Cooperation*; Oye, K.A., *Cooperation under Anarchy*, 1986, Princeton: Princeton University Press; and Waltz, *Theory of International Politics*.

way. Others may consider drug trafficking as a societal threat, or a social problem. The policy of a state on drug control will depend on their understanding of drug trafficking. In other words, it depends on the perception of the cocaine threat by each state. In the international community, however, there might be other elements states might need to consider, including status and identity.

This chapter has provided a theoretical explanation of non-traditional security threats and how states conceptualise the threat. It has argued that the securitisation of non-traditional security threats requires examination of the influences on wider aspects than just the physical survival of a state. This is because state interests are multi-faceted. At the same time, this chapter has established a framework for analysis for this book. In the following chapters, the impact of cocaine trafficking in the European Union and the United States will be examined. These chapters will assess the impact of cocaine trafficking using the four aspects of state functions presented in this chapter as a template. This will lead to the investigation of the EU and US policies on drug control in the Andes.

Chapter 2

The 'Securitisation' of Cocaine Trafficking in the European Union

Introduction

A security threat, as argued in the previous chapter, is constructed through the uncertainty and fear of something or someone different from 'self'. The construction of a threat might depend on the nature of the problem, and will determine a state's actions against the phenomenon. This chapter will examine the securitisation of cocaine trafficking from an EU perspective, and will contrast it with the American perspective outlined in the following chapter. In order to examine the securitisation of cocaine trafficking, the implications of the cocaine trade in EU member states will be investigated. Through the examination of the implications of the cocaine trade, this chapter will attempt to determine to what extent the EU member states regard cocaine trafficking as a threat. As discussed in chapter 1, due to the complex nature of the cocaine trade, the analysis of securitisation will be based on four aspects of state functions: economic, political, public order and diplomatic.

The economic aspect will examine the impact of the cocaine trade on the legal national economy of EU member states. Cocaine trafficking can cause a financial loss to the European governments through the reduction of revenues and increased expenditure on law enforcement and treatment programmes. Money laundering, also, is a concern of the EU member states as there are two major off shore centres in the European Community. The political aspect will explore drug-related corruption and the issue of state legitimacy. This section will examine corruption in various government institutions, such as officials at the 'frontline' (law enforcement agencies and Customs), and politicians. In the section on violence and public order, the influence of cocaine trafficking on the safety and stability, and health issues related to cocaine use, in a state will be analysed. The expansion of the West European cocaine market has led to high competition among the traffickers, who use violence to protect their turf. Health issues are varied, including the increasing numbers of cocaine addicts and the spread of infectious sexual diseases, and also drug-related deaths. The addicts are regarded as a nuisance due to the consumption of illicit substances and the acquisition crimes they are likely to commit. The diplomatic aspect will investigate the indirect impact of cocaine trafficking, with the focus on EU regulations against cocaine trafficking and the sovereignty of the EU member states. The EU is trying to establish co-ordinated policies among the EU member states to curb cocaine flows to and within the European Community. However, such efforts contradict some member states' laws and policies.

Economic Impact

This section will examine the impact of cocaine trafficking on the national economies of EU member states. The impact is both direct and indirect from the activities of criminal organisations. For example, governments suffer financial losses due to the sale of cocaine, the growth of narco-businesses and the pursuit of money laundering. On the other hand, government expenditures on drug control and treatment for drug addicts constitute a form of indirect losses. In order to examine how cocaine trafficking affects state economies, this section will focus on the following elements: the losses of government revenues caused by untaxed expenditures on cocaine; money laundering operations by criminal organisations; and the costs of government counter-drug policies.

The Loss of Government Revenues

The cocaine trade in Western Europe until the 1980s was a discreet business because of the relatively small number of addicts and the manner in which the traffickers operated. One of the reasons for this is Europe's geographical remoteness from Latin America. The majority of cocaine supplied to European consumers is produced in the Andes, and distributed by the Colombian drug cartels.[1] A change, however, occurred in the mid-1980s. The introduction of the Schengen Agreement in 1985, and the full implementation of the Schengen Treaty in 1995 opened a window of opportunity to cocaine traffickers because it enabled free movement within a major part of Western Europe.[2] Thereafter, the Colombians regarded Western Europe as a 'single market', with potential for profitable business opportunities.[3] Consequently, the import and consumption of the drug increased at an alarming rate.[4]

---

1 Interview with Mr Vos at the European Council in Brussels on 8 July 2002. See also the Introduction for cocaine trafficking in Latin America.

2 Interview with an official at the European Commission in Brussels on 15 January 2002. The European Union, *Schengen Treaty Free Movement of Persons within the European Union*, http://europa.en.int/en/agenda/shengen.html (Accessed 3 November 2004).

3 Paoli, L., Güller, N., and Palidda, S., *Pilot Project to Describe and Analyse Local Drug Markets: First Phase Final Report: Illegal Drug Markets in Frankfurt and Milan*, 2000, European Monitoring Centre for Drug and Drug Abuse Scientific Report, EMCDDA/EPI/CT.99.EP.06/2000, Lisbon: European Monitoring Centre for Drug and Drug Abuse, p. 49; and van Doorn, J., 'Drug Trafficking Networks in Europe', *European Journal on Criminal Policy and Research*, Vol. 1, No. 2, 1993, p. 101.

4 According to reports by the United Nations Drug Control Policy, the seizures made in Europe between 1988 and 1991 recorded an average annual growth rate of 21%, and the total cocaine seizures made in Western Europe in 1999 were over 43 tonnes, which is about one third of the total seizures in the United States. Also, following increased demands from the market, larger cocaine loads were transported by sea vessels, in addition to the shipments via air transport. Between 1988 and 1991, the average weight of a seizure in Europe was 142.29kg by sea transport compared with 3.79kg by air. van Doorn, 'Drug Trafficking Networks in Europe', pp. 100–101; United Nations Drug Control Policy, *World Drug Report 2000*, 2000, Oxford: Oxford University Press, p. 44; United Nations Drug Control Policy, *Global Illicit Drug Trend 2001*, 2001, New York: United Nations Drug Control Policy,

For a state, a booming industry is usually a welcome event, however this is not the case for the growth of the cocaine trade. One of the reasons is that cocaine is illegal therefore governments cannot tax it, despite the fact that the profits generated via cocaine trafficking are enormous. This means that the governments are losing revenue. According to British Home Office estimates in 2002, the size of the illicit drugs market (including both heroin and cocaine) is £6.6 billion, which is slightly smaller than the tobacco industry.[5] About 200 tonnes of cocaine is believed to be smuggled into Europe annually, which is sold for about £60 per gram on the street.[6] The British and Spanish cocaine markets are the largest in Europe, and surveys indicate that users spend an average of £15,000 annually on cocaine consumption.[7]

The influence of the cocaine trade on the national economies of EU member states varies because criminal organisations in each state have different degrees of involvement. For example, Italy reports its cocaine problem as a minor issue and does not have strong evidence that points to the growth of the cocaine trade on its territory.[8] On the other hand, the Netherlands, Spain and Britain report the seriousness of the cocaine problem in their states. They are known as major cocaine importing states and have experienced a rapid increase in the amount of cocaine seized on their

---

p. 127; Plan nacional sobre drogas, *Spain: Drug Situation 2000*, 2000, REITOX REF/2000, http://www.emcdda.org/multimedia/publications/national_reports/NRspain_2000.PDF, p. 34; Farrell, G., Mansur, K., and Tullis, M., 'Cocaine and Heroin in Europe 1983-1993: A Cross-National Comparison of Trafficking and Prices', *The British Journal of Criminology*, Vol. 36, No. 2, Spring 1996, p. 275; The General Secretariat, 'Cocaine: European "drug of the year"', *International Criminal Policy Review*, May–June, 1989, p. 24; and OIDT, *Italy: Drug Situation 2000*, 2000, REITOX REF/2000, http://www.emcdda.org/multimedia/publications/national_reports/NRitaly_report_2000.PDF (Accessed 14 March 2003) p. 87.

5   For example, see National Criminal Intelligence Services, *UK Threat Assessment 2003*, 'Main Threats', 3.37, http://www.ncis.co.uk/downloads/CADT_Org_Imm_Crime.pdf (Accessed 20 March 2005); Islam, F., 'Class A capitalism', *The Observer*, 21 April 2002; and cf. Jordan, D.C., *Drug Politics: Dirty Money and Democracy*, 1999, University of Oklahoma Press: Norman, p. 78.

6   Islam, op cit.

7   A survey in North-West England of a sample of continuing crack users found that they spend an average of over £20,000 a year, ranging from £1,000 to £71,000. The amount for new users, who have taken crack in the past six months, vary from £500 to £140,000 a year, at an average of £15,000. The amount includes estimated values of both cocaine and crack consumed by both regular and occasional users. Bramley-Harker, E., *Sizing the UK Market for Illicit Drugs*, 2001, RDS Occasional Paper 74, London: Home Office, p. 27; Brian, K., Parker, H., and Bottomley, T., *Evolving Crack Cocaine Careers: News Users, Quitters and Long Term Combination Drug Use in N.W. England*, 1998, Manchester: University of Manchester Press, pp. 46–66.

8   OIDT, *Italy: Drug Situation 2000*.

territories.[9] This reflects their policy against drugs,[10] their geographical locations and connections to Latin America and the Caribbean[11] respectively.

Among the three major cocaine importers, the situation in Spain is considered to be the worst because of its cultural, linguistic and historical ties with Latin America and its location between Africa and Europe.[12] In addition, Spain's membership in the EU is a positive incentive for the Colombian traffickers to use it as a transit state. The EU offers a borderless economic zone to the traffickers once they are inside one of its member states. These factors are seen as advantages by the Colombian cocaine traffickers, and hence they have used Spain to expand their networks to other parts of Western Europe.[13] In other words, Spain became a transit state to the European market, as Mexico has been the one to the US market.[14] Colombian cartels have established a monopoly over European cocaine supply at a regional level through alliances with local criminal organisations.[15] By the mid-1990s, members of the Cali cartel were believed to be working in 'virtually every country' in the European Union.[16]

One of the factors that enabled the Colombians to monopolise the European Community was the lack of indigenous European criminal organisations within the cocaine market.[17] Historically, as Mack argues, the trafficking of illicit goods was not the core of European criminal organisations' activities. Trafficking

---

9 Interview with an official at the European Commission in Brussels on 15 January 2002.

10 The Dutch government's policy on Marijuana smoking is believed to be luring traffickers of hard drugs, such as cocaine and heroin. It has led to a more active drug trade. The Dutch cocaine market in the 1990s was operated by over 420 criminal groups with different ethnic backgrounds. van Doorn, op cit., pp. 96–104.

11 In Britain, crack and cocaine are largely distributed by Jamaican illegal immigrants. Home Affairs Committee, *Drug Trafficking and Related Serious Crimes Vol. II; Minutes of Evidences and Appendices*, HC 370-II, 1989, London: HMSO.

12 Interview with an official at the European Commission in Brussels on 15 January 2002. Latin American drug lords have cultivated connections in Spain since the 1970s to expand their business free from the pressures of the Drug Enforcement Agency. In the mid 1980s, Jorge Luis Ochoa and Gilberto Rodriguez-Orejuela fled Colombia to Spain, and they organised drug trafficking networks in Spain before they were arrested and extradited to Colombia in 1986. Resa-Nestares, C., 'Transnational Organised Crime in Spain: Structural Factors Explaining its Penetration', in E.C. Viano (ed.), *Global Organized Crime and International Security*, 1999, Aldershot: Ashgate, pp. 52–53; and Plan nacional sobre drogas, *Spain: Drug Situation 2000*, p. 32.

13 The Galician clans, Spanish criminal groups, played a key role in the mid-1980s to distribute cocaine to the Spanish market. The Colombians expanded their business to the Mediterranean coast with collaboration from French and Italian criminal organisations.

14 See introduction for the details.

15 van Doorn, op cit., p. 100.

16 Freemantle, B., *The Octopus: Europe in the Grip of Organised Crime*, 1995, Orion: London, p. 52; and Resa-Nestares, 'Transnational Organised Crime in Spain ', pp. 48–54.

17 Dorn, N., Murji, K., and South, N., *Traffickers: Drug Markets and Law Enforcement*, 1992, London: Routledge, p. xi.

activities tended to be conducted by small, criminal groups acting independently.[18] European governments, thereby, did not have the know-how to prevent the Colombian domination in the European cocaine trade. Local criminal organisations became involved in the cocaine trade following the expansion of the Colombian cocaine business in Europe, realising its profitability.[19] As a result, the European cocaine network now consists of linkages between Colombian cocaine trafficking organisations and various European criminal groups, such as Italian, French and Albanian criminal organisations.[20]

By the late 1990s, the increased availability of cocaine was recognised widely in Western Europe. For example, in Britain, cocaine became available through well-connected networks of traffickers, and hence, the customers did not need to wait to receive the supply of cocaine.[21] It also meant that the traffickers started to form a structure to make the supply mechanism function more efficiently and profitably – to some extent, more 'organised' cocaine supply routes, with a division of tasks among the traffickers.[22] In EU member states, most criminal organisations operate independently and on a small scale without formal structures for drug trafficking. The Italian Mafia is an exception.[23]

---

18 European criminal groups have been involved in illicit trafficking. The involvement of French criminal organisations in the illicit trafficking of drugs and humans was recorded as early as the 1950s alongside money laundering. Mack, J.A., with Kerner, H-J., *The Crime Industry*, 1975, Westmead: Saxon House, pp. 34–36, and 63–64.

19 UNDCP, *World Drug Report 2000*, p. 44.

20 The importation of cocaine used to be in small quantities carried by 'mules' using commercial flights from the West Indies or the East Coast of the United States. However, recent trends show that more cocaine now comes directly from South America, for example Colombia, Venezuela, Panama, Brazil, Argentina, and even the Caribbean states. The trafficking routes via southern and western Africa and increasing use of the Balkans and Eastern Europe have been indicated by seizures made in these regions. Also some criminal groups in London, such as Yardies, are conducting Italian Mafia style cocaine trafficking operations on a smaller scale, but their activities remain within national boundaries. Paoli *et al.*, *Pilot Project to Describe and Analyse Local Drug Markets*, pp. 66–67; Dorn *et al.*, *Traffickers*, p. 41; Edmunds, M., Hough, M., Urguía, T.N., *Tackling Local Drug Markets*, 1996, Crime Detection and Prevention Series Paper 80, London: Home Office, pp. 10–33; Dorn, N. and South, N., 'Drug Market and Law Enforcement', *The British Journal of Criminology*, Vol. 30, No. 2, 1990, p. 176; Freemantle, op cit., p. 61; Bean, P., 'Cocaine and Crack: The Promotion of an Epidemic', in Bean, P. (ed.), *Crack and Cocaine: Supply and Use*, 1993, London: Macmillan, p. 67; DrugScope, *United Kingdom: Drug Situation 2000*, 2000, REITOX REF/2000, http://www.emcdda.org/multimedia/publications/national_reports/NRuk_2000.PDF (Accessed 14 March 2003), p. 42; Plan nacional sobre drogas, op cit., p. 35.

21 Bean, P. and Pearson, Y., 'Crack and Cocaine Use in Nottingham 1989/90 and 1991/92', in Mott, J. (ed.), *Crack and Cocaine in England and Wales*, 1992, RPU Paper 70, London: Home Office, p. 27; and Brian et al., *Evolving Crack Cocaine Careers*, pp. 70–77.

22 Ruggiero, V. and South, N., *Eurodrugs: drug use, markets and trafficking in Europe*, 1995, London: UCK Press, p. 129; and Parker, H., and Bottomley, T., *Crack Cocaine and Drugs – Crime Careers*, 1996, London: Home Office, p. 64.

23 The Mafia use pre-existing heroin trafficking routes and their connections in America to traffic cocaine. According to Becchi, however, there is no monopoly of the Italian drug

Money Laundering

Whilst the cocaine market grows, traffickers require a mechanism to launder large sums of narco-money, in order to transfer their money from the illegal economy to the legal one. Since the narco-money cannot be used in the legal economy without laundering, money laundering has been considered as: 'the meeting point between criminality and the legal economy and marks the entry of mafia power into the world of business.'[24] In other words, money laundering is the lifeline for their activities and contributes to the enrichment of the cocaine traffickers; and it is the beginning of the illicit penetration into the legal economic and financial system.[25]

The methods commonly used for money laundering are investments in legitimate businesses and transactions through several banks to erase the illicit origins. Criminal organisations often use legitimate businesses as their 'shell corporation'[26] and 'front company' to launder money and to cover their illicit activities.[27] These are the traffickers' first steps of rooting themselves into the legitimate economy. Different types of businesses are chosen to serve their purposes: to deliver cocaine under the concealment of a delivery of a legal commodity and to deposit narco-money together with a legal income.[28] Considering the services required for the cocaine traffickers, the business involved in transportation and international trading[29] and businesses

---

market because this picture of Mafia control is an illusion manufactured by politicians. In fact, there are lots of competitors and many dealers, and many different actors are involved in the Italian drug trade, such as the Italian Mafia, foreign mafia, and urban gangsters. Clutterbuck, R., *Drug, Crime and Corruption*, 1995, New York: New York University Press, p. 143; Jamieson, *The Modern Mafia: Its Role and Record*, Conflict Studies 224, 1989, London: Centre for Security and Conflict Studies, pp. 20–29; The General Secretariat, 'Cocaine', p. 23; Becchi, 'Italy: Mafia-dominated Drug Market?' in Dorn, N., Jepsen, J., and Savona, E. (eds), *European Drug Policies and Enforcement*, 1996, London: Macmillan, pp. 123–128; and Paoli *et al.*, *Pilot Project to Describe and Analyse Local Drug Markets*, pp. 66–67.

24 Report by the *Guardia di Finanza* in March 1989 cited in Jamieson, *The Modern Mafia*, p. 33.

25 However, according to a British government source, the methods and processes are not known to government authorities except for the general use of banks and front companies for the purpose. NCIS, *United Kingdom Threat Assessment of Serious and Organised Crime 2003*, http://www.ncis.co.uk/downloads/CADT_Org_Imm_Crime.pdf (Accessed 20 March 2005).

26 Shell corporations are fictitious and exist only on documents without commercial purposes. Through these corporation narco-dollars are deposited in the disguise of legally earned money.

27 Sometimes, traffickers buy bankrupt companies in order to launder money, for instance, the Italian Mafia bought a company called *Manifattura Fedelma* in Prato. Savona, E.U., and De Feo. M.A., 'International Money Laundering Trends and Prevention/Control Policies', in Savona, E.U. (ed.), *Responding to Money Laundering: International Perspectives*, 1997, Amsterdam: Harwood Academic Publisher, p. 17.

28 Other businesses criminal organisations utilise for this purpose can be van hire firms and dealerships, restaurants, and amusement arcades.

29 For example, import and export companies, commodity trading, and cargo businesses.

presenting possibilities to deal in relatively large sums of cash[30] are employed as their front companies.[31] For instance, some British criminal organisations are mainly associated with the import-export business, which could support their imports of illicit goods as well as legitimate goods.[32] Mafia groups are involved in a wider range of legal economic activities. Criminal groups in Turin have developed and penetrated into industrial sectors, and have become established as 'industrial productive capital' for the state.[33]

In the legitimate economy, the development of front companies and the increasing influence of the cocaine traffickers via their companies directly affects the national economies of EU member states. The growth of front companies leads to the creation of wide-ranging jobs and contributes to the local economy. The injection of some of the enormous wealth at the disposal of criminal organisations into the legal economy can lead to positive consequences by strengthening some industries, and increasing productivity. However, it could mean that the state economy is increasingly dependent on narco-money and increases the influence of cocaine traffickers within a states' economic system. In Spain, according to Resa-Nestares, money-laundering operations by drug traffickers played a significant role in the strong economic growth of the 1980s. Resa-Nestares claims the growth was 'made possible mainly by a revaluation of assets due to large investments in real estate for money-laundering purposes'.[34] Also, the investments of the cocaine traffickers contributed to the development of the Spanish national economy by moving 'into sophisticated production, even into high technology'.[35]

Narco-dependency in the national and local economy can lead to a worse scenario in which traffickers gain popular support and are seen as benefactors. If criminal organisations provide jobs and services to local communities, it is because they seek advantageous returns.[36] The Galician clans in Spain, for example, invested 'generously' in social infrastructures that increased the efficiency of their illicit operations.[37] Also, the Italian mafia groups provided market protection for domestic entrepreneurs from foreign competitors by price fixing to eliminate competition so that they could also protect their own businesses.[38]

---

30 Such as car, art and antiques dealers and bureaux de change.

31 'NAO report links money-launderings to gambling', *VNU Network*, 14 January 2005, http://www.pcmag.co.uk/print/bf/1139158 (Accessed 21 February 2005).

32 Ruggiero *et al.*, *Eurodrugs*, p. 191.

33 Sicilian Mafias are influential in construction business in southern Italy, and are trying to expand their business to the north. Varese, F., paper given at the Security Conference at the University of Cambridge on 30 October 2004; and Ruggiero *et al.*, *Eurodrugs*, p. 191.

34 Resa-Nestares, 'Transnational Organised Crime in Spain', pp. 60–61.

35 Ruggiero, V., 'The *Camorra*: 'Clean' Capital and Organised Crime', in Pearce, F. and Woodiwiss, M. (eds), *Global Crime Connection*, 1993, London: Macmillan, pp. 154–155.

36 The Neapolitan Camorra was a provider of employment until the 1970s, and substantial numbers of Naples' economically activated population were employed by contraband operations. Ruggiero, 'The *Camorra*', pp. 149–150.

37 Resa-Nestares, 'Transnational Organised Crime in Spain', p. 53.

38 Gambetta, D. and Reuter, P., 'Conspiracy among the many: the mafia in legitimate industry', in Fiorentini, G. and Peltzman, S. (eds), *The Economics of Organised Crime*, 1995,

In respect to regulating banks to prevent money laundering, European banks have been reluctant to act against suspicious transactions. This is partly because of the weakness of government regulation on bank transactions. Despite the EU directive in 2001,[39] the government approach to controlling money transactions via banks is not co-ordinated among the EU member states. For example, the lack of strong legislation against money laundering in Spain has provided a relatively easy environment for criminal organisations to conduct money laundering using Spain's financial and banking systems.[40] Also, due to the financial power of the banks and the wealth at the disposal of traffickers, it has been difficult to limit banks' freedom to accept customers.

The difficulties in regulating money laundering stem from the economic partners of the EU, such as Switzerland and Liechtenstein. They are not EU members, but they have close connections to the EU politically and economically. Hence, bank policies in these states can affect the economic transactions of the EU member states. This also means that their policy would limit the EU efforts to control illicit money flow.

Some banks, such as Swiss, Liechtenstein and Luxembourg banks, consider bank secrecy an important policy. These banks with secrecy policies generate illicit money within the European Community and enable deposits to be transferred to other banks without criminal trace.[41] Bank secrecy, designed to protect client information, has enabled criminal organisations to establish bank accounts without the risk of disclosures being made to the law enforcers.[42] The lack of effective legislation combined with financial secrecy has allowed Luxembourg and London – the EU's financial capital – to grow to become the largest off-shore centres in the world.[43] Taking advantage of the weak government control to prevent money transactions, criminal organisations, particularly drug trafficking organisations such

---

Cambridge: Cambridge University Press, p. 128.

39 Directive 2001/97/EC of the European Parliament and of the Council of 4 December 2001 amending Council Directive 91/308/EEC on prevention of the use of the financial system for the purpose of money laundering – Commission Declaration, *Official Journal*, L 344, 28/12/2001 P. 0076 – 0082, http://europa.eu.int/smartapi/cgi/sga_doc?smartapi!celexapi !prod!CELEXnumdoc&lg=EN&numdoc=32001L0097&model=guichett (Accessed 3 March 2005); Council of Europe, *Convention on Laundering, Search, Seizure and Confiscation of the Proceeds from Crime*, Strasbourg, 8.XI.1990, http://conventions.coe.int/treaty/en/ Treaties/Html/141.htm (Accessed 20 February 2005); Ludford, S., *EU Money Laundering Rules - Tough Implementation Needed*, 'We'll Make Europe Work for You', 18 October 2001, http://www.sarahludfordmep.org.uk/news/306.html (Accessed 20 February 2005); and EFE, 'Los Quince acuerdan ampliar su lucha contra el blanqueo de dinero', *El Mundo*, 16 October 2001, http://www.elmundo.es/elmundo/2001/10/16/enespecial/1003245309.html (Accessed 1 March 2005).

40 Resa-Nestares, 'Transnational Organised Crime in Spain', pp. 57–60.

41 Sherwell, P., 'Liechtenstein 'a magnet for money launderers'', *Telegraph*, 23 January 2000, http://www.telegraph.co.uk/htmlContent.jhtml?html=%2Farchive%2F2000%2F01%2 Fwliech21html (Accessed 21 February 2005).

42 Resa-Nestares, 'Transnational Organised Crime in Spain,' pp. 57-60.

43 UN Office for Drug Control, *World Drug Report*, 1997, http://www.unodc.org/adhoc/ world_drug_report_1997/CH4/4.6.pdf (Accessed 21 February 2005), p. 141.

as Colombian cartels, receive their payments through European financial channels. In 2001, Spanish authorities cracked down on a money laundering route of cocaine cartels in Medellín via banks in Sevilla.[44]

Once criminal groups set up their bank accounts, the wealth will be deposited and the money gains legality. Despite its illicit origin, the large sums of money provide criminals with credit and influence in the legitimate economy through financial power backed up by the bank. For instance, Ruggiero maintains that the Camorra, which successfully launder their illicit profits into the Italian national financial system, has gained influence and easy access to money because of its status as a privileged customer with the banks.[45]

Narco-money in the national economy might provide the impression of contributing to the financial system, but it is often transferred and invested internationally. Access to the national financial systems enabled criminals to transfer their deposits to off-shore tax havens, such as Panama, to escape from tax collectors as well as law enforcers. The local economy, therefore, actually does not benefit from the wealth of criminal organisations. Ruggiero argues that vast amounts of money do not usually stay in local surroundings for long: 'dealing had not stimulated their local economy; rather it was impoverished as money was taken out of the area.'[46]

Expenditures on Drug Control Policies

A further economic impact of cocaine trafficking on EU member states is the cost of drug control and rehabilitation policies. The cocaine market exists on the principle of the capitalist market: where there is demand, there is supply. According to EU officials, demand reduction and rehabilitation should be the way to diminish cocaine supply.[47] The weakness in this approach is the cost. British government reports claim that counter-drug efforts, such as law enforcement and prevention programmes, are costly.[48] The expenditure required to maintain effective anti-drug operations

---

44 EFE, 'Desmantelan una red de tráfico de cocaína distribuida en locales de lujo', *El Mundo*, 26 February 2001, http://www.elmundo.es/elmundo/2001/02/26/sociedad/983201993. html (Accessed 1 March 2005); Jamieson, *The Modern Mafia*, p. 33; and Savona, E., 'Money Laundering, the Developed Countries and Drug Control: the New Agenda', in Dorn, N., Jepsen, J., and Savona, E. (eds), *European Drug Policies and Enforcement*, 1996, London: Macmillan, p. 216; Cf. EFE, 'La policía desarticula un grupo dedicado a lavar dinero procedente del narcotráfico', *El Mundo*, 17 September 2003, http://www.elmundo.es/elmundo/2003/09/16/ madrid/1063713774.html (Accessed 1 March 2005).

45 Ruggiero, 'The *Camorra*', p. 153.

46 Ruggiero *et al.*, *Eurodrugs*, p. 132.

47 Interviews with officials at the European Commission in Brussels in on 23, 24 and 25 April and 8, 9 and 11 July 2003.

48 Wagstaff, A. and Maynard, A., *Economic aspects of the illicit drug market and drug enforcement policies in the UK*, Home Office Research Study 95, 1988, London: HMSO, p. 4; House of Commons, Home Affairs Committee, Session 1988-89, Seventh Report, *Drug Trafficking and Related Serious Crime*, Vol. 1, 1989, London: HMSO.

and treatment programmes are not easily afforded by either local or national governments.[49]

Since the 1980s, the cocaine market has grown rapidly, and government expenditures on drug related issues have been increasing significantly. In an attempt to reduce the size of the cocaine market, according to a 1997 UNDCP report, OECD countries spend about US$120 billion annually on controlling drug abuse (including expenditure on law enforcement, prevention programmes and health care for drug related diseases).[50] The British government, for example, allocated an annual budget of £142 million for drug treatment problems[51] in 2001.[52] The government expenditure on drug treatment, however, increased rapidly and it was expected to reach £300 million in 2005.[53] The British government allocated £398 million for drug treatment in the fiscal year 2007.[54]

In respect to the cost of treatment for cocaine addicts, it is hard to make an estimate, as there is no agreed medication to substitute for cocaine. According to *The Economist*, the estimated cost of cocaine treatment is equivalent to that of heroin – at least £10 billion per year.[55] In addition, considering the increase of cocaine imports, it is likely that there will be a growing number of cocaine addicts who require treatment. According to the British government, the number of cocaine addicts who require treatment has been rising at an alarming rate: there was an increase of 70%

---

49 British Customs and Excise estimated the expenditure necessary for customs alone for fiscal year 1993 at £120–150 million. Some local governments, such as the city councils of Zurich (Switzerland) and Hull (the United Kingdom), had difficulty supplying sufficient services to sustain effective anti-drug operations There are arguments whether the cost of drug related issues could be reduced by the legalisation of the drugs. For the details, see the arguments of, for example, Mishan, Saffer and Chaloupka. *HM Customs and Excise Annual Report*, cm. 2352, October 1993, London: HMSO; Mishan, E.J., 'Narcotics: The Problem and the Solution', *Political Quarterly*, 1990, Vol. 61, No. 4; Saffer, H., and Chaloupka, F., 'The demand for illicit drugs', *Economic Inquiry*, Vol. 38, No. 3, July 1999; Thompson, T., 'Hull is Britain's new drug capital', *The Observer*, 12 May 2002; and Fahrenkrug, H., 'Drug Control in a Federal System: Zurich, Switzerland', in Dorn, N., Jepsen, J., and Savona, E. (eds), *European Drug Policies and Enforcement*, 1996, London: Macmillan.

50 United Nations Drug Control Policy, *Report on the Economic and Social consequences of drug abuse and illicit trafficking*, 1997, New York: United Nations Drug Control Policy.

51 The document does not specify the types of substances treated in the programme.

52 The National Treatment Agency for Substance Misuse, *National Programme Funding*, 18 October 2004, http://wwwnta.nhs.uk/programme/national/funding_intro.htm (Accessed 20 February 2005).

53 Audit Commission, *Health Data Briefings: 2 Drug Treatment Services*, October 2007, http://www.audit-commission.gov.uk/Health/Downloads/HealthDataBriefing_DrugTreatmentServices1.pdf (Accessed 19 October 2007).

54 Ibid. In 2003, the British government launched a three-year programme called the *Criminal Justice Interventions Programme* (CJIP) with funding of £447 million in order to reduce the effects of drug-related crime on the community. This programme aims to 'get drug-misusing offenders out of crime and into treatment'. *Tackling Drugs, Out of crime, into treatment*, http://www.drugs.gov.uk/WorkPage/DrugInterventionsProgramme/Otherstakeholder/CJIP_ForTheCourts.pdf (Accessed 20 February 2005), p. 2.

55 'It's all in the price', *The Economist*, 8 June 2002, p. 28.

between 1993 and 1999.[56] This sharp increase of cocaine addicts, according to the studies of European local drug markets, is not only a trend in Britain, but also in other EU member states, such as Germany and Italy.[57]

To sum up, the economic impact of the cocaine trade on EU member states is not simply a matter of financial damage, although losses of financial resources caused by cocaine trafficking are substantial. The penetration of the cocaine traffickers into the legitimate economy is regarded as the more serious harm. Accumulation of wealth may allow them to negotiate in the legal economy. With large sums at their disposal, the cocaine traffickers can dominate financial sectors and the local community: they can be privileged customers for banks, and can provide jobs and services to the local community. The competition between legitimate corporations and criminal organisations in legal markets, however, undermines the growth of the national economy since the legitimate corporations cannot afford to spend the same level of resources that criminal organisations do.

Political Impact

Corruption plays an important role in the world of European drug trafficking as the financial power of criminal organisations penetrates states both economically and politically. 'Collaboration' by authorities ensures the safety of, and profits from, illicit businesses.[58] In Europe, the enforced criminalisation of the drug trade could result in 'a massive increase of criminal violence and an insidious spread of corruption at all levels of officialdom' as has happened in the drug scene in the United States.[59]

Corruption of the political system affects state decision making in a liberal democracy, although the influence of corruption is difficult to identify. This is because the influence of narco-corruption usually appears mostly on matters related to the cocaine trade and money laundering. One of the indicators of the manipulation of decisions, according to Newell, can be the amount of legislation against crime and corruption.[60] The Italian parliament, for example, passed anti-corruption and organised crime laws after the end of World War II; however, their implementation and enforcement have not always been effective.[61] It is believed

---

56 Home Affairs Select Committee, Third Report: *The Government's Drugs Policy: Is It Working?* 9 May 2002, http://www.publications.parliament.uk/po/cm200102/cmselect/cmhaff/318/31808.htm.

57 Paoli *et al.*, *Pilot Project to Describe and Analyse Local Drug Markets*, pp. 39–42.

58 Passas, N., 'Globalization and Transnational Crime: Effects of Criminologic Asymmetries', *Transnational Criminal Organization*, 1998, Vol. 4, Nos 3&4, Autumn/Winter, p. 27.

59 For the details of US cocaine market, see chapter 3 of this book. Mishan, 'Narcotics', p. 462.

60 Newell, J.L., *Corruption mitigating policies in Italy*, a paper presented at the 53rd PSA Annual Conference at the University of Leicester, 15–17 April 2003.

61 For example, la legge n. 1720 in 1948, la legge 31 maggio 1965 n.575 (Disposizioni contro la mafia) in 1965; la legge n.646 del 13/9/1982 (or known as 'legge Rognoni-La Torre') in 1982; and *LEGGE 1o ottobre 1996*, n. 509. Camera dei Deputati, *Conoscere Le Mafie Costruire La Legalita*, http://www.camera.it/_bicamerali/antimafia/sportello/dossier/

to be the proof of the Mafia's influence on state decision making that the leading party (Christian Democratic Party) are linked with Mafia groups as a known fact in Italy, and connections of Mafia groups with government authorities have been exposed particularly in Sicily.[62] The breadth of the Mafia's political influence was brought to light in the early 1990s through the 'Clean Hands' judicial investigation,[63] and numbers of politicians were forced to resign. In 1993, one third of the national Parliament was charged with corruption, and the head of a national media company was under investigation in connection with a criminal organisation.[64]

Another indicator of corruption in the Italian government is the amount of information on its cocaine market that is provided in the report to the European Monitoring Centre for Drugs and Drug Addiction (EMCDDA). This report compares the drug problems of EU members.[65] The unwillingness of the Italian government to provide information might be related to the Mafia involvement in cocaine trafficking and Mafia connections to the politicians.[66]

Turning to the influence of the cocaine traffickers on other government agencies, the officers at the 'front-line' of combating drug trafficking (such as customs, immigration services, and the judicial system including police and prisons) face higher risks of being targeted for bribery.[67] The degree of corruption, however, may vary in agencies as well as states. For example, some states with economically powerful criminal organisations, such as Italy, have high corruption rates but other states with smaller criminal groups, like the Netherlands, tend to have low rates.[68]

---

dossier1_4.html (Accessed 20 February 2005); Abbate, L., 'La Caccia al tesoro della mafia', *Polizia di Stato*, http://www.poliziadistato.it/pds/primapagina/parliamo_di/caccia_tesoro_mafia.htm (Accessed 20 February 2005); '7. Mafia, 1982-1988', *LutherBlissett.net*, http://www.lutherblissett.net/archive/078-08_it.html (Accessed 20 February 2005); and Istituzione di una Commissione parlamentare d'inchiesta sul fenomeno della mafia e delle altre associazioni criminali similari, *LEGGE 1o ottobre 1996, n. 509*, http://www.camera.it/_bicamerali/antimafia/legge.htm (Accessed 20 February 2005).

62 Lea, J., *Organised Crime, the State and the Legitimate Economy*, http://www.bunker8.pwp.blueyonder.co.uk/orgcrim/3806.htm (Accessed 30 July 2004).

63 The politicians caught in this investigation were accused of criminal conspiracy, extortion, corruption and association with organised crime.

64 Della Porta, D., and Vannucci, A., 'The resources of corruption: some reflections from the Italian case', *Crime, Law & Social Change*, Vol. 27, Nos 3-4, 1997, p. 233.

65 Osservatorio italiano per la verifica dell'andamento del fenomeno delle droghe e delle tossicodipendenze, *Italy: Drug Situation 2000*; and Paoli *et al.*, *Pilot Project to Describe and Analyse Local Drug Markets*, pp. 105–108.

66 Clutterbuck, R., *Drug, Crime and Corruption*, 1995, New York: New York University Press, p. 143; Stenson, K., 'Beyond histories of the present', *Economy and Society*, Vol. 27, No. 4, 1998; and Stille, A., 'All the Prime Minister's Men', *The Independent*, 24 September 1995.

67 NCIS, *United Kingdom Threat Assessment of Serious and Organised Crime 2003*, http://www.ncis.co.uk/downloads/CADT_Org_Imm_Crime.pdf (Accessed 20 March 2005).

68 According to Transparency International (TI), the Netherlands is given CPI 2004 score of 8.7 out of 10 for cleanness of the system, the UK got 8.6, Spain 7.1 and Italy 4.6 from an expert survey. Also looking at the perception of the degree of corruption in national institutions and sectors, the general public in Italy and Spain are more sceptical about

The influence of the Colombian cartels has infiltrated into Spain. One EU official claimed that Spain has received the most serious damage from cocaine traffickers among EU member states.[69] It is mostly because the Colombian cocaine cartels have established their European headquarters in Spain, and imported methods that rely on corruption and intimidation as they do in Colombia. The influence of the cartels is widespread in the financial and judicial spheres – Spanish professionals, such as lawyers, bankers and economists are bribed for their operations.[70] In 2003, a lawyer, ex-secretary of the Chamber of Commerce of Vilagarcía de Arousa (Pontevedra), and ex-vice president of the Chamber of Commerce of Vilagarcía were found guilty of being involved in the international cocaine trafficking network in the early 1990s and of attempting to import 2 tonnes of cocaine.[71]

In Italy, the existence of influential criminal organisations in the area is a predicament for law enforcers. In order to conduct police operations and effective arrests, it is necessary for the police to have a 'peaceful' relationship[72] with the local Mafia groups. The relationship is maintained through bribery of the police officers and exchange of information and favours: information on illicit activities of rival criminal organisations from the Mafia groups to the police, and information on forthcoming law enforcement operations from the police to enable the Mafia to avoid arrest. In some regions, such as Palermo, Mafia members are frequent visitors to the police headquarters.[73] The judgement and decisions of Italian law enforcers, therefore, could be favourable to criminal groups because they are either under the financial influence of the Mafia or in fear of the Mafia.[74]

In Britain, cocaine traffickers are also in contact with the police. Corrupt police officers and detectives undermine law enforcement operations with their involvement

---

corruption than that in the Netherlands. Although the data analysed by TI does not focus on corruption related to organised crime, the result seems to be applicable to the case of cocaine trafficking. Transparency International, *Transparency International Corruption Perceptions Index 2004*, 2004, Berlin: Transparency International, p. 4; and Transparency International, *Transparency International Global Corruption Barometer 2004*, 2004, Berlin: Transparency International, p. 18.

69 Interview with an official at the European Commission in Brussels on 11 July 2003.

70 Europa Press, "El Negro' era el 'delegado' del cártel de Bogotá en España y ponía precio a la cocaína', *El Mundo*, 8 March 2002, http://www.elmundo.es/elmundo/2002/03/07/espana/1015518180.html (Accessed 1 March 2005).

71 EFE, 'El abogado Pablo Vioque pide que testifique Liaño en el juicio al que se le someterá por narcotráfico', *El Mundo*, 14 January 2003, http://www.elmundo.es/elmundo/2003/01/13/sociedad/1042486158.html (Accessed 1 March 2005); and Agencia, 'Huyen tres 'narcos' justo antes de que la Audiencia Nacional les condene por un alijo de 1991', *El Mundo*, 20 June 2003, http://www.elmundo.es/elmundo/2003/06/19/sociedad/1056019909.html (Accessed 1 March 2005).

72 This means that the police are not in dispute or conflict with the local mafia groups that are involved in drug trafficking.

73 Private conversation with an Italian scholar at ECPR conference at Marburg, Germany, September 2004.

74 Briquet, 'The Hidden Aspect of Democracy', *Nuove Effemeridi*, No. 50, 2000/II.

in the protection of traffickers by forging documents and re-selling seized cocaine.[75] In addition to selling cocaine and protecting traffickers on the street, some police officers provide services to drug traffickers. As the *Guardian* reports, police drafted several letters to reduce prison sentences after a bribe of £5,000, and attempted to sabotage major court cases after a bribe of £100,000.[76] Scotland Yard announced that there were 134 officers (and 11 ex-officers) charged with corruption offences related to drug trafficking. More than 80 officers were suspected of these offences in March 2000.[77]

In the Netherlands, systemic bribery of front-line officers by criminal organisations and individual traffickers is rare. According to van Duyne, there is some corruption within the police at lower levels, but no systemic corruption of customs officers, except at Schipol airport where some officers are under pressure to let drugs into the country.[78] The reason why there is little corruption, van Duyne claims, is that the traffickers are 'relying on their smuggling skills' rather than on bribery, and it is difficult to reach higher ranking officials to gain sufficient returns (information and protection) to merit the amount spent on bribery.[79] Considering the fact the Dutch cocaine market is operated by large numbers of small criminal groups, the amounts smuggled at any one time may be small enough to go through customs undetected. Individual traffickers may think bribery is an unnecessary expense for their operation.

There is some evidence that criminal organisations active in Europe corrupt government officials and private sectors, such as banks.[80] Corruption related to criminal organisations in Western Europe, however, does not seem to be widespread or have serious effects on judicial and political affairs. Even Italy, which has a higher corruption score than other EU member states in Transparency International Reports, has a lower score than the Andean countries.[81] Fijnaut claims that there is no 'systemic corruption of police officers and other government officials'.[82] The reason why most EU member states do not suffer from corruption is, as Dorn and South maintain, that law enforcement operations are conducted by several agencies with

75 Thompson, T., 'Corrupt police split reward cash with fake informants', *The Observer*, 17 December 2000.

76 Hartley-Brewer, J., 'Police held in drug case', *The Guardian*, 25 September 1999, http://www.guardian.co.uk/Archive/Article/0,4273,3905553,00.html.

77 Gillard, M.S. and Flynn, L., 'Corruption squad under fire', *The Guardian*, 4 March 2000, http://www.guardian.co.uk/Archive/Article/0,4273,3970352,00.html.

78 van Duyne, 'Organized crime, corruption and power', *Crime, Law & Social Change*, Vol. 26, No. 3, 1997, pp. 206–207.

79 Ibid., p. 211.

80 Mickey Green, the leader of one of the largest British cocaine trafficking organisations, was reported to have 'had a string of detectives on his pay-roll', and has been charged for 'fixing' witnesses at an inquest. Thompson, T., 'Deadly cargo', *The Observer*, 21 April 2002.

81 *TI Global Corruption Barometer 2004*, and *TI Corruption Perceptions Index 2004*.

82 Fijnaut, C., 'Organized Crime: A Comparison Between the United States of America and Western Europe', *The British Journal of Criminology*, Vol. 30, No. 3, 1990, p. 331; and Dorn, N., Murji, K., and South, N., *Traffickers: Drug Markets and Law Enforcement*, 1992, London: Routledge, p. x.

multiple and overlapping jurisdiction.[83] Therefore, bribery of government authorities may turn out to be rather costly for criminal organisations.

Impact on Public Order

The cocaine trade undermines citizens' trust in the safety of their community. According to the British government, there are several risk factors for the community with increasing numbers of drug related activities, including community divide, mobility among residents, and the availability of firearms.[84] For both local and national governments of the EU member states, instability of their communities and fear of widespread infectious sexual diseases, such as AIDS, are unwelcome by-products from the cocaine trade. Through this section, the risks society faces from the escalation of cocaine related problems: namely, the use of violence, drug abuse and infectious diseases, and drug related crime, will be investigated as symptoms of the disruption of public order posed by cocaine trafficking.

The Use of Violence

After the European cocaine market increased in size, according to the British government, the use of violence has changed.[85] Throughout the 1990s, violence associated with the drug markets escalated rapidly alongside the increased appearance of firearms. For example, the British cocaine market came to register a higher use of violence by traffickers than in the 1980s.[86] Within a decade, the victims of murder and attempted murder related to the cocaine trade have risen sharply, although most victims are likely to be drug users in debt to traffickers, and betrayers of criminal organisations.[87] The criminal organisations engaged in cocaine trafficking have increasingly come to resemble their Latin American counterparts in the formation of their organisations, the operation of their businesses, and the use of violence.[88]

---

83 Dorn *et al.*, 'Drug Market and Law Enforcement', p. 184; and Dorn, N. and South, N., 'After Mr Bennett and Mr Bush: US Foreign Policy and the Prospects for Drug Control', in Pearce, F. and Woodiwiss, M. (eds), *Global Crime Connection*, 1993, London: Macmillan, p. 82.

84 *Drugs and Community Safety: the Strategic Challenge*, Report of a Local Government Forum Conference held on 10 December 1997, 1998, London: HMSO, p. 7.

85 NCIS, *United Kingdom Threat Assessment of Serious and Organised Crime 2003* (Accessed 30 July 2004).

86 Mack *et al.*, *The Crime Industry*, pp. 57–58.

87 There were 21 people killed during the dispute over turf, and an additional 67 attempted murders occurred in 2001 in London alone. Hopkins, N., 'Crack dealers threaten more cities with violence', *The Guardian*, 25 June 2002; Hopkins, N., 'Growing impact of drug from abroad', *The Guardian*, 25 June 2002, http://www.guardian.co.uk/drugs/Story/0,2763,743343,00.html (Accessed 3 May 2003); and Bean *et al.*, 'Crack and Cocaine Use in Nottingham', p. 27.

88 Dorn, N., Oette, L., and White, S., 'Drug Importation and the Bifurcation of Risk: Capitalization, Cut Outs and Organized Crime', *The British Journal of Criminology*, Vol. 38, No. 4, Autumn 1998, pp. 550–557.

In the past, the European cocaine market was operated without much violence, or at least not as visible as that in the Latin American countries.[89] European traffickers used violence only on very limited occasions, and kept their guns for 'status symbols' rather than for actual use.[90] It is generally considered that the drug traffickers do not apply violence in a visible manner in public because they do not want to attract the attention of law enforcement agencies to their activities.[91]

Cocaine traffickers, to some extent, enforce *de facto* law and order in the market and in their communities, through the use of violence to ensure their business. The cocaine traffickers have acquired guns and come to use them for protecting their business. The use of violence is not a peculiar feature to some organisations known to be aggressive in nature. In most violence-related cases, those involved in the incident are drug traffickers and consumers trying to settle disputes over turf, payment and other problems due to the way some British drug distribution groups, as well as the Italian Mafia, operate.[92]

Furthermore, the use of violence increased in the 1990s, as competition in the cocaine market became more intense. The involvement of foreigners into the European cocaine markets is perceived partly as a result of increasing numbers of illegal immigrants and the EU policy on free movement. For example, as Spain has become a transit state for cocaine across Europe, its problems spread to neighbouring European states.[93] Cocaine trafficking drove illegal immigrants to the European Community because the cocaine trade provides more jobs and a means for survival to the illegal immigrants as it expands. The increasing numbers of cocaine dealers, however, will lead to competition to ensure profits.[94] The growing numbers of immigrants participating in the cocaine trade increased the visibility of foreigners dealing in cocaine, and contributed to escalation in violence. The community in Romagna, Italy, was alarmed by the rise of the murder rate between 1991 and 1994, which jumped from 4.8% to 15% following a nine-fold increase

---

89 For the details on Latin American cocaine trafficking organisations, see introduction.

90 Mack *et al.*, *The Crime Industry*, pp. 84–90.

91 NCIS, *United Kingdom Threat Assessment of Serious and Organised Crime 2003* (Accessed 30 July 2004); van Duyne, 'Organized crime, corruption and power', p. 211.

92 Dorn *et al.*, *Traffickers*, p. 48.

93 Reports of the United Nations and the European Monitoring Centre for Drug and Drug Abuse (EMCDDA) indicate that the majority of illicit drugs in Europe transit through and are seized in Spain. Cocaine seizures in Spain increased by 55% in 1998/99, and 63% of total European cocaine seizures were made in Spain and the Netherlands. Other major importers of cocaine are the United Kingdom and Germany. UNDCP, *World Drug Report 2000*, p. 44; Plan nacional sobre drogas, *Spain: Drug Situation 2000*; and Trimbos-instituut, *The Netherlands: Drug Situation 2000*, 2000, REITOX REF/2000, http://www.emcdda.org/ multimedia/publications/national_reports/NRnetherlands_2000.PDF (Accessed 14 March 2003), p. 67.

94 Ruggiero *et al.*, *Eurodrugs*, p. 137; and Bean, 'Cocaine and Crack', pp. 74–75; and Dorn *et al.*, *Traffickers*, p. 3.

in foreign participation in the drug business.[95] Victims of the murders were mostly other immigrants.[96]

The growth of the cocaine market has brought a change to EU member states, not only in terms of the profits cocaine traffickers can generate, but also in their manner of operation. Previously, cocaine in Europe was sold by Bohemian-style dealers, who used cocaine and shared it with their peers.[97] Cocaine dealers were not apparent in the local community, and the purchase of cocaine was impossible without contacts.[98] It is, however, evident that the increasing numbers of cocaine traffickers has led to competition and the higher visibility of the trade on the streets – operating in a less secretive and more aggressive manner. Spanish criminal groups, for instance, came to adopt Colombian-style tactics and were willing to use violence. In 1995, it appeared that the Colombians killed a Galician gang and a Spanish lawyer who wanted to repent of their crimes. Later the same year, four Colombians were found dead, and the deaths were alleged to be caused by retaliation from the Galicians.[99] Similarly in Italy, the cocaine market became more open and competitive from the mid-1990s due to the crackdown on drug dealing enterprises by southern Italian Mafia groups. Following the end of the domination by Mafia groups, local cocaine markets became less organised and more violent. According to a dealer for the Fiore organisation in Milan, this was when the criminal group's members were arrested and lost control over most of their territories.[100]

---

95 Balloni *et al.*, 'The Infiltration of Organised Crime in the Emilia-Romagna Region: Possible Interpretations for a New Social Defence', in Viano, E.C. (ed.), *Global Organized Crime and International Security*, 1999, Aldershot: Ashgate, p. 36.

96 This trend has been recognised widely in Western Europe: in Britain the majority of the street dealers are blacks and other minorities. In Germany, police statistics in the 1990s show that more than 75% of suspects of drug dealing and trafficking were non-German. (N.B., There is a criticism of the statistics that the police have a tendency to suspect and capture foreigners compared with those of German nationality, and therefore the statistics may not illustrate an accurate picture of the German cocaine scene.) In Italy, some Albanian immigrants control a share of cocaine distribution in the Romagna region, and the increased numbers of foreigners have replaced the jobs Italians that used to occupy in cocaine distribution networks. Ruggiero *et al.*, *Eurodrugs*, p. 119; Paoli *et al.*, *Pilot Project to Describe and Analyse Local Drug Markets*, p. 56; and Balloni *et al.*, 'The Infiltration of Organised Crime in the Emilia-Romagna Region', p. 37.

97 Paoli et al., *Pilot Project to Describe and Analyse Local Drug Markets*, p. 97; and European Monitoring Centre for Drug and Drug Abuse, *Annual Report on the State of the Drugs Problem in the European Union 2001*, 2001, Luxembourg: Office for Official Publication of the European Communities, p. 36.

98 See also the research on the hidden economy by Henry, which resembles the old style cocaine trade. The hidden economy of illicit trades include, for instance, smuggling wine bought in France to the UK and selling them to friends and neighbours at untaxed prices. Henry, S., *The Hidden Economy: The Context and Control of Borderline Crime*, 1978, Oxford: Martin Robertson, chapter 2; and cf., Paoli *et al.*, *Pilot Project to Describe and Analyse Local Drug Markets*, p. 113.

99 Resa-Nestares, 'Transnational Organised Crime in Spain', p. 56.

100 Paoli *et al.*, *Pilot Project to Describe and Analyse Local Drug Markets*, pp. 113–114.

Drug Abuse and Related Problems

Cocaine availability in Europe increased dramatically in the 1990s, and consumption of the drug was accelerated by the decline of prices. The dramatic drop of cocaine prices[101] and rising purity[102] made it as popular and cheap as 'ecstasy'.[103] As the price fell, cocaine came to be consumed by a wide-range of people, in contrast to the trend described by Lewis in the period prior to the 1980s – limited consumption among rich and higher-class people.[104] Regarding the growing share of cocaine in the European drug market, Parker and Bottomley express its popularity as: 'Rock and crack cocaine is one of a new generation of designer products which has arrived in the UK for the 1990s' – and the rest of Europe.[105] Widespread cocaine consumption has caused concerns on health and moral grounds as well as divisions in the community. According to EU officials, it is perceived that the social fabric and sense of values of a society are challenged by cocaine abuse.[106]

The change in the cocaine trade was dramatic. Despite the fear of some European states of a 'cocaine epidemic' based on the amounts of seized cocaine, the number of addicts statistically remained small until the mid-1990s.[107] Since the late 1990s,

---

101 The price of cocaine dropped by over 50% in the 1980s, and in the 1990s declined even further. In 1989, cocaine in Germany cost €66.5 per gram, and in 2003 in Britain cost £50 per gram. EMCDDA, *Annual Report 2001*, p. 35; Paoli *et al.*, *Pilot Project to Describe and Analyse Local Drug Markets*, pp. 72–73; Maynard, A., 'The economics of drug use and abuse', in Ciba Foundation, *Cocaine: Scientific and social dimensions*, Ciba Foundation Symposium, 1992, West Sussex: John Wiley and Sons, p. 247; Bramley-Harker, *Sizing the UK Market for Illicit Drugs*, 2001, p. 23; and Shapiro, H., 'Where Does All the Snow Go? The Prevalence and Pattern of Cocaine and Crack Use in Britain', *Crack and Cocaine: Supply and Use*, in Bean, P. (ed.), 1993, London: Macmillan, p. 11.

102 Due to competition, the purity of cocaine in Europe has increased. For example, the average purity of cocaine remains between 40–69%, but the purity of crack is about 80–100% in the UK. Crack is a processed form of cocaine and usually dealers manufacture it with other chemicals. DrugScope, *United Kingdom: Drug Situation 2000*, p. 41.

103 Cocaine availability in Britain was about 60% in the early 1990s, and high availability was confirmed in a 1992 survey. Users can purchase the drug almost 24 hours a day, 7 days a week. Paoli *et al.*, *Pilot Project to Describe and Analyse Local Drug Markets*, pp. 88–97; Dean, A., Carvell, A., Green, A., Pickering, H., and Stimson, G.V., 'Crack and Cocaine Use in Britain in 1990: First National Report', in Mott, J., (ed.), *Crack and Cocaine in England and Wales*, 1992, RPU Paper 70, London: Home Office, p. 14; Bean *et al.*, 'Crack and Cocaine Use in Nottingham', p. 27; and Edmunds *et al.*, *Tackling Local Drug Markets*, pp. 10–33.

104 Lewis, R., 'European Market in Cocaine', *Contemporary Crises*, Vol. 13, 1989, p. 36; Paoli *et al.*, *Pilot Project to Describe and Analyse Local Drug Markets*, pp. 42, and 82; and DrugScope, *United Kingdom: Drug Situation 2000*, p. 39; and Hartnoll, R., Avico, U., Ingold, F., Lange, K., Lenke, L., O'Hare, A., and de Roij-Motshagen, A., 'A multi-city study of drug misuse in Europe', *Bulletin on Narcotics*, Vol. XLI, Nos 1/2, p. 9.

105 Parker *et al.*, *Crack Cocaine and Drugs*, p. 9.

106 Interviews with the officials at the European Commission between April and July 2003.

107 Shapiro, 'Where Does All the Snow Go?', pp. 12–19; The General Secretariat, 'Cocaine', p. 23; Cooperation Group to Combat Drug Abuse and Illicit Trafficking in Drugs

however, international organisations, such as the United Nations Office on Drugs and Crime, alerted European states about the increase in cocaine addicts. According to a United Nations Drug Control Programme[108] report in 2000, European cocaine abuse has intensified in comparison to the mid-1990s.[109] Following the report from UNDCP, the International Drug Inspection Board presented the estimated number of cocaine addicts in Europe at about 2 million. 'Of Europe's two million cocaine consumers, Spain and Germany account for some 500,000 and Italy 300,000.'[110]

At the national level, the information governments hold on their drug problems varies. For example, the British government indicated its awareness of the increase of cocaine addicts, but had insufficient data to make reasonable estimates on the degree of cocaine penetration into the community.[111] According to Shapiro, the fact that cocaine users who can afford private treatment for their addiction without notifying their habit publicly, have made it difficult to obtain accurate data on addiction.[112] States reporting high cocaine consumption, such as Spain and Germany, have been trying to build a database for cocaine abuse and the cocaine market to improve their policy making on drug control.[113]

Due to the increasing numbers of users, the cocaine trade has become more open. Sales are not always in a discreet manner, as it used to be, and cocaine abuse has become more noticeable in the local community. At the same time, areas in which cocaine is traded have grown increasingly unsafe because of crime related to the cocaine trade, such as prostitution and the illegal holding of firearms. In some cities, parents do not allow their children to go to the local playground 'because of the used needles and condoms lying around' as a trace of the cocaine abuse from the previous night.[114] As such problems surface, governments come under pressure to address the problem and seek solutions.

The major problems related to cocaine abuse are health issues and acquisitive crime to support a cocaine habit. The arguments over health problems caused by cocaine have been divided in Europe.[115] Haasen and Krausz, for instance, argue

---

(Pompidou Group), *Multi-City Study: Drug misuse trends in thirteen European Cities*, 1994, Strasbourg: Council of Europe Press; and Dorn, N. and South, N., 'After Mr Bennett and Mr Bush: US Foreign Policy and the Prospects for Drug Control', in Pearce, F. and Woodiwiss, M. (eds), *Global Crime Connection*, 1993, London: Macmillan, p. 76.

108 UNDCP has changed its name to UNODC (United Nations Office on Drugs and Crime).

109 UNDCP, *World Drug Report 2000*, p. 65.

110 Carneiro, L., *Report: Transnational organised Crime*, RRI435185 EN.doc, PS301.427, 15 March 2001, p. 3.

111 DrugScope, *United Kingdom: Drug Situation 2000*, p. 42.

112 Shapiro, 'Where Does All the Snow Go? ', p. 23.

113 Plan nacional sobre drogas, *Spain: Drug Situation 2000*, p. 86.

114 Lee, M., 'London: 'Community Damage Limitation' through Policing?', in Dorn, N., Jepsen, J., and Savona, E. (eds), *European Drug Policies and Enforcement*, 1996, London: Macmillan, p. 36.

115 Interviews with officials of the European Commission in Brussels on 15 January 2002, 8 July 2002, and interview with an official at the United States Mission to the European Union in Brussels on 25 April 2002.

that cocaine and crack use does not cause instant addiction, cocaine babies or crack epidemics. It is, therefore, not an immediate danger to health and it is unnecessary to overreact to the phenomenon.[116] For example, the number of cocaine-related deaths in England increased by five times between 1993 and 2001, although this is less than one-tenth of the deaths caused by heroin.[117] Statistically, cocaine related mortality is trivial. On the other hand, Stevenson maintains: 'Heavy cocaine users are prone to psychological and behavioural disorders.'[118] Other research also suggests psychological and physical damages caused by cocaine consumption, such as paranoia and aggression,[119] infectious sexual diseases and tuberculosis through injection of the drug, damage to the nasal bone (bone perforation or pneumotherax) by snorting, and bronchitis and pneumonia through smoking.[120] According to research in Spain, the increase in cocaine use was followed by an increase in non-fatal emergency cases of these problems.[121]

The more serious issue related to cocaine use and health may be infectious sexual diseases that could be spread to communities through needle sharing and prostitution. Infectious sexual diseases, such as HIV/AIDS and hepatitis, spread rapidly in communities with high drug user rates. This has made the governments take drug issues seriously. Diseases, such as AIDS/HIV, are transferred among cocaine users through sharing needles for cocaine injection, and through sexual activities.[122] In Spain, HIV infection increased rapidly throughout the 1990s. According to the Spanish government, this was caused particularly because of the spread of HIV among cocaine injectors.[123] By the mid-1990s, Spain experienced over 7,000 newly diagnosed HIV patients and more than 5,000 deaths annually. HIV infection reached

---

116 Haasen, C., and Krausz, M., 'Myths versus Evidence with Respect to Cocaine and Crack: Learning from the US Experience', *European Addiction Research*, 2001, Vol. 7.

117 The number of cocaine related deaths in 2001 was 96, and that of heroin and morphine was 889. NTA, *Drug-related deaths*, http://www.nta.nhs.uk/programme/drd2.htm (Accessed 20 February 2005).

118 Stevenson, R., *Winning the War on Drugs: To Legalise or Not?* Hobart Paper No. 124, 1994, London: The Institute of Economic Affairs, p. 26.

119 17% of the samples admitted the tendency to be aggressive after using cocaine, and among them 33% become frequently aggressive, 20% intermediately, and 10% infrequently.

120 Plan nacional sobre drogas, *Spain: Drug Situation 2000*, pp. 88–89; Erickson, P.G., Adlaf, E.M., Murray, G.F., and Smart, R.G., *The Steel Drug: Cocaine in Perspective*, 1987, Lexington, Mass: Heath; and Fagan, J., 'Intoxication and Aggression', in Tonry, M. and Wilson, J.Q. (eds), *Drugs and Crime: Crime and Justice: A Review of Research*, 1990, Chicago: The University of Chicago Press, p. 256.

121 Treatment for cocaine problems increased three times in a three-year period between 1996 and 1999, alongside non-fatal emergency cases, which increased from 30% in 1997 to 37.2% in 1998. Despite these increases, the number of deaths caused by overdoses has declined since 1995, unlike the 1980s, when they rose. Plan nacional sobre drogas, *Spain: Drug Situation 2000*, pp. 21–22.

122 Cocaine, in particular, is used to increase sexual pleasure, and also heavy users tend to be involved in prostitution to support their habit.

123 Ministerio de Sanidad Y Consumo, *HIV and AIDS in Spain 2001*, 2002, Madrid: Ministerio de Sanidad Y Consumo Centro de Puvlicaciones, p. 3.

about 32% of drug users.[124] The costs for health care related to drug consumption, as García-Altés *et al.* claim, were estimated at 31,080 million pesetas out of the total social costs, 88,800 million pesetas (US$ 467 million), in 1997.[125]

According to EMCDDA, HIV infection among drug injectors in the majority of the EU member states, however, is below 5%.[126] The United Kingdom, for example, has only 1% of HIV infection among drug injectors.[127] This lower rate of HIV infection is regarded as a consequence of harm reduction and prevention programmes.[128] The British government was reluctant to tackle the drug problem prior to the discovery of the connection between cocaine use and HIV. It then switched to a priority of law enforcement, demand reduction, and education of the nation based on Harm Reduction Programmes.[129]

Another problem that may be brought by the increase of cocaine abuse is the higher crime rate in some communities. Increase in crimes, such as theft and burglary, undermines personal safety and trust within a community. The connection between drug use and crime is established by the research of the British government as well as Brain *et al.*[130] Drug use is often associated with acquisitive crime committed by users to maintain their habit.[131] According to a British Home Office report, approximately 78% of the expenditures on cocaine and heroin in Britain are financed by money obtained through criminal activities.[132]

---

124 EMCDDA, 'Annual report on drugs in the EU – 2000: Problem Drug Use – Changing Trends', *News Release*, No. 5/2000 – 11 October 2000, Lisbon: EMCDDA, p. 2.

125 This data includes all illegal drug use in Spain, not just cocaine. Hence the social cost of cocaine consumption can be smaller than the numbers given here. García-Altés, A. Ma Ollé, J., Antoñanzas, F., and Colom, J., 'The social cost of illegal drug consumption in Spain', *Addiction*, Vol. 97, No. 9, September 2002, pp. 1145–1147.

126 The exceptions are Spain and Portugal (27%). EMCDDA, *News Release*, No. 5/2000, p. 2.

127 See also, Office for National Statistics, *Diagnosed HIV-infected patients: by probable routes of HIV infection and region of residence when last seen for care in 2002: Regional Trend 38*, http://www.statistics.gov.uk/STATBASE/ssdataset.asp?vlink=7762 (Accessed on 2 March 2005); Office for National Statistics, *Diagnosed HIV-infected patients: by probable routes of HIV infection and region of residence when last seen for care in 2001: Regional Trend 37*, http://www.statistics.gov.uk/STATBASE/ssdataset.asp?vlink=5933 (Accessed on 2 March 2005); and Meikle, J., 'Drug injectors still sharing equipment', *The Guardian*, 20 December 2003, http://society.guardian.co.uk/drugsandalcohol/story/0,8150,1110697,00.html (Accessed on 3 March 2005).

128 The United Kingdom Harm Reduction Alliance, *Submission to The Home Affairs Select Committee on the Government's drug policy*, July 2001, http://www.ukhra.org/statements/select_committee.html (Accessed on 2 March 2005); Advisory Council on the Misuse of Drugs, *Report: AIDS and Drug Misuse Part 1*, 1988, London: Her Majesty's Stationery Office.

129 Stevenson, *Winning the War on Drugs*, p. 46.

130 Brian *et al.*, *Evolving Crack Cocaine Careers*, pp. 86–88.

131 Bockma, H., 'Distributing Heroin to addicts is pointless' (interview with J.P. Grund), *International Journal on Drug Policy*, Vol. 3, No. 4, 1992, p. 193.

132 Home Affairs Select Committee, *Third Report.*

Several states recognise the connection between the rise of cocaine use and criminal rates in their cities.[133] The increase in availability and abuse of cocaine tend to lead to the rise of the crime rate. For example, street robberies in Bristol rose by 77% between 2001 and 2002 following the increased availability and use of cocaine.[134] Kingston-upon-Hull known for the highest seizures in Britain, recorded the worst levels of car crime and the highest per capita drug-related death rates.[135] In Spain, crime rates that were related to cocaine derivatives rose by about 3% between 1998 and 1999.[136] Although acquisitive crime may not have as strong an impact as predatory crime, the notion of 'living in a safe community' can be lost. Parker and Bottomley, therefore, conclude: 'if we are concerned with the impact of drug driven crime on the wider community in terms of people feeling their cars and homes are safe, then this is a perspective to be taken seriously.'[137]

As a part of their drug control policy, some governments have considered an effort to rehabilitate and restrict the increase of cocaine addiction and trade by creating a drug bloc in a community, in which those involved in drugs can gather. Care facilities for cocaine addicts could lure more addicts as well as dealers since not all addicts can successfully be rehabilitated.[138] Also, some care facilities for addicts are considered as 'disruptive to the local community and encourage casual drug use' because used syringes are thrown into rubbish bins in parks and shopping centres and there is drug use in public places.[139]

The creation of areas for cocaine addicts and dealers to congregate for their trade could lead to social exclusion of particular groups as other local residents may wish to disassociate themselves from the problem in that particular area – the social exclusion of a community.[140] The high participation rates of foreigners is noticeable and alarms a local community more than native cocaine traffickers might do because they are regarded as 'alien'. For example, areas with a high population of immigrants and social minorities are likely to be the targets for this. This is because these immigrants are likely to be low income, and it is believed that 'crack cocaine … tends to a disproportionate degree, although not exclusively, to be a problem for poorer communities'.[141] In Britain, Black communities were regarded as a possible source of the cocaine epidemic.[142] This prejudice comes not only from their economic situation, but also from a high presence of Jamaican illegal immigrants in the British cocaine trade.[143] Pearson *et al.* believe that the alienation of a community could be

---

133 See also, EMCDDA, *Annual Report 2003: the state of the drugs problem in the European Union and Norway*, 2003, Luxembourg: Office for Official Publications of the European Community, p. 33.

134 Hopkins, 'Growing impact of drug from abroad'.

135 Thompson, 'Hull is Britain's new drug capital'.

136 Plan nacional sobre drogas, *Spain: Drug Situation 2000*, p. 29.

137 Parker *et al.*, *Crack Cocaine and Drugs*, p. 52.

138 Fahrenkrug, 'Drug Control in a Federal System', p. 183.

139 Bean *et al.*, 'Crack and Cocaine Use in Nottingham', p. 32.

140 Dorn *et al.*, 'After Mr Bennett and Mr Bush', p. 76.

141 Hopkins, 'Crack dealers threaten more cities with violence'.

142 Dorn *et al.*, 'After Mr Bennett and Mr Bush', p. 76.

143 Hopkins, 'Crack dealers threaten more cities with violence'.

'obstructing not only the movement towards racial justice but also the quest for an effective drug control policy'.[144]

Considering the impact of cocaine trafficking on a community, there is a possibility of social instability through the creation of a social divide, prejudice to foreigners, crimes and a polluted environment. The existence of an active cocaine market in the community leads those involved in the cocaine trade to that particular area, and can become a source of challenge to the moral values of the community. This is because cocaine trafficking is regarded as immoral and against the beliefs of community life.

Diplomatic Impact

This section will examine the issues associated with the limitation of state sovereignty affected by the international regulations on drug prohibition. Drug related issues were not policy priorities for West European states and accordingly for the European Union until the late 1980s or early 1990s. Since the 1990s, however, the European Union has recognised drug related issues as a significant global concern, and undertaken to fight against illicit drugs based on the principle of shared responsibility.[145] By the end of the 1990s, almost all EU member states ratified the United Nations Conventions against drug trafficking and abuse.

The drug control efforts of the EU member states were not considered to be sufficient by the International Narcotics Control Board (INCB). In relation to the counter-drug efforts made by EU member states, there is little progress in law enforcement measures to curb the inflow of cocaine from Latin America. This is borne out by the estimated amount of cocaine sold in Western Europe and the growing number of addicts. The INCB, therefore, has been dissatisfied with the approaches and efforts of Western Europe, arguing that there was little evidence of successful counter-drug measures, particularly by the Dutch and Portuguese. This is because these two states are not following the 1988 UN convention against illicit drug traffic in narcotics and psychotropic substances. Portugal does not criminalise possession of illicit drugs under its domestic law, and the Netherlands allows consumption of marijuana.[146]

The pressure on the European Union is not only from international organisations but also from the United States. According to US officials, although there is a document stating EU-US co-operation against transnational organised crime, the projects have

---

144 Pearson, G., Mirza, H.S., and Phillips, S., 'Cocaine in Context: Finding from a South London Inner-City Drug Survey', in P. Bean (ed.), *Crack and Cocaine: Supply and Use*, 1993, London: Macmillan, p. 125.

145 *COM (79) 670 final*, Luxembourg: Office for Official Publication of the European Communities, p. 12.

146 The United Nations, *United Nations Convention against Illicit Traffic in Narcotic Drugs and Psychotropic Substances 1988*, article 3 paragraph 2; and INCB, *The International Narcotics Board Annual Report 2001*, 2002, New York: UN Official Publications, p. 74.

yet to materialise.[147] The United States has been asking for European co-operation in drug control operations, as it believes such measures will be beneficial to every state. The slow decision-making process in the EU is seen by the US as evidence of a lack of enthusiasm to fight against cocaine trafficking. The EU member states are, to some extent, expected to act as a unified actor to contribute and comply with cocaine regulation. In other words, the EU member states are expected to co-ordinate their policies to that of the European Union rather than pursuing national drug control.

The difficulty for the European Union may lie in differences of individual states' understanding and recognition of the drug issues. The EU member states have all committed themselves to the fight against drugs, but the drug policies of each member state of the European Union vary. Drugs tend to be regarded as health issues, not criminal ones. The Dutch and Portuguese do not have laws explicitly prohibiting the sale of drugs.[148] The Scandinavians take almost the opposite stance on drugs from these two states – namely, strict prohibition. As for the British approach, drug legislation in Britain has been influenced by US legislation, and drug related offences are tried in criminal courts.[149] In this sense, the European Union does not seem to have a coherent drug policy. Nevertheless, the member states of the European Union have agreed to undertake efforts to reduce the consumption of cocaine, which may be regarded as a harmonisation of policies. According to a European Council official, this is how the EU introduces co-ordinated laws to the member states: wait until the member states are accustomed (or 'communised' in EU jargon) to the idea of criminalisation of cocaine trafficking.[150] The EU allows sufficient time for the idea of criminalisation of illicit drugs to be established in each member state, and domestic laws to regulate drug trafficking to be enacted voluntarily by them.

Slow progress in the criminalisation of cocaine and the enforcement of the law reflects cocaine's lower market share in the European illicit drug market in the 1990s.[151] Although Western Europe is the second largest cocaine market in the world, its total seizures remain 13% of world-wide seizures, compared to 75% of seizures being in the United States.[152] On the other hand, heroin seizure in Europe reached 28.1% of word-wide seizure, of which 80% comes from the largest heroin-producing region of Asia via the *Balkan route*.[153] Considering the geographical proximity, the

---

147 Interview with an official at US Mission to the European Union in Brussels in April 2002.

148 Interview with Mr Vos at EU Council in Brussels on 8 July 2002.

149 Dorn *et al.*, 'Drug Market and Law Enforcement', p. 173.

150 Interview with Mr Vos; and Interview with an official at European Commission in Brussels on 9 July 2002.

151 EMCDDA, 'Table Markets-6. Quantities of cocaine seized (kgs). Part (ii) 1985 to 2002', *Statistical Bulletin 2004*, http://stats04.emcdda.eu.int/index.cfm?fuseaction=public. Content&nNodeID=5362 (Accessed 3 March 2005).

152 Interpol,   *Cocaine*,   http://www.interpol.org/Public/Drugs/cocaine/default.asp (Accessed 3 March 2005).

153 Heroin seizures in Asia make up 52.5% of world-wide seizures, and it produces 98% of heroin. The size of the European heroin market is estimated at 120–150 tonnes annually. Interpol, *Heroin*, http://www.interpol.int/Public/Drugs/heroin/default.asp (Accessed 3 March 2005); and The Commission on Narcotic Drugs, *World drug situation with regard to drug*

number of heroin addicts and the ease of transportation of drugs, the EU has regarded heroin from Asia as higher priority than cocaine from Latin America.

According to an official of the European Commission, although the amount of cocaine smuggled into the European Union might appear to be less significant than that of heroin, it has the other related issue of illegal immigrants.[154] It has been considered that illegal immigration from Latin America increases as the amount of the cocaine imported to Europe rises. Due to the policy on freedom of movement within the EU member states, criminals and illegal immigrants can be widespread within the European Union after entering from Spain. The official claim is that the regulations and co-operation against cocaine trafficking will inevitably restrict both illegal immigration and cocaine imports to Western Europe.[155]

The mechanism for cocaine control co-operation with Latin America has existed in the form of bi-regional co-operation between the EU and the Caribbean and Latin America since 1987.[156] The emphasis for support, however, has been on the projects with the Caribbean states that are used as transit states for international cocaine trafficking. This is because there are some EU member states with colonial ties with the Caribbean states, such as the Dutch and British government, and they sponsored the projects.[157]

Another reason for this slow progress in a unified approach to drugs in the European Union is because drugs come into the judicial sphere. In order to harmonise the laws of the member states, it is necessary for the states to give up some of their sovereignty to set laws, and follow the EU guideline. Co-operation in the fight against drug trafficking within the EU has been established through the Amsterdam Treaty, Article 29, in the field of co-operation in Justice and Home Affairs (JHA) in order to provide citizens with safety through 'an area of freedom, security and justice'. It has been a sensitive issue for member states to co-operate over law enforcement issues and, therefore, they are reluctant to advance their co-operation under this framework of the EU. The Action Plan to Combat Drugs for the period between 2000 and 2004, however, does appear to show EU influence over national policy making in the member states.[158] The Action Plan goes closer to harmonisation of policies by stating that the 'approximation of rules on criminal matters in the Member States' would take place if necessary.[159]

trafficking: report to the Secretariat, the United Nations, Economic and Social Council, Vienna: the United Nations.

154 Interview with an official at the European Commission in Brussels on 15 January 2003.

155 Ibid.

156 Interview with Mr Vos.

157 Interview at the European Commission on 15 January 2002.

158 Boekhout van Solinge, T., *Drugs and Decision-Making in the European Union*, 2002, Amsterdam: CEDRO/Mets en Schilt, p. 141.

159 *COM (1999) 239 final*, Luxembourg: Office for Official Publication of the European Communities, p. 10.

One such effort is the establishment of the European Monitoring Centre for Drugs and Drug Addiction (EMCDDA), which has been operational since 1995.[160] The EMCDDA has two roles: one is to provide more accurate information on the drug problems the EU member states are facing.[161] The other is to function as a mediator between 'science, practice, and policy' through monitoring and analysing the impact of the drug situation and the impact of drug control policies and strategies at both national and EU levels.[162] The EMCDDA produces various reports concerning drug control and drug problems of the EU and its member states.

The reason for the member states' reluctance is that the consequence of co-operation is a hand-over of their authority on policing and law making in relation to transnational crime. The limitation of abilities on law making, law enforcement and border control are all fundamental aspects of state sovereignty. However, being a member state of the EU means that they have to accept EU policies as their own. As Monar suggests, therefore, the concept of sovereignty might be less meaningful in a globalised and interdependent world.[163] The member states, however, remain concerned that their sovereignty is being eroded, particularly in the judicial sphere. However, the EMCDDA could be an advantage for the EU member states in controlling drug. The real value of the EMCDDA may be its capability to provide information to the EU member states. Through the EMCDDA, the EU member states have an opportunity to learn about the drug situations and drug control strategies and policies of other EU member states' and compare them to their own.

Conclusion

The European Community has perceived the threat posed by the cocaine trade in health, crime, and moral issues. Considering the impact of cocaine trafficking to the EU member states, it is regarded as a societal security threat rather than a national security threat. A societal security threat, as discussed in chapter 1, does not affect a state's borders and its functions in a fundamental way, but it can harm the social

160 Estievenart, G., *The Agencies of the European Community: European Centre for Drugs and Drug Addiction*, http://europa.eu.int/agencies/emcdda/index_en.htm (Accessed 3 March 2005); Council Regulation (EEC) No 302/93 of 8 February 1993, *Official Journal L 036* , 12/02/1993 P. 0001 – 0008, http://europa.eu.int/smartapi/cgi/sga_doc?smartapi!celexap i!prod!CELEXnumdoc&lg=en&numdoc=31993R0302&model=guichett (Accessed 3 March 2005); and 'Council Regulation (EC) No 3294/94 of 22 December 1994', *Official Journal L 341, 30/12/1994 P. 0007 – 0007*, http://europa.eu.int/smartapi/cgi/sga_doc?smartapi!celexap i!prod!CELEXnumdoc&lg=en&numdoc=31994R3294&model=guichett (Accessed 3 March 2005).

161 EMCDDA, *About the EMCDDA*, http://www.emcdda.eu.int/index. cfm?fuseaction=public.Content&nNodeID=373&sLanguageISO=EN (Accessed 3 March 2005).

162 EMCDDA, *National and EU drug strategies and policies*, http://www.emcdda.eu.int/ index.cfm?fuseaction=public.Content&nNodeID=2176&sLanguageISO=EN (Accessed 3 March 2005).

163 Mitsilegas, V., Monar, J., and Rees, W., *The European Union and Internal Security: Guardian of People?* 2003, London: Palgrave Macmillan.

environment, moral values and well being of a community. From this perspective, the cocaine trade is affecting the social fabric and harmony in communities as well as in nations as a whole.

Cocaine trafficking generates large amounts of money and employs many people both directly and indirectly. Through income from the cocaine trade, traffickers can penetrate the legal economy and influence national industries, although it might not be noticeable to the general public. Also, the ability to employ a work force has been supporting illegal immigrants by allowing them to earn an income from the cocaine trade and survive in the European Community. This could lead to two issues for governments. First, there will be increasing numbers of illegal immigrants able to settle in the EU member states due to the income they can generate from cocaine trafficking. Second, the active cocaine market could destabilise and undermine the safety of local communities. This may be caused by the mistrust and misperception of foreigners led by the high participation rate of illegal immigrants in the cocaine trade. Misperception and negative sentiment against particular social groups could lead to social conflicts and division in a community in economic and racial terms, since poorer areas are more vulnerable to the drug trade.

The increase in the numbers of cocaine dealers and users can spread violence and infectious diseases. At the same time, the active involvement of dealers and users will make their presence in the community more visible. The trace of cocaine abuse (for instance, discarded needles and cylinders) can be seen in public places, such as parks. The expansion of the cocaine market increases competition among dealers, which has led to the increase in the use of violence to protect their interests. Although the victims of gunfights tend to be those involved in the cocaine business, the death toll reported in the media generates fear among the citizens. It is possible that the use of violence may escalate in the future. Cocaine trafficking challenges the well-being of the state and society, and the cultural values they possess. The dealing in, and the use of, illegal substances affect respect for law and the judicial system of the nation, as well as the moral and cultural development of children.

To the government, the wide spread cocaine market could undermine its international identity as a moral and law-abiding nation with adequate control over its own well-being. In addition, domestic cocaine abuse could lead to international interference in drug control over the state territories, such as pressure to enforce law and to establish legislation against cocaine trafficking from the United States and international organisations. Such interference could be regarded as a violation of sovereignty, or a state being forced to give up some of its sovereignty to comply with an international trend. To disregard the international trend in drug control, however, might undermine the ability of European leaders to conduct co-operative policies to solve global problems. The European approach to drug control, therefore, is a socio-economic project based on their understanding of cocaine as a societal security threat. This will be examined further in chapters 4 and 6. For the EU member states, cocaine trafficking is caused by social factors, including poverty, education, health and moral misdirection.

Chapter 3

The 'Securitisation' of Cocaine Trafficking in the United States

Introduction

This chapter will concern itself with how the United States sees the threat from cocaine trafficking. As argued in chapter 1, non-traditional security threats, such as drug trafficking, do not damage the physical existence of a state, but affect various state functions. An analysis of America's conceptualisation of the cocaine threat is a necessary step in examining its drug control policy, which we will do in a later chapter. This is because the US understanding of cocaine trafficking influences its particular approach to drug control in the Andes. In order to determine the damage posed to the United States by the cocaine trade, this chapter will investigate four aspects in state affairs that could be affected by cocaine trafficking following the framework for analysis set in chapter 1.

First, it will examine the economic impact of both the cocaine business and law enforcement efforts to control the domestic flow of cocaine. Government finance is affected by lost tax income, health costs, and law enforcement budgets. Also, the national financial and banking sectors are used for money laundering by the traffickers. Second, the political impact will be examined through the analysis of the relationship between law enforcement and corruption. In order to ensure the illicit trade, bribery is a necessary tool for cocaine traffickers. Those working for law enforcement and ports of entry tend to be targeted. Third, this section will analyse the impact of cocaine trafficking on public order, such as drug-related crimes, health issues and the limitation of civil rights. The cost of cocaine trafficking extends to national well-being and the operation of the judicial system. Fourth, this section will investigate the diplomatic impact related to cocaine trafficking by focusing on foreign traffickers working to smuggle cocaine into the United States, and the way these traffickers are punished. It will also examine US efforts to ensure Latin American states control cocaine trafficking through the use of narcotic certification.

Economic Impact

Cocaine traffickers are attracted to the United States because of its economic power. The expansion and penetration of the cocaine business affects legal economic activities in both the state and society. This section focuses upon two issues. First, the operation and expansion of the cocaine business will be examined. The cocaine trade, after all, is a matter of money: 'drug money, rather than drugs, is the root of the evil.'[1] The expansion of the cocaine business allows traffickers to 'buy' businesses in the legal economy as well as exert influence through corruption. Although there is debate over the precise size of the cocaine market, it is sufficient to generate large sums of money. Narco-dollars penetrate and manipulate the national economy.

Secondly, the cost of controlling cocaine will be investigated. Cocaine prohibition is a significant drain on the United States. Since the prohibition of cocaine, the government has been allocating large amounts of the budget to execute law enforcement. Its emphasis on law enforcement increased the number of inmates and prisons, which is known as the 'prison-industry complex'. Considering the numbers of cocaine addicts and the amount of cocaine available in the United States, the cost effectiveness of law enforcement has been questioned.

The Underground and Upperground Economies

The cocaine trade is a lucrative business. Prohibition of cocaine and law enforcement has led to higher prices and to a larger cocaine industry.[2] According to Wisotsky, prohibition pushed up the prices of pharmaceutical cocaine by 40 to 60 times in the late 1980s, and consequently allowed an annual $80–$100 billion flow of cocaine-dollar circulation in the underground economy.[3] During the last two decades, however, cocaine prices fell by nearly 70%. As reports to the Office of National Drug Control Policy indicate, it has reduced US expenditure on cocaine, which was estimated as $35.3 billion in 2000.[4]

As for the quality of cocaine, despite the decline in price, its purity increased from 10% to 20% to about 70% by the end of the 1980s,[5] and reached higher purity throughout the 1990s.[6] A minimal amount of cocaine on the street can be purchased for as little as $3 in a package of 0.1 to 0.5 grams, and pure cocaine was available at around $90 to $100 per pure gram in the late 1990s.[7] Since the 1990s, cocaine is

---

1   Wisotsky, S., *Beyond the War on Drugs: Overcoming a Failed Public Policy*, 1990, New York: Prometheus Books, p. xxxi.

2   Ashley, R., *Cocaine: Its History, Uses and Effects*, 1975, New York: St. Martin's Press, pp. 93–105; and Naylor, R.T., *Wages of Crime: Black Markets, Illegal Finance, and the Underworld Economy*, 2002, Ithaca: Cornell University Press, p. 34.

3   One ounce of pharmaceutical cocaine cost $50, but prohibition caused it to rise to between $2,000 and $3,000. Wisotsky, *Beyond the War on Drugs*, p. xxxvii.

4   Rhodes, W., Langenbahn, S., Kling, R., and Scheiman, P., *What America's Users Spend on Illegal Drugs, 1988-1995*, 29 September 1997, Washington DC: ONDCP, http://www.whitehousedrugpolicy.gov/publications/drugfact/retail/contents.html, p. 6 (Accessed 30 April 2003); Abt Associates Inc., *What America's Users Spend on Illegal Drugs 1988-2000*, December 2001, http://www.whitehousedrugpolicy.gov/publications/pdf/american_users_spend_2002.pdf, p. 3 (Accessed 30 April 2003).

5   Interview with an official at the Office of National Drug Control Policy in Washington DC on 28 May 2003; Office of the Attorney General, *Drug Trafficking – A Report to the President of the United States*, 1989, Washington, DC: The White House, p. 7.

6   Interview with officials at ONDCP in Washington DC on 28 May 2003.

7   DEA, 'Cocaine: Trafficking by Colombian and Mexican Organizations', in *Drug Trafficking in the United States*, September 2001, http://www.dea.gov/pubs/intel/01020/

more affordable for a greater percentage of the population and, moreover, the higher purity of cocaine allows purchasers to 'cut'[8] and resell it in lower but still acceptable purity for other users. This made the cocaine trade an inexpensive business to start for those requiring an income.[9]

In order to increase their earnings, poor minority groups in inner-cities often seek involvement in cocaine businesses. According to McCoun and Reuter, estimates based on the arrests related to drug offences showed that one-third of black males born in the 1960s in inner-city Washington DC engaged in drug dealing between the ages of 18 and 24.[10] The cocaine business, as Brownstein argues, could provide not only immediate cash gains but also 'opportunities for ownership, control and autonomy to anyone who could afford to purchase even a minimal amount of cocaine'.[11] It is, however, not easy to be successful in the cocaine trade, partly because of the competitiveness of the market.

Those who are successful in dealing cocaine may establish 'crack houses' and may be involved in more organised forms of the trade. Williams observed the changes and developments in the New York cocaine trade: the cocaine business became complex, dangerous and competitive by the mid-1980s. Successful operation in the cocaine business meant 'diversifying' and required involvement in real-estate dealings in order to run profitable crack houses with larger numbers of crews.[12] By the early 1990s, the New York cocaine business was more organised and seemed to take the form of corporation-style business operations.

In order to return the illicit earnings into the legal economy, the traffickers or dealers erase the trace of criminality through bank transfers and the purchase of legitimate companies. Money laundering has been criminalised by the government because it legitimises illicit gain and provides financial power in the legal economy to drug traffickers. However, money laundering did not attract much attention until the 'the Bank of Credit and Commerce International (BCCI) scandal'[13] in 1988.

---

index.html#cocaine (Accessed 30 April 2003); and ONDCP, *The Price of Illicit Drugs: 1981 through the Second Quarter of 2000*, October 2001, Washington, DC: Abt Associates Inc., http://www.whitehousedrugpolicy.gov/publications/pdf/price_illicit.pdf, p. 7 (Accessed 30 April 2003).

8   To 'cut' cocaine means mixing cocaine with other chemical substances to reduce purity.

9   See also the section in the Introduction titled 'The Nature of Latin American Cocaine Trafficking' for details of the cocaine industry. Bell, D., 'Crime as an American Way of Life', *Antioch Review*, June 1953.

10 MacCoun, R.J. and Reuter, P., *Drug War Heresies: Learning from Other Vices, Times, and Places*, 2001, Cambridge: Cambridge University Press, p. 22.

11 Brownstein, H.H., *The Rise and Fall of a Violent Crime Wave: Crack Cocaine and the Social Construction of a Crime Problem*, 1996, New York: Criminal Justice Press, p. 38.

12 Williams, T., *The Cocaine Kids: The Inside Story of a Teenage Drug Ring*, 1992, Cambridge, Mass.: Perseus Books, p. 123.

13 See below for the details.

For banks, accepting deposits is the way to operate their business, and they earn up to 3% in commission on each transaction for transferring money.[14] Frequent requests to transfer large sums of money by the drug traffickers represent more business opportunities for banks. Some banks, therefore, keep laundering narco-dollars, despite its illegality.[15] The BCCI, for example, was accused of supporting money laundering more than once. It faced disclosure of the fact that it had been laundering narco-dollars for Colombian cocaine cartels and General Manuel Noriega of Panama in 1988. BCCI was accused of knowingly laundering $14 million out of $32 million in cocaine profits.[16] Again in 1991, the accusation of BCCI money laundering returned with the claim of laundering $23 million dollars for General Noriega.[17]

The Flagship National Bank in Florida was accused of accepting deposits and transferring narco-dollars in the 1980s. According to a court document, the cash deposited was, sometimes, powdery with cocaine left on the notes.[18] Considering the state of the notes brought to the bank, the origin of the money might be evident. However, the bank continued to accept the money, and failed to report these suspicious transactions to the government. This may be sufficient to believe that the bank took the money despite knowing its origin.[19]

In respect of front companies and money laundering, cocaine traffickers use businesses that deal with large amounts of cash, such as jewellers. In Los Angeles, wholesale jewellery companies were contracted for laundering money. Ropex Corporation and Andonian Brothers Manufacturing Company were assisting traffickers with money laundering and transferring the money internationally under the disguise of legal trade.[20] In Miami, a travel agency and *casa de cambio* (money exchange) owned by Mauricio Lehrer and Oscar Cuevas, respectively, were used to launder the narco-dollars for the Cali cartel.[21] The money was transferred through

---

14 Woodiwiss, M., Crime, *Crusades and Corruption: Prohibitions in the United States, 1900-1987*, 1988, London: Pinter Publishers, p. 195.

15 Grosse, R.E., *Drugs and Money: Laundering Latin America's Cocaine Dollars*, 2001, Westport: Praeger, pp. 198–203.

16 Getler, W., 'A Major Bank Accused by U.S. Of Laundering Cocaine Profits', *International Herald Tribune*, 12 October 1988.

17 Friedman, A., and Waters, R., 'US indicts BCCI officials on drug money charges', *Financial Times*, 6 September 1991.

18 *Mariano H. Ospina, Petitioner v. United States of America*, No. 90-6719, October Term, 1990, http://www.usdoj.gov/osg/briefs/1990/sg900324.txt (Accessed 7 March 2005).

19 The persons who took money to the bank identified themselves as undercover government officials. The bank argued the case on this point, but the court rejected it. *State v. Hernando Ospina*, 798 F.2d 1579 (1986).

20 Parker, III, W., *Testimony*, 20 April 1999, http://financialservices.house.gov/banking/42099par.htm (Accessed 21 February 2005).

21 Castillo, F., *Los Jinetes de la Cocaína*, 2001, chapter 3, http://www.derechos.org/nizkor/colombia/libros/jinetes/cap3.html (Accessed 7 March 2005); chapter 4, http://www.derechos.org/nizkor/colombia/libros/jinetes/cap7.html (Accessed 7 March 2005); 'Con un pie en avión de la DEA', *PostNuke*, 6 November 2004, http://www.diariooccidente.com.co/printarticle4939.html (Accessed 7 March 2005); and Duque Gómez, D., 'El Presidente debe ser

local banks, such as a Miami bank and Citibank to the accounts of shell corporations in South America, London, and Switzerland.

After successfully laundering money, drug traffickers purchase legal business corporations and properties to increase their access to the legitimate economy. In Miami, about 20% of all real estate in the region was owned by various drug traffickers in the 1980s.[22] The drug traffickers used 'shell corporations' based in the Netherlands Antilles for the purchase in order to conceal their connection.[23] The large sums of cash at their disposal allow drug traffickers to be in an advantageous position in competition for businesses in the legal economy compared to the legal corporations.[24]

The penetration of cocaine traffickers into the legitimate economy may not be visible on the surface due to their disguise by using shell corporations. However, the inflow of 'dirty money' to the national economy and its removal to foreign banks can affect the credibility of the national financial market and banking system. At the same time, it will strengthen traffickers' financial power in the legal economy. The financial power of cocaine traffickers can lead to domination of certain businesses, such as ownership of land and properties. This could provide the traffickers with influence and control over the areas to establish secure operational ground for their illicit business.

The Cost of Drug Control

The financial losses related to cocaine consumption are not limited to untaxed sales in the cocaine market for the government. There are those arising from the prohibition of drugs and the drug control policy.[25] According to Perl, drug abuse costs the US

---

juzgado', *Colombia Analitica*, 14 June 2001, http://colombia.analitica.com/politica/3171552. asp?frameactive=0 (Accessed 7 March 2005).

22 Richards, J.R., *Transnational Criminal Organization, Cybercrime, and Money Laundering*, 1999, Boca Raton: CRC Press, p. 56; and Savona, E.U., and De Feo, M.A., 'International Money Laundering Trends and Prevention/Control', in Savona, E.U. (ed.), *Responding to Money Laundering: International Perspectives*, 1997, Amsterdam: Harwood Academic Publisher, pp. 28–31.

23 The 'true' identity of the owners of these corporations was not revealed until the investigation went through three levels of shell corporations.

24 Ianni, F.A.J., 'Formal and Social Organization in an Organized Crime 'Family': A Case Study', *University of Florida Law Review*, 1971, Vol. 24, p. 31.

25 Dennis argues that legalising drugs in the 1980s could have saved about $25 billion for the government. Dennis, R.J., 'The economics of legalizing drugs', *The Atlantic*, Vol. 266, 1990, p. 128.

$160 billion annually[26] because of the costs required for treatment of drug users ($14.9 billion), the criminal justice system, and social welfare ($35 billion).[27]

Drug control policy is based upon two programmes: law enforcement operations (supply reduction), as well as the education and treatment of addicts (demand reduction). Drug control still focuses heavily on law enforcement to reduce the supply of cocaine, although the balance between supply and demand reduction has been reconsidered since the Clinton administration.[28] This is partly because law enforcement operations can be regarded as self-sufficient, due to the fact that the seized assets are used to fund further law enforcement, as detailed below.[29] Due to the cost of drug law enforcement, there are criticisms of its cost effectiveness,[30] but a DEA report claims that law enforcement operations have reduced cocaine use by 75% in the last 15 years.[31]

The seizures and confiscation of the cash and assets of convicted dealers and traffickers by law enforcement agencies and customs can bring generous revenues to the government. A part of confiscated assets, then, will be re-distributed to the law enforcement agencies as a reward to motivate the officers to pursue other dealers and traffickers and to provide resources for future operations. This system is supported by law: federal and state laws permit law enforcement agencies to earn money from seizures. It is, therefore, said that drug law enforcement operations are run on the wealth confiscated from drug traffickers. For example, Florida, with its high drug trafficking rates, earned enough to build a mini-jail with drug money.[32] According

---

26 The economic costs of drug abuse increased rapidly. In 1992, it was $98 billion, and $110 billion in 2000. Pickering, T.R., Testimony at Joint Hearing on *Supplemental Request for Plan Colombia* before the Senate Subcommittee on Foreign Operations, Export Financing, and Related Programs; defense; and Military Construction, Committee on Appropriations, 106 Congress, 2nd Session, 24 February 2000, http://frwebgae.access.gpo.gov/cgi-bin/getdoc.cgi?dbname=106_senate_heringsedocid=f:63941.pdf (Accessed 16 May 2003), p. 12; National Institute on Drug Abuse, *Economic Costs of Alcohol and Drug Abuse Estimated at $246 billion in The United States*, 13 May 1998, http://www.nida.nih.gov/MedAdv/98/MA-513.html (Accessed 9 March 2005); and Harwood, H., Fountain, D., and Livermore, G., & the Lewin Group, *The Economic Costs of Alcohol and Drug Abuse in the United States 1992*, NIH publication No. 98-4327, Rockville, MA: National Institute on Drug Abuse, chapter 1.

27 Perl, R., *Drug Control: International Policy and Approaches*, CRS Issue Brief IB88093, 7 April 2003, http://www.house.gov/htbin/crsprodget?/ib/IB88093 (Accessed 2 May 2003), p. 2.

28 Interview with an official at ONDCP in Washington DC on 28 May 2003.

29 Rydell and Everingham estimated that to reduce the same amount of cocaine consumption, law enforcement would cost the government about 10 times more than that of demand reduction. To reduce cocaine consumption by 1%, treatment programmes may cost about $34 million, and law enforcement may cost $246–366 million. Rydell, P. and Everingham, S., *The cost of cocaine control*, 1994, Santa Monica, CA: RAND.

30 Williams, *The Cocaine Kids*, p. 7; and Wisotsky, op cit., p. 106.

31 Hutchinson, A., *DEA and Doctors: Cooperation for the Public Good*, Speech at American Pain Society, 14 March 2002, http://www.usdoj.gov/dea/speeches/s031402.html (Accessed 30 April 2003).

32 Starita, J., 'Drug Dealers Pay in Jail, Out of Wallet', *Miami Herald*, 18 October 1982, section A.

to a report by the US Department of Justice, the government distributed one-third of the total seizures ($4 billion) to federal and local law enforcement agencies in 1994.[33] The distribution of money to agencies depends on the amount of seizures made in the previous year, hence 'the more seizures, the more money'.[34]

This system seems to function well. The prospect for extra budgets will certainly give law enforcers greater incentives to tackle cocaine problems in their jurisdiction. Also, the money earned from the law enforcement operations can support further operations against the cocaine trade. As Naylor points out, however, this system has a danger that the law enforcers focus on seizing and confiscating cash from the traffickers and dealers rather than cocaine *per se*.[35] Thereby, there is a concern that the targets of law enforcement operations could be not 'the most serious offenders but on the most lucrative prospects'.[36] In other words, the priority for law enforcement may not be justice but money. Regarding this concern, the ex-members of Los Angeles elite squad, 'the Majors', admitted that they began targeting larger sums of cash seizures for their department (the Sheriff's department).[37] This is because the police departments were expected to seize money to make their budget.[38]

The earnings from the seizures, however, are not sufficient to cover the cost of law enforcement operations. MacCoun and Reuter estimate that the cost of drug control programmes increased by 3.5 times in the mid-1990s compared to the 1980s.[39] One of the reasons for this is the expansion of law enforcement operations. The number of law enforcers has continued to rise in order to cope with cocaine control, plus the fact that the number of inmates increases as a result of law enforcement. It requires more facilities and money to manage the 'prison-industry complex'. This started with the increase in arrests and the resulting lack of prison facilites. The need for more prisons encouraged the building industry, and created more jobs.[40] Consequently, building prisons became 'big business' in the United States. For example, California built twenty prisons between 1984 and 1999, and this became 'California's leading

33 US Department of Justice, *Audit report: Asset forfeiture program - Annual financial statement*, 1995, Washington DC: US Department of Justice.

34 MacCoun, R.J. and Reuter, P., *Drug War Heresies: Learning from Other Vices, Times, and Places*, 2001, Cambridge: Cambridge University Press, p. 119.

35 Naylor, *Wages of Crime*, p. 247.

36 MacCoun *et al.*, *Drug War Heresies*, p. 119; and Gregorie, D., *Frontline: Drug Wars Interview*,   http://www.pbs.org/wgbh/pages/frontline/shows/drugs/interviews/gregorie.html (Accessed 4 October 2004).

37 Garner, D., from comments during the TV programme *Frontline: When Cops Go Bad*, original air date 16 October 1990, http://www.pbs.org/wgbh/pages/frontline/shows/drugs/archive/copsgobad.html (Accessed 8 March 2005).

38 Gates, D., from comments during the TV programme *Frontline: When Cops Go Bad*, original air date 16 October 1990, http://www.pbs.org/wgbh/pages/frontline/shows/drugs/archive/copsgobad.html (Accessed 8 March 2005).

39 MacCoun *et al.*, *Drug War Heresies*, p. 24.

40 Moor, M.H., 'Supply Reduction and Drug Law Enforcement', in Tonry, M and Wilson, J.Q. (eds), *Drug and Crime: Crime and Justice A Review of Research*, Vol. 73, 1990, Chicago: The University of Chicago Press, p. 115.

'public work' program'.[41] The newly built prisons need to be maintained by sufficient numbers of staff, and hence have provided job opportunities to local populations around the new prisons.

The increase of law enforcement officers and the high incentives for arresting drug offenders has raised the general prison population. The number of prisoners in the United States (both federal and state) has been increasing since the 1970s. Following the increase in the number of prisoners, the Reagan administration requested a 48% increase in the budget for the US Bureau of Prisons in 1989 'in order to accommodate an anticipated increase in federal prisoners from 44,000 today to 72,000 by 1995'.[42] The number of inmates, however, exceeded the estimate made in 1989, and reached 1.8 million by the end of 1998.[43] In the mid-1990s, drug offenders in federal prisons represented 50% of the total inmates.[44]

The high population of cocaine offenders within prisons has been the consequence from drug law enforcement, as cocaine users do not amount to 50% of the total American population. This trend is also recognised in local arrests: according to Zimring and Hawkins, 'more than 75% of all male arrests in New York City tested positive for cocaine' in the early 1990s, although only 10% of the local population were cocaine users.[45] The high incarceration rates of drug offenders reflect the focus of law enforcement operations. In 1998, 59% and 21% of federal and state prisons respectively were occupied by drug offenders.[46] The government expenditures on correction and incarceration of drug offenders in 1996 amounted to over $68 billion.[47]

The budgets and personnel have kept on increasing since the Reagan administration's expansion of agencies to fight the War on Drugs after 1982.[48] For example, the size of the Drug Enforcement Agency has more than doubled in the last two decades. The budget has increased 6.7 times since 1983, reaching nearly $19 billion in 2003.[49] Furthermore, the government has broadened the engagement in cocaine control. According to Gray, the government allocated the budget for law

---

41 Gray, J.P., *Why Our Drug Laws Have Failed and What We Can Do About It: A Judicial Indictment of the War on Drugs*, 2001, Philadelphia: Temple University Press, pp. 33–34.

42 Wisotsky, op cit., p. xix.

43 Gray, op cit., p. 29; and New York County Lawyer's Association, *Report and Recommendation of the Drug Policy Task Force*, 1996 (October), New York: New York County Lawyer's Association, p. 5.

44 MacCoun *et al.*, *Drug War Heresies*, p. 26.

45 Zimring, F.E., and Hawkins, G., *The Search for Rational Drug Control*, 1992, Cambridge: Cambridge University Press, p. 138.

46 Drug offenders include poly-drug users and those who use other drugs, not only cocaine. Walters, J.P., *Fact Sheet: Drug Treatment in the Criminal Justice System*, March 2001, Washington DC: ONDCP, p. 2, http://www.whitehousedrugpolicy.gov/publications/factsht/treatment/index.html (Accessed 19 September 2004).

47 Ibid., p. 2; For the cost of keeping prisoners, see also: Gray, op cit., pp. 34–37.

48 Reagan, R., *Presidential Statement of 14 October 1982*.

49 In 1983, the number of DEA officials was 4,013, but in 2003, the DEA has registered 9,629 officials and received $1,897.3 million for its budget. DEA, *DEA Staffing & Budget*, http://www.usdoj.gov/dea/agency/staffing.htm (Accessed 9 May 2003).

enforcement operations to various departments, which do not seem to be related directly to drugs, such as the Department of Land Management.[50]

In relation to demand reduction, Caulkins *et al.* argue that treatment programmes to reduce consumption among cocaine users may achieve higher cost-performance than law enforcement. According to their analysis, $1 million invested in treatment programmes could lower cocaine consumption by 104 kg, but arrests of distributors would only cut supply by 13 to 26 kg.[51] Applying their data to the estimated annual consumption of pure cocaine, the cost to reduce cocaine consumption would be about $336 million, which is considerably lower than the cost of law enforcement.[52]

One of the problems of demand reduction, however, is that the number of addicts accessible for treatment is limited.[53] According to a report from the Federal Bureau of Prisons, there were about 34,000 drug addicts treated in prison programmes in 1998.[54] Compared to the numbers of imprisoned drug abusers this is only a small amount, so the treatment projects may need expansion to include more inmates. MacCoun and Reuter maintain that cocaine addicts undertaking treatment were estimated to be only 10% or less of cocaine addicts in 1995.[55] The criminality attached to the use of cocaine may have made the addicts difficult to treat except while in custody.

In sum, the impact of the cocaine trade is complex in economic terms. The losses from the cocaine trade are costly, although not all the losses are visible. The cocaine economy provides wealth to those who are remote from legitimate economic gains, and it could even bring them an opportunity to climb up the social ladder in society. The advance of traffickers and dealers into legal economic activities funded by narco-dollars could escape notice until the influence of traffickers became unavoidable in the legal economy. It is possible that the legal economy is damaged by the lack of fair competition in markets. Legitimate corporations funded by narco-dollars also obscure the border between criminal activities and legal activities.

Concerning law enforcement operations, federal and state governments obtain extra revenues through law enforcement directed against cocaine offenders. Additional income supports further operations. Considering these facts, cocaine control seems to

---

50 Gray, op cit., p. 42.

51 Caulkins, J., Rydell, P., Schwabe, W.L., and Chisea, J., *Mandatory minimum drug sentences: Throwing away the key or the taxpayers' money?* 1997, Santa Monica, CA: RAND.

52 Data from ONDCP indicates annual consumption of pure cocaine is between 270–400 tonnes. The calculation is made on 350 tonnes. Rhodes, W., Layne, M., Johnston, P., and Hozik, L., *What America's Users Spend on Illegal Drugs 1988-1998*, December 2000, Washington DC: ONDCP, http://www.whitehousedrugpolicy.gov/publications/drugfact/american_users_spend/section1.html (Accessed 19 September 2004), Section 1; and also 'Antidrug idea: more tests in U.S.', *The Miami Herald*, 28 November 2002, http://www.miami.com/mld/miamiherald/news/columnists/andres oppenheimer/4622170.htm?template =contentModules/printstory.jsp (Accessed 19 September 2004).

53 Also, there is no specific treatment for cocaine addiction.

54 Federal Bureau of Prisons, *Substance Abuse and Treatment Programs in the Federal Bureau of Prisons: Report to Congress*, January 1999, Washington DC: US Department of Justice.

55 MacCoun *et al.*, *Drug War Heresies*, p. 33.

be a self-sufficient policy for the United States because law enforcement operations can earn their way with seized assets. Moreover, successful law enforcement can provide increased job opportunities to citizens. There is, however, danger in this approach: one is that economic incentives in law enforcement tend to mislead personnel to pursue money rather than justice.[56] In such cases, law enforcement operations could damage the accountability of the justice system. The other is that there is potential for 'partnership' between drug businesses and law enforcement operations being established to sustain the prison-industry complex. As Wisotsky warns: 'Drug enforcement could easily become a perpetual motion machine, with drug dealers and drug agents operating in a state of symbiosis: black market profits can finance both the police and the policed in mutual prosperity forever after.'[57]

Political Impact

This part will examine how cocaine traffickers affect government through the use of bribery. According to Simpson, prohibition of a commodity spawns corruption and undermines credibility of the government's institutions. The prohibition of liquor in the 1920s, he claims, did 'more than anything else in American history to corrupt the police and to destroy respect for the law,'[58] and the equivalent today is believed to result from 'the prohibition of cocaine and other drugs.'[59] Under drug prohibition, the problem of corruption is inevitable, particularly for those working in law enforcement.[60] The UN Drug Control Programme noted 'Wherever there is a well-organized, illicit drug industry, there is also the danger of police corruption'.[61] Bribery may reach personnel in the government from law enforcement officials to politicians. The effects of corruption are not always visible, but will undermine the institutional functions and operational processes, and will taint law enforcers (including customs officers) and politicians.

Those most likely to be targeted by cocaine traffickers are law enforcement officers, such as agents of the DEA, the Federal Bureau of Investigation (FBI), the Central Intelligence Agency (CIA) and judicial figures. The nature of their work and expertise makes them useful targets for drug traffickers. In the case of the CIA, its agents were known to have connections with Colombian cartels involved in cocaine

---

56 Gregorie, D., *Frontline: drug wars: Interview*, http://www.pbs.org/wgbh/pages/frontline/shows/drugs/interviews/gregorie.html (Accessed 4 October 2004).

57 Wisotsky, op cit., p. 175.

58 Simpson, A., *The Literature of Police Corruption*, 1977, New York: John Jay Press, p. 93.

59 Wisotsky, op cit., p. 149.

60 Woodiwiss, op cit., p. 8.

61 UNDCP, *Technical Series Report No. 6, Economic and Social Consequences of Drug Abuse and Illicit Trafficking*, 1998, New York: UNDCP, p. 38.

trafficking.[62] In 1988, two CIA agents were arrested for assisting both cocaine and arms trafficking for a Colombian cartel in exchange for $225,000.[63]

One of the cases that created suspicion of corruption inside the DEA and CIA was that of BCCI. It exposed negligence by the DEA in the form of passive involvement in money laundering as well as the supply of information to traffickers by the CIA. It was reported that although the money laundering operations via BCCI were known to the law enforcement agency, the cocaine traffickers and the banks got away with impunity. According to Robinson, an investigation revealed that the DEA and the US Inland Revenue Service (IRS) knew that there were more than 125 transactions of cocaine-dollars through BCCI between 1985 and 1990, but no action was taken against them.[64] During the investigation, suspicion of CIA involvement in tipping-off the cocaine traffickers arose because of the mysterious disappearance of $23 million from BCCI before seizures of its assets took place.[65]

The influence of Colombian traffickers even reached to government officials within the United States, and led to business relationships being established. As a result of Operation Cornerstone in 1995, the connections of lawyers to officials in the US government to the Cali cartel of Colombia were disclosed.[66] Among them, there was a former director of the Justice Department's Office of International Affairs, Michael Abbell, and a former prosecutor, William Moran, who used to fight against the Cali Cartel.[67] Abbell was known to engage in the cocaine business by abusing his position as a defence attorney for Gilberto Rodriguez Orejuela and the Cali cartel. Another example of such corruption investigated by Marshall is the case of an organisation called 'The Company' which was established in 1986 and consisted of former law enforcement officials and military officials.[68] The Company dealt drugs and arms with guerrilla groups as well as Latin American cocaine traffickers through the members' connections to drug trafficking organisations and foreign insurgency groups established during their government service.

Customs officers might be involved in corruption by turning a blind eye to cocaine smuggling in order to earn some extra money. Although they are expected to halt the flow of cocaine into the United States at the border, the temptation of cash might be too strong to resist. According to a Government Accounting Office report, there were some cases of corruption related to drug trafficking by the Immigration

---

62 Scot, P.D., and Marshall, J., *Cocaine Politics: Drugs, Armies, and the CIA in Central America*, 1991, Berkeley, CA: University of California Press.

63 Honey, M., 'CIA and rebels linked to Colombian cocaine cartel', *The Times*, 30 June 1988.

64 Robinson, S., 'US narcotics agents knew of drug links', *Daily Telegraph*, 6 September 1991.

65 Friedman, A., 'Inquiry into BCCI 'tip-off' to drug dealers', *Financial Times*, 28 October 1991. As for the BCCI scandal, see the section on Economic Impact above.

66 'Cali Cartel: Do they really run the business?' *Latin American Regional Report: Andean group*, 29 June 1995.

67 Zengerle, P., 'Defendant vanishes in Miami lawyer's drug trial', *Reuters*, 17 July 1998.

68 Marshall, C., *The Last Circle*, 1994, http://www.lycaeum.org/books/books/last_circle/circle!.htm (Accessed 3 September 2004), chapter 5.

and Naturalization Service and customs officers. They were involved in ensuring safe passage and disclosing drug intelligence to traffickers.[69] Those corrupt officials received, as an FBI Special Agent revealed, about double their annual salary for waving trucks through customs.[70] For example, a border patrol agent in Arizona who agreed to assist the safe passage of a cocaine load through the United States Border Patrol checkpoint was receiving $3,000 to $10,000 for each passage.[71]

Another example is that at the border between San Diego and Tijuana, according to Carman, an ex-Customs Special Agent in San Diego, there is systemic corruption in the Custom Services.[72] Carman was told to accept the situation by his superior in the office. The Customs officials receive routine payoffs from the cocaine traffickers and let the drugs into the United States.[73] The officials also provide information on air surveillance to assist the traffickers' escape from detection. He also points out the corruption of the Commissioner of Customs and Secretary of Treasury who chose to ignore corruption lower down within the service.

On the street, bribery takes a more discreet form but has a higher involvement of police officers. A 1998 report by the GAO indicates that half of all the police officers convicted in corruption cases between 1993 and 1997 involved drug-related offences.[74] Generally, drug related police corruption involved small groups or individual officers conducting unconstitutional searches and seizures, protecting traffickers and providing false crime reports or testimony.[75] In the 1980s, a group of Miami police officers stole large amounts of cocaine and money from a trafficker's boat.[76] At that time, it is believed that 10% of the Miami police department was corrupt. Stealing from seized money and cocaine occurred relatively often during

---

69 GAO, *Drug Control: INS and Customs Can Do More To Prevent Drug-Related Employee Corruption*, March 1999, GAO/GGD-99-31, GAO: Washington DC, p. 12.

70 NPR, 'Corruption at the Gates', *All Things Considered*, 12–13 September 2002, http://www.npr.org/programs/atc/features/2002/sept/border_corruption/ (Accessed 4 October 2004).

71 Office of the United States Attorney District of Arizona, 'Corrupt former U.S. border patrol agent sentenced to 9 years in prison', *Press Release*, 9 February 2004, Case No. CR-00-1346-TUC-FRZ.

72 *Complaint by John Carman v. the United States*, Case No. 00 CV 1215 JM (NLS), 30 July 2001, http://www.narconews.com/carmancomplaint.html (Accessed 8 March 2005); Al Giorno, 'Narco-Corruption at U.S. Customs Services', *The Narco News Bulletin*, 2 August 2001, http://www.narconews.com/Issue13/carmanstory1.html (Accessed 8 March 2005).

73 The amount varies from $50,000 a car to $250,000 a tanker. The passing of information about surveillance was agreed with large sums of payment as well.

74 GAO, Report to the Honorable Charles B. Rangel, House of Representatives, *Law Enforcement: Information on Drug-Related Police Corruption*, May 1998, GAO/GGD-98-111, GAO: Washington DC, p. 35.

75 Ibid., pp. 3–8.

76 Olkon, S., 'Well-known Miami lawyer released while waiting for trial on money-laundering, obstruction charges', *The Miami Herald*, 20 February 2005, http://www.miami.com/mld/miamiherald/news/breaking_news/11016577.htm (Accessed 8 March 2005).

the law enforcement operations.[77] In Los Angeles, a former police department officer admitted stealing $500 and cocaine from a suspect.[78]

There are different levels of corruption. For example: 'on-the-scene release, where the suspect offers the officer money or drugs to let him go without arrest'[79] revealed by an informant system, which was often used in the US judicial system to capture drug traffickers.[80] More systemic forms of bribery include the supply of information relating to wiretaps, search warrant applications, planned arrests, names of informants, surveillance operations, and related sensitive information in exchange for periodic payments or a percentage of sales and revenues so that the traffickers can avoid arrest.[81] In one of the cases in the Los Angeles police department corruption scandal, a former officer admitted at the court that the money seized from suspected cocaine traffickers was not officially recorded.[82] Instead, it was used to make the suspect's family work as informants to testify against other suspected traffickers. Corrupt law enforcement officials will compromise the results of the law enforcement operations before they even start. The failure of operations costs the government in financial terms as well as in the credibility of its justice system.

Regarding corrupt politicians, the influence of cocaine traffickers on members of Congress was suspected in 1999. The Republican chairman of the Senate Intelligence Committee in 1999 was criticised for 'soften[ing]' a drug control bill that 'would expand economic sanctions against drug traffickers and the businesses that work with them.'[83] Critics of the bill said that 'in this Congress … we are not insulated by the efforts of the [drug] kingpins to buy influence and corrupt [American] political institutions' because the narco-lobbyists were believed to be paid by the drug traffickers.[84] The evidence of corruption among politicians is hard to identify because it is difficult to be certain about the influence on government decision-making.[85]

Corruption seems likely to persist as long as the cocaine trade remains illegal. Moreover, tougher law enforcement and harsher punishments can drive the traffickers to bribery in order to obtain 'protection' from corrupt officials. As Woodiwiss argues 'expanded enforcement and severe penalties' bring the United States to the stage of

---

77 'When Cops Go Bad'.

78 CNN, '6 more convictions overturned in LAPD corruption scandal', *CNN*, 23 March 2000, http://archives.cnn.com/2000/US/03/23/lapd.probe/ (Accessed 8 March 2005).

79 Wisotsky, op cit., p. 146.

80 Goddard, D., *Easy Money*, 1978, New York: Farrar, p. 164.

81 'When Cops Go Bad'.

82 '6 more convictions overturned in LAPD corruption scandal'.

83 Weiner, T., and Golden, T., 'Bill to Combat Drug Traffic Caught in Lobbying Battle', *New York Times*, 4 November 1999, http://www.nytimes.com/library/world/americas/110499drug_sanctions.html (Accessed 11 November 1999).

84 Ibid.

85 It might be possible to figure out through careful analysis of the numbers and details of bills. Newell, J., 'Corruption Mitigating Policies in Italy', and Allum, F., 'The Struggle Against Organised crime in Italy,' both are papers presented at 53rd Annual PSA Conference: Democracy and Diversity, 15–17 April 2003.

further lawlessness, that is to say, 'corruption, betrayal, deception, chaos and terror have become an institutionalized part of the drug law enforcement world.'[86]

Impact on Public Order

This section concerns the disturbance in communities resulting from the use of violence related to the cocaine trade. Violence related to cocaine seems to come from two places: the traffickers and law enforcement officers. This part recognises aggressive law enforcement operations as an indirect element caused by the cocaine trade, and hence, considers it as an impact of cocaine trafficking. In order to analyse the impact of violence and cocaine abuse, this section will be divided into two parts: firstly, crime and the use of violence on the cocaine scene will be examined. The use of violence is an inevitable feature of the cocaine trade because of its illegality. The traffickers use violence to protect their business and profits. Also, the abuse of cocaine and the crimes stemming from cocaine habits are also sources of concern for a community from health and safety perspectives. Secondly, the limitation of civil liberties led by the law enforcement efforts against cocaine abuse will be investigated. The enthusiasm to control cocaine has damaged civil rights.

Crime and Violence related to Cocaine

The use of violence by traffickers and dealers is a common feature in the cocaine trade. However, some argue that violence in cocaine trafficking is not as high as it is reported by the media. Brownstein maintains that cocaine-related violence is a social construction of politicians, policy-makers and law enforcers through the media in order to promote a drug scare and to encourage public support for the expansion of law enforcement and the contraction of civil liberties.[87] Also, Zimring and Hawkins maintain that the cocaine trade may play a substantial role in predatory crime in the United States, yet there is not enough evidence to prove causality.[88]

Violence seems to play a significant role in the cocaine trade, although some facts reported by the government could have been exaggerated. MacCoun and Reuter identify the potential causes of violence at drug scenes, particularly crack and cocaine, as: the youthfulness of participants; the value of the drugs themselves; the intensity of law enforcement; and the indirect consequence of drug use.[89] For the dealers and traffickers, violence is a necessary means to protect their business because of its illegal nature.[90]

---

86 Woodiwiss, op cit., p. 196.
87 Brownstein, op cit., pp. 80–88.
88 Zimring *et al.*, op cit., p. 151.
89 MacCoun *et al.*, *Drug War Heresies*, p. 123.
90 Chaiken, J.M., and Chaiken, M.R., 'Drugs and Predatory Crime', in Tonry, M and Wilson J.Q. (eds), *Drug and Crime: Crime and Justice A Review of Research*, Vol. 73, 1990, Chicago: The University of Chicago Press, pp. 213–214; and Shapiro, B., 'How the War on Crime Imprisons America', 1996, *The Nation*, Vol. 262.

In respect to the use of violence in the cocaine trade, according to Goldstein *et al*, between 1984 and 1988 drug and alcohol-related homicides increased by 11%.[91] Among the homicide cases, systemic homicides tripled in 1988 in comparison to 1984, and 88% were related to either cocaine or crack dealings.[92] The increase of systemic homicides related to the cocaine trade could result from the expansion of the cocaine market as well as the Colombian distribution networks. At the higher levels of the cocaine distribution system, the cell managers of the Colombian cartels apply violence as punishment and as warnings. Fuentes believes that: 'A respected manager with the effective use of violence tends to have less betrayal by both customers and workers.'[93] For the cell managers, violence is a tool to keep order and enforce the rules to operate their transaction successfully.

The individual dealers at the lower levels of the cocaine distribution system use violence in the same manner to ensure payment from customers and to protect their own turf. At the street level dealings of cocaine, dealers purchase the drug on either a 'cash' or 'consignment' basis through their own networks.[94] Making deals in this manner often is a cause of violent disputes over the payment because the customers fail to return with the rest of the payment by the agreed date. This kind of operation through loose individual connections with weak hierarchical structures is known as the 'freelance model'.[95] Curtis and Wendel describe the characteristics of cocaine dealing in this manner as:

> Freelancing tends to be the most visible, disruptive, and violent form of market organization. Socially bonded organizations are based on social ties, such as kinship, ethnicity, and neighborhood. They are held together by personal relationships, are often discreet about their sales practices (for example, they tend not to advertise drugs openly in the street), and are often less violent and disruptive to their communities than are other types of drug-dealing organizations.[96]

---

91 In 1984, drug/alcohol related homicides were 42% and in 1988 were 53% of all homicides. In 1984, systemic homicides were only 21% but it rose to 74% in 1998. Goldstein, P., 'The drug/violence nexus: A tripartite conceptual framework', *Journal of Drug Issues*, Vol. 14, 1985; and Goldstein, P., Brownstein, H.H., Ryan, P.J., and Bellucci, P.A., 'Crack and homicide in New York City, 1988: A conceptually based event analysis', *Contemporary Drug Problem*, Vol. 16, 1989.

92 Ibid.

93 Fuentes, J., *Life of a Cell: Managerial Practice and Strategy in Colombian Cocaine Distribution in the United States*, 1998, Washington, DC: National Institution of Justice, http://www.ncjrs.org/pdffiles1/nij/grants/194608.pdf, pp. 202–204 (Accessed 30 April 2003).

94 A consignment basis transaction is similar to a loan or partial payment for cocaine/crack. The seller will provide cocaine in exchange for 50–70% of its total value, and then the customer will bring the rest of the payment by the agreed date.

95 Johnson, B.D., Hamid, A., and Sanabria, H., 'Emerging Models of Crack Distribution', in Mieczkowski, T. (ed.), *Drugs, Crime, and Social Policy: Research, Issues, and Concerns*, 1992, Boston: Allyn and Bacon, p. 60.

96 Curtis, R., and Wendel, T., unpublished paper referred in National Research Council, Manski, C.F., Pepper, J.V., and Petrie, C.V. (eds), *Informing America's Policy on Illegal Drugs: What We Don't Know Keeps Hurting Us*, 2001, Washington DC: National Academy Press, p. 163.

The lack of ties between individual dealers and the community to which they belong made them indifferent to others, and apply violence frequently. Therefore, Goldstein concludes that homicides in the drug scene are more likely to be a result of 'illicit drug market disputes rather than psychopharmacological effects of crack'.[97]

Turning to the relationship between law enforcers and some local communities, there are conflicts between them, particularly within inner-cities. This is because the local people have felt abused by the law enforcers. It relates to the anti-loitering laws that give the law enforcement agents the right to arrest suspected drug-related offenders based solely on profiles. Impressions from the profiles can be largely influenced by personal beliefs and values. As Glasser and Siegel point out, this operation contains the danger of twisting the facts with prejudice residing in officials.[98] It creates the risks of cocaine related arrests being the result of prejudice in the law enforcement agents.[99]

For example, since there is a perception that the cocaine trade is largely controlled by the Hispanic and black population, there is prejudice against these minority groups. The prejudice has shaped particular trends that do not fit the profile of American cocaine use. The controversy in the trends is that the majority of cocaine users are white middle-class suburbanites and the majority of cocaine arrests are unemployed black males.[100] Due to such prejudice in the law enforcers, in some inner cities, such as Baltimore, more than 50% of the black male population between the ages of 18 and 35 were imprisoned.[101] Furthermore, in 1989, black and Hispanics constitute 92% of all those arrested as drug offenders, although government statistics show that blacks constitute only 15–20% of US drug users.[102]

Arrest without warrant based on police suspicion of cocaine dealing may be effective to capture people, but at the same time, it can increase distrust of law enforcement enforcers. Such sentiment can increase hostility toward law enforcers. McCoun and Reuter argue that the dispute between the communities and law enforcers is evident because the ways in which some police officers treat cocaine offenders were so inhumane that conflict between inner-city citizens and the police emerged.[103] It is likely that the cocaine scene is associated with violence by the traffickers to protect their deals, although the frequency and level of violence could vary. McKenan reports that hostility and violence against the police is so fierce that no police officers can enter some areas.[104] Following the absence of official law

97 Goldstein *et al.*, 'Crack and Homicide in New York City', p. 120.

98 Glasser, I., and Siegel, L., 'When Constitutional Rights Seem Too Extravagant to Endure: The Crack Scare's Impact on Civil Rights and Liberties', in Reinarman *et al.* (eds), *Crack in America: Demon Drugs and Social Justice*, 1997, Berkeley: University of California Press, p. 238.

99 Interview with a Mexican official at Secretaria de Relatciones Exteriores in Mexico City on 14 June 2003.

100 Glasser *et al.*, op cit., p. 234.

101 Gray, op cit., p. 44.

102 Duster, D., 'Pattern, Purpose, and Race in the Drug War: The Crisis of Credibility in Criminal Justice', in Reinarman *et al.* (eds), *Crack in America*, p. 264.

103 MacCoun *et al.*, *Drug War Heresies*, p. 120.

104 McKernan, V., 'The Real War on Drugs', *Newsweek*, 21 September 1992, p. 14.

enforcement mechanisms, the areas tend to be ruled by the drug traffickers. Under such circumstances, there are possibilities that bystanders will be the victims of shootings between cocaine traffickers.[105]

Although there are cases of violence in some areas, it usually targets particular people, such as traitors to the trafficking organisations, and politicians and law enforcers acting against traffickers' interests. The possibility of cocaine users getting involved in violent crime, such as homicide, is low, but usually they are more likely to be involved in property crime and theft in order to obtain financial resources to use drugs.[106] The neighbourhood of the areas with large numbers of cocaine users suffer from higher rates of petty crime, such as burglary and theft. The police are reluctant to answer non-drug related cases when they are called. As a consequence, statistics released by the Los Angeles Times state that 'only about 47% of all slayings from 1990 and 1994 were even prosecuted in Los Angeles County, compared with about 80% in the late 1960s.'[107] This approach appears to be over emphasising the drug related cases and neglecting other criminal cases.

In addition to the insecurity arising from the increase of violence associated with cocaine trafficking, the government has been seriously concerned about the harm to health posed by the use of cocaine. The number of cocaine users peaked in the 1990s, and then started to decline.[108] Following the trend of decline, according to reports from the DEA and ONDCP, the statistics indicate that cocaine users (including both heavy and casual) remain about 2.4% of the total population.[109] The health problems related to the cocaine trade are more likely to be caused by the related activities of the cocaine addicts, such as prostitution. Therefore, the high HIV positive rates among US cocaine users have been regarded as a consequence of needle sharing since other developed countries in which the government offers harm reduction programmes[110] register lower rates.[111] Some cocaine addicts tend to engage in prostitution to support

---

105 Wisotsky, op cit., p. 152.

106 Chaiken *et al.*, 'Drugs and Predatory Crime', p. 211.

107 Gray, op cit., p. 70.

108 Williams, *The Cocaine Kids*, p. 7; and Hutchinson, A., *DEA and Doctors: Cooperation for the Public Good*, Speech at American Pain Society, 14 March 2002, http://www.usdoj.gov/dea/speeches/s031402.html (Accessed 30 April 2003).

109 The calculation is based on the figure given above as the number of hard core cocaine users and population from The International Institute of Strategic Studies, *The Military Balance 2002-2003*, 2002, Oxford: Oxford University Press, p. 243; Rhodes *et al.*, *What's America's Users Spend on Illegal Drugs*; Abt Associates Inc., op cit., p. 8; and Rhodes, W., Layne, M., Johnston, P., and Hozik, L., *What America's Users Spend on Illegal Drugs 1988-1998*, December 2000, Washington DC: ONDCP, http://www.whitehousedrugpolicy.gov/publications/pdf/spending_drugs_1988_1998.pdf, p. 8 (Accessed 30 April 2003).

110 The programme based on rehabilitation and treatment frequently applied in European states to cocaine abusers. It contains projects to treat cocaine abusers and to provide a facility for supplying clean needles.

111 Reinarman, C., and Levine, H.G., 'The Crack Attack: Politics and Media in the Crack Scare', in *Crack in America*, p. 45.

their habit.[112] Through these, the cocaine addicts may spread infectious diseases such as HIV/AIDS and other sexual diseases to the community. For example, Colorado Springs, which is known for high infection rates of HIV in the community, has a large number of prostitutes and injecting drug users.[113] According to the research by Neaigus *et al.*, the sample of injecting drug users contained 40% HIV seropositive, a disease that is transmitted by syringe sharing and sexual behaviours.[114] These studies indicate that the existence of a large community (network) can trigger the rapid spread of HIV.

There are also dangers to health associated with cocaine use. However, the harm of actual cocaine use (such as instant addiction and death), according to Baum, has been exaggerated by the government.[115] There are certainly health problems caused by the frequent use of cocaine. Those consuming cocaine excessively over long periods of time may experience paranoia, hallucinations and physical damages, and also tend to become aggressive.[116] Cocaine is not a physically addictive substance like opium, and normally death is caused by an overdose. The media has sensationalised information related to cocaine and crack by showing 'crack babies' being 'addicted' to cocaine in their mother's womb.[117] In reality, the influence of cocaine on unborn babies has yet to be proved.

The Limitation of Civil Liberties

The United States has a reputation for widely accepted civil liberties and protected civil rights. However, Americans have much less personal autonomy in comparison to during the period before the War on Drugs.[118] The war on drugs is regarded as a means

---

112 Hunt, D.E., 'Drugs and Sensual Crimes: Drugs dealings and prostitution', in Tonry, M and Wilson, J.Q. (eds), *Drug and Crime: Crime and Justice A Review of Research*, Vol. 73, 1990, Chicago: The University of Chicago Press.

113 Rothenberg, R.B., Woodhouse, D.C., Potterat, J.J., Muth, S.Q., Darrow, W.W., and Klovdahl, A.S., 'Social Networks in Disease Transmission: The Colorado Springs Study', in Needle, R.H., Coyle, S.L., Genser, S.G., and Trotter II, R.T. (eds), *Social Networks, Drug Abuse, and HIV Transmission*, Research Monograph, Number 151, 1995, http://www.nida. nih.gov/pdf/monographs/151.pdf (Accessed 9 March 2005).

114 Neaigus, A., Friedman, S.R., Goldstein, M., Zldefonso, G., Curtis, R., and Jose, B., 'Using Dyadic Data for a Network Analysis of HIV Infection and Risk Behavior Among Injecting Drug Users', in Needle, R.H., Coyle, S.L., Genser, S.G., and Trotter II, R.T. (eds), *Social Networks, Drug Abuse, and HIV Transmission*, Research Monograph, Number 151, 1995, http://www.nida.nih.gov/pdf/monographs/151.pdf (Accessed 9 March 2005).

115 Baum, D., *Smoke and Mirrors: The War on Drugs and the Politics of Failure*, 1997, Boston: Little Brown.

116 Carbajol, C., 'Psychosis Produced by Nasal Aspiration of Cocaine Hydrochloride', in Jeri, F.R. (ed.), *Cocaine 1980*, 1980, Lima: Pacific Press, pp. 128–132.

117 Morgan, J.P., and Zimmer, L., 'The Social Pharmacology of Smokeable Cocaine: Not All It's Cracked Up to Be', in Reinarman et al. (eds), *Crack in America*, p. 151.

118 Interview with an official at the Department of State in Washington DC on 27 May 2003.

to protect American values and morals.[119] This is because the cocaine situation in the late 1980s was regarded as an opportunity for institutionalising the judgements and tactics through public support during the 1990s. The cocaine epidemic in the 1980s was driven by the fear of disruption to the American social structure by the mass flow and use of cocaine.[120] Politicians kept appealing to citizens to preserve morals and values in American society, and made them believe that tolerance to cocaine, such as legalisation, is equal to the 'advocacy of international narco-terrorism'.[121] The government claimed to be committed to 'America's moral regeneration'.[122]

The willingness of the US to limit its own freedoms for the sake of drug control appeared to be a consequence of the claim by the government: '[Americans] should be extremely reluctant to restrict [drug enforcement officers] within formal and arbitrary lines.'[123] At the height of the War on Drugs, Americans were willing to sacrifice their own civil liberties. Opinion polls revealed that they even approved of extreme measures, such as: giving up some freedoms (62%), using the military to control the domestic drug trade (82%), letting police search homes of suspected drug dealers without a warrant (52%), and reporting drug users to the police (83%).[124] Not only the public but also the Supreme Court is supportive of limiting civil rights in exchange for fighting the war on drugs. The Supreme Court ruled that 'government agencies can evict tenants in public housing even when the resident is unaware that a visiting family member or relative is using drugs'.[125] Zimring and Hawkins claim that: 'Public support for extreme governmental responses to drugs is higher than for authoritarian countermeasures to any other social problem.'[126] It is considered that 'Americans have opposed drug use and feared drug experiences because they seemed to threaten a generally accepted set of values and aspirations that dated from the beginnings of the national experience.'[127]

The restrictions on freedom for the fight against drugs are understood: as drugs forced the United States 'to strike a new balance between order and individual

---

119 Gumble, A., 'Bush appoints moral crusader to fight drugs', *Independent*, 1 May 2001; Roosevelt, M., 'The war against the war on drugs', *Time Magazine*, 1 May 2001; Marquis, 'Tough Conservative Picked for Drug Czar', *New York Times*, 26 April 2001.

120 Musto, D.F., *The American Disease: Origins of Narcotic Control*, 1987, Oxford: Oxford University Press, p. 345.

121 Dorn, N., and South, N., 'After Mr Bennett and Mr Bush: US Foreign Policy and the Prospects for Drug Control', in Dorn, N. and South, N. (eds), *Global Crime Connection*, 1993, London: Macmillan, p. 80.

122 Woodiwiss, op cit., p. 199.

123 White House, *National Drug Control Strategy*, September 1989, pp. 7–8.

124 Ibid.

125 'Supreme Court OKs Public-Housing Drug Eviction', *The Associate Press*, 26 March 2002, http://www.phs.bgsm.edu/sshp/rwj/GranteeResources/Newsreports/02march.htm (Accessed 3 October 2004).

126 Zimring *et al.*, op cit., p. 21.

127 Morgan, H.W., *Drugs in America: A Social History, 1800-1980*, 1981, New York: Syracuse University Press, pp. ix–x.

liberties.'[128] To some extent, the end has come to justify the means in the War on Drugs. The beginning of America's sacrifice of civil rights was marked by an executive order for urine-tests to be conducted on all civilian federal workers to ensure they were not drug users.[129] Some private companies followed the government direction, and requested their employees take the test. Although the urine test was eventually withdrawn from the drug control policy, it seemed that there was little opposition to such a test among Americans. As a consequence, drug testing of students has been operated consistently, and Supreme Court Justice A.M. Kennedy did not accept the challenge of a high school student against urine testing in 2002.[130]

In respect to legislation, the punishments for cocaine and crack offences are decided by the Federal Sentencing Guidelines and Omnibus Anti-Drug Abuse Act of 1988.[131] These laws impose mandatory minimum imprisonment[132] on the offenders and prohibit parole.[133] At trial, according to Sterling, the President of Criminal Justice Policy Foundation, it is unnecessary for the police, federal agents, and prosecutors to present hard evidence against a suspect for prosecution.[134] The testimony of 'co-operating individuals', the 'snitch', against the suspect will be enough to convict.[135] The only way for drug offenders to receive a reduced sentence is to assist the government as an informant.[136] Considering the desperation of the convict to minimise the sentence, the information provided to the government could be unreliable. Gray maintains that: '[the] War on Drugs has made [the United States] and its institutions so desperate that our judgement and our reason have been seriously clouded.'[137]

The war on drugs and the claim of moral regeneration brings the risk of tighter government control on individuals, the loss of civil liberties, and injustice under the uniform mandatory minimum sentencing. The information provided through such

---

128 Krausse, H., 'FBI Director Says Drugs, Terrorism To Force New Balance of Law, Liberty', *Austin American Statesman*, 11 February 1989, p. C37.

129 Woodiwiss, op cit., p. 212.

130 'Supreme Court Justice Lashes Student Challenging Drug Tests', *Boston Globe*, 20 March 2002, http://www.phs.bgsm.edu/sshp/rwj/GranteeResources/Newsreports/02march. htm (Accessed 3 October 2004).

131 Zobel, R.W., *An Overview of the United States Sentence Guidelines*, from the public lecture organised by ACPF, UNAFEI, and JCPS on 10 February 1999 at the Ministry of Justice, Japan, http://www.acpf.org/Activities/Activities(Homepage3)/public%20lecture1999/ SentenceGuidelines.html (Accessed 10 March 2005).

132 An offender with 5g of crack or 500g of powder cocaine will be sentenced to a 5 year mandatory minimum. The punishment will depend on the amount of the substance. This difference between powder cocaine and crack has been criticised as disproportionate. Zobel, op cit.

133 United States Sentencing Commission, *Report to the Congress: Cocaine and Federal Sentencing Policy*, 2002, Appendix A.

134 Sterling, E., comment in *Frontline: Snitch*, air date 12 January 1999, http://www.pbs. org/wgbh/pages/frontline/shows/snitch/etc/script.html (Accessed 8 March 2005).

135 Kinzley, D., comment in *Frontline: Snitch*.

136 *United States Sentencing Guidelines of 1998*, section 5K 1.1.

137 Gray, op cit., p. 101.

policies could lead to limited understanding of the cocaine trade and the nature of substances.

Diplomatic Impact

The expansion of the cocaine trade has been affecting the United States through increasing the number of addicts and weakening public order. The United States regards cocaine trafficking as an alien conspiracy to undermine its power because of the origin of cocaine and the ethnicity of those engaged in the trade.[138] The cocaine traffickers, known as 'Drug Lords', remain in their own countries to ship cocaine to the United States. The US government is unable to reach them to exert punishment. For the government it has been a serious concern to prevent foreign criminals establishing any connections and to ensure the protection of its citizens and communities through drug control. In order to prevent further development of the cocaine trade and to restore order, the government has been keen to stretch its drug control to countries associated with cocaine production.

In this section, the diplomatic and international relationships regarding cocaine trafficking will be examined. Cocaine trafficking has influenced the relationship between the United States and the Latin American states through the activities of the criminal organisations and US counter-measures. Firstly, the increase in immigrants from Latin America supported by cocaine trafficking will be examined. Secondly, money laundering and the linkage between criminal groups will be investigated. The United States regards money laundering as a means to expand criminal organisations and create regional instability through its influence and connection with insurgency groups. Thirdly, the US process of Narcotics Certification and the tension it has aroused with Latin American governments will be investigated. Fourthly, the implications of the trials of foreign criminals under the US judicial system will be examined. The United States and some Latin American states ratified the extradition treaties, but sending cocaine traffickers to the United States for trial is not always possible for Latin American governments. In some cases, the US determination to try the traffickers under its system became a cause of disharmony.

Cocaine Trafficking as a Foreigner's Business

The cocaine 'epidemic' and the introduction of prohibition laws coincide with the rise of particular social groups in the United States. During the period in which the Harrison Narcotics Act of 1914 was introduced, the whites in the south of the United States feared the growing social power of the blacks and tried to curb their social progress.[139] About four decades later, the cocaine trade was associated with the Mafia, and the government promoted the 'view of an alien Mafia conspiracy as

---

138 See also introduction.

139 Brecher, E.M., *Licit and Illicit Drugs*, 1972, Boston: Little, Brown, pp. 275–276; and Musto, op cit., p. 11.

the cause and explanation'.[140] Then, in the 1980s, the black and Hispanic immigrants in inner-city neighbourhoods were blamed for the 'cocaine epidemic' in the United States.[141]

Some argue that the prohibition of cocaine and other narcotic drugs such as opium stemmed not from their dangers or chemical effects but from political reasons, such as the alienisation of minority groups and concealment of other social problems. Considering the immigrant participation in the cocaine trade, a Mexican official maintains, it has been regarded as a problem brought by minority groups.[142] According to Musto, drug control alienates certain minority groups because: 'The energy that has given impetus to drug control and prohibition came from profound tensions among socio-economic groups, ethnic minorities, and generations – as well as the psychological attraction of certain drugs.'[143]

Cocaine distribution is indeed mainly operated by foreigners, such as Hispanic immigrants, Latin Americans operating from their homeland, and the Italian Mafia. In the 1960s, illegal businesses were owned by Mafia families, consisting mainly of those of Italian and Sicilian descent, although the cocaine market was still small.[144] Currently, the majority of cocaine trafficking is, as illustrated in chapter 1, controlled by Latin American drug trafficking organisations via networks in Latin America and branches in the United States. The long borders between the United States and Mexico are difficult to patrol and have made the United States vulnerable to the smuggling of illicit goods from the South.[145] In addition, Mexico's membership

---

140 Smith, Jr., D.C., 'Paragons, Pariahs, and Pirates: A Spectrum-Based Theory of Enterprise', *Crime and Delinquency*, Vol. 26, July, 1980, p. 374.

141 Reinarman *et al.*, 'Crack in Context: America's Latest Demon Drug', in Reinarman, C., and Levine, H.G. (eds), *Crack in America: Demon Drugs and Social Justice*, 1997, Berkeley: University of California Press, p. 2.

142 Interview with a Mexican government official in Mexico City on 14 June 2003.

143 Musto, op cit., pp. 244–245.

144 Cressey, D., 'Methodological Problems in the Study of Organized Crime as a Social Problem', 1967, *Annuals of the American Academy of Political and Social Science*, Vol. 374, pp. 103–104.

145 The Mexican routes were particularly important for the smugglers in the aftermath of the 11 September terrorist attacks. This is because all international ports of entry were under tight security measures at the time, and smugglers had to traffic their goods over land via Mexico to avoid seizures. Interviews with a Coast Guard official at the Office for National Drug Control Policy, Washington DC on 28 May 2003; US General Accounting Office, *US-Mexican Border: Issue and Challenge Confronting the US and Mexico*, GAO/NSIAD-99-190, July 1999, Washington DC: GAO; and US General Accounting Office, *Border Control: Drug Interdiction and Related Activities Along the Southwestern US Border*, GAO/GGD-88-124FS, September 1988, Washington DC: GAO; Gonzalez, S., *DEA Statement* before the US House of Representatives Committee on Government Reform Subcommittee on Criminal Justice, Drug policy, and Human Resources, 15 April 2003, http://www.usdoj.gov/dea/pubs/cngrtest/ct041503.html (Accessed 30 April 2003); and *Anthony, R.,* 'Farmgate-to-Street Model of Narcotics Trafficking', paper presented at Roundtable entitled *Business Practices of Narcotics Trafficking Enterprises*, at the Library of Congress on 29 January 2003, http://www.loc.gov/rr/frd/Drug_conference/pdf-files/Farmgate-to-Street-Model-of-Narcotics-Trafficking.pdf, p. 9 (Access 30 April 2003).

in the North America Free Trade Agreement (NAFTA) is another advantage for the Latin American cocaine traffickers.[146] Cocaine became widely available and affordable through systemic distribution developed alongside the rise of Colombian drug cartels in the 1970s. Their establishment of 'cells'[147] in the United States in the 1980s repaints the picture of the American cocaine scene.[148]

In the US cocaine market, the Colombians have established distribution networks through immigrant communities, and held the north-eastern part of the United States and the cities on the eastern coastline[149] under their control.[150] The cocaine distribution in other parts of the United States, however, is controlled by different trafficking organisations such as the Mexicans and the Dominicans in co-operation with the Colombians.[151] They controlled the high levels of the distribution system (broker and wholesaler) through their well-placed cells.[152] The operations at the two bottom levels (retail and street) are run by different ethnic groups, such as immigrants from the Dominican Republic, Puerto Rico, Mexico and Colombia as well as Americans (mainly blacks).[153] This is one of the reasons the US government has established links between inner cities, where these minorities live, and the cocaine trade.

---

146 In 2002, there were 9.6 million pedestrians and 15.3 million vehicles crossing the border every day despite tighter security measures after the terrorist attack on 11 September 2001. Koppel, T., 'Illegal Drugs, Mexico, and NAFTA: Rise in Illegal Drugs Entering U.S. From Mexico', *ABC*, 6 May 1997, http://more.abcnews.go.com/onair/nightline_new/transcripts/ntl0506.html (Accessed 4 November 1999); and Gonzalez, op cit.

147 Cells are the equivalent of local branches in the cocaine trafficking network. They are structured around kinship and friendship, and 'the recruitment of cell workers follows ethnic and cultural lines'. Each cell operates independently from others and focuses exclusively on increasing its productivity. For further details, see Lyman, M., 'Business Principles of Modern Narcotics Trafficking Operations', *paper presented at Roundtable* entitled *Business Practices of Narcotics Trafficking Enterprises*, at the Library of Congress on 29 January 2003, http://www.loc.gov/rr/frd/Drug_conference/pdf-files/Business-Principles-of-Modern-Narcotics-Trafficking-Operations.pdf, p. 4 (Access 30 April 2003).

148 Fuentes, op cit., p. 276.

149 For example, Boston, Miami, Newark, New York, and Philadelphia.

150 DEA, 'Cocaine: Trafficking by Colombian and Mexican Organizations', in *Drug Trafficking in the United States*, September 2001, http://www.dea.gov/pubs/intel/01020/index.html#cocaine (Accessed 30 April 2003).

151 Ibid.; and Lyman, M., *Business Principles of Modern Narcotics Trafficking Operations*, *paper presented at Roundtable* entitled '*Business Practices of Narcotics Trafficking Enterprises*', at the Library of Congress on 29 January 2003, http://www.loc.gov/rr/frd/Drug_conference/pdf-files/Business-Principles-of-Modern-Narcotics-Trafficking-Operations.pdf, pp. 12–14 (Accessed 30 April, 2003).

152 Fuentes, op cit., pp. 14–17.

153 It is known that distributors buy kilograms and sell ounces at the retail level and buy ounces and sell grams at street level. *Anthony, R., Farmgate-to-Street Model of Narcotics Trafficking*, paper presented at Roundtable entitled '*Business Practices of Narcotics Trafficking Enterprises*', at the Library of Congress on 29 January 2003, http://www.loc.gov/rr/frd/Drug_conference/pdf-files/Farmgate-to-Street-Model-of-Narcotics-Trafficking.pdf, p. 4 (Accessed 30 April 2003); Reuter, P., *Do Middle Markets for Drugs Constitute an Attractive Target for Enforcement?* Paper presented at Roundtable entitled '*Business Practices of Narcotics*

Following the rapid spread of cocaine in the cities in the 1980s, the International Narcotics Control Strategy Report (INCSR) reported the 'most intense and immediate problem is inner-city crack use'.[154] Regarding the government's emphasis on the cocaine problem, some believe that it is a political tactic to divert public attention from other social issues, such as poverty. To some extent, cocaine policy has been a political tool: 'a scapegoat substance to a troubling subordinate group – working-class immigrants, racial or ethnic minorities, rebellious youth.'[155] Reinarman and Levine criticise the government for ignoring the fundamental problems in society, as 'supporting the drug war became extremely useful politically ... because, among other reasons, it provided a convenient scapegoat for enduring and ever growing urban poverty.'[156] Also, Woodiwiss argues that the government blamed cocaine for being a cause of problems (such as violence and poverty) in the post-Vietnam War America. It was considered that: '[t]he use of drugs was an easy way to explain the rise in violent crime and theft in the cities and also the growing disaffection of many young, white Americans.'[157] Magruder, however, maintains the links between cocaine and social problems were exaggerated by the government.[158]

It is possible that the government focused on cocaine trafficking as a significant political issue in order to conceal serious and fundamental problems in society. At the same time, the United States has perceived its situation as facing large numbers of illegal immigrants coming from Latin America, and they have the potential to become involved in cocaine trafficking.

Money Laundering and Global Crime Connections

One of the US government's serious concerns related to cocaine profits is to prevent money laundering and the enrichment of criminal organisations. Also, the connection between the cocaine trafficking organisations and insurgency groups in Latin America could lead to instability in that region. As government officials that were interviewed claim, instability in Latin America could be a serious issue for the United States as a neighbouring state.[159]

Trafficking Enterprises', at the Library of Congress on 29 January 2003, http://www.loc.gov/rr/frd/Drug_conference/pdf-files/Do-Middle-Markets-for-Drugs-Constitute-an-Attractive-Target-for-Enforcement.pdf, p. 3 (Accessed 30 April 2003); and Williams, *The Cocaine Kids*, p. 51.

154 Office of National Drug Control Policy, *National Drug Control Strategy*, 1989, Washington, DC: Government Printing Office, p. 4; and National Commission on Marijuana and Drug Abuse, *Second Report: Drug Use in America: Problem in Perspective*, 1973, Washington, DC: Government Printing Office.

155 Reinarman *et al.*, 'Crack in Context', p. 1.

156 Reinarman *et al.*, 'The Crack Attack', p. 19.

157 Woodiwiss, op cit., p. 166.

158 Magruder, J.S., *One Man's Guide to Watergate*, 1974, London: Hodder & Stoughton, pp. 103–105.

159 Interviews with US government officials at the Department of States and the ONDCP in Washington DC on 27 and 28 May 2003 respectively.

Controlling money laundering for the United States is to control illicit cash flow into the financial systems as well as to control the activities of drug trafficking organisations and insurgency groups around the world. According to Marshall, the cocaine traffickers are using the US financial system to launder vast amounts of cocaine dollars, and are expanding their capability.[160] Money laundering brings large amounts of money into the US financial system, but initial deposits of money tend to be made in Latin America, particularly in Mexico. The Mexican banking system has been employed by the cocaine traffickers as a useful means to transfer illicit profits into legal economic mechanisms.

When considering the harm that money laundering causes to the US financial system[161] and the potential it has to enlarge criminal organisations, the United States applies anti-money laundering policies to 'improve' Latin American banking systems through the domestic laws regarding international trade and narcotics control.[162] This is because regulations on Latin American financial systems could advance US counter-narcotics measures as well as fight transnational organised crime.[163]

The significance of controlling money laundering also stems from the connection between the drug trafficking organisations and the insurgency groups. The United States believes that the laundered drug money is supporting the activities of insurgency groups and will have the potential to increase international terrorism, such as the expansion of the activities of *Fuerzas Armadas Revolucionarios de Colombia* (FARC) to other states supported by narco-dollars.[164] The increasing financial power of insurgency groups in Latin America could result in regional instability. Since the terrorist attacks of 11 September 2001, the United States put further emphasis on money laundering and connections between criminal groups because narco-guerrilla alliances can strengthen not only the production of cocaine but also the financial power of both drug trafficking organisations and insurgency groups.[165]

A Colombian government official claims that all insurgency groups in Colombia are supporting their activities with drug income.[166] The major insurgency groups were estimated to earn $500–600 million annually from drug trafficking, and

---

160 Marshall, D., DEA Congressional Testimony, *US Law Enforcement Response to Money Laundering Activities in Mexico*, before the Subcommittee on General Oversight and Investigation of the Committee on Banking and Financial Services, 5 September 1996, http://www.usdoj.gov/dea/pubs/cngrtest/ct960906.htm (Accessed 4 September 2004).

161 For example, it could undermine the credibility of the system by accepting illicit dollars.

162 For example, the United States applies guideline for narcotics certification and the International Emergency Economic Power Act, and also its influence in the International Monetary Fund.

163 Grosse, op cit., p. 201.

164 Interviews with US government officials at the Department of State in Washington DC on 27 May 2003.

165 Casteel, S.W., DEA Testimony, *Narco-Terrorism: International Drug Trafficking and Terrorism – a Dangerous Mix*, before the Senate Committee on the Judiciary, 20 May 2003, http://www.usdoj.gov/dea/pubs/cngrtest/ct052003p.html (Accessed 11 October 2004).

166 Interview with a Colombian government official at the Embassy of Colombia in Brussels, 10 July 2002.

have gained sufficient influence to negotiate with the Colombian government.[167] As a consequence, the FARC obtained control over about 40% of Colombian territory, and engages in cocaine trafficking via connections with Mexican and Central American drug trafficking organisations.[168] Worse, Ejército de Liberación Nacional de Colombia (ELN) also demands the same territory as the FARC. With the expanding financial power of the insurgency groups, the Colombian government is experiencing difficulties in settling peace talks with the insurgency groups and regaining control over the territories.[169]

In addition, the activities of insurgency groups and immigration at the border areas have been creating conflicts of interests between Colombia and neighbouring states, such as Venezuela. In the areas of guerrilla control, there are frequent disputes over territories and operations in cocaine trafficking among insurgency groups and cocaine trafficking organisations. Violence in these areas created large numbers of refugees and immigrants within Colombia as well as in neighbouring states.[170] In the areas where immigrants, drug traffickers and insurgency groups gather, there is a tendency for insecurity to increase, caused by the high crime rates and frequent use of violence. This has been a cause of discord between Colombia and its neighbouring states.

Annual Narcotics Certification

The US Narcotics Certification is a policy to reduce drug flow into the United States by supporting counter-narcotics operations in the major drug production areas. At the same time, the narcotics certification is a way to coerce Latin American states to commit to drug control by reducing and halting economic aid. The United States has been supporting states fighting against drug production and trafficking with generous funding. The states to be assisted are chosen through the certification process. The states that receive US aid, not only for counter-drug measures but also for trade benefits, are determined in the process of the Narcotics Certification Process by the president and released as the 'Majors List' from 2003.[171] The aim of the United

---

167 GAO, *Drug Control: Narcotics Threat from Colombia Continues to Grow*, Report for Congressional Requesters, June 1999, GAO/NSIAD-99-136, Washington DC: GPO, p. 9.

168 Casteel, *Narco-Terrorism*.

169 GAO, *Drug Control: Narcotics Threat from Colombia Continues to Grow*, p. 10.

170 Chomsky, N., *Rogue States: The Rule of Force in World Affairs*, 2000, Cambridge, MA: South End Press; and Hinton, H.L., *Drug Control: Counternarcotics Efforts in Colombia Face Continuing Challenges*, Testimony before the Committee on International Relations, House of Representatives, 26 February 1998, GAO/T-NSIAD-98-103, Washington DC: GPO.

171 This is a list of major illicit drug-producing countries and transit countries, and contains 23 countries, including Bolivia, Colombia and Mexico. White House Office of Press Secretary, Statement by the Press Secretary: Annual Presidential Determinations of Major Illicit Drug-Producing and Drug-Transit Countries, *White House Press Release*, 31 January 2003, http://www.state.gov/g/inl/rls/prsrl/17092.htm (Accessed 9 May 2003); and Simons, P., *Briefing on the President's FY 2003 Narcotics Certification Determinations*, 31 January 2003, http://www.state.gov/g/inl/rls/rm/17110.htm (Accessed 9 May 2003). The

States in the Narcotics Certification is to encourage Latin American states to crack down on cocaine cartels and to reduce the inflow of cocaine by downsizing their processing and transporting capabilities.

The states on the list have been evaluated according to their efforts against the cocaine industry, and are notified whether they are certified or decertified for the next fiscal year. Previously, the countries certified by the United States were evaluated by their efforts in drug control through co-operation with the US drug control policy. The procedure of Annual Narcotics Certification Determinations, however, has been modified from 2003 following legislation by the Foreign Relations Authorisation Act, 2002-2003.[172] This is because of criticisms against the method of evaluation.[173] The new procedures have decided that states' efforts in drug control will be measured by performance over the past 12 months. If their performance is judged by the United States to not be satisfactory, the source countries are disqualified from receiving US foreign aid.[174] For the United States, Narcotics Certification is a process to ensure the effective use of its resources to reduce cocaine through assessing operations and fund management by the recipients of its aid.

The Narcotics Certification is a cause of discord with the Andean states due to the evaluation process applied by the United States. Narcotics Certification is regarded as a means employed by the United States to impose its policy upon states using its economic power. Walker argues that Certification is forcing other states to comply with US-style drug control, whereas those governments might have more pressing matters in their countries.[175] For the Latin American countries, being decertified by the United States is equivalent to losing possible economic means of survival. For example, the Peruvian government was refused US military aid for drug control for two years. The government, however, had to revise its policy due to economic

---

Narcotics Certification existed from earlier. After a few years without the Certification due to international criticism, the government modified the procedure, which applied from FY 2003 Certification.

172 Bureau for International Narcotics and Law Enforcement Affairs, *Fact Sheet: FY 2003 Narcotics Certification Process*, 31 January 2003, http://www.state.gov/g/inl/rls/fs/17010.htm (Accessed 9 May 2003).

173 Interview with a US government official at the US Mission to the European Union in Brussels on 25 April 2002.

174 According to the Fact Sheet 2003, 'Countries found to have 'failed demonstrably' are ineligible for many types of U.S. foreign assistance: sales or financing under the Arms Export Control Act; provision of agricultural commodities, other than food, under the Agricultural Trade Development and Assistance Act of 1954; financing under the Export-Import Bank Act of 1945; and most assistance under the Foreign Assistance Act. This prohibition would not affect humanitarian, counternarcotics, and certain other types of assistance that are authorized notwithstanding any other provision of law.' INL, *Fact Sheet: FY 2003 Narcotics Certification Process*.

175 Walker III, W.O., 'US Narcotics Foreign Policy in the Twentieth Century: An Analytical Overview', in R.F. Perl (ed.), *Drugs and Foreign Policy*, 1994, San Francisco: Westview Press, p. 33.

difficulty caused by the withdrawal of economic assistance and trade benefits from the United States.[176]

Furthermore, the pursuit of certification also aroused criticisms against US double-standards: Latin American states are 'judged' by the United States, but it does not produce any review on the performance evaluation of its own drug control efforts.[177] According to Hakim considering the increasing sentiment against the way the United States employs Narcotics Certification, pushing compliance to US drug control policy could cause damage to future counter-narcotics co-operation with other states.[178]

Trials of Foreign Suspects in the US Justice System

Cocaine trafficking affects the law of the United States, and its government tries to punish cocaine traffickers operating outside US territories. For example, Pablo Escobar, who was known as a leader of the Medellín cartel in Colombia, exported cocaine to the United States. Since drug cartels are not physically operating on the US territory, the government needs to rely on Latin American governments for punishment. The Latin American counterparts, however, are not reliable in prosecuting cocaine traffickers because of widespread corruption and fear among officials.[179] As a result, the United States can ensure justice to the cocaine traffickers. In order to try criminals in other countries, the United States has arranged extradition treaties with Latin American countries.

Not all Latin American countries were willing to sign an extradition treaty due to domestic circumstances. For example, the Paz Zamora administration of Bolivia hesitated to renew the extradition treaty with the United States because it was not supporting US led drug control.[180] The Bolivians preferred to try the traffickers under Bolivian laws, despite some faults in their judicial system. Knowing Bolivia's economic dependence on US aid, the United States announced the halt of $44 million until extradition arrangements were agreed.[181]

The agreement of an extradition treaty with the United States is not easy for Latin American governments. Although trying traffickers in the United States is a solution to their malfunctioning judicial system, there are problems posed by the

---

176 Ibid., p. 31.

177 Interviews with Colombian and Mexican officials and CICAD official on 10 July 2002, 14 June 2003, and 29 May 2003 respectively.

178 Hakim, P., *US Drug Certification Process Is in Serious Need of Reform*, http://www.foreignpolicy-infocus.org.

179 Moore, M., 'Mexican Stunned by Killing of Police Chief', *The Washington Post*, 29 February 2000, http://www.washingtonpost.com/wp-srv/Wplate/2000-02/29/0791-022900-idx.html (Accessed 29 February 2000); Davison, P., 'Escobar's hand seen in Bogota bomb atrocity', *Independent*, 1 February 1993; and Ross, T., 'Colombian judges court death', *Independent*, 18 November 1998.

180 Isikoff, M., 'Bolivia Offers Non-Extradition Deal to Traffickers', *The Washington Post*, 19 July 1991.

181 Menzel, S.H., *Fire in the Andes: US Foreign Policy and Cocaine Politics in Bolivia and Peru*, 1996, New York: University Press of America, p. 94.

cocaine cartels.[182] These examples of corruption and threats in Latin American countries, and the creation of an image of an extradition treaty as an example of 'Yankee imperialism', appealed to the sentiment against the United States to prevent the traffickers being extradited.[183] Consequently, despite the existing extradition treaties, there is no guarantee in the extradition treaty that the United States will obtain its objective.

Since the US government is unsure of extraditing traffickers, it has employed more forceful measures. It has abducted wanted traffickers in a policy known as 'state-sponsored abduction'. According to Herrera, this was accomplished by federal law enforcement agencies, such as the DEA with support from the justice system, which disregarded the illegality of the process.[184] Many traffickers are forced to travel to the United States, and tried in the US court for punishment. Despite this being a clear violation of human rights and international law, the US court records indicate that these arrests are made outside its own territory but also within the legal process.

Such violation of human rights and other states' sovereignty is ignored because the United States believes that only it can provide justice. Such belief was supported by President G. Bush who made a statement regarding the trial of General Manuel Noriega of Panama, to 'give Noriega a fair trial in the United States', and bring justice to the criminals.[185] Moreover, human rights are violated further. The rule of 'innocent until proven guilty' does not apply to foreign cocaine suspects who are treated as criminals rather than suspects. General Noriega was 'indicted by grand juries in Miami and Tampa' during the BCCI scandal in 1988, although there was no proof of his laundering money through BCCI at that time.[186]

The forceful manner of the United States judicial process towards the Latin American states created resentment and distrust of US intentions. The US emphasis on controlling cocaine at source, as Pujalte points out, has been criticised as the United States are '[trying] to transfer the economic, social and political costs abroad'.[187] Also, Toro points to the activities of some US agencies that 'were less willing to accept national jurisdiction as a limit to their activities and tried to 'work

---

182 Interview with an official at the Mexican Foreign Ministry, 14 June 2003.

183 Lee, R.W., 'Policy Belief: Making the most of Colombia's Drug Negotiations', *Orbis*, Vol. 35, No. 2, Spring 1991; Tulis, L., *Unintended Consequences: illegal drugs & drug policies in nine countries*, 1995, Colorado: Lynne Rienner; and Menzel, S.H., *Cocaine Quagmire: implementing the US anti-drug policy in the north Andes – Colombia*, Maryland: University Press of America, 1997.

184 Herrera, H.A., 'Kidnapping Policy During the Drug War Era: Ethical and Legal Implications,' *Low Intensity Conflict & Law Enforcement*, Vol. 5, No. 3, Winter 1996, pp. 492–493.

185 Ibid., p. 497.

186 Getler, W., 'A Major Bank Accused by U.S. of Laundering Cocaine Profits', *International Herald Tribune*, 12 October 1988.

187 Pujalte, C., Remarks in Caucus on *International Narcotics Control of The United States*, The Congressional Research Service, 8 May 1987, Washington DC: Government Printing Office, p. 8.

on their own".[188] The lack of respect for the sovereignty of Latin American states indicates that the United States does not regard them as its equals.

There is a fear of regional instability posed by the increasing financial power of criminal organisations in Latin America. Also, the criminal organisations are using the US economic and financial system to increase their assets through transferring money from Latin American banks. In order to fight against foreign criminals in Latin America, the US government has been employing methods to enforce its own domestic laws to Latin American states. It is unusual to apply domestic laws to regulate other states' activities. The United States, however, does not appear to have much hesitation in doing so. The United States is concerned only for its own interests regardless of international law, other state's sovereignty, or human rights. US enthusiasm to eliminate cocaine trafficking to the United States has led it, since the 1980s, to pursue counter-narcotics programmes internationally with enormous sums of money. Despite US support to Latin American countries, these countries are uneasy with American-style operations, and they fear US interference in their domestic matters and the US's lack of respect for their sovereignty.

Conclusion

The United States considers cocaine trafficking as a national security threat. This is because it sees cocaine trafficking as a potential harm to the US national economy and moral values, as well as potential support to international terrorism and regional instability. In the United States, cocaine trafficking is experienced in a combination of direct and indirect harms. Although the supply and consumption of cocaine affect various aspects of national life, the impact of counter-narcotics measures cannot be disregarded. This is because the activities of criminal organisations and law enforcement agencies are, to some extent, inter-related, and the impact of these two different activities are part of the threat posed by cocaine trafficking. The criminal activities and law enforcement operations, however, affect the state in different ways. Tandy, the chief of the DEA, expresses the threat posed by cocaine trafficking as: 'Drug trafficking organizations attack the soul and fabric of America in pursuit of … money.'[189] On the other hand, Reinarman and Levine claim that US drug control policies have caused more damage through racism, poverty and misinformation.[190]

The impact of the cocaine trade in the United States is more closely linked to the consequences of law enforcement than the nature of trafficking organisations. Although the US government justifies the significance of strict legislation against cocaine and crack,[191] Brownstein maintains that the 'crack crisis' and 'crack epidemic' were inventions to justify 'the massive expansion of the criminal justice

---

188 Toro, M.C., *Mexico's 'War' on drugs*, 1995, London: Lynne Rienner, p. 32.

189 Tandy, K.P., *United States Efforts to Combat Money Laundering and Terrorist Financing*, Before the US Senate Caucus on International Narcotics Control, 4 March 2004.

190 Reinarman et al., 'The Crack Attack', pp. 14 and 46.

191 Musto, op cit., p. 11.

system and the loosening of restrictions on law enforcement that were central to the justice juggernaut'.[192]

The US government regards cocaine as a 'foreign' enemy to its economy and society due to its origin and the fact that those actively involved in the cocaine trade are likely to be Latin Americans and other ethnic minorities. The large sums of narco-dollars laundered into the US national economy support ethnic minorities and illegal immigrants, allowing them to survive and enrich themselves in the United States. At the same time, the social and economic costs from the increasing number of cocaine addicts are expanding. In the cocaine trade, the United States is losing both financial and human resources. In addition, there is a fear in the US government that narco-dollars can fuel regional instability in Latin America, particularly in Colombia. The terrorist groups in Latin America might be able to expand their activities from the domestic to the international level supported by narco-dollars. Such regional instability will cause damage to the United States both politically and economically.

Drug control in general, therefore, is regarded as a policy that alienates some minority groups. The image attached to each drug remains vivid to the Americans: it is believed to be a rampant substance in black and Hispanic communities although the majority of users are white. The cocaine trade is dominated by Hispanic populations because most cocaine is produced in Latin America and distributed through immigrant communities in the United States. The law enforcers, therefore, target particular communities for cocaine arrests, and in doing so, the disregard for human rights has created tension with local communities. As a result, some communities in inner cities are ruled by the cocaine traffickers – the emergence of 'states within a state'. Law enforcement targeting often depends on profiling such things as ethnicity and the assets of suspects.

The law enforcement agencies can earn their operational funding from seizures of assets and arrests of cocaine traffickers. This system of providing seized assets as rewards to the law enforcement agencies spawned injustice and corruption among the agents. Law enforcement officers steal confiscated assets and make illegal arrests and house searches, as well as receiving cash from the traffickers. At the higher levels, investigations are neglected. These cases could be concealed from the public, but when they are exposed, it leads to distrust of the authorities. As a result of the War on Drugs, 'the entire criminal justice system has been losing credibility'.[193]

Turning to the diplomatic impact, the United States fears regional instability fuelled by narco-dollars, as well as the massive flow of cocaine from Latin America. In order to reduce cocaine production, the United States is actively involved in extradition and bilateral efforts to control cocaine from source countries. The US approach to drug control, however, sometimes disregards the sovereignty of other states and international law. Narcotics Certification can develop negative responses from Latin American states because US foreign narcotics policies towards Latin America have been insensitive to sovereignty issues. This can trigger discord, and

---

192 Brownstein, op cit., p. 42.
193 Gray, op cit., p. 35.

make bilateral co-operation difficult, even though Latin American states heavily depend on the United States for economic support.

Overall, cocaine trafficking to the United State has been perceived as a threat, which directly and indirectly affected the economic and public order of its domain. The War on Drugs is supposed to protect America from danger, but ironically, it creates more danger to the society and eventually to the state. Fierce law enforcement practices have brought more violence than the cocaine trade originally did, and restricted the liberty of citizens in the name of protection and justice. Furthermore, aggressive and coercive drug control policy towards Latin America has been making co-operation with other states more difficult.

Chapter 4

EU Drug Control Policy Towards the Andes

Introduction

This chapter concerns itself with European Union drug control policy towards the Andes and its consequences. The chapter focuses on the political aims, objectives and interests of the EU in drug control policy as well as the consequences from, and the responses to, actual executions of drug control programmes. Since the 1980s, the illicit importation of cocaine from Latin America has been increasing dramatically and the EU has allocated relatively large sums of money for drug control efforts in the region. The EU strongly believes that economic, social and political reform to eliminate poverty is the key to curbing cocaine production. This approach reflects the nature of the cocaine problem that the EU member states are facing. As examined in chapter 2, the EU member states regard cocaine as principally a societal security threat, or a health and social problem rather than a national security threat.[1] Therefore, their understanding of cocaine control is to support the economic and social systems of Andean states in order to provide sufficient resources and educate people.

In order to examine EU anti-drug co-operation with Andean states, this chapter will be divided into four sections. First, it will investigate the background of EU involvement in cocaine control in the Andes through the development of co-operation between the EU and the Andean states for drug control purposes. The EU's connection to the Andes is not strong except in the case of a few EU member states that had colonial ties to Latin American states. However, the EU supports drug control in the Andes with relatively large amounts of funding. Second, the chapter will examine the EU approach to drug control. The EU perceives the solution to reduce cocaine trafficking from a particular angle, that is to say, a matter of economic and political development. Through the examination of the way the EU plans and delivers a drug control project in the Andes, this section will attempt to grasp EU beliefs on effective cocaine control. This section will be divided into two sub-sections: alternative development and other projects related to trade, political and social affairs. Alternative development (crop substitution) is the EU's main effort to control cocaine. It is a way to introduce a new economic mechanism in targeted areas. In the other section, EU projects to support drug control in the Andes from trade, political and law enforcement spheres will be investigated. The EU alternative

---

1   The EU declared transnational organised crime and drug trafficking as security threat in 2003. For further details, see *A Secure Europe in the Better World: European Security Strategy*, 12 December 2003.

development programme for drug control contains wide-ranging projects. Alongside alternative development (crop substitution) projects, the EU is supporting political development and trying to establish law enforcement co-operation with the Andean states via Europol, although these efforts are yet to be developed further. In short, the EU alternative development programme is aiming at introducing new commercial products (legal crops) and industries to coca growing areas as alternative economic means to coca cultivation, and supports the new economic system through projects concerning political and social development. Third, the details of the EU alternative development programme will be examined, following that in Bolivia. Bolivia has received several programmes emphasising drug control from the EU compared with other Andean states. Fourth, this chapter also elaborates the EU attempt to a bi-regional co-operation mechanism for drug control in Latin America. The EU puts emphasis on a regional approach to transnational issues, and this approach is also applied to the relationship with the Andes, and more widely with Latin America. This section will investigate the EU's efforts to establish a regional mechanism in Latin America in order to deal with transnational issues.

Background

Since the attack on 11 September in the US, the EU seems to have more direct and significant interest in supporting the fight against heroin in Asia, due to the size of the European heroin market and its geographical proximity to the producing states. This is because, according to an official of the European Council, cocaine is not as big a problem as heroin coming from Asia, which is geographically closer to Europe.[2] The European Council official maintains that the possible damage posed to Europe is greater from the activities of Al Qaeda, supported by heroin production, than from the FARC supported by cocaine production. The European Union, therefore, lacks the motivation to invest more effort in countering cocaine imported from the Andes.

Although some EU member states (such as Spain, Portugal and the United Kingdom) have colonial and historical ties to Latin America and the Caribbean, Latin America does not seem to have exercised much political and economic influence on post-war Europe. The Permanent Mechanism of Political Consultation and Co-ordination, known as the Rio Group, acting as collective body of political co-operation on behalf of Latin American and the Caribbean states negotiated with the EU for closer relationships and greater co-operation in economic and political spheres, beginning in 1990.[3] The agreement on co-operation between them reflects such a situation, and has therefore made an emphasis on historical and cultural ties between Europe and Latin America in order to cultivate their relationships.[4]

---

2   Interview with Mr Johannes Vos at the European Council in Brussels on 8 July 2002.

3   Sosa, A.J. and Dallanegra Pedraza, L., *El Groupe de Los Ocho y el Futuro de America Latina*, http://www.amersus.org.ar/PolInt/GrupoRio.htm (Accessed 4 January 2005).

4   *Rome Declaration on Relations Between the European Community and the Rio Group*, pp. 91–90, Brussels, 20 December 1990. The first meeting of the Rio Group with the EU

Despite its geographical distance and relatively weak connections to the region, the EU recognised the 'potential for a rich institutional relationship between Europe and Latin America'.[5] In pursuit of this aim, the EU became involved in Latin America and the Caribbean both economically and politically. Co-operation between the European Union and Latin American countries developed in the 1970s, and by the end of the 1980s Latin America received '45.5% of its direct foreign investment from Europe and 43% from the United States'.[6] Between 1990 and 1994, 925 million ECU was spent in co-operation with Latin America.[7]

The Andean countries did not enjoy economic and trade benefits with the European Union until the modification of the Andean Pact in 1993. This was in contrast to its counterpart Mercosur – South America's largest economic institution.[8] As the European Union effort to control cocaine increased in the 1990s, European support to the Andes rose substantially. This aroused criticism from other Latin American countries, who claimed that the European Union has been over-emphasising the problems related to cocaine in the Andean community, and neglecting other parts of Latin America.[9] In the late 1990s, however, the Andean community's biggest trading partner was still the United States, and the trade volume of the EU was merely one-third that of the US.[10]

Dorn argues that: 'Unlike the US, the EU has few strategic security concerns in South America generally or in the Andes especially.'[11] European attitudes toward the cocaine problem, and the drug problem in general, are not national security issues but social and health issues.[12] If European criminal organisations expand their networks and volume of cocaine imports further, this situation could change. The problems caused by cocaine trafficking could be then perceived as security concerns for the EU, such as street violence, crimes, the spread of contagious sexual diseases, addiction, illegal migration, and the economic costs of law enforcement.

Due to the rapid growth of the European cocaine market, the EU began to become involved in cocaine control. The EU approach to cocaine control is to foster

---

consisted of Argentina, Brazil, Bolivia, Chile, Colombia, Ecuador, Mexico, Paraguay, Peru, Uruguay and Venezuela, and also included some Caribbean states at a later stage.

5   Patten, C., *A Common Foreign Policy for Europe: relations with Latin America*, 9 November 2000, SPEECH/00/427, http://europa.eu.int/comm/external_relations/news/patten/speech_00_427.htm (Accessed 28 October 2001).

6   *The EU and Latin America: The Present Situation and Prospects for Close Partnership 1996-2000*, http://europa.eu.int/comm/dg1b/pol_proentations/den_com95945.htm (Accessed 28 October 2001), pp. 10–14.

7   Ibid.

8   *Outcome of Proceedings of Working Party on Latin America*, 10196/94, ill/JF/mn, Brussels, 19 October 1994.

9   Interview with an official at the Mexican embassy in Brussels, 23 January 2002.

10   *Andean Community: Indicative Multiannual Guidelines*, 12 March 1998, Brussels, IB/1038/98, p. 2.

11   Dorn, N., 'Borderline Criminology: External Drug Policies of the EU', in Dorn, N., Jepsen, J., and Savon, E. (eds), *European Drug Policies and Enforcement*, 1996, a, London: MacMillan, p. 259.

12   See chapter 2 for the details.

development and trade policies towards the Andes. In other words, EU policies toward the Andes are shaped by developmental considerations rather than military-oriented law enforcement programmes.[13] This is partly because the EU is an international organisation and lacks a significant military capability. Its lack of capability has made the EU difficult to achieve a consensus amongst the member states about militarised drug control. Through support for development, the EU tackles cocaine trafficking in the Andes by promoting crop substitution, infrastructure improvement, and strengthening local government and communities. The EU support is entitled 'alternative development programmes' because the main project is to promote economic activity in the recipient state by introducing legal crops that can substitute coca and cocaine production.

Focusing on cocaine control through economic development comes from the EU's understanding of economic difficulties and their relation to criminal activities. According to EU officials, poverty is the cause of increasing coca and cocaine production, as well as the misuse of the drugs.[14] They believe that those who abuse or produce drugs are often pushed into it by their social environment, poverty, marginalisation and unemployment. According to this interpretation, without the elimination of poverty, there will not be success in drug control.[15] An official of the European Commission maintains that one of the EU's priorities in alternative development, therefore, is to reinforce the legal economic activities of the poorest sectors in the Andean countries in order to prevent them from engaging in illicit drug trafficking or cultivation.[16]

The EU views violence in Latin American countries as a by-product of poverty. Active guerrilla groups and paramilitaries are strengthened by narco-dollars. Hence, the large amounts of money in drugs and money-laundering have attracted, to a certain extent, terrorist movements and paramilitary organisations seeking funds with which to purchase arms. Their targets are generally areas where the social fabric has already been torn apart by poverty and political instability. As a result, violent conflict is a constant threat all along the main drug routes to Europe: the cocaine road from Latin America.[17] The EU concludes that: 'The problem of consumption and production would only be resolved ... if economic and social marginalisation were reduced, especially in drug-producing countries.'[18] The EU sees its fight against drugs as a fight against poverty in the drug producing countries.

---

13 For details of EU drug control projects, see below. The approach to drug control by law enforcement will be examined in the following chapter.

14 Interviews with officials at the European Commission and the European Council in Brussels on 22–23 April 2002 and 8–10 July 2002.

15 Interview with an official at the European Commission in Brussels, 8 July 2002.

16 *The EU's priorities for future drugs cooperation in Latin America*, 6838/98 DG H II, Brussels, 12 March 1998, Paragraph 4.

17 *Communication from the Commission on Conflict Prevention*, COM (2001) 211 final, 11 April 2001, Brussels, p. 16.

18 EMCDDA, *Euro-Ibero American Seminar: Cooperation on Drugs and Drug addiction Policies (Conference Proceedings)*, 1999, Luxembourg: Office for Official Publication of the European Communities, pp. 13–14.

Due to its awareness of the complex nature of drug problems in the Andes, the European Union has decided to carry out drug control in the Andes with a holistic and cross-pillar approach. This consequently provided authority to a working group under the Committee of Permanent Representatives (COREPER), known as the Horizontal Drugs Group (HDG). This was created by COREPER in February 1997 to cover the cross-pillar drug policies. As a consultation group for drug related issues, it covers wide-ranging policies and came to be involved in various roles.[19] This is because drug trafficking is on the agenda for all three pillars of the European Union introduced by the Maastricht Treaty. The first pillar concerns economic and health issues, the second pillar is on the Common Foreign and Security Policy, and the third pillar is on Justice and Home Affairs. In drug control, the first pillar brings out the issues related to development co-operation and the health measures within the Community. The second pillar concerns dialogues with third countries and the relationship with the United Nations, but it does not have concrete projects on security and drugs. According to Boekhout van Solinge, the role of the second pillar in drug related issues are political and diplomatic rather than pragmatic.[20] In the third pillar, the fight against drug trafficking and transnational organised crime is dealt with through law enforcement.

The original role for the working group is as a consultation body for COREPER before it brings proposals to the European Council. However, the HDG expanded its role in the co-ordination of projects and policies in the three pillars. The HDG go through all drug related documents before they are submitted to COREPER and then the Council, and adjust and co-ordinate proposals from different pillars for a project package in order to use EU resources effectively. Due to the decision-making mechanisms in the Council, the consensus on a proposal is reached at an early stage, at the HDG and COREPER.[21] The Council, therefore, tend to approve the proposal coming up from COREPER fairly swiftly.[22] With the expertise on drug related issues, the HDG has also come to be involved in policy-making, such as the Drugs Strategy Plan under the British Presidency. In co-operation and co-ordination on drug control

19 COM (1999) 239 final, Brussels, 1999, Luxembourg: Printing Office for the European Communities.

20 Boekhout van Solinge, T., *Drugs and Decision-Making in the European Union*, 2002, Amsterdam: CEDRO/Mets en Schilt, p. 33; see also, Bewley-Taylor, B.D., Fazey, C.S.J. with Boekhout van Solinge, T., 'The Mechanism and Dynamics of the UN System for International Drug Control', *Forward Thinking on Drugs: A Release Initiative*, 14 March 2003, http://www.forward-thinking-on-drugs.org/review1-print.html (Accessed on 9 January 2005).

21 For decision-making, the Council requires unanimous voting. Due to the complex mechanism of EU decision-making, the process tends to be time consuming, and in order to accelerate the process, they try to reach consensus before the final decision by the Council. For the details on EU decision-making, see Boekhout van Solinge, *Drugs and Decision-Making in the European Union*.

22 There are some occasions when the Council rejects the proposals, but it tends to be the period the EU is drafting in its policy priorities. The Council respects the expertise of the HDG, and usually adopts its proposals. Interview with Mr Johannes Vos at the European Council in Brussels on 8 July 2002.

with Latin America and the Caribbean in 1998, the HDG decided the EU priorities in drug control to cover all the issue areas with which the EU is concerned.[23]

The EU recognition of the cocaine threat, as examined in chapter 2, is moderate. As cocaine is categorised as a societal security threat, it is more concerned on health and social problems related to cocaine abuse and trade. This is reflected in the HDG dealing more with the first and third pillar issues: the second pillar does not have a budget for implementing projects.[24] In addition, some EU member states regard cocaine trafficking as a problem for other member states, and are sceptical of how far drug control efforts in Latin America would reduce the cocaine supply from the Andes when there is a continuous increase of cocaine seizures in Europe.[25] The cocaine related problems, therefore, do not convince the EU member states of the need to extend the drug control operation through external drug control policy toward the Andes. There seems to be the notion among the EU member states that cocaine control can remain internal and it is not necessary to conduct it in the Andes. Particularly after the terrorist attacks of 11 September 2001, the Council began to emphasise the importance of drug control in Asia out of Community security concerns regarding active insurgency groups funded by drug trafficking and the possibility of Asian drugs coming through the Balkans.[26]

The EU concerns about Asian drugs seem to be reflected in the steady increase in the co-operation with Asian countries.[27] Budget line B7-6310 (North-South Cooperation in the fight against drugs) is addressed to financing projects to fight drugs in developing countries. During 2001, €2 million were invested in drug control efforts in Latin America and the Caribbean out of the North-South Cooperation budget.[28] The following year, despite the fact that the Budget line covers projects undertaken in all developing countries, the funding allocated to it declined dramatically from €10 million in the mid-1990s to €1.9 million.[29] The reduction of the budget in B7-6310 did not halt the projects in the Andes as the money was brought from other budget lines. However, such a rearrangement has affected other projects by reducing the money for non-drug related projects.[30] The reduction from

---

23 Boekhout van Solinge, op cit., pp. 52–53.

24 Ibid., p. 34.

25 Interviews with officials at the European Commission and the European Council in Brussels on 22–23 April 2002 and 8–10 July 2002. For cocaine supply in Europe, see Chapter 2 of this book.

26 Interview with Mr Johannes Vos at the European Council in Brussels on 8 July 2002.

27 The European Council, *Economic and Financial Affairs Budget*, 26 November 2004, Press: 322, No. 14617/04; The European Council, *Economic and Financial Affairs Budget*, 24 November 2003, Press: 331, No. 14939/03; The European Council, *Economic and Financial Affairs Budget*, 11 December 2002, Press: 390, No. 15373/02; and The European Council, *Economic and Financial Affairs Budget*, 26 November 2001, Press: 424, No. 14157/01.

28 An unpublished EU document on the budget obtained during an interview at the European Commission in Brussels on 23 April 2002.

29 The data is from 7 January 2002. In 2001, the budget was €5.5 million.

30 For instance, despite the decline of the budget for the fight against drugs, from which projects in the Andes were supported, there was not much increase in the finance for co-operation with Latin America in the line of B7-31 for economic co-operation. According to

the Budget line B7-6310, therefore, may affect ongoing projects in the Andes. This means alternative development programmes and other development programmes in the Andean region have been financed at the expense of reducing funding to non-drug related programmes.

Despite these internal criticisms, the EU recognises the significance of co-operation in 'the fight against international organised crime, in particular drug trafficking and fraud at [international] level'.[31] The EU argues that its drug control policies in Latin America and the Caribbean are based on the concept of 'shared responsibility' under the international drug prohibition. The EU official point of view to anti-drug operations is that: 'The Union's self-interest and duty are indivisible when it comes to fighting drug production and trafficking, as dictated by the principle of co-responsibility between producer and consumer countries.'[32]

The concept of shared responsibility (or co-responsibility) has formed the basis of the Declaration of Cochabamba in 1996 and 1998 at the Rio Group meeting, an initiative taken by Latin American states, and has been internationally recognised at the UN General Assembly in June 1998.[33] According to a Colombian official source, Latin American countries intended to emphasise the implicit role that Western society, the consumers of cocaine, takes in cocaine trafficking by introducing shared responsibility.[34] It was also an attempt by the Latin Americans to engage the European Union in cocaine control, and to increase developed countries' awareness of their obligations to be more active in cocaine control. This is because Latin American states are aware that West European states are more concerned with heroin, and reluctant to become involved in drug control in Latin America.[35]

To some extent, the EU regards cocaine trafficking not as a regional but as a global problem for which it shares part of the burden through its creation of a cocaine market in Europe.[36] The EU is trying to establish itself as a role model for political actors with respect for international order and community spirit. As Manners argues, the EU can be an example of the compatibility between regionalism and multilateralism, and to promote inter-state co-operation through wider interests for the international community.[37] The idea behind supporting cocaine control in the

---

an EU official, those used for supplements are Budget line B7-310 (Financial and Technical Cooperation with Latin America) and B7-311 (Economic Cooperation with Latin America). Unpublicised budget details obtained in an interview with an official at the European Commission on 23 April 2002; See also footnote 27 on the budget.

31 *The EU and Latin America*, p. 5.

32 Patten, C., *3rd Meeting of the Support Group of the Peace Process: Colombia: A European contribution to peace*, http://europa.eu.int/comm/externall_relations/colombia/3msg/template_copy(1).htm.

33 EMCDDA, *Euro-Ibero American Seminar*, p. 13.

34 Interview with an official at the Colombian embassy in Brussels on 10 July 2002.

35 Ibid.

36 COM (97) 670 final, Luxembourg: Office for Official Publication of the European Communities, p. 12.

37 Manners, I., 'Normative Power Europe: a contradiction in terms?', *Journal of Common Market Studies*, Vol. 40, No. 2, 2002, p. 253; The European Commission, *The EU international policy on drugs*, July 2003, http://europa.eu.int/cgi-bin/etal.pl (Accessed 9 January 2005).

Andes, according to an EU official, is the sense of participation and responsibility as a member of international society and compliance with international laws.[38] It is important for the European Union to be involved in Latin American cocaine control not for the primary reason that cocaine is a serious and urgent issue in Europe but because the international community, led by the United Nations, is supporting cocaine control.[39] At the same time, the EU expects the host states to obey the UN ruling and international norms.[40] This emphasis on UN conventions and international laws is to show the importance of being law abiding and co-ordinating with the international community, in order to lead the host states to respect them. This is what Manners calls normative power supported by the ability to shape conceptions of what is 'normal' in a society.[41]

Latin American officials claim that if European efforts to curb cocaine production in the Andes are in accordance with the notion of shared responsibility, then there might be other ways to comply.[42] Precursor chemicals are used to extract cocaine from coca paste. Such precursors are essential ingredients for cocaine production. Therefore, export controls on precursor chemicals from Europe have been requested by not only the Andean countries but also other Latin American countries.[43] These chemicals are produced mainly in Europe, particularly in Germany and the Netherlands, and smuggled into the Andes.[44] The Latin American countries criticise the lack of control of precursor chemicals. 'People never talked about the actual producers of the chemical precursors for the drug trade.'[45] Without precursor chemicals from Europe, Latin American drug trafficking organisations cannot produce cocaine from coca leaves or paste. Hence, stricter control of chemicals on the European continent could reduce cocaine production in Latin America.

According to a Mexican official, they suspect that the reluctance of the EU to regulate illicit chemical flows reflects their unwillingness to risk their economic performance and offend the large and influential European chemical industry.[46] Regarding this EU reluctance, Latin American states have felt that monitoring the flow of chemicals is a feasible way to contribute to drug control within the territories of the EU member states. It does not deny that there is substantial effort made in

---

38 Interview with an official at the European Commission in Brussels on 10 July 2002.

39 Smith, K., *European Union Foreign Policy in a Changing World*, 2003, Oxford: Polity Press, p. 203.

40 Interview at the European Commission on 10 July 2002.

41 Manners, 'Normative Power Europe', p. 240.

42 Interviews with Mexican and Colombian officials in Brussels on 23 January and 10 July 2002 respectively.

43 *Record of the third meeting on precursors and chemicals frequently used for the illicit manufacture of narcotic drugs or psychotropic substances*, 28 March 2000, http://europa. eu.int/comm/external_relations/andean/doc/lima.htm; EUR-Lex Document 295A1230 (10); and *OJL* 324 30.12.1995, p. 1.

44 *Text: Rep. Gilman Urges European Cooperation in Drug Control Efforts*, 21 February 2001, http://usinfo.state.gov/topical/global/drugs/01022310.htm (Accessed 8 May 2002).

45 EMCDDA, *Euro-Ibero American Seminar*, p. 51.

46 Interview with a Mexican official at the embassy in Brussels, 23 January 2002.

the Andes in the form of alternative development programmes.[47] However, Latin American states believe that if the EU is taking shared responsibility seriously, it could have made more effort to control precursor chemical flow from Europe to Latin America. Latin American governments, therefore, feel that the EU still considers cocaine as the other region's problem and not really theirs.[48]

According to the theories examined in chapter 1, the EU's interest in cocaine control is not clear in the Realist sense. In relation to EU drug control policy in the Andes, the EU motivation might be too weak to be justified by Realist explanations of self-interest because Europe is geographically remote from Latin America. Also, the most important drug in Europe is not cocaine, but heroin from Asia. Hence, there seems to be insufficient reason for the EU to spend hundreds of millions of ECU in the Andes.

However, the EU may see drug prohibition as its contribution to the international community. In this sense, the EU's perception of its participation in cocaine control may be explained by a Liberal theory of compliance with international norms. According to a Liberal explanation, the EU is urging and supporting the Andean countries to comply with the international order as a member of the United Nations. It is possible to apply a liberal explanation to the EU. The aim of the EU is to develop the capabilities of the Andean states in order for them to be competent to comply with drug prohibition. The EU sees the problem of the Andean states as a lack of capability to control their territory due to weak political and economic systems.

As for social constructivists, the EU policy is based on its belief and image.[49] The EU operations in the Andes come from its notion of its duty as a member of international society. It may mean that there have not been vital interests for the EU in Latin American cocaine control. The EU, in fact, is executing its drug policy in Latin America in order to restore regional stability, which contributes to international stability. Wendt claims this is an important feature in 'Kantian international relations' – taking a holistic view of self-interest and considering others' interests as one's own.

The European Approach to Drug Control

The aims of the EU in supporting the fight against drugs in the Andes are: to reduce cocaine exports from the Andes; and to prevent destabilisation of Latin American counties, which may be caused by guerrilla groups and paramilitaries, financed by narco-dollars.[50] The latter does not have an urgent or direct impact on EU interests, but the EU is concerned about the influence Latin American instability could have on other parts of the world. The EU's commitment to control the cocaine trade is

---

47 See below.

48 Interview with officials at Mexican embassy and Colombian embassy in Brussels on 23 January 2002 and 10 July 2002 respectively.

49 Wendt, A., *A Social Theory of International Politics*, 1999, Cambridge: Cambridge University Press.

50 Interview with an official of the European Commission in Brussels, 9 July 2002.

not simply for the regional interests of Europe but for the wider interests of the international community.

The EU understanding of the nature of the drug problems in the Andes has made the fight against poverty synonymous with the control of cocaine. This understanding may have reflected the cocaine problems in Western European states as analysed in chapter 2. The Western European states have experienced economic and social problems, but not violence and epidemic corruption. Considering how the illegal cocaine trade affects consumers and the national economy, the EU seeks a solution in economic and social improvement in the Andes. The tools for the fight are development projects rather than militarised law enforcement.

The EU approach to control cocaine production through the elimination of poverty in the Andean states sounds like a promising plan, combining state's economic growth, political reform and drug control, which could solve the problem at its deepest level. However, Billings and Blee argue that the elimination of poverty cannot succeed by market economic policies and the preservation of cultural strategies to a few areas unless such efforts are 'supported and strengthened by linkages to similar efforts throughout the nation'.[51] To raise the economic performance of a particular community proved to be difficult in their study of a US town. The mining town remained in poverty despite several attempts at regeneration throughout the 20th century.[52] Despite twenty-year efforts to improve national economic and living conditions, Bolivia remains in poverty – 70% of its population are in extreme poverty.[53] This suggests that the war on poverty cannot be successful just by introducing some projects to promote the production of marketable crops in one region. In the light of these findings, alternative development programmes might require wider international support to drug control projects along with a much greater transference of resources to developing countries.

In order to tackle cocaine control through the elimination of poverty, a declaration to 'undertake to cooperate in the struggle against the illicit production, illegal traffic, sale, distribution and consumption of narcotics, including the traffic of precursors and the laundering of money, in line with the provisions of the 1988 Vienna Convention' was adopted by the EU and the Rio Group at the high-level meeting in 1990.[54] There are several detailed possible co-operation areas listed in the declaration. For example: alternative development, appropriate legislation, co-operation between law enforcement agencies, prevention and education, and rehabilitation programmes. Their intentions, at the second meeting, even went further to promote the distribution of information though the media 'with full respect for freedom of the press and of information' in each region.[55]

---

51 Billings, D.B., and Blee, K.M., *The Road to Poverty: The Making of Wealth and Hardship in Apparachia*, 2000, Cambridge: Cambridge University Press, p. 356.

52 Billings *et al.*, op cit., p. 356.

53 The European Commission, *Rural Development Policy and Strategic Framework: Bolivia Pilot Study*, October 2000, http://europa.eu.int/comm/development/rurpol/outputs/bolivia/bolivia.pdf (Accessed 12 January 2002).

54 *Rome Declaration*.

55 *Conclusions of the Second Institutionalized Ministerial Meeting Between the European Community and the Rio Group, Held in Santiago de Chile on 28 and 29 May 1992*, 7111/92

According to the officials of the European Commission, the EU approaches co-operation with Latin American states as an assistant in a project rather than as the executor.[56] This is because the EU considersthat the initiatives belong to the host state (or the 'owner' of the project) and this influences the progress and outcome of the project. The EU claims that it does not 'negotiate' with the Latin American countries to sponsor a project, but they 'discuss' the priorities and requests from the Latin American governments. It means that the EU approach is more recipient-orientated rather than sponsor-led. What the EU emphasises is the 'ownership' of the projects, that is to say, whichever project is supported by the EU will receive the full commitment of the host states. This is because the EU considers that the initiative of the host state is the key to the success of the project.[57] Also, the EU regards co-operation in drug control projects as an educational opportunity for Latin American states to learn project planning and management skills from the EU.[58]

Through the meetings, the EU provides a place for discussions for the Latin American countries.[59] The issues brought to the meeting are not necessarily drug related matters because, for the EU-Latin America relationship, drug control is an issue area within a larger context of co-operation. It means that the EU is supporting Latin America not only in the fight against drug trafficking but also to support their needs in general.[60] The regular dialogues at difference levels give opportunities for the Andean and other Latin American countries to reveal their concerns in different spheres, and deepen mutual understanding about their national circumstances. Dorn approves of such an EU approach in terms of its communication and flexibility of decision making: 'The lessening of the rhetorical pressure on the Latin American countries opens up for the [EU] the opportunity to deepen its understanding of development needs and drug problems.'[61]

The perception of the process, however, is different in the eye of Latin American officials. A Colombian official source maintains that there is 'negotiation' to gain EU approval of their proposals.[62] According to the source, the process goes as follows. The EU offers certain amounts of money that are planned to be spent on a recipient, then the list of proposals from potential recipients will be examined. The decision on projects is expected to be made jointly as it is stated in the EU country strategy paper,[63]

(Press 108), Santiago, 29 May 1992, pp. 10–11.

56 EU approval for projects is given in accordance with the principles of the '3Cs' – known as 'the Maastricht Treaty principles of co-ordination, complementary and coherence'. Interviews with officials conducted between April and July 2002 at the European Commission in Brussels; and *Evaluation of EU development aid to ALA states: Phase III – Synthesis Report (Final Report)*, 15 March 1999, European Commission Joint Relex Service For the Management of Community and to Non-Member Countries.

57 Interview with an official of the European Commission in Brussels, 9 July 2002.

58 Interview with an official of the European Commission in Brussels, 24 April 2002.

59 Ibid.

60 Ibid.

61 Dorn, 'Borderline Criminology: External Drug Policies of the EU', p. 262.

62 Interview with an official at Colombian embassy in Brussels, 10 July 2002.

63 *Country Strategy Paper: Colombia 2001-2006*, http://europa.eu.int/comm/external_relations/colombia/csp/02_06en.pdf (Accessed 26 June 2003).

however, in reality there are cases where the EU simply sends out its decision. There seems to be feeling among Latin American officials that the EU does not regard them as its equals and that some of their concerns are not taken seriously.[64]

In addition, not all projects are funded by the EU but many are sponsored by aid from the member states. This means that a project proposed by Latin American countries will not be carried out unless one of the member states volunteers to sponsor it, despite the approval from the EU.[65] The sponsors of projects for drug control in Latin America and the Caribbean seem to be limited to several states, such as Spain, Germany, and the United Kingdom as far as the funding of the projects decided in 2000.[66] An official of the European Council confirms that there is a relative lack of interest from member states when it comes to drug related issues.[67] This means that the opportunity for Latin American countries to realise their wishes can be very limited unless their proposal captures major European supporters of drug control policies.

Once a proposal is accepted, conditions required for the implementation of the project will be set out. However, in the case of the EU, the conditions will be the nature of community participation and sustainability of the project, for example, maintenance of the social infrastructure introduced by the project. These conditions are aimed at the sustainability of the projects and the maintenance of the facilities established, and they are therefore flexible.[68]

There is dissatisfaction among Latin American officials regarding the process and the way in which the EU handles the situation. Opportunities for discussions and dialogue are appreciated because both sides could use the opportunity to reveal their concerns before the actual project is decided and put into operation. This may contribute to more effective and smoother alternative development programmes in the Andes due to the EU's awareness of the situation in the recipient states.

Alternative Development Alternative development, according to Friedmann, is a process that seeks the empowerment of households though their involvement in socially and politically relevant actions as well as through improving their living conditions. Alternative development policies need to be adjusted to 'the prevailing historical and cultural circumstances.' What is essential in each case is to construct and strengthen the political community to support people's lives and to ensure the success of each project.[69] Moreover, developing a rural infrastructure needs to be a major emphasis in alternative development policies, alongside the creation of non-agricultural jobs.[70]

---

64 Interview with a Latin American official in Brussels, 23 January 2002.

65 Ibid.

66 *Consejo de la Unión Europea: Proyectos propuestos por los Estados miembros y la Comisión*, 6008/01, Bruselas, 8 de febrero de 2000.

67 Mr Johannes Vos of the European Council, 8 July 2002.

68 Interview with an official of the European Commission, 9 July 2002.

69 Friedmann, J., *Empowerment: The Politics of Alternative Development*, 1992, Oxford: Blackwell, pp. 33–41.

70 Ibid., p. 106.

The effect of alternative development is multidimensional. Alternative development in food security can provide not only sustainability to households, but also the improvement of agricultural production systems in the target areas. The success of this type of alternative development project, however, is not easy to achieve. This is because in order to carry out successful empowerment in food security, the alternative development projects may need to satisfy conditions such as: sufficiency, reliability, autonomy (or self-determination), long-term stability, and equity.[71] The problem for the recipient of aid is that all the requirements are difficult to fulfil for an economically weak state without foreign support.

Although it may be a demanding programme to sustain, once the alternative development programme has achieved its goals, it can empower the national government in three ways: '(a) by disengaging the state from problems that are better dealt with at local and regional levels; (b) by creating institutions that can be responsive to the diversity of locally and regionally articulated needs; and (c) by stabilizing the political system.'[72] In short, alternative development may support positive economic growth and strengthen a state following the empowerment of local government.

The execution of alternative development, however, needs careful planning. Concerning political perspectives, for example, what it requires for effective operation of a project is: collaboration between the host nation and the donor, the host nation's strong will to proceed with empowerment, and stability in the state at regional and national political arenas.[73] From economic perspectives, the allocation and scale of funding may affect the outcome of an alternative development project. Investment in some sectors, such as export industries, may 'contribute to economic growth' whereas investments in highly protected industries may cause 'a net loss of foreign exchange for the host country'.[74] The failure of alternative development may mean the collapse of one economic sector and the regional economy. This would affect individuals as well as the national economy. A weakened economy can make a state vulnerable to the increase of activity by guerrilla groups.

Other factors that influence the success of alternative development are the possibility of self-expanding processes of economic growth and the possibilities of self-sustained growth in the programme. The possibilities as such are limited in primary production activities, for instance, agriculture. Barkin argues: 'To ensure the success of such a process, it is often essential for the government to provide special subsidies and infrastructure investments. This help is often not enough, however, and additional measures for protecting the initial high-cost production may have to be combined with more coercive policies...'[75] Economic protectionism, which is

---

71 Ibid., pp. 127–178.

72 Ibid., p. 134.

73 Ibid., p. 7.

74 Balassa, B., 'The Process of Industrial Development and Alternative Development Strategies', *Essays in International Finance*, No. 141, December 1980, Princeton: Princeton University Press, p. 3.

75 Barkin, D., 'Rural Development Effects', in Downing, T.E., Hecht, S.B., Pearson, H.A., and Garcia-Downing, C., *Development or Destruction: The Conversion of Tropical Forest to Pasture in Latin America*, 1992, Colorado: Westview Press, p. 239.

against the current international trend in trade policy, should be allowed to promote the development of certain economic sectors until they reach sufficient levels of competitiveness.

Although alternative development can strengthen a state both politically and economically, the elimination of poverty (or development of a state) takes a long time. Rostow illustrated the process of state development through five stages, which could mislead one to assume that development will follow a mechanistic path once it is started.[76] As a critique to Rostow, Faaland and Parkinson claim that 'a century or more must pass' before the development process brings 'the standard of life in backward countries' to that of developed countries, although there are countries that managed to achieve rapid economic growth in the post-war period.[77] The EU acknowledges that the nature of drug control required in the Andes and Latin America requires a long-term commitment. This is essential for sustainable economic, political and social development in the region.[78] The important point here is whether the EU is prepared to maintain its policies with consistency throughout the development process of the recipients. Keeping member states' attention on cocaine control might be difficult if there is no obvious reason for them to continuously support the policies.

There may be two possible dangers in alternative development. First, the project may not really reflect the needs of the host state. There were criticisms of foreign aid in the past that the projects proposed and financed by the donor are based on the donor's views about what is required without much regard to the situation in the host state. The result was failure.[79] This is because the interest of the donor is 'to influence the economic policies of the recipient countries in the direction of the donor countries' and agencies' thinking'.[80] In such cases, the project may not be the one the recipient wishes to extend or promote.[81] Also a lack of knowledge of the circumstances in the target region and a lack of participation at local level may prevent the successful operation of a project.[82] An alternative development project should emphasise the situation in the host state rather than the interests of the donor.

The second danger is that it is difficult to sustain the economic system established in alternative development projects. Mansfield and Sage claim that alternative development creates a misperception that it can bring economic alternative development to coca cultivation.[83] They assert that the failure of

---

76 Rostow, W.W., *The Stages of Economic Growth*, 1963, Cambridge: Cambridge University Press.

77 Faaland, J., and Parkinson, J.R., *The Political Economy of Development*, 1986, London: Frances Pinter, p. 247.

78 *The EU and Latin America*, p. 17.

79 Washimi, K., *ODA (The reality of ODA projects)*, 1989, Tokyo: Iwanami.

80 Faaland *et al.*, op cit., p. 233.

81 Ibid., p. 236.

82 Dorner, P., and Felstenhaousen, H., 'Agrarian reforms and employment - the Colombian case', Land Tenure Centre, University of Wisconsin, LTC Reprint no.66, 1970, p. 228.

83 Mansfield, D. and Sage, C. 'Drug Crop Producing Countries: A Development Perspective', in Coomber, R. (ed.), *The Control of Drugs and Drug Users: Reason or*

alternative development stems from the issues dealt with in the programme, namely crop substitution.[84] In the case of drug control, such a failure will force people back to the cocaine trade for survival. Stevenson maintains that: 'Crop substitution programmes will also be ineffective unless the acreage under cultivation can be controlled, which is difficult in an industry where the factors of production are abundant so that supply is highly elastic.'[85] Alternative development might succeed in establishing a new economic system in a host state, but its sustainability may be questionable.

Moreover, according to Atkins, there are four possible problems, related particularly to the EU alternative development projects aimed at fighting cocaine trafficking.[86] First, lowering trade barriers tends to benefit large-scale agricultural producers, not small farmers. Legal crop markets are highly competitive and those that turned from coca to legal crops are unlikely to be successful or earn much.[87] Second, the drug-linked cultivation areas are remote from markets, both domestic and international, and farmers lack facilities to transport their crops.[88] Third, Bolivia and Peru produce three-quarters of the coca in the Andes, but they did not benefit from EU trade concessions until 1993.[89] This means that Bolivia and Peru could not have secured the markets to sell their products produced from alternative development. Fourth, 'while trade concessions have been in place, other processes have continued to undermine the validity of legal rural enterprises in the Andean regions. The farmers may need to compete with cheap imported goods.'[90] The traditional coca cultivation areas and high land in Bolivia and Peru have difficulty in producing legal crops due to their severe environmental conditions. The crops that grow in the areas are limited: they need to survive at a high altitude and in poor soil conditions. In addition, poor infrastructure prevents the farmers from transporting their products.

As the above critique suggests, although introducing alternative crops may be easy, consolidating and sustaining the new production system with sufficient profits may be harder. The capacity and potential of the markets for alternative crops could be the key to successful sustainable development in the Andes. The predicament, however, is that it might be difficult for the new producers to compete in the well-established markets without some sort of protection for their products, such as concessions on tariffs. The protection scheme on alternative crops cannot bear fruit without support from the donor and other developed countries at the cost of their own

---

Reaction? 1998, Harwood Academic Publishers: Amsterdam.

84 This is because these projects introduce a few legal crops to the region, and the production will exceed the demand. There is no market to support newly introduced products in the region, and there is a lack of means to export such products outside the region.

85 Stevenson, R., *Winning the War on Drugs: To Legalise or Not?* Hobart Paper No. 124, 1994, London: The Institute of Economic Affairs, p. 35.

86 Atkins, A., *European Drug-Control Policy and the Andean Region*, Narcotics and Development Discussion Paper 6, 1993, London: Catholic Institute of International Relations, pp. 22–23.

87 Ibid., p. 22.

88 Ibid., p. 22.

89 Ibid., p. 23.

90 Ibid., p. 23.

trade benefits. Lee and Clawson conclude that 'crop substitution is not a promising strategy for reducing coca cultivation in the Andes'.[91]

Despite these criticisms, the EU continues to pursue its alternative development projects in the Andes. It is aware of the first criticism, and regulated its approach to a project it supports by Community Regulation. According to the regulation, priority support is given to North-South co-operation in the field of drug control 'at the request of the partner country for the preparations of national plans in the campaign against drugs'.[92] Further, the EU and Rio Groups have adopted several concepts forming the basis of EU drug control efforts in Latin America in the 1990 Rome Declaration, such as their respect for 'the purposes and principles of the UN charter' and support of 'democracy and the rule of law, respect for human rights and promotion of social justice, respect for sovereignty, self-determination and non-intervention'.[93]

The EU's concerns about sustainability, expansion and further development of the projects are expressed in the following way:

> ... the drugs issue must be accepted as a cross-cutting issue in all international debates, whether the focus is on sustainable development or on security issues. In this context, priority should be given to schemes designed to foster cooperation and encourage response from host countries, rather than those which imply unilateral actions.[94]

The EU repeatedly emphasises the importance of consistency and coherence in its policies. It fears the possibility that 'Crop substitution in one country may just create new problems in the neighbouring country' and the success of crop substitution is vital to 'many drug-producing countries dependent on agricultural exports'.[95] In order to promote the economies of the recipients of alternative development projects, the EU addresses the need to 'promote an open and increasingly productive and equitable international economy, in which specific attention will be given to the interests of the less developed countries.'[96]

The programmes supported and proposed by the EU seem to follow the principles that were claimed by the scholars of development studies such as communication with recipients and executing projects to encourage activities in not only economic but also political and social spheres. The following sections will investigate the content of the EU alternative development programmes and their results.

---

91 Lee, R. and Clawson, P., *Crop Substitution in the Andes*, December 1993, Washington DC: ONDCP.

92 *Community Regulation (EC) No. 2046/97 of the Council*, 13 October 1997.

93 *Rome Declaration*.

94 *COM (97) 670 final*, p. 13.

95 Hart, R., *Drugs and its impact on crime: Europe's response*, 526th Wilton Park Conference, 6–8 April 1998, http://www.wiltonpark.org.uk/conference/reports/wp536report. html (Accessed 25 August 2002).

96 *Rome Declaration*.

EU Alternative Development Programmes

The co-operation programmes of the EU with Latin America and the Caribbean had expanded to wider coverage than crop substitution and drug related issues. In 1998, the EU's drug control co-operation with Latin America and the Caribbean was executing 66 recommendations related to: alternative development (crop substitution), cultivation, production and transport, precursor chemicals, government organisation against drugs, legislation, law enforcement, judicial organisation, information/ intelligence, money laundering and seizure of assets, corruption, prevention and rehabilitation.[97]

Although the EU budget for drug control has declined,[98] EU support to Latin America, particularly to the Andes, has continued. The Panama Plan (the comprehensive action plan on drugs endorsed at the Rio Summit in June 1999) deals with the following areas: demand reduction, supply reduction, judicial, police and custom co-operation and illegal trade in arms, money laundering, and legislation on drugs and the strengthening of institutions. During 2000–2001, the EU had 58 activities underway and also suggested 33 projects.[99]

Case Study: Alternative Development Programme in Bolivia

The EU alternative development programme in the Andes was operated only in Bolivia until the early 2000s. This does not mean that the EU did not support development in Colombia and Peru. There has also been technical support and political, social and economic support to them. This is because these two countries have influential cocaine trafficking organisations and insurgency groups. They are capable of violent attacks on personnel in an effort to prevent progress. It is, therefore, believed that operating a long-term agricultural project to destroy coca fields and replace them with legal crops is too dangerous.[100] The development programmes in Colombia and Peru have been supporting education, technical support, and developing social infrastructure.[101] According to Vogel of the European Commission, an alternative development scheme requires relatively peaceful conditions. Successful projects may be possible in Bolivia, Peru and Ecuador but may be difficult in Colombia because of its internal conflicts.[102] The EU does not have the means to ensure the security of the projects and areas for the project workers since it does not possess its own military. The current success in Bolivia mainly depends on the relationship between the government and the drug cartels, and the absence of strong revolutionary groups.

---

97 *The EU's priorities for future drugs cooperation in Latin America*, Paragraph 1.

98 See sections above.

99 *Coordination and Cooperation Mechanism on Drugs Between The EU, Latin America and the Caribbean: Annual Report 2000-2001*, Obtained during an interview in Brussels; and *Consejo de la Unión Europea*.

100 Interview with Mr K. H. Vogel of the European Commission in Brussels, 23 April 2002.

101 Interview with an official at the European Commission in Brussels on 9 July 2002.

102 Interview with Vogel at the European Commission in Brussels on 23 April 2002.

In the case of Peru, the weakness of the revolutionary groups led the EU to agree to establish aid programmes.

In Bolivia, an EU alternative development programme consisting of three projects is in progress. Bolivia is considered a successful example of the EU alternative development programmes in the Andes. The relative success may result from the fact that Bolivia's political stability satisfies one of the key conditions required by the EU.

The alternative development programme in Bolivia targeted the illicit coca cultivating areas of the Chaparé, and was allocated €30 million for a four-year period.[103] The programme has two objectives, to improve economic and social conditions. In order to improve the economic condition of the region, alternative development is introduced. The alternative development is based on four actions: improving basic infrastructure, access to credit for production purposes, formal establishment of ownership and land registration, and improving management of natural resources. As for social conditions, development of facilities for production and social purposes, such as education and health, are planned. The aim is to prevent migration from some areas to the coca cultivating areas by improving their surroundings.

The alternative development programme consists of three projects targeting different areas: PRAEDAC, PRODEVAT and APENIN. All projects contain several aims and subprojects to achieve their goals. For example, the 'Support to Mining Areas of the Altiplano' (APENIN) the budget of €5 million has objectives to control migration to big cities from mining areas by creating jobs locally.[104] Many miners went into coca cultivation after the closure of tin mines, and therefore providing alternative economic opportunities means miners can end their involvement in the cocaine trade. In this section, the activities and results of the two major projects will be examined.

First, the 'Programa de Apoyo a la Estrategia de Desarrallo Alternativo en el Chaparé' (Alternative Development support programme in the Chaparé – PRAEDAC).[105] This had a budget of €19 million over four years between 2001 and 2004.[106] PRAEDAC is believed to be a feasible operation because of its geographical advantages. Its location is a reasonable distance for shipping to two big cities, Cochabamba and Santa Cruz, as well as being connected to Chile and Argentine

---

103 *Minutes of the Fourth High-Level Meeting*, p. 7.

104 *European Community Support for the Fight Against Drugs in Bolivia.*

105 The areas included in the execution of the programme are: Villa Tunari (Provincia Chaparé), Chimoré and Puerto Villarroel (Provincia Carrasco), and subregion of Shinahota (Provincia Tiraque) and Entre Ríos (Provincia Carrasco), covering about 37.930 Km², including 35,000 families. *PRAEDAC: Potencialidades de los Productos Forestales No Maderables en el Tropico de Cochabamba*, Publicación No RN-002/2001, Agosto 2001, Cochabamba: Comision Europa, p. 6.

106 PRAEDAC was signed on 8 April 1997. The project was established on the budget of €24,100,000. The EU financed 80% and the Bolivian government, 20%. *Programa de Apoyo a la Estrategia de Desarrollo Alternativo en el Chapare – PRAEDAC*, http://europa.eu.int/ comm/external_relations/bolivia/intro/praedac.htm (23 March 2002); *European Community Support for the Fight Against Drugs in Bolivia.*

by air and roads. The other is the low cost of production in Cochabamba and the large availability of land, as well as favourable weather condition for substitute crops.[107] The four main objectives of PRAEDAC are planned to influence different spheres of the local community. First, in order to empower the local government and improve living conditions, the development of basic infrastructure and services needs to be achieved. Second, secure credit for small farmers and enterprises to promote alternative crops and economic activities. Third, land registration should be formalised to clarify and provide security in land ownership. Fourth, it is necessary to strengthen the capability of conserving natural resources to ensure protection of the environment and sustainability.

Through PRAEDAC, the EU is aiming at increasing the ability of the local governments to be capable of planning, preparing and managing the development of programmes with the funding they received in the context of judicial, socio-economic and community support.[108] The improvement of social infrastructure, such as community buildings, hospitals, schools, water and sewer systems, and land registry has increased respect and support for the local government from the community.[109] Additionally, in order to ensure popular support to the project, it was necessary for the EU to negotiate with the coca producers union to establish agreements on policies and the acceptance of protection.[110] As for land registry and restructuring, it is expected to increase productivity in the region and help control population movements for illicit drug production purposes. Although the project is relatively successful, more co-operation and commitment from the local governments are required to cover wider areas of the region.[111] Consequently, as la Misión de Evaluación de Medio Término (Mission of mid-term evaluation – MEMT) suggests, there are possibilities for the region to develop further projects such as agro-industries (fruit processing), and ecotourism through initiatives from the local authorities and the request of the communities.[112] With sufficient capability, the local governments may be able to promote more development in their local communities.

The second project, the 'Development of the Andean Valleys of Arque and Tapacarí' (PRODEVAT) has prevented migration to the coca cultivating areas. In the past, the high migration rates from the target areas led to more people becoming involved in the area of coca cultivation.[113] With a budget of €6 million, the project

---

107 Alternative crops the project is planning to promote are rice, yucca, maize, and other priority crops, such as banana, corn, citrus and pineapple. *PRAEDAC: Potencialidades de los Productos Forestales*, pp. 6–7.

108 Unpublished EU working paper, 2002, p. 3.

109 Ibid., p. 2.

110 Unpublished EU Working Paper, 1999, pp. 10–12.

111 The project has achieved reform of 20,000 hectares of land at the first stage of the operation, and 80,000 hectares at the second stage. Unpublished EU working paper, 2002, p. 5.

112 Ibid., p. 4.

113 The advantage Arque and Tapacarí have is their proximity to Cochabamba, the largest city in the province.

intends to improve agricultural and livestock production, access to markets, health and education services, and management capacity of local authorities.[114]

The general aim of the project is to improve the living standard within the region, which is currently very low due to its extreme poverty. PRODEVAT reached the goals defined in Plan Operatión Global (1998–2003) by the Bolivian government, but the extension of the project to March 2005 was been recommended to the EU due to the lack of progress with the project.[115] This was, according to Vogel, because of the need to provide further assistance for social and economic infrastructure and monitoring the progress of facilities introduced by the project.[116]

The project has succeeded in drawing attention to health, education and basic infrastructure, but it could not satisfy local needs. For example, there are schools and a hospital in Tapacarí, and a service water system that provided for only 3% of the region in 1992 was extended to cover 21% by 2002, in co-operation with the Family and Health International (FHI) and The United Nations Children's Fund (UNICEF). Also, 72 kilometres of road was provided by the project, but it was far below the actual local demand of 450 kilometres.[117]

In respect of progress monitoring, Vogel refers to anxiety over consolidating economic activities using newly introduced facilities. For example, the project introduced a price monitoring system and irrigation system to expand productivity in a few areas. The price monitoring system is to check on the price changes in the target markets for local products. This system intends to provide higher competitiveness to the local farmers in local and regional markets with the capacity to access information on demands at different places and redirect the products to various markets nearby.[118] With the irrigation system, 2,640 families benefit from more productive agricultural operations and are expected to achieve commercial surpluses within a few years.[119] The combination of two systems could improve the trade performance of the communities and the region. The difficulty for the farmers who participate in this project is that they do not have sufficient savings to survive for a few years with small incomes. Vogel, therefore, claims that this project needs more assistance from the EU until the system can ensure sufficient improvement and economic stability to the communities involved.

Alongside efforts to activate the local infrastructure and economy, PRODEVAT also tried to reinforce the management abilities of the local authorities on such issues as natural resource management and road maintenance. To support this scheme, the EU has allocated €998,000.[120] While the project is trying to encourage agricultural production for commercial purposes, it also encourages non-agricultural products to be commercialised, such as craftsmanship and ecotourism.[121] The geographical

---

114 *European Community Support for the Fight Against Drugs in Bolivia.*
115 Unpublished EU Working Paper, 2002, pp. 7–8.
116 Interview with Vogel at European Commission on 23 April 2002.
117 Unpublished EU working paper, 2002, pp. 8–9.
118 Ibid., p. 11.
119 The irrigation system covers 660 hectares of land. Ibid., p. 11.
120 Ibid., pp. 10–11.
121 Ibid., p. 12.

location of the region is suitable for day-trippers and adventure trippers from Cochabamba, if roads are improved.

Recognising the progress and influence of the project in the region, MEMT has, however, questioned the result in preventing migration to the coca cultivation area. There are still relatively large numbers of people moving into the coca cultivation areas according to estimates. Population growth in the area increased by 25% in the period of 1992–2001.[122] From the long-term perspective, it is believed that the projects in Bolivia may achieve satisfactory results by introducing and establishing legal crop cultivation and social, economic and political infrastructures. In addition, the EU has approved the extension of the project, PRODEVAT, for the period of 2006–2009. Although no decision for the budget has made, PRODEVAT is expected to achieve its objectives in a more socially rooted manner.[123]

Other EU Projects on Trade, Political and Social Affairs

The EU approach to alternative development programmes is broad and one programme contains several different projects. There are, however, some common elements in each project, such as improving infrastructure, including land reform, strengthening local political institutions, and law enforcement co-operation. All the projects are supported by the EU trade policies to expand and protect the markets for the commodities produced from alternative development projects. The main elements of EU alternative development (economic tools such as General System of Preference and co-operation between companies in Europe and the Andes; land and infrastructure reform; law enforcement co-operation) and their function in the programme are examined below.

Economic Measures   The EU has been applying the General System of Preference (GSP) to products from the Andes. Due to this scheme, nearly 80% of Andean countries' industrial and agricultural goods can enter the EU duty-free.[124] From 1995, the EU introduced a new system called 'Multi-annual Scheme of Generalised Tariff Preferences' for the Andean countries for ten years (1995–2004) as a special scheme for the drug producing countries. As a result of this scheme, due to the encouragement and promotion given to the Andean countries, their exports to European markets grew by 60%. About 90% of the Andean products sold in the EU are exempt from custom duties.[125] The Commission has requested that the GSP scheme be continued to promote the products from alternative development programmes, and also the increase of special development projects in the Andean region.[126]

---

122 Ibid., 2002, p. 7.

123 Interview with K.H. Vogel of the European Commission, Brussels, 23 April 2002.

124 *European Community Support for the Fight Against Drugs in Bolivia*, http://europa. eu.int/comm/external_relations/bolivia/intro/drugs.htm (Accessed 23 March 2002).

125 *The Andean countries benefit from the EU's 'Drugs' Generalised System of Preferences (GSP)*, http://europa.eu.int/comm/external_relations/andean/intro/index.htm (Accessed 25 August 2002).

126 *The EU and Latin America*, p. 18.

Atkins' criticism, noted above, refers to the exclusion of Bolivia and Peru from the GSP scheme. There were also allegations from the Commission that Colombia was regarded as ineligible for the GSP scheme.[127] The next GSP scheme was for the period 1 January 2002 to 31 December 2004, however, all three states were included in the status of the special drug related GSP scheme, under which 'three-quarters of Colombia's exports to the EU are exempt from custom duties.'[128]

Alongside the GSP scheme, the EU also promotes business alliances between European and Andean corporations through a project started in 2001. According to EU statistics, this project called 'EU-Andean AL-Partenariat' involves 75 European corporations and 404 Andean counterparts and 'offer[s] … co-operation in technology, products, financing, and services related to the alliances'.[129] This may contribute to creating off-farm jobs in order to absorb the excess work force in the Andean countries. The support for economic growth and sustainability in the Andes is essential for the success of the EU drug control policies. Commissioner Chris Patten said that EU economic support is 'the corollary to political backing'.[130]

The GSP scheme has covered the major drug producing countries in the Andes since 2002. It will increase competitiveness of the Andean products in European markets. At the same time, it will decrease the competitiveness of European products, and it may be difficult to gain popular approval in Europe. As for the AL-Partenatiat project, this also needs to be supported by the EU to secure markets until their products become sufficiently competitive to compete against products from other parts of the world. To some extent, those economic policies should be the backbone of EU alternative development programmes to be sustainable, although this policy could work against the interests of EU member states by protecting Andean products in the European markets.

Infrastructure and Land Reform   To increase the competitiveness of farmers in the Andes, it is necessary to improve local infrastructure, particularly roads and paths linking the regional and national markets and also schools and hospitals. For farmers and other producers, the high accessibility to the markets is a prerequisite for the increase of commercial activities. Some rural areas do not have well-established roads and paths to transport commodities to the market.

Land reform and registration is not a priority in EU alternative development, but does have significant influence on local productivity. Within the alternative development programme, land reform is used to control migration, particularly migration into the illicit coca growing areas. Furthermore, it has the effect of motivating farmers by providing them with full responsibility for a certain area.[131]

---

127 Patten, C., *Colombian international commitment to peace*, 30 April 2001, http://europa.eu.int/comm/external_relations/news/patten/speech_01_192.htm   (Accessed   25 August 2002).

128 *Council Regulation (EC) No 2501/2001 of 10 December 2001*, http://europa.eu.int/comm/external_relations/andean/doc/gspreg01_en.pdf (Accessed 25 August 2002).

129 *AL-Investment*, http://europa.eu.int/comm/europeaid/projects/al-invest/index_en.htm (Accessed 25 August 2002).

130 Patten, C., *Colombian international commitment to peace*.

131 Mr K.H. Vogel of the European Commission in Brussels, 23 April 2002.

Land reform in the Andes is a key to successful alternative development programmes because the persistence of a feudal structure in land ownership was an obstacle to increasing productivity. Land reform, however, was not on the agenda until the 1960s, and then its significance in productivity became recognised in the 1970s. Dorner and Felstenhaousen, for example, criticised the development plan in Colombia in the 1960s for ignoring the fundamental problem at the local level, that is, land reform.[132] Since the 1960s, there have been some projects to replace feudalism; for example, the Cornell Vicos Project in Peru intended to convert a 'feudal' estate into a 'community farm' enterprise.[133]

The collapse of feudalism following land reform was regarded as an opportunity for the Andes to reinforce their economic growth. The expectation of the change was as follows:

> If such a social and economic transition could occur widely in the Andean region, its serious agricultural problems might be solved ... then the entire population of the region could move ahead more rapidly into the industrial, more affluent, and in many respects more egalitarian society emerging on the coast and in some jungle-colony areas. The Vicos case holds regional significance because this experience has proved that socio-political techniques are already at hand to solve many of the socio-economic problems most characteristic of the Andean area.[134]

Modernisation of land registration and infrastructure could raise productivity in the Andes because many rural areas do not have sufficient access to fundamental facilities. Land reform may encourage farmers and also control the movement of people.

Strengthening Political Institutions As discussed in the sections on development, the stability and function of political institutions in the target region of an alternative development project play a significant role in alternative development programmes. This is because they are in charge of the management of the programme, particularly after the EU project team hands over the operation. In other words, the sustainability of the mechanism introduced by the project, such as agricultural production systems and public infrastructure, depends on the capability of local authorities. In addition, Billings and Blee claim that the local government is 'not simply a passive reflection of economic conditions, but a significant factor in its own right in shaping the course of rural social development'.[135] Without long-term vision and management and planning capabilities of the institutions, elimination of poverty cannot be achieved.[136]

---

132 Dorner *et al.*, *Agrarian reforms and employment*, p. 224.

133 Harvey, C., Jacobs, J., Lamb, G., and Schaffer, B., *Rural Employment and Administration in the Third World: Development Methods and Alternative Strategies*, 1979, Farnborough: Saxon House, p. 1.

134 Holmberg, A.R., and Dobyns, H.F., 'Case Study: The Cornell Program in Vicos, Peru', in Wharton, C.R. (ed.), *Subsistence Agriculture and Economic Development*, 1969, Chicago: Aldine Press, p. 410.

135 Billings *et al.*, op cit., p. 320.

136 Ibid., p. 320.

Therefore, 'Supporting the establishment and operation of democratic institutions is … a priority for Community aid, both directly, in the form of projects supporting such institutions, and indirectly, through action against destabilising forces such as drug trafficking.'[137]

According to EU officials, the EU prioritises support to local governments and non-governmental organisations working for rural communities in order to establish political structures that will grow from small scale to the national level.[138] In this manner, there is less risk of intervening with national government, and thereby the EU's position in a supporting role to the government is maintained. In addition, reform of local government and increased political participation in a village appear to be a more feasible project than national government reform. Other reasons why the EU targets local communities is that without sufficient political power at a local level, the projects carried out in the areas may not be sustained effectively.[139]

Law Enforcement Co-operation   In respect to law enforcement co-operation, the EU is taking the initiative, particularly as an information sharing system. The EU is keen to organise seminars and conferences to create opportunities for law enforcement agents from different parts of the world to meet and get to know each other as well as exchange their knowledge and experiences.[140] The aim of the EU is to promote the acquaintance of agents and agencies working in the field of drug control in different countries, and widen their networks. This project, however, differs from a conventional form of law enforcement co-operation as these officials do not leave their countries to make arrests but provide information either voluntarily or on request.

The EU's efforts have borne fruit in the form of the Andean liaison officer network and international network of law enforcement officials.[141] With the expansion of such a network, it may be possible to increase the numbers of seizures of drugs and prevent illicit movements of narcotics internationally.[142] For example, if Colombian officials noticed suspicious shipping from its ports to one of the European countries, then they could just send a message to agents in Europe to which the ship may travel to inform them of its existence. Those agents at the destination state may be able to investigate or even capture the criminals.

As the result of the expanded network of anti-drug agents, it may be possible to chase and control illicit drug shipments more easily and frequently. The aim of the EU is to increase the efficiency in arrests of drug traffickers and have closer communication among law enforcement institutions in different countries. At the

---

137 *Multiannual Guidelines For Community Aid Colombia*, IB/1035/98-EN, 12 November 1998, Brussels: European Commission.

138 Interviews with officials at European Commission and European Council on 23–25 April and 8–11 July 2002.

139 Interview with Mr Vogel of European Commission on 24 April 2002.

140 Interview with an official of European Commission on 10 July 2002; Community Regulation (EC) No. 2046/97.

141 *Minutes of the Fourth High-Level Meeting of Drug Expert of the Andean Community and the EU, 29-30 March 2000*, Brussels, 12 April 2000, 7688/00, p. 9.

142 Interview with an official of the European Commission in Brussels, 9 July 2002.

moment, there are a few projects between Europol and law enforcement agencies in the Andes and other Latin American countries.[143] They are still at the preparation stage for the projects. If it starts functioning, this network could expand and strengthen the law enforcement network internationally.

In sum, the projects themselves as well as the alternative development programme as a whole cover various sectors of the local community. Also, the non-military approach of the EU seems to promote popular participation and support from local communities. This is, however, a weakness of the EU project because officials do not have any means of protecting themselves and the progress of a project. They need to rely on the host state to create stability and ensure their safety.

The wide-ranging projects of the EU are built around crop substitution. An alternative development programme cannot succeed by itself as discussed above. Therefore, in one programme, economic development needs to be protected by securing markets domestically and internationally; social infrastructures need to be established for productivity and efficiency; and local government needs strengthening to maintain stability in the areas. If this programme can progress at a certain level, it might assist the creation of a developed country and the reduction of cocaine production. This process, however, may be time consuming and may cost substantial amounts of money. It would be questionable to assume that Europeans are willing to create economically strong and stable states in order to reduce the import of cocaine from the Andes.

Inter-regional Co-operation

Another tool for the EU to use in curbing cocaine trafficking in Latin America is to create a regional co-operation mechanism. What the EU is aiming at is strengthening regional co-operation in a wider context. Beyond the European continent, the EU model can serve as an example for other regions in encouraging states to reduce political tension, to increase economic interdependence and to create greater mutual trust between countries.[144] In order to encourage regional and sub-regional co-operation against cocaine trafficking, the EU has created a mechanism that involves not only the EU and the Andes but also other Latin American countries and the Caribbean.

Regarding the transnational nature of cocaine trafficking, the EU takes the view that a regional approach to control cocaine may work more effectively than bilateralism. As Manuel Marín González, the vice-president of the European Commission remarked at the Euro-Ibero American Seminar in 1999, 'regional cooperation is the only way to combat money laundering, to control precursors and to harmonise legalisation.'[145] Also, experiences from the past have confirmed

---

143 *Consejo de la Unión Europea.*
144 *COM (2001) 211 final*, p. 8.
145 EMCDDA, *Euro-Ibero American Seminar*, p. 14.

that: 'tackling this problem in one country alone merely serves to transfer it to neighbouring countries.'[146]

The concept of bi-regional co-operation mechanisms was adopted in the 1999 Panama Comprehensive Action Plan for EU/Latin America Counter-Drug Assistance as the priorities for action to reinforce Latin American countries to 'play a key role in the new mechanism on drug cooperation/co-ordination between Europe and Latin America/Caribbean countries'.[147] Following the intention to strengthen the bi-regional mechanism, aid from the Commission and the member states is expected to focus particularly on reinforcement of 'the inter-regional cooperation between Latin America and the Caribbean as well as between the various Latin American sub-regional groups'.[148] At the same time, the EU has suggested it holds high-level meetings of the bi-regional co-operation mechanism among the EU, Latin America and the Caribbean.[149]

By the summer of 2002, the bi-regional co-operation mechanism was established, and was ready for action. As the officials of both regions revealed, however, there is no project or funding to operate the mechanism.[150] Although the bi-regional mechanism is appealing to the Latin American countries, it lacks concrete projects to materialise the ideas. One Latin American official confessed that the offer of the EU sounds ideal, but what Latin American countries really need are concrete and practical projects to improve the situation in the region.[151]

Conclusion

The EU's involvement in drug control in the Andes has been motivated by its desire for shared responsibility in the international society and drug prohibition. The EU's lack of material interest in the Andean region makes it difficult to justify its initiatives and the allocation of money to drug control from a Realist perspective. On the other hand, reluctance to adequately control precursor chemicals also makes it difficult to fit its behaviour into the Liberal approach.

European perception of the drug problem, as analysed in chapter 2, as a health and social issue may have gained support to tackle the drug control from humanitarian aspects (development, human rights and elimination of poverty). The EU has carried out alternative development programmes in the Andes to fight against poverty, which is believed to be the main cause of the cocaine trade. The EU, also,

---

146 *European Parliament resolution on Plan Colombia & support for the peace process in Colombia*, 1 February 2001, http://europa.eu.int/comm/external_relations/colombia/doc/ep01_02_01.htm (Accessed 17 October 2002).

147 *Declaration of Rio de Janeiro*, 29 June 1999, http://europa.eu.int/comm/external_relations/andean/doc/rio_prio06_00.htm (Accessed 17 October 2002).

148 *COM (1999) 239 final*.

149 *EU-Rio group: Santiago Declaration/Xth institutionalised ministerial meeting*, 28 March 2001, http://europa.eu.int/comm/external_relations/andean/intro/santiago28_03_01.htm (Accessed 17 September 2003).

150 Interview with Mr Johannes Vos of the European Council in Brussels, 8 July 2002.

151 Interview with a Latin American official in Brussels, 23 January 2002.

has invested in alternative development, in order to re-establish a legal economic system in coca growing regions. The EU emphasis on the economic aspect, namely poverty reduction, to tackle cocaine trafficking has come from its perception of the cocaine problem as a societal security threat. From an EU perspective, improvement of economic standards would allow coca-growing areas to develop better social infrastructure, which would reduce the necessity to continue cultivating coca. An economic approach to control cocaine is reflected in the change in allocation of budgets. The budget lines for economic co-operation have received the continuous support, but the budget exclusively on drug control in the Andes has declined. Consequently, budgets for economic co-operation have expanded the projects to be covered.

The EU drug control programmes contain various components to support state development, in addition to crop substitution there are economic, political and social components. The alternative development programmes seem to have been planned thoroughly according to the claims of scholars of development studies. This may also be because of the awareness of the EU of the complexity of the nature of cocaine trafficking. The efforts in these fields, however, are yet to be developed. For example, law enforcement co-operation through Europol and the Andean law enforcement agencies has progressed only slowly because of insufficient development in EU law enforcement co-operation. It seems that the weakness in the EU non-economic co-operation in drug control also comes from its focus on poverty reduction. Political and social projects may be positioned in a supportive role to assist the function of economic projects by establishing the necessary infrastructure and management authorities. In order to ensure effectiveness and profitability, the project area requires facilities for modern cultivation and transportation for markets. Also, for the sustainability of a project, it is necessary to train local authorities to ensure continuation of the mechanisms introduced by the project. The EU programmes show the importance of both a holistic approach to alternative development and support to issues surrounding cocaine control.

Despite some weaknesses in the EU programmes, this approach can be a new tool to combat drug trafficking by attacking the origin of the problem, if every drug producing state is as stable as Bolivia. Moreover, the EU values consultation with the recipient states in order to decide the types of projects and support required by them. The sense of ownership of drug control programmes would secure the progress and maintenance of projects by the Andean governments. However, alternative development programmes take a long time to achieve results, and those results might be rather obscure, as some EU officials believe what they are trying to achieve is to the change the way of thinking of people in the Andes. In reality the programmes are costly and they may be difficult to sustain, and they are also without the means to protect the projects areas from those who are against coca eradication. One of the keys to successful alternative development programmes may be popular participation, but also ensuring financial resources. The weakness of the EU can be its absence of a budget to spend, and its reliance on funds from member states. At the same time, it could be a strength to have several potential donors to sustain its projects. For example, if one state lost its interest in supporting one project, there might be other state willing to sponsor it.

In order to offset its weakness, it would be beneficial for the EU to co-operate with other international actors that could provide security measures for EU projects. This is because in order to maintain peace and order, sometimes coercion is required to those who disregard the rules in the society. Alternative development can provide new economic mechanisms and social infrastructure to a local community, but it is difficult to maintain peace and stability if there are armed traffickers. However, attempting to conduct multiple operations is costly for bilateral co-operation. Therefore, participating in an international operation for drug control, such as Plan Colombia, could have been an opportunity for the EU to pursue a project in co-ordination with other projects.

Chapter 5

US Drug Control Policy Towards the Andes

Introduction

This chapter will analyse the US counter-narcotics policy towards the Andes, looking at the emergence of the policy; US projects in the Andean countries and the consequences for the countries involved. The chapter will examine how the United States has tried to curb the flow of cocaine from the Andes through its foreign narcotics policy. The US drug control policy affected the cocaine industry in the region, the relationship between the United States and the Andes, and the domestic political, social and economic situations of the recipient states.[1]

As noted in chapter 3, the United States has regarded cocaine trafficking as a national security threat and launched a war against its source in the Andes. The US approach to drug control differs from that of the European Union: whilst the EU focuses exclusively on alternative development programmes, the United States has pursued crop eradication, drug interdiction and alternative development. However, the principal US effort has been law enforcement operations and the use of armed forces. This is because, from the US perspective, supply reduction in the Andes is the key to curbing the flow of cocaine. Military involvement in drug control has been to ensure the operation of law enforcement activity, particularly those of eradication and interdiction in the Andes, by protecting personnel and equipment involved in these schemes. Engaging the military in drug control, however, has been challenged in terms of its legitimacy and effectiveness.

US drug control, particularly in Latin America has been criticised and considered a failure because cocaine continues to be smuggled into America and the price of cocaine and crack have been declining. Furthermore, as a US official admits, the US drug control policy has led to instability in some coca growing areas in the Andes, because of strong resistance against coca eradication by the coca growers.[2] Despite criticism, the US government is determined to pursue its policy.

In order to analyse US drug control policy and its consequences, this chapter is divided into two parts. First, the US narcotics policy toward the Andes, called the 'Andean Narcotics Strategy', will be examined in terms of its historical background and changing trends, in order to illustrate how current US foreign narcotics policy was formed. Through the examination of its historical background, the analysis

---

1   For a detailed discussion on the implications of cocaine trafficking in the Andes, see the Introduction in this book.

2   Interview with an official at USAID in Washington DC on 27 May 2003.

will explain the reasons why the US government came to develop and expand its foreign narcotics policy toward the Andes. Thereafter, each major component in the US 'Andean Narcotics Strategy' will be investigated to identify the strengths and weaknesses of its approach. In both sections, the relationship between the Andean states and the United States are explored because US drug control in the region cannot be implemented without co-operation from the Andean governments.

The second part of this chapter will focus on eradication, interdiction and alternative development, components of US drug control policy because American policy makers believe a three-prong approach is the most effective way to tackle cocaine trafficking. The emphasis is, however, not equal among the three elements of the strategy. The US emphasis is on the programmes directly targeting the cocaine trade, eradication and interdiction. Alternative development is regarded as having only a supportive role.

The US Foreign Narcotics Policy: The Andean Strategy

The cocaine trade, as discussed in chapter 3, has been recognised as a 'threat' to the United States due to the large sums of money at the disposal of drug trafficking organisations and their capability to exert influence on the political and economic systems. In addition, there is the potential that insurgency groups empowered by narco-dollars could cause regional instability. The nexus of drug trafficking organisations and insurgency groups can be a predicament to law enforcement operations in the Andean states due to the violent attacks agents might face during the operations. The growing influence of the drug trafficking organisations might lead a state to become uncooperative towards the US drug control policy.[3] It is partly in considering such possible dangers, the origin of cocaine and the nationalities of those who engage in the cocaine trade that cocaine trafficking was categorised as a national security threat from foreign states – an alien conspiracy to harm the social fabric and economic well-being of the US. This notion of a foreign conspiracy established a priority in the fight against cocaine trafficking, focusing on the external enemy (the supply of cocaine) rather than internal problem (the demand for cocaine).

The US government has decided to control the supply of drugs because of the nature of the capitalist economy. There are two ways to control the cocaine market: one is to reduce demand, because if there is no demand, then there will be no supply. The other is to reduce supply in order to increase the price at the market and discourage consumers from purchases, following the rule of 'invisible hand'.[4] The US argument on demand reduction is that by reducing supply: the price will rise and the consumers will not be able to afford cocaine.[5] In the case of illicit commodities,

---

3   Reagan, R., *National Security Directive 221*, Narcotics and National Security, 8 April 1986.

4   According to Smith, there is a point at which consumers and suppliers agree on a commodity price, and above or below that point, the trade would not exist. Smith, A. *The Wealth of Nations*, [1776] 1993, Oxford: Oxford University Press.

5   Interviews with officials at the ONDCP in Washington DC on 28 May 2003.

this argument is much more difficult, as US officials admit, because the reduction of cocaine production is not easy to achieve.[6]

According to Carpenter, the US supply reduction policy was formed mainly because policy makers experienced little success in controlling the demand for drugs. Hence, they attempted to control supply in the source countries.[7] In order to reduce cocaine supply, the United States has tried to seize cocaine and eradicate coca fields in producer and transit states. It has also tried to weaken the influence and financial power of drug trafficking organisations.

It was the Reagan and Bush administrations in the 1980s that shaped a policy toward the Andes that became known as the 'war on drugs' or 'drug war American style'. The US emphasis on supply reduction, however, has a longer history dating from the Nixon administration in the late 1960s. In this part of the analysis, the emergence and establishment of the current drug control policy in the US, and the significance of the policy to the US government will be examined in two sections. One section will investigate the historical background and the other will explain the issues related to the militarisation of drug control.

The Emergence of the Andean Narcotics Strategy

The Andean states hold major significance for the US foreign narcotics policy as the source of cocaine since the 1960s. In the 1970s, the Ford and Carter administrations extended the interdiction operations and programmes to eradicate drugs in the Andean states and Mexico. The foreign narcotics policies of Ford and Carter, however, were modest compared to those of Reagan and Bush. It was the Reagan and Bush administrations that established the emphasis controlling supply rather than demand.[8] The introduction of the Andean Strategy in the mid-1980s enabled the United States to be more active and to militarise its operations. The militarisation of drug control in the Andean Strategy has created a strong image of US drug control.

The Andean Strategy stemmed from the Reagan administration's supply control policy, which consisted of 'three major components: eradication, interdiction and alternative development'.[9] It was thought that drug control could only be effective with the combination of these three components. However, the emphasis on the three elements of drug control reflected the economic and political situation of the time, and 'the answer to the curse of narcotics trafficking' changed in accordance with the government priority.[10] For instance, the Reagan administration was not a keen supporter of economic aspects because it pursued the policy of 'zero tolerance' to cocaine and those involved in the cocaine trade. On the other hand, the Bush

---

6   In 2002, US statistics recognise a slight decline in cocaine imports after three decades of drug control efforts. Statistical data obtained in an interview with an official at the ONDCP in Washington DC on 28 May 2003.

7   Carpenter, T.G., *Bad Neighbor Policy: Washington's futile war on drugs in Latin America*, 2003, New York: Palgrave, pp. 20–21.

8   Ibid., p. 18; and Craig, R., 'La Campaña Permanente: Mexico's Antidrug Campaign', *Journal of Interamerican Studies and World Affairs*, Vol. 20, No. 2, May 1978, pp. 101–121.

9   Carpenter, *Bad Neighbor Policy*, p. 21.

10   Ibid., p. 91.

administration recognised the significance of supporting the economy of the source in order to prevent re-cultivation of coca after eradication was executed.[11]

The Bush administration adopted a US $270 million supply reduction policy in the Andes in 1989, describing it as 'balanced, decisive, effective and achievable'.[12] The plan aimed at reducing the supply of Andean cocaine to the United States by 60% by 1999.[13] This Andean Strategy led to even larger sums of money being allocated. In fiscal year 1991–1992 over US$ 600 million (59% of the total US international drug control budget) went to the Andean states, Bolivia, Colombia and Peru. This was a large increase from that of the Reagan administration's $5 million budget.[14]

The dramatic increase in budget for the Andean strategy during the Bush administration resulted not only from an emphasis on drug control policy but also from the militarisation of foreign narcotics operations. In the early 1990s, military aid to the Andes rose sharply to over US $100 million to each state.[15] Between 1990 and 1998, the United States spent a total of US $731 million in supporting the Colombian national police and military in drug control.[16] However, the amount of funding allocated to drug control projects in the region was hardly sufficient to pursue effective operations. Bolivian officials reckoned that alternative development schemes for coca farmers alone required about US$300 to 500 million annually.[17] Despite Bush's awareness of the significance of economic support and approval of the Andean Strategy, social and economic development projects were still secondary concerns of US drug control goals.

The change in US drug control policy came when Bill Clinton became president in 1993. The following year, the US drug control strategy registered a shift of emphasis from supply reduction to demand reduction. This was regarded as a more sophisticated approach than simply attacking the source.[18] Such demand reduction efforts are considered more liberal than others as: 'The US has shifted its strategy

---

11 Bagley, B.M., 'Dateline Drug Wars: Colombia: Support Package Strategy', *Foreign Policy*, No. 77, Winter 1989–1990, p. 163.

12 Shannon, E., 'Attacking the Source', *Time*, 28 August 1989, p. 19.

13 WOLA, *Going to the Source: Results and Prospects for the War on Drugs in the Andes*, WOLA Policy Brief, 7 June 1991, http://www.lindesmith.org/news/news.html (Accessed 20 November 1999), Section I.

14 GAO, *Drugs: International Efforts to Attack a Global Problem*, June 1993, Report to the Chairman and Ranking Minority Member, Committee on Foreign Affairs, House of Representatives, GAO/NSIAD-93-165, Washington DC: GAO, pp. 10–15; and Andreas, P.R., Bertram, E.C., and Sharpe, K.E., 'Dead-end Drug Wars', *Foreign Affairs*, Winter 1991–1992, No. 85, p. 106.

15 During the Reagan administration, the largest recipient, Colombia, had support of $20 million. WOLA, *Going to the Source: Results*, Section II; and Bagley, 'Dateline Drug Wars', p. 163.

16 GAO, *Drug Control: US Counternarcotic Efforts in Colombia Face Continuing Challenges*, Report to Congressional Requesters, GAO/NSIAD-98-60, February 1998, Washington DC: General Accounting Office, p. 3.

17 Shannon, 'Attacking the Source', p. 19.

18 Perl, R.F., 'Clinton's Foreign Drug Policy', *Journal of Interamerican Studies and World Affairs*, Vol. 35, No. 4, winter 1993–1994, pp. 150–151.

from the past emphasis on transit interdiction to a more balanced effort with source countries to build institutions, destroy trafficking organizations and stop supplies.'[19] As Naylor argues, the reduction of demand might be a more effective approach to decrease the cocaine trade according to the theory of capitalist economics.[20] By 1996, however, the Clinton administration had to adjust its policy to emphasise supply reduction more than the administration wished due to political pressures.[21] By the end of the term, the Clinton administration made a decision to support Colombia's drug control programme, Plan Colombia, with over $1 billion military aid.[22] The US could not get away from Reagan's militarised supply reduction.

The reform of the Andean Strategy by the Clinton administration was not only a shift of emphasis but also an attempt to increase Andean compliance with US drug control. The Clinton administration prioritised eradication and activated a certification process to ensure the host governments' participation in the operations.[23] The US aim of controlling the supply of cocaine was not always compatible with the interests of Andean countries.[24] For the Andean states, the cocaine industry was a problem they needed to deal with, but not necessarily the highest priority in their policies. Bolivia and Peru were not keen on a militarised eradication programme because of their economy's high dependence on the coca industry.[25] Hence, the United States has been securing co-operation from the Andean states to its drug

---

19 The White House, *A National Security Strategy of Engagement and Enlargement*, February 1995, p. 11.

20 Naylor, R.T., *Wages of Crime: Black Markets, Illegal Finance, and the Underworld Economy*, 2002, Ithaca: Cornell University Press, p. 11; and also see articles by Bargley and Lee.

21 The US war on drugs could not end or change direction easily because there are lots of related interests involved. The reduction of the supply of military equipment provided to Latin American states, such as helicopters, is a serious issue to the US military industry. In addition, there are large numbers of personnel involved in drug control and the law enforcement institutions have been expanding, such as the Drug Enforcement Administration (DEA). Furthermore, US sponsored drug control operations and programmes in the Andes are mainly managed and carried out by US subcontractors, such as Dyncorp. ONDCP, *The National Drug Control Strategy 1996*, Washington DC: US Government Printing Office; Brooke, J., 'Bogotá Journal: A Captain in the Drug War Wants to Call it Off', *The New York Times*, 8 July 1994; and DEA Intelligence Division, *The Drug Trade in Colombia: A Threat Assessment*, March 2002, DEA-02006, http://www.usdoj.gov/dea/pubs/intel/02006/indexp.html (Accessed 16 May 2003).

22 DeYoung, K., 'Clinton Pledges To Keep U.S. Out Of Colombia War; Visit Highlights Anti-Drug Support', *The Washington Post*, 31 August 2000, p. A.01; Dudley, S., 'Battle Brews Over Plan Colombia; U.S.-Backed Program to Eradicate Drug Crops Faces Gathering Opposition', *The Washington Post*, 20 September 2000. p. A.29; and DeYoung, K., 'Colombia to Get Fewer, Stronger Helicopters; White House Modifies Anti-Drug Aid in Face of Criticism From GAO, Congress', *The Washington Post*, 13 October 2000, p. A.18.

23 ONDCP, *The National Drug Control Strategy 1996*.

24 Lee, R.W., *The White Labyrinth: Cocaine and Political Power*, 1989, New Brunswick, NJ: Transaction, p. 2.

25 For details, see chapter 2, and Clawson, P.L., and Lee III, R.W., *The Andean Cocaine Industry*, 1998, New York: St Martin's Griffin.

control operations more through 'sticks' (coercion and sanctions, such as reducing aid) than 'carrots' (granting economic aid) since the early 1990s.[26]

The tool the Clinton administration used to ensure the compliance of Andean states with its drug control policy was annual narcotic certifications, explained below. Although narcotics certification was introduced earlier, it did not have any actual impact on the Andean states until the Clinton administration in the mid-1990s. Due to their political and strategic significance to the US, the government did not apply sanctions to the Andean states in practice. The Clinton administration believed that the tough use of the certification process brought successes in drug control. For example, the decertification of Colombia led to an increase in the number of arrests of drug traffickers and improved Colombian counter-narcotics performance.[27] Consequently, as a Colombian government official maintained, the Clinton administration became the first (and so far only) administration that actually decertified any Latin American states since the Reagan administration introduced the process.[28]

By the time George W. Bush became president in 2001, the Andean Strategy was allegedly making progress and illicit coca fields in Peru and Bolivia had been eradicated. According to US government statistics, coca production in Bolivia and Peru was declining, whilst that in Colombia was expanding.[29] As a result of drug control operations supported by the US, coca cultivation in these states has reduced and the power of the drug cartels has been weakened. Beers, thereby, claims that drug traffickers in Bolivia and Peru no longer represented a national security threat to the United States.[30]

Following the change of situation in the Andes, the Andean Strategy was broadened by the Bush administration in the 2000s to include not only drugs, but also two additional elements, democracy and development.[31] This was called the '3Ds' of the Andean Strategy. Through support to the 3Ds in the Andes, the aim is at solving: 'all problems and threats to the Andean region, and indirectly to the United States.'[32] This led to the shift of emphasis in US policy toward Bolivia and Peru

26 Carpenter, *Bad Neighbor Policy*, p. 123.

27 Bouley, Jr., E.E., 'The Drug War in Latin America: Ten Years in a Quagmire', in Gerber, J., and Jensen, E.L. (eds), *Drug War American Style: The Internationalization of Failed Policy and Its Alternatives*, 2001, New York: Garland Publishing, p. 179.

28 Interview with an official at the Embassy of Colombia in Brussels on 10 July 2002.

29 The Bureau for International Narcotics and Law Enforcement Affairs, *International Narcotics Control Strategy 2002*, March 2003, http://www.state.gov/g/inl/rls/nrcrpt/2002/html/17944.htm (Accessed 12 August 2003), Section on 'South America'.

30 Beers, R., *Statement* before the Senate Armed Service Committee, 4 April 2000, http://www.state.gov/www/policy_remarks/2000/000404_beers_sasc.html (Accessed 5 May 2002).

31 The Andean Strategy changed its name to the Andean Regional Initiative, and came to include projects for strengthening democratic institutions and improving their ability to deliver services, strengthening the judicial system, protecting human rights, reducing corruption and creating legal employment opportunities for the locals.

32 Brownfield, W.R., *On the Record Briefing: Andean Region Initiative*, 16 May 2001, http://www.state.gov/g/inl/narc/rm/2001/may_aug/index.cmf?docid=2925 (Accessed 12 June 2002).

from security to economic assistance. The balance of security support and economic assistance were reversed: Peru received US$ 75,000 and about US$ 120,000 for security and economic support respectively, and Bolivia received US$ 48,000 and approximately US$ 75,000.[33] By expanding projects, the US attempts to pursue a balanced approach between security and socio-economic programmes.[34] According to Carpenter, however, the ultimate goal of the US government was 'to encourage, persuade, bribe, or coerce foreign governments into joining the US-led drug war'.[35]

The annual narcotics certification process has been a tool to secure co-operation from the Andean states (and other drug producing states) with the US drug control policy since the early 1980s. This process is a determinant of drug control assistance, and consequently, all other types of support to the source countries. The US president assesses the drug control performance of the source countries and decides whether to certify them for funding for the following fiscal year.[36] For the decertified states, there are sanctions, such as: 50% suspension of all US assistance for the current fiscal year; 100% suspension of all US assistance in the following fiscal year, unless the state is re-certified; and voting against loan applications from the multinational development banks and International Monetary Fund.[37] The state may also lose competitiveness in the US market because the US government would remove its trade preference from decertified countries.[38] A decertified state needs to improve its drug control performance without any support from the United States.[39]

The repercussions of decertification can be severe on the Andean states because they are poor. Peru and Colombia both struggled from decertification for two years in the 1990s. During the decertification period, the Colombian government decided to involve its military in drug control. This cost the government over US $100 million to purchase suitable equipment – high-performance utility helicopters – in order to secure US approval for its drug control policy.[40] Bolivia, which is the second poorest state in the western hemisphere and highly dependent on US support, feared decertification so much that co-operating with US drug control became its policy priority. For the Bolivia-US relationship, cocaine dominates the agenda and drug

---

33 Department of State Office of Press Secretary, *Fact Sheet: Andean Region Initiative*, 23 May 2002, http://www.state.gov/p/wha/rls/fs/8980.htm (16 May 2003).

34 Department of State Office of Press Secretary, *Fact Sheet: Andean Region Initiative*.

35 Carpenter, *Bad Neighbor Policy*, p. 21.

36 *The US Foreign Relations Authorization Act.*

37 Tammen, M.S., 'The Drug War vs. Land Reform in Peru', *Cato Policy Analysis*, No. 156, 10 July 1991, http://www.cato.org/pubs/pas/pa-156.html (20 May 2003); and Simons, P., *Briefing on the President's FY 2003 Narcotics Certification Determinations*, 31 January 2003, http://www.state.gov/g/inl/rls/rm/17110.htm (Accessed: 11 September 2003).

38 This will increase the import duty by 50%. Tammen, 'The Drug War vs. Land Reform in Peru'.

39 The United States has the largest quota in the International Monetary Fund, World Bank and other multinational banks, and thereby it is possible for it to oppose applications for funding and investments.

40 Gelbard, R.S., *U.S. Counternarcotics Policy Toward Colombia*, Statement to the House Committee on International relations, 11 September 1996, http://www.fas.org/irp/congress/1996_hr/h960911g.htm (Accessed 18 November 2000).

control efforts for the Bolivian government were almost a condition for receiving aid from the US.[41] As Lane *et al.* maintain, to co-operate with the US drug control is 'the only way [Bolivia] can get help in the problems that really concerns [it'].[42] To some extent, the United States has succeeded in securing co-operation from the Andes through setting these states the target of engagement with US drug control as a condition for its support in other spheres, such as trade and economics.

This has given the impression that the United States is imposing its policy on Andean states through coercion. The narcotics certification process for the United States is a means to make Andean states engage in its drug control operations. Regardless of their domestic situation, the Andean governments were pushed to prioritise US style drug control in their own policies in order to secure economic support from the United States.[43] The domestic instability provoked by the forced drug control operation caused Latin Americans to view the approach as a failure.

The failure of drug control is caused by the contradiction in supply reduction efforts and the condition of drug control for providing economic aid.[44] The halt and reduction of US aid due to poor drug control performance undermined the legal economy of Andean states. Some considered that sanctions against source countries should not be applied. Instead, the United States should provide the means to stabilise the economic situation in those states in order to ensure progress in drug control.[45] As a US government official remarked, however, the Andean Strategy was initiated to pursue US interests.[46] Therefore, the United States only approves policies that are considered to advance American interests. This is the reason why US drug control places more emphasis on law enforcement than development projects.

The Militarisation of Drug Control

Having examined the general principles and development of the Andean Strategy, the focus moves on to the militarisation of drug control operations. The militarisation of cocaine control began in the late-1980s. The introduction of armed forces into drug control operations generated caution amongst the Andean governments and influenced their relationship with the United States. In this section, two issues will be examined: firstly, the reasons why the United States decided to involve the military

41 Williams, J., *Waging the War on Drugs in Bolivia*, 20 February 1997, Washington DC: Washington Office on Latin America, p. 8.

42 Lane, C., Waller, D., Larmer, B., and Latel, P., 'The Newest War', *Newsweek*, 13 January 1992.

43 Schulz, D.E., *The United States and Latin America: Shaping an Elusive Future*, March 2000, http://www.carlisle.army.mil/ssi/pubs/2000/uslatin/uslatin.pdf (Accessed 16 May 2003), p. 39.

44 García Argañarás, F., 'The Drug War at the Supply End', *Latin American Perspectives*, Issue 96, Vol. 24, No. 5, September 1997, p. 77.

45 Perl, R.F., *88093: Drug Control: International Policy and Options Update*, 7 January 1997, Washington DC: Department of State.

46 Interview with an official at the US Department of State in Washington DC on 27 May 2003.

in its drug control operations; and secondly, the implications of the militarisation of the war on drugs on Andean-US relations.

The militarisation of the war on drugs was confirmed when George Bush stated in his presidential speech of 5 September 1989 that states fighting against drugs may be provided with military aid if they request it. By the late 1980s, violence in the Latin American cocaine trade escalated. Some Americans involved in drug control operations were killed and due to the hostile environment their operations could not progress satisfactorily.[47] Despite the risks associated with drug control, there was not much hope for protection from the host states, which were not adequately equipped to deal with drug traffickers and insurgency groups armed with sophisticated high-tech weaponry. This was partly because US law prohibited weapon sales to the countries that had strong criminal organisations and insurgency groups. For example, before the Andean Strategy was agreed, the United States amended its law so as not to sell military and high-tech equipment, such as radar, to Colombia out of fear of selling to the drug traffickers and insurgency groups.[48] Consequently, Colombia, which suffered severe attacks from the Medellín drug cartel, could not equip itself to fight or even protect its citizens from drug traffickers. Colombia found itself at a disadvantage in its violent confrontation.[49] The lack of adequate equipment, as a Colombian government source confirms, rendered the Colombian government unable to ensure the safety of its citizens and drug control projects. Carpenter claims that it was the frustration of the agencies involved that gave rise to the idea of using the military as a panacea for the war on drugs.[50]

Once the US government decided to include a military component in its foreign narcotics policy, it sent generous amounts of equipment to the states concerned. However, the way in which the US government provided the equipment was ineffective because it did not respect the needs of the recipients. For example, Colombia asked for equipment for its police and military and funding to establish a system to protect its judiciary. The United States dispatched US $65 million worth of military equipment that was not suitable for the Colombian police in 1989.[51] In such cases, according to a Colombian government official, the Colombian government did not have personnel with adequate knowledge to operate the equipment, and therefore the aid was not supporting drug control operations.[52]

---

47 For the details, see the section on eradication below.

48 Claudio, A., 'United States-Colombia Extradition Treaty: Failure of Security Strategy', *Military Review*, December 1991, p. 70.

49 Some officials express concerns on safety issues because of Columbia's insufficient ability to control the violent situation. Interview with K. Vogel at the European Commission on 23 April 2002, and a Colombian government official at the Colombian Embassy in Brussels on 10 July 2002.

50 Carpenter, *Bad Neighbor Policy*, p. 34.

51 Treaste, J.B., 'US Gives Wrong Equipment to Fight Drugs, Bogota Says', *New York Times*, 12 September 1989; GAO, *Drug Control: US Counternarcotic Efforts in Colombia Face Continuing Challenges*, Report to Congressional Requesters, GAO/NSIAD-98-60, February 1998, Washington DC: General Accounting Office, p. 4.

52 Interview with a Colombian government official at the Colombian Embassy in Brussels on 10 July 2002.

In order to maximise the benefits from these resources, the United States should have consulted with the Colombian government. According to Latin American official sources, the way the United States provides support to drug control in source countries depends more on US internal affairs than the needs of actual projects in Latin America.[53] For example, project budgets and equipment are approved and delivered in accordance with the US fiscal calendar without agreement from the host state. The Paz Zamora administration experienced having US Green Berets sent from the United States before the Bolivian Congress had approved their reception.[54] Even when the host and sponsor reached agreement on the contents of an aid package, the contents may be changed in accordance with US domestic circumstances. For instance, the type and numbers of helicopters received can be changed without notice because of lobbying and negotiation within the US government.[55] Such incidents may be caused by the lack of US respect for Andean states. As some US government sources admit, the US government takes the acceptance of host states for granted, and treats supply reduction projects in a similar manner to its domestic policies.[56]

The reluctance of Andean states' towards the US militarization of drug control stemmed from their concerns about the role of the military in their own countries. Having experienced frequent coup d'états in their history, Andean states are sensitive about the balance of civil-military control, and cautious about increasing the authority of the militaries. As Bagley claims, careless empowerment of the military for drug control could pose a risk to weak democratic constitutions in Latin America.[57] This is because military aid to the Andes can destroy the balance between civil and military control in the recipient states. Some Latin American states, particularly in the Andes, are surviving as democratic states but with a fragile balance of civil-military power. The US government, however, was willing to extend the authority of the US military and enable it to undertake the arrest of drug traffickers. For example, in order to capture and try Pablo Escobar in the United States, the US government authorised

---

53 Ibid., Interview with a Mexican government official at the Ministry of Foreign Affairs in Mexico City on 14 June 2003, and an official of the Organization of American States at its headquarters in Washington DC on 30 May 2003.

54 Washington Office for Latin America, *Going to the Source*, p. 3; Gamarra, E.A., 'US-Bolivia Counternarcotics Efforts During the Paz Zamora Administration: 1989-1992', in Bagley, B.M. and Walker III, W.O. (eds), *Drug Trafficking in the Americas*, 1996, Miami: North South Center Press, p. 229; WOLA, *Clear and Present Dangers: The US Military and the War on Drugs in the Andes*, 1991, Washington DC: WOLA, p. 71; 'US troops expelled', *International Herald Tribune*, 24 July 1992; and Shannon, 'Attacking the Source', p. 10.

55 The helicopters usually offered to the host state are Huey and Blackhawk, but the numbers of these helicopters can be changed after negotiations and discussions among the US politicians that are supported by the manufacturers.

56 Interviews with US government officials at the ONDCP in Washington DC on 28 May 2002.

57 Bagley, B.M., 'The Use of Armed Forces in Drug Interdiction: The Strategic Context', in Manwaring, M.G. (ed.), *Security and Civil-Military Relations in the New World Disorder: The Use of Armed Forces in the Americas*, September 1999, http://www.carlisle.army.mil/ssi/pubs/1999/newworld/newworld.pdf (16 May 2003), pp. 58–59.

the military to arrest him in Panama in 1989, despite the fact that US domestic law prohibits law enforcement by the military.[58]

Andean states were not supportive of the US plan. Colombia made it clear that foreign troops were not needed to solve its drug problems.[59] In Bolivia, citizens did not approve of the government decision to allow the US military to operate in their country, and protested by demonstration. The US pressure on the government 'left a feeling of bitterness, of weakness, of dependency that has been reflected in the press and in public opinion'.[60] However, the difference in economic and political power between the host and sponsor states, as Latin American officials agree, allows host states little room for negotiation.[61] A Colombian police general confirmed that the confrontation between the Andean states and the United States remained until the host governments accepted the US policy in order to secure the flow of US aid and trade benefits.[62] Due to their dependence on the US, according to a Mexican official source, the Latin American states are obliged to comply with US drug control operations, considering the repercussion of refusal on their economic and political situations.[63] Latin American scepticism about 'military aid' is rooted in their fear of US violation of their sovereignty. The Latin American governments are concerned that the United States may violate their sovereignty based on its interpretation of US national and international security interests.[64]

The problem of militarization of drug control was a concern not only to the host states but also to the US Department of Defence (DoD). The nature of drug control contradicts the role of the US military because, as Mabry points out, '[t]he US military is forbidden to enforce US civilian laws'.[65] This means that the US military does not have adequate authority to conduct drug control. Therefore, the US military's role in drug control is limited to: supporting other agencies by providing necessary equipment and assisting the host nations to build social infrastructure as

58 For the details, consult: Carpenter, *Bad Neighbor Policy*, p. 39.

59 Gusheko, J., 'Colombia Asks Help in Protecting Judges', *The Washington Post*, 30 August 1989.

60 'Sensación de debilidad', *Siglo 21*, March 1991.

61 Interviews with a Colombian government official at the Colombian Embassy in Brussels on 10 July 2002, and Mexican officials at the Mexican Embassy in Brussels on 23 January 2002, and Ministry of Foreign Affairs in Mexico City on 14 June 2003.

62 Interview with a police general of Colombia at the Colombian Embassy in London on 17 January 2002; and WOLA, *Going to the Source*, Section IV.

63 Mexico experienced coercive persuasion by the United States to co-operate in Operation Intercept (1969) and Operation Condor (1975). At that time, its high economic dependency and weak position limited Mexico's ability to negotiate with the US on these issues. Interview with a Mexican government official at the Ministry of Foreign Affairs in Mexico City on 14 June 2003.

64 Tokatlián, J.G., 'National Security and Drugs: Their Impact on Colombian-US Relations', *Journal of Interamerican Studies and World Affairs*, Vol. 30, No. 1, Spring 1988, p. 140.

65 Mabry, D.J., 'Andean Drug Trafficking and the Military Option', *Military Review*, March 1990.

a part of an alternative development programme.[66] New roles have permitted the expansion of some divisions of the military in the post-Cold War era, such as the US Southern Command (SouthCom) based in Panama.[67] In the mid-1990s, the DoD has adopted a non-active policy in drug control, except for some divisions, because of the limited roles the military could perform.[68] The withdrawal of the DoD from drug control was implicitly accepted by government officials. There was a recognition that 'the heart of the struggle [was] economic, not military' despite the increasing military assistance to the Andes.[69]

Another possible reason why the DoD decided to withdraw from drug control could be the ineffectiveness of military operations. Militarised drug control has generated scepticism about its cost effectiveness. From an economic perspective, the military was considered to be a poor option for narcotics control policy. An evaluation by a US think-tank, RAND, of the militarisation of drug control, maintains that the military would be an ineffective tool for drug control because the expense is too high.[70] Also, the DoD realised the difficulties in supporting drug control. As Ford reports in his testimony to the House of Representatives, the DoD's operation was undermined as a result of political dialogue between the United States and the Andean states.[71] This was caused by the host state's inability to operate and repair equipment provided by the United States, and limited information sharing with the host states. The supply of parts and goods required for maintaining operations was refused by the US government because the host state did not meet the conditions and requirements for receiving aid.[72] Disruption was caused by political interference,

---

66 Ford, J.T., *Drug Control: DoD Allocates Fewer Assets to Drug Control Efforts*, Testimony before the Subcommittee on Criminal Justice, Drug Control and Human Resources, Committee on Government Reform, House of Representatives, 27 January 2000, GAO/T-NSIAD-00-77; Wilson, G.C., 'Cheney Pledges Wider War on Drugs', *The Washington Post*, 19 September 1989; and Sheridan, B.E., 'DoD's Restructured Counterdrug Policy', *Defense Issues*, Vol. 9, No. 21, 1994.

67 The increased significance of SouthCom in Latin America can be traced to its sharply increased budget from US$ 230 million in fiscal year 1990 to over US$ 430 million in fiscal year 1991. Matthews, W., 'Special Report: U.S. Southern Command', *Army Times*, No. 52, Vol. 13, p. 16; and WOLA, *Going to the Source*, Section II.

68 Following this change of policy, the DoD reduced the budget it spent on drug control operations by 24% between 1993 and 1999, and some agencies, such as US Southern Command, received only 43% of the requested funding for operations. Ford, *Drug Control: DoD Allocates Fewer Assets to Drug Control Efforts.*

69 Isikoff, M., 'DEA in Bolivia: Guerrilla Warfare', *The Washington Post*, 16 January 1989.

70 Reuter, P., *et al.*, *Sealing the Borders: The Effect of Increased Military Participation in Drug Interdiction*, RAND Report, R-3594-USDP, January 1988, Santa Monica, CA: RAND Corporation.

71 Ford, *Drug Control: DoD Allocates Fewer Assets to Drug Control Efforts*, pp. 12–13; and Pitts, P., 'Fighting Drugs at the Source', *Proceedings*, July 1994, p. 55.

72 Ibid.

and there was tension between the military involved in drug control at the frontline and the political officials back in the US.[73]

Despite the restriction over US military operation, the Andean governments are concerned about strengthening their militaries. This fear stemmed from the fact that, as US government officials confirmed, US troops require co-operation from counterparts in the host state.[74] In addition, the US government used it as an opportunity to test new equipment and personnel.[75] This could empower the military in the Andean states and, as feared by Latin American governments, could jeopardise democracy and civilian control.[76] However, as Carpenter observes, Americans have fewer concerns about the use of the military in the international war on drugs and this explains why the government was in favour of the military operations in the Andes.[77]

The Three-Prong Strategy to Fight Cocaine Trafficking

Although US drug control is often associated with the use of the military, it is portrayed as a 'three-prong strategy' combining three programmes: eradication, interdiction and alternative development.[78] The Andean Strategy is a multi-agency operation executed through loosely inter-connected agency networks, based on the idea of 'one team, one fight'.[79] This represents the idea that agencies with various expertise working together will more effectively tackle cocaine trafficking. Within the three-prong strategy, eradication and interdiction are aimed directly at the cocaine industry by eradicating coca fields and intercepting cocaine en-route to the United States. Alternative development programmes are aimed at providing alternative economic means for coca farmers in order to prevent them from cultivating coca bushes. As US government sources confirm the chief focus is on eradication and interdiction compared to alternative development, because the US emphasis is on halting cocaine supply to its homeland.[80]

In this part of the analysis, the implication of the three-prong strategy for the Andean states and the relationship between the Andes and the United States will be examined. This strategy is the backbone of US drug control in the Andes. Firstly, the

---

73 Interviews with officials of the Coast Guard and the DEA at the ONDCP in Washington DC on 28 May 2003.

74 Interviews with government officials at the ONDCP in Washington DC on 28 May 2003.

75 Carpenter, T.G., and Channing Rouse, R., 'Perilous Panacea: The Military in the Drug War', *Cato Policy Analysis* No. 128, 15 February 1990, http://www.cato.org/pubs.pas.pa128.html (20 May 2003).

76 Mabry, 'Andean Drug Trafficking and the Military Option'.

77 Carpenter, *et al.*, 'Perilous Panacea'.

78 The US has been supporting alternative development in the Andes for two decades, and interdiction and eradication for nearly three decades.

79 Schneider, A., and Copeland, P., 'With little fanfare, US goes to war', *The Washington Times*, 5 July 1992.

80 Interviews with officials at the ONDCP, the Department of State, and the USAID between 27–29 May 2003 in Washington DC.

eradication programme to destroy coca fields will be examined. Coca eradication aims to eliminate the raw material of cocaine in producer states. Secondly, the interdiction programme to intercept cocaine before it reaches the United States will be investigated. This programme targets activities of drug trafficking organisations directly, and tries to seize cocaine shipments. Both of these programmes involve military operations. Thirdly, the alternative development programme will be examined. This is a programme to support economic and social development of the community by encouraging cultivation of legal crops as substitutes for coca and the construction of social infrastructures. Alternative development is supportive of the other two programmes.

Eradication

The US government regarded eradication of coca fields as the most effective way to weaken the cocaine industry because cocaine could not be produced without coca leaves. The eradication programme in the 1980s, however, did not have the expected impact on the cocaine supply chain, and the policy appeared to be a failure.[81] The US effort to destroy coca fields continues to the present day with the introduction of new approaches and techniques, such as aerial fumigation. The size of coca fields eliminated in one operation, according to a government official, has increased as a consequence of the changes.[82] This section will examine the impact of the eradication programme in the Andes. The eradication programme has the widest impact among the three programmes in drug control policy because the eradication of coca fields affects the farmers' livelihoods, and has significant repercussions for the host states.

This section looks at three types of eradication programmes: manual eradication, aerial eradication and voluntary eradication. Manual and aerial eradication programmes are part of the law enforcement project with the military. These operations can be a cause of discord between the United States and the host country. Early on, manual eradication was the standard operation in the Andes because of the terrain where the coca fields were located. In the 1990s, however, eradicating coca fields by aerial fumigation of chemicals became the norm, due to the need to avoid the risk of sending agents on the ground into areas protected by armed traffickers and insurgency groups. Voluntary eradication was part of the alternative development programme. It was promoted by the Bolivian government to avoid conflicts with farmers and reduce illicit coca production peacefully, but it was funded by the United States. In some cases, eradication and alternative development can be two sides of the same coin.

Manual and Aerial Eradication   Eradication projects performed as part of law enforcement are, sometimes, described as an 'aggressive' approach because of the impact and the manner in which they are carried out. Also, the militarisation of operations, when it is not favoured by the host state, is regarded as a necessary

81 ONDCP, *National Drug Control Strategy 2003*, 2003, Washington DC: GPO.
82 Interview with an official at the ONDCP in Washington DC on 28 May 2003.

protective means for personnel working for coca eradication. This comes from the nature of the operation. The US and host governments both agree that military equipment is essential for personnel vulnerable to the attacks by those who are protecting the coca growing sites.

Manual eradication of coca fields is not a favoured option because it is labour intensive and dangerous. According to a US government source, manual eradication is an expensive operation because it requires large numbers of personnel in coca fields (or small groups working long term) and there is a high possibility of attacks by drug traffickers.[83] Through manual eradication, only a few hundreds hectares a month can be destroyed at best. However, there are places that can only be targeted by manual eradication.

The Upper Huallaga Valley in Peru, for instance, is too steep to take planes for fumigation, and therefore manual eradication is the only option. The risk of performing the operation in the area was high because of the presence of both drug traffickers and guerrilla groups, who could be acting in unison.[84] During the first half of 1988, 32 eradication workers and 6 development officials were killed by the guerrillas and the drug traffickers.[85] Despite the danger, the US government was determined to fight against coca cultivation in the Upper Huallaga Valley.

The US government continuously invested in the eradication programme in Peru. Under the Bush administration in the early 1990s, *Coca Eradication in the Upper Huallaga Valley* (CORAH) was allocated $16.9 million for the manual eradication of coca fields.[86] The results of the project were uncertain in terms of hectares of coca fields eradicated and its impact on the Andean cocaine industry.[87] A US State Department Report released in March 1990 indicated that cultivation of coca in Peru was stable, and that there had been an increase in the total Andean coca production in comparison with the previous year.[88] The US government believed that there were direct and indirect returns from those operations, and kept funding drug control operations in Peru.[89]

Eradication by the aerial spraying of chemicals can wipe out large numbers of coca fields in one operation. Fumigation, as both Colombian and US officials agree, is the most effective means for the governments to eradicate large numbers of coca fields with the minimum danger to personnel.[90] The United States enabled

83 Interview with an official on the Colombian issue at the ONDCP in Washington DC on 28 May 2003.

84 See Latin American cocaine trafficking in Introduction.

85 Smith, M., 'Peru Calls for US to Join Tougher Anti-Coca Effort', *The Washington Post*, 5 August 1988.

86 This project also included demolishing clandestine airstrips used by drug traffickers.

87 GAO, *Drug Control: US Antidrug Efforts in Peru's Upper Huallaga Valley*, December 1994, GAO/NSIAD-95-11, Washington DC: US Government Accounting Office, p. 5.

88 Sciolino, E., 'World Drug Crop Up Sharply in 1989 Despite US Effort', *The New York Times*, 2 March 1990.

89 GAO, *Drug Control: US Antidrug Efforts in Peru's Upper Huallaga Valley*, p. 5.

90 Interviews with officials at the Colombian Embassy in Brussels on 10 July 2002, at the Mexican Ministry of Foreign Affairs in Mexico City on 14 June 2003, and at the ONDCP in Washington DC on 28 May 2003.

the Andean states to operate aerial spraying by providing the necessary equipment, such as helicopters and chemicals, and to increase the number of operations.[91] Nevertheless, it is an expensive operation because of the equipment required and the cost of maintenance. According to Colombian and US sources, fumigation is not an affordable operation for Colombia without US funding and the supply of equipment.[92] All the parts for repairing helicopters and fuel to fly needs to be brought from the United States, and daily operations with helicopters is too costly for the Colombian government.

This expensive and massive eradication operation still does not assure the decline of coca production in the Andes. Aerial spraying increased the number of eradicated coca fields, but total cultivation in the Andes remained stable until 2002. The reasons for this could be a *balloon effect* and the failure of converting farmers from coca cultivation to legal crop cultivation. The balloon effect is a phenomenon by which the crop cultivation moves from one place to the other, due to drug control operations. The traffickers try to avoid eradication, and change the location of their cocoa fields to remote areas and neighbouring countries. Consequently, successful eradication projects in Bolivia and Peru in the late 1990s pushed coca cultivation into Colombia. According to US agencies, statistics showed that coca cultivation in Bolivia and Peru was declining steadily until 2001, but in Colombia it was increasing steadily to maintain the total coca cultivation in the region.[93] Then, in 2000, Colombia launched a large-scale drug control programme[94] designed to reduce coca fields by 15% through intensive operations.[95] The coca production, however, has already increased in Bolivia and Peru by 23% and 8% respectively.[96] Although this setback was expected, from past experience, maintaining the decrease of the total coca production in the Andes is a serious challenge to US drug control.

91 For the details on fumigation, see the case of Colombia in chapter 6.

92 Interviews with officials at the Colombian Embassy in Brussels on 10 July 2002, and at the ONDCP in Washington DC on 28 May 2003.

93 In the Chapare, the Bolivian government reduced illicit coca fields from 33,900 hectares to 5,400 hectares by June 2001. The US government expressed its approval of the Peruvian coca eradication efforts, which have continuously reduced coca production in the state by more than 20% every year since 1998. Between 1996 and 1998, on the other hand, Colombia's coca cultivation increased steadily from 67,200 hectares to 101,800 hectares. Rubin, J.P., *Peru's Coca Reduction Efforts*, US Department of State Office of the Spokesman Press Statement, 12 January 2000, http://secretary.state.gov/www/briefings/statements/2000/ps0001126.html (Accessed 14 June 2000); GAO, *Drug Control: Narcotics Threat From Colombia Continues to Grow*, Report to Congressional Requesters, GAO/NSIAD-99-136, June 1999, Washington DC: GAO, p. 17.

94 It is called Plan Colombia, and for the details, see chapter 6.

95 ONDCP, *2002 Annual Assessment of Cocaine Movement*, March 2003, ONDCP-03-01, Washington DC: ONDCP; DEA, *Drug Intelligence Brief: Changing Dynamics of Cocaine Production in the Andean Region*, June 2002, http://www.usdoj.gov/dea/pubs/omte;/02033/02033p.html (Accessed 16 May 2003); and ONDCP, *Major Narcotics Producing Nations: Cultivation and Production Estimates 1998-2002*, 2003, Washington DC: ONDCP.

96 ONDCP, *2002 Annual Assessment of Cocaine Movement*; DEA, *Drug Intelligence Brief*; and ONDCP, *Major Narcotics Producing Nations*.

One of the efforts aimed at preventing coca farmers from re-cultivating coca is an alternative development programme. As a USAID official confirms, the eradication programme is carried out with the backup of alternative development programmes to seize the situation after eradication and to lead the target areas to legal crop cultivation.[97] However, the official claims that the speed of destroying coca fields by fumigation is so fast that alternative development programmes cannot reach their target, and some places are left without any alternative means for living. Furthermore, the damage to soil caused by chemicals prevents alternative crop cultivation because the chemical that killed coca also kills legal crops.[98]

A drawback of aerial spraying is damage caused to the environment by the chemicals. The Andean states were concerned about the impact of aerial spraying on the natural environment, livestock and human beings, and refused to carry out eradication in such a manner throughout the 1980s.[99] Not only were the Andean states concerned about the impact of spraying herbicides, but the manufacturers of the chemical were also concerned. The manufacturers of herbicides tebuthiuron (called *Spike* and *Spike 20P*) refused to sell the product for aerial spraying because the chemical 'may also be dangerous to agricultural crops, wildlife, fish, and even humans'.[100] The products were not meant for direct contact with humans or for spraying wide areas indiscriminately. Although the US government assured the safety of chemical use for fumigation, scepticism and suspicion remained strong among concerned parties.

Nevertheless, the Andean states accepted US-led eradication projects because of their dependency on the United States. Opposing eradication has not been an option.[101] According to Colombian and Mexican government sources, Bolivia's high dependency on foreign aid makes it more vulnerable than other Andean states in relations with the United States because the United States is not only influential in the bilateral relationship but also in international organisations, such as the International Monetary Fund.[102] The Bolivian government has, under such conditions, been accepting US drug control operations in order to secure economic

97 Interview with an official at the USAID in Washington DC on 27 May 2003.

98 Ibid., and Interviews with officials at the European Commission in Brussels on 10 July 2002.

99 Fellon, M. 'Bush Turns to Military Aid to Stanch Narcotics Flow', *Congressional Quarterly Weekly Report*, 9 September 1989.

100 Lee III, R.W., 'Why the US Cannot Stop South American Cocaine', *Orbis*, Vol. 32, No. 4, Fall 1988, p. 514; and Blueston, K., and Blickman, T., 'Lessons to Learn', *The World Today*, Vol. 54, No. 6, June 1998, http://www.lindesmith.org/news/news.html (Accessed 5 November 1999).

101 See Introduction for the details; and Liddy, G., *Will: The Autobiography of G. Gordon Liddy*, 1980, New York: St Martin's Press, p. 135.

102 The IMF grants aid through voting, and the US can prevent it by voting against the proposal. Interviews with officials at the Colombian Embassy in Brussels on 10 July 2002, and at the Mexican Ministry of Foreign Affairs in Mexico City on 14 June 2003; 'US Pressure forces minister to quit', *Latin American Andean Group Report*, 4 April 2000, p. 7.

aid.[103] The first militarised eradication operation was Operation *Blast Furnace* in 1986, and subsequently Operation *Snowcap* in 1988.[104] The Bolivian government was concerned that military involvement in drug control could provoke the local population unnecessarily and risk disputes.[105] Operation *Blast Furnace* caused fierce opposition from the coca Union in the region and after 4 months, the military forces were sent back to the United States.[106] For Operation *Snowcap*, the Bolivian government could not publicise the operation because the atmosphere in the Chapare would have been too hostile.[107] Although the Bolivian government successfully eradicated 80% of the illicit coca bushes from the Chapare, it caused massive social disruption and endangered the Bolivian democratic political system.[108]

Not only in Bolivia, but also in other Andean coca producing states, eradication made farmers hostile to the government and its operations, and led to support for guerrilla groups and drug trafficking organisations.[109] Some farmers had their legal crops eradicated by aerial spraying, and coca growers were furious because their fields were damaged. In addition, they frequently encountered harassment by the military and armed drug law enforcement agents.[110] Militarised and rapid eradication of coca fields provoked those who were engaged in the cocaine industry and led to social protests.

In Bolivia, the 'Néstor Paz Zamora' insurgency movement emerged in 1990, in Chaparé, as a reaction to the US-led drug control and military presence in the country. There are frequent disputes in the Chaparé and Yungas, the major coca producing areas, over coca eradication between coca farmers and the Special Rural Mobile Force (UMOPAR) that is in charge of executing coca eradication and law enforcement.[111] The farmers were seeking to protect their coca fields as well as themselves from harassment by the UMOPAR. As American style drug control continued, the opposition grew stronger.[112] Since the end of Bolivia's largest drug

103 *La Paz 4839 Cable Text* for the meeting between the Bolivian President Jorge Quiroga and the US President George W. Bush during Quiroga's visit to the United States, Meeting on 6 December 2002, FOIA 200201357, http://jeremybigwood.net/FOIAs/US2Tuto/images/US-Tuto-1.jpg (Accessed 4 July 2003), pp. 3–7.

104 Both of them are eradication project in Chapare involving the military.

105 Youngers, C., 'A Fundamentally Flawed Strategy: The US 'War on Drugs' in Bolivia', *Issue in International Drug Policy*, Issue Brief #4, 18 September 1991, Washington DC: Washington Office on Latin America, p. 9.

106 Carpenter, *et al.*, 'Perilous Panacea: The Military in the Drug War'.

107 The operation was conducted by about 100 DEA and UMOPAR of Bolivia trained by the DEA for counter-narcotics operations. Isikoff, 'DEA in Bolivia: Guerrilla Warfare'; and Shannon, 'Attacking the Source', p. 20.

108 *La Paz 4839 Cable Text*, pp. 3–7.

109 Reuter, P., 'The Limits and Consequences of US Foreign Drug Control Efforts', *The Annals*, No. 521, May 1992, p. 162.

110 Coffin, P., 'Coca Eradication', *Foreign Policy in Focus*, Vol. 3, No. 29, October 1998, http://www.lindesmith.org/news/news.html (Accessed 5 November 1999).

111 Youngers, 'A Fundamentally Flawed Strategy', p. 9.

112 This was partly because of the violation of human rights by the UMOPAR. The UMOPAR has been reported for rape, tortures, and violent attacks against the civilian population. Spedding, A.L., 'Cocataki, Taki-Coca: Trade, Traffick, and Organized Peasant

control programme, *Plan Dignity* in 2000, there have been continuous demonstrations and road blockades against coca eradication and the government came close to declaring a state of martial law.[113]

In Peru and Colombia, the focus of criticism was on the involvement of the US military in drug control operations. Insurgency groups were using 'Yankee imperialism' to justify their anti-regime movements, claiming that this was a form of US control over their countries.[114] The Peruvian government was aware that eradication and interdiction programmes worked to 'strengthen cooperation between the coca growers and the communist guerrillas'. Peru, however, needed to accept American style drug control because of the Anti-Drug Abuse Act of 1986 and 1988, which makes economic aid conditional on drug control performance.[115] After refusing military assistance offered by the United States, Peru suffered from a lack of funding for economic and security affairs. By the mid-1990s, drug control in Peru and Colombia faced difficulties managing effective operations due to the activities of the guerrilla groups enriched by the cocaine trade.[116]

Voluntary Eradication Not all eradication programmes are coercive. In order to avoid confrontation with the coca farmers caused by coercive eradication, the Bolivian government launched a programme of cash compensation for eradicating coca fields. Between 1987 and 1998, the Bolivian National Directorate for Agricultural Reconversion paid $2,000 per hectare to coca growers who voluntarily eradicated their coca fields. The expenditure for the programme reached approximately US $100 million.[117] During this period, most funds given to the Bolivian government by the United States were spent on this project. It was successful in the sense that many farmers participated, and it did not lead to confrontation between the government

---

Resistance in the Yungas of La Paz', in Léons, M.B., and Sanabria, H. (eds), *Coca, Cocaine and the Bolivian Reality*, 1997, New York: State University of New York Press, p. 122; Farthing, L., 'Social Impacts Associated with Antidrug Law 1008', in Léons, M.B., and Sanabria, H. (eds), *Coca, Cocaine and the Bolivian Reality*, 1997, New York: State University of New York Press, p. 264; Menzel, S.H., *Fire in the Andes: US Foreign Policy and Cocaine Politics in Bolivia and Peru*, 1996, New York: University Press of America, p. 33; Human Rights Watch, *Bolivia Under Pressure: Human Rights Violation and Coca Eradication*, Vol. 8, No. 4, 1996, http://www.hrw.org/hrw/summaries/s.bolivia965.html (Accessed 25 April 1999).

113 Associated Press, 'Farmers block key road in Bolivia to protest eradication of coca', *CNN*, 17 April 2000, http://www.cnn.com/2000/WORLD/americas/04/17/bolivia.protests.ap/index.html (Accessed 17 April 2000).

114 Youngers, C., 'The War in the Andes: The Military Role in US International Drug Policy', *Issues in International Drug Policy*, Issue Brief #2, 14 December 1990, Washington DC: Washington Office on Latin America, p. 3.

115 Tammen, 'The Drug War vs. Land Reform in Peru'.

116 Hinton, Jr., H.L., *Drug Control: Observation on US Counternarcotics Activities*, Testimony before the Subcommittee on Western Hemisphere, Peace Corps, Narcotics, and Terrorism, Committee on Foreign Relations; and the Caucus on International Narcotics Control, US Senate, 16 September 1998, GAO/T-NSIAD-98-249, Washington DC: GAO, p. 7.

117 GAO, *Drug Control: Efforts to Develop Alternatives to Cultivating Illicit Crops in Colombia Have Made Little Progress and Face Serious Obstacles*, GAO-02-291, February 2002, Washington DC: US General Accounting Office, p. 23.

and farmers. However, according to a US government source, it did not reduce the number of coca fields.[118]

A 1987 State Department progress report from the Bureau for International Narcotics Matters states: 'Optimism about the future must be tempered by the reality that has actually occurred in Bolivia since 1980. 'Voluntary' campaigns ... have not worked. Far from reducing total hectares, Bolivia's coca cultivation expand[ed] during 1986 by at least 10%.'[119] This is because the farmers that participated in the voluntary eradication programme replanted coca bushes in other fields, often in more remote areas, or in land owned by different family members.[120] The expenditure and numbers of fields eradicated increased but there was no reduction in the total production of coca. Furthermore, farmers planted coca bushes in order to ask for compensation to eradicate them. Coca farmers diversified their business by adopting alternative crops, but they continued to grow coca. This is because it is the way farmers minimise risk in production. The legal crops have uncertain success, especially at the outset of change, so the farmers would not wish to eradicate their most reliable cash crop, coca, immediately.[121]

In sum, all three measures of eradicating coca did not reduce cocaine production. Hence, the eradication policy that did not reduce coca cultivation, even after three decades, was regarded as a failed policy.[122] Rabasa and Chalk register their scepticism about fumigation efforts by the United States by questioning its ineffectiveness and whether it is linked to workable alternative development programmes to prevent re-cultivation of coca in different places.[123] Some farmers claim that they would be more willing to co-operate and eradicate coca bushes with the gradual reduction and competitive prices of legal crops introduced as an alternative. Herbicides only push farmers to militancy or to support for guerrilla groups.[124] The problem lies in the fact that farmers are not willing to eradicate coca until alternative development proves to be a secure means to another income.[125] Aerial spraying tends to be indiscriminate in

---

118 Interview with an official at the US Department of State in Washington DC on 27 May 2003.

119 Kline, D., 'How to Lose the Coke War', *Atlantic Monthly*, May 1987, p. 27.

120 Interview with an official at the US Department of State in Washington DC on 27 May 2003.

121 Interview with an official of the CICAD/OAS in Washington DC, 29 May 2003; and Franco, A.A., *Testimony* before the House Appropriations Committee on Foreign Operations US Assistance to Colombia and the Andean Region, 10 April 2002, http://www.state.gov/press/spe_test/testimony/2002/ty020410.html (Accessed 20 May 2003).

122 Bullington, B., 'All About Eve: The Many Faces of United States Drug Policy', in Pearce, F., and Woodiwiss, M. (eds), *Global Crime Connections*, 1993, London: Macmillan, p. 42.

123 Rabasa, A., and Chalk, P., *Colombian Labyrinth*, 2001, Pittsburgh: RAND, pp. 94–95.

124 Weisman, A., 'The Cocaine Conundrum', *Los Angeles Times Magazine*, 24 September 1995, http://www.worldcom.nl/tni/drugs/links/lt950924.htm (Accessed 24 July 1998).

125 'Growers dismayed by 5-year strategy', *Latin American Regional Group - Andean Group*, 27 January 1998, pp. 2–3; and 'Bánzer sets record eradication target', *Latin American Weekly Report*, 1 June 1999.

spraying herbicide over the legal crops.[126] This happens because the planes cannot fly low enough to be precise, due to fear of being shot down by the traffickers and guerrillas. In some areas, the alternative crops were planted side by side with coca bushes.[127] The success of alternative crops is sometimes endangered by eradication programmes.[128]

Interdiction

The interdiction programme directly targets drug trafficking organisations and their activities by breaking the lines of the cocaine supply chain and dismantling production. The main focus of this programme is to seize cocaine before it comes into the United States, and remove the traffickers from cocaine trafficking.[129] The programme contains various operations, such as the interception of coca products and cocaine, and the capture and extradition of drug traffickers. Interdiction is the preferred policy of the Andean states, over eradication. The drug trafficking organisations are a nuisance in source countries, but tackling cocaine cartels by themselves is a difficult task to accomplish because of the economic and political influence drug trafficking organisations possess. By the mid-1980s, the Andean states were suffering from the growing political and financial power of the drug trafficking organisations.[130]

In this section, US efforts to crack down on cocaine trafficking in the Andes will be investigated. Firstly, the operations to crack down on cocaine trafficking organisations by the Drug Enforcement Administration (DEA) will be examined. Secondly, a programme known as *Air Bridge Denial*, to shoot down cocaine carriers in order to disrupt transportation, will be assessed. US co-operation and support for interdiction programmes are essential for the Andean states to succeed in tackling cocaine trafficking organisations in their territories. As a Colombian government source confirms, US aid is vital to carry out and maintain operations because the Andean states lack technology and knowledge to fight against drug trafficking organisations by themselves.[131]

Cracking Down on Cocaine Cartels   The DEA has two missions in Latin America: to dismantle cocaine trafficking organisations, and to support the development of

---

126 USAID, *Evaluation of Alternative Development Strategy in the Andes and Bolivia Program Challenge*, USAID-INL Briefings, 17 January 2003, PowerPoint Document, obtained during an interview at USAID on 27 May 2003.

127 Interviews with officials at the Department of States and the ONDCP in Washington DC on 27–28 May 2003.

128 See section below for the details.

129 The White House, *National Drug Control Strategy 2003*, February 2003, Washington DC: Government Printing Office, p. 32.

130 For details, see chapter 2.

131 Interview with a police general at the Colombian Embassy in London on 29 January 2002.

their Latin American law enforcement organisations.[132] The operations of the DEA outside the United States have unique features.[133] Officially, the DEA supports the operations of the host states and offers advanced techniques and expertise to capture or demolish drug trafficking organisations. Furthermore, DEA involvement in the Andes can only be executed by joint operations with their counterparts in the host state. During the operation, DEA personnel reside, and work closely with the local police and within the legal system of the host state.[134]

In order to crack down on Latin American cocaine trafficking, the DEA has used the Consolidated Priority Organisation Target (CPOT) list and *Priority Strategy* (previously known as the *Kingpin Strategy*) since the early 1990s.[135] This policy aims to target those who are regarded as 'the most influential traffickers' and organisations in the cocaine trade, and seeks to weaken the cocaine supply networks by removing them from the chain. This strategy has been the 'DEA's top priority and its primary enforcement approach for addressing the national priority of reducing the availability of illegal drugs in the United States'.[136]

In respect of the assistance to the Latin American anti-drug law enforcement agencies, the roles of the DEA are to support and train local police for law enforcement operations. The priorities of DEA operations since the late 1990s are to teach expertise on drug-related investigations and to crack down on trafficking organisations.[137] The DEA offers intelligence for investigations and analysis of the seizures in order to support and plan future operations with other law enforcement agencies.[138] The DEA shares information and expertise with its counterparts in the Andes, such as the Special Investigation Unit (SIU) of the Colombian National Police (CNP).[139]

---

132 'Text: DEA's Marshall Testifies on Law Enforcement Aspects of Plan Colombia', *Washington File*, 20 February 2001, http://usinfo.state.gov/regional/ar/colombia/plan28c.htm (Accessed 18 January 2005).

133 Interview at the ONDCP with Envoy from the Drug Enforcement Administration on 28 May 2003.

134 DEA personnel in host states are not always received well. This is because the community was sceptical about US drug control operations, and in the past, the DEA personnel were not covered by the local legal system. For example, the DEA officers in Mexico carried guns under US regulations rather than following Mexican gun regulations. Interview with Mexican Foreign Ministry official on 14 June 2003 in Mexico City.

135 The list is created by the agencies involved in law enforcement: the DEA, the FBI, the Multiagency Special Operation Division, and the Department of Justice. The White House, *National Drug Control Strategy 2003*, pp. 28–29; also see The White House, *National Drug Control Strategy 2002*, February 2002, Washington DC: Government Printing Office.

136 GAO, *Drug Control: DEA's Strategies and Operations in the 1990s*, GAO/GGD-99-108, July 1999, Washington DC: US General Accounting Office, p. 48.

137 Interview at the ONDCP with the Envoy from the Drug Enforcement Administration on 28 May 2003.

138 Ibid.

139 Marshall, D., *DEA Congressional Testimony* before the Subcommittee on National Security, International Affairs and Criminal Justice, 9 July 1997, http://www.usdoj/dea/pubs/cngrtest/ct970709.htm (Accessed 29 October 1999).

These forms of assistance and training reflect the US aim of expanding the capacity and ability of law enforcement institutions in the Andean states to ensure the control of cocaine at the supply end. One of the agencies receiving such training and support is the Special Drug Police Force (EFLN) of Bolivia. The EFLN has expanded its size and capacity in law enforcement and established specialised operational units,[140] thereby enabling joint operations between Bolivia and the United States.

Since the mid-1990s, EFLN, with support of the DEA and the DoD, conducted complex investigations to dismantle major cocaine trafficking organisations, resulting in the arrest of key traffickers, the destruction of drug processing laboratories and seizures of cocaine.[141] The increased access to information on the business transactions of cocaine cartels through international co-operation enabled the Bolivian police to successfully halt several cocaine shipments. In September 1995, the joint investigation by Bolivian authorities and the DEA involving an aircraft carrying about 5 tonnes of cocaine from Peru revealed that Bolivian police and airport personnel were involved in the cocaine trade. This finding led to the reform of the EFLN.[142] On another occasion, the EFLN seized 5 tonnes of cocaine, destined for Spain, in Santa Cruz acting on the information provided by the DEA and Spanish Police.[143]

Regarding operations conducted with the Colombian authorities, the DEA have arrested major drug traffickers and supported intelligence sharing mechanisms with Colombia. Operation *Selva Verde* was carried out by bi-lateral co-operation between the CNP and the DEA.[144] The aims of the operation were to locate and destroy clandestine laboratories, airstrips and storage sites of the Cali cartel; and to form a strong narcotics intelligence and operational alliance between the DEA and the Colombian government.[145] The DEA assisted with intelligence analysis and identified cocaine-processing facilities, rather than actively leading the operation. Through this

140 US Department of State, *International Narcotics Control Strategy 2002*, March 2003, http://www.state.gov/g/inl/rls/nrcrpt/2002/html/17944.htm (Accessed 14 August 2003).

141 Constantine, T.A., *DEA Congressional Testimony* before the Subcommittee on Western Hemisphere House International Relations Committee, 7 March 1996, http://www. druglibrary.org/schaffer/dea/pubs/cngrtest/ct960307.htm (Accessed 14 April 2000).

142 US Department of State, *International Narcotics Control Strategy Report 1995*, March 1996, http://www.hri.org/docs/USSD-INCSR/95/OtherUSG/DEA.html (Accessed 15 August 2003).

143 'Bolivia Seizes 2 Tons of Cocaine Meant for Spain', *Reuters*, 2 August 2003, http:// www.washingtonpost.com/wp-dyn/articles/A13626-2003Aug1.html (Accessed 4 August 2003); 'Bolivian Police Seize 2 Tons of Cocaine', *Associated Press*, 1 August 2003, http:// www.washingtonpost.com/wp-dyn/articles/A13626-2003Aug1.html (Accessed 4 August 2003); and 'Bolivia seizes 5 Tons of Cocaine in Record Bust', *Reuters*, 3 August 2003, http:// www.washingtonpost.com/wp-dyn/articles/A16638-2003Aug3.html (Accessed 4 August 2003).

144 ONDCP, *The National Drug Control Strategy 1997*, http://www.ncjrs.org/htm/dea. htm (Accessed 15 August 2003).

145 GlobalSecurity.org, *Operation Selva Verde*, http://www.globalsecurity.org/military/ tps/selva_verde.htm (Accessed 18 January 2005).

operation, Colombia's Information Analysis and Operation Centre for drug control increased its ability to share intelligence and act as an analysis institution.[146]

Operation *Millennium* commenced in 1999 targeting one of the cocaine trafficking groups of Medellín, and its associates in Mexico and the United States. This international operation tackled several multinational drug trafficking organisations operating in Colombia and Mexico with the co-operation of various agencies in Colombia, Mexico and the United States, such as the CNP, the Colombian Prosecutor General's Office, the DEA, the US Attorney's Office, and the Department of Justice Criminal Division.[147] The consequence of phase one was the arrest of influential cocaine traffickers in Colombia and Mexico.[148] Among the arrests, there was Alejandro Bernal Madrigal, the head of a cocaine trafficking organisation and an influential figure in Medellín since the later 1990s.[149] The US sought for extradition of captured traffickers to try them in a US court under the extradition treaty with Colombia. The trial of key cocaine traffickers in Latin America has been one of the main tools to dismantle cocaine trafficking organisations. Therefore, Colombia's co-operation to extradite these two traffickers was regarded as 'evidence of the Colombian government's commitment' to drug control.[150]

Continuous operations to prevent cocaine trafficking and tackle drug trafficking organisations have not made a dramatic change in the cocaine industry, but some differences have been made by interdiction. In Bolivia, drug trafficking organisations were so weakened that they have not been the main concern of the Bolivian government since the mid-1990s. Also in Colombia, the organisation of the cocaine trade has changed due to a series of successful operations to wipe out two major cartels. The crackdown on the Cali and Medellín cartels in the mid-1990s brought a

---

146 Washington Office on Latin America, *Drug, Democracy and Human Rights: US Law Enforcement Overview 2002: Colombia*, http://www.wola.org/publications/ddhr_law_enforcement_overview_colombia.htm (Accessed 18 January 2005).

147 The operation resulted in the arrest of one of the remaining leaders of the Medellín cartel, Fabio Ochoa-Vasquez, and large amounts of cocaine. Ledwith, W.E., *DEA Testimony* before the House Government Reform Committee, Subcommittee on Criminal Justice, Drug Policy and Human Resources, 15 February 2000, http://www.usdoj.gov/dea/pubs/cngrtest/ct021500.htm (Accessed 14 August 2003).

148 La Procuraduría General de la República, *Boletín*, No. 333/99, 15 October 1999, http://wwwpgr.gob.mx/cmsocial/bol99/oct/b0033399.htm (Accessed 18 January 2005); 'Text: U.S. and Colombia Authorities Deal Major Blow to Drug Traffickers', *Washington File*, 13 October 1999, http://www.fas.org/irp/news/1999/10/D13_drugs20_usia.htm (accessed 18 January 2005); 'Golpe contra las redes de lavados de activos al servicio del narcotrafico', *El Espectador*, 16 January 2002, http://www.mindefensa.gov.co/prensa/temas/narcotrafico (Accessed 18 January 2005).

149 CNN, *Alejandro Bernal Madrigal: Reputed Drug Lord*, http://edition.cnn.com/interactive/specials/0008/colombia.key/bernal.html (Accessed 18 January 2005); Sierra Bedoya, Z.A., 'Fabio Ochoa busca recursos para evitar cadena perpetua', *El Colombiano*, 15 August 2003, http://www.elcolombiano.com/historicod/200308/20030815/nnh001.htm (Accessed 18 January 2005).

150 DEA, 'Head of One of the World's Largest Cocaine Transportation Organizations Extradited to the United States', News Release: Immediate Release, 30 October 2001, http://www.usdoj.gov/dea/pubs/pressrel/pr103001.html (Accessed 18 January 2005).

decentralisation of the Colombian cocaine trade, but did not diminish it. According to Lyman, decentralisation of the trade has allowed an increased number of smaller trafficking organisations to become active, and made it more difficult for the law enforcement agents to tackle them.[151] As proof of this, a large quantity of cocaine is still smuggled into the United States.

DEA support in terms of intelligence and expertise is appreciated by the law enforcement agencies in the Andes.[152] The Andean authorities, particularly the police forces, are willing to receive DEA support for their operations.[153] Latin America has a different understanding of the role of the DEA. The DEA sees its role as supporting Latin American law enforcement organisations, but for the Latin Americans, the DEA has a leading role in operations due to its advanced expertise in operation planning, investigation and analysis. Such respect has been a significant element in managing joint operations effectively.

Air Bridge Denial Air bridge denial is an operation started in 1995 to shoot down aircraft transporting cocaine to Mexico from Colombia, Bolivia and Peru. For example, planes suspected of carrying cocaine into Colombia are shot down in Peruvian airspace to cut the air transport network. It has forced traffickers to find alternative routes and methods – such as using better communication security during their flights, flying closer to the Peruvian borders and through Brazilian airspace, and using different routes.[154] Air bridge denial is supported by the Colombian and Peruvian authorities because it targets drug traffickers exclusively. Both governments believe that the operation increases the risks to cocaine trafficking and reduces the coca trade in the regions in which the air bridge denial operates. It may motivate farmers to move to alternative crops in order to support their lives.[155] Another reason the Colombian and Peruvian governments value air bridge denial is that they do not lose support from farmers because of this drug control operations. This is because it clearly targets not farmers but drug traffickers.

Air bridge denial is also an operation that suits US interests: it directly attacks transportation networks of cocaine trafficking. US support for air bridge denial allows it to be 'aggressive' and effective.[156] In order to assist the Colombian and Peruvian

---

151 Lyman, M., 'Business Principles of Modern Narcotics Trafficking Operations', *paper presented at Roundtable* entitled *Business Practices of Narcotics Trafficking Enterprises*, at the Library of Congress on 29 January 2003, http://www.loc.gov/rr/frd/Drug_conference/pdf-files/Business-Principles-of-Modern-Narcotics-Trafficking-Operations.pdf, p. 6 (Accessed 30 April 2003).

152 Interview with a Colombian Police General at the Embassy of Colombia in London, 14 January 2002.

153 Ibid.

154 Marshall, D.R., *DEA Testimony* before Committee on Government Reform Subcommittee on Criminal Justice, Drug Policy and Human Resources, 2 March 2001, http://www.ict.org.il/documents/documentdet.cfm?docid=61 (Accessed 15 August 2003).

155 GAO, *Drug Control: Efforts to Develop Alternatives to Cultivating Illicit Crops in Colombia Have Made Little Progress and Face Serious Obstacles*, p. 37.

156 US Department of State, *International Narcotics Control Strategy Report 1999*, March 2000, http://www.state.gov/g/inl/rls/nrcrpt/1999/903.htm (Accessed 15 August 2003).

governments, the United States provided intelligence and equipment. For example, Operation *Pajarito* was a high frequency radio intercept programme to support the Peruvian air bridge denial operation.[157] As a result of this operation, they captured 24 aircraft and confiscated approximately 13 tonnes of cocaine base and powder in 1995. Also, the Colombian authorities were supported by their US counterparts to tackle the air transport networks of the Cali cartel in Operation *Skyweb* in 1995.[158]

The result of air bridge denial was satisfactory to all those concerned: in Peru, for example, it succeeded in reducing narcotics related flights by 50%.[159] Donnie Marshall of the DEA testified that the reduction of Peruvian coca cultivation between 1995 and 2000 was a result of air bridge denial operations. This helped to keep the coca price low and reduced the profit from it.[160]

Coca cultivation in Peru, however, increased from 2001. An increase in coca cultivation resulted from the suspension of air bridge denial after an accident. In 2001, the Peruvian authority mistakenly shot down an aircraft carrying a family of American missionaries. This incident was widely covered by the US media, and led to major criticism. After the accident in Peru, the United States suspended the operation.[161] According to a GAO report, however, such an accident was expected to happen. The GAO reported on the pilot scheme for the air bridge denial, claiming that only one-third of suspected aircraft were actually carrying drugs. Therefore, there was a high possibility that innocent planes were shot down just because they were suspected of possessing cocaine loads.[162]

Despite the decision by the US government, the governments of Colombia and Peru were keen to continue the operation in order to obstruct cocaine trafficking. In 2003, Colombia reached an agreement with the United States to resume the operation, but Peru could not gain approval from the US for the operation.[163] There is persistent opposition against air bridge denial in the United States because of the accident that killed American civilians. The actual operation of air bridge denial is highly dependent on equipment and financial resources from the United States. Consequently, the power to decide whether to proceed with the operation or not remains in US hands.

The Andean states and the United States, in sum, have more harmonised policies in interdiction than in eradication. A critique of the militarisation of drug control, however, claims that air bridge denial has made the drug cartels equip themselves

---

157 US Department of State, *International Narcotics Control Strategy Report 1995*.

158 Ibid.

159 Constantine, *DEA Congressional Testimony*, 7 March 1996.

160 Marshall, *DEA Testimony*, 2 March 2001.

161 Simons, P.E., 'US Narcotics Control Initiative in Colombia', *Testimony* before the Senate Drug Caucus, 3 June 2003, http://www.state.gov/g/inl/rls/rm21203.htm (Accessed 19 August 2003).

162 Isikoff, M., 'Suspected Planes May Become Targets', *The Washington Post*, 17 September 1989.

163 Mohammed, A., 'US, Colombia Near Agreement on Anti-Drug Fights,' *Reuters*, 15 July 2003, http://www.washingtonpost.com/wp-dyn/articles/A61589-2003Jul15.html (16 July 2003); and 'Colombian drug flights 'to resume'', *BBC*, 5 August 2003, http://news.bbc.co.uk/2/low/americas/3127125.stm (Accessed 19 August 2003).

with heavier weapons.[164] The increasing militarisation of the war on drugs can lead to the militarisation of society through the increasing use of violence by law enforcement agents and cocaine traffickers, and this poses threats to the political stability of the Andean states. Despite the criticism, operations such as air bridge denial reflect the interests of both parties directly, which made it easier for them to co-operate and co-ordinate their policies. Also, international co-operation allows the governments to achieve better law enforcement performance due to the greater amounts of information they can access. In respect of interdiction, despite the US dominance in policy determination, the United States and Andean states may have more sense of co-operation rather than coercion.

Alternative Development

Alternative development programmes consist of two elements: crop substitution and social projects. These programmes are positioned in a supportive role to ensure the success of other programmes, particularly eradication. Alternative development provides economic assistance in the areas growing coca that are affected by eradication. For the United States, alternative development programmes have a low priority compared with other drug control programmes.[165] Therefore, the budget allocated for alternative development has been less than for the other two programmes.[166] The emphasis on eradication and interdiction still remains in the three-prong strategy, although the contribution of alternative development has come to be recognised in cocaine supply reduction. Unlike the Europeans, who set a high priority on economic and social development in their drug control operations, economic projects were not valued by the United States.[167]

The success of alternative development, according to the United States Agency for International Development (USAID) responsible for the programme, depends on the efforts of eradication and interdiction.[168] Economic support provided through alternative development functions as 'carrot' to both the host state and the coca growers, in contrast to the 'sticks' of law enforcement and punishment. Alternative development projects are closely linked to the host state's law enforcement performance. Since the mid-1990s, the United States has set the conditions that alternative development support will be determined by the host state's law

---

164 Acción Andina-Transnational Institute, *The Drug War in the Skies The US Air Bridge Denial Strategy: The Success of A Failure*, 1999, Cochabamba: TNI, Part II.

165 Interview with an official at the USAID in Washington DC on 30 May 2003.

166 The budget for alternative development in the late 1980s was $23 million, and increased to $230 million in 2001. In 2002, the budget was about $397 million. GAO, *Drug Control: Efforts to Develop Alternatives to Cultivating Illicit Crops in Colombia Have Made Little Progress and Face Serious Obstacles*, pp. 7 and 22; Office of the Press Secretary, *Andean Regional Initiative*, 23 March 2002, Washington DC: the White House, http://www.state.gov/p/wha/rls/fs/8980.htm (Accessed 18 March 2005).

167 See the previous chapter for the details of the EU drug control operations in the Andes.

168 GAO, *Drug Control: US-Supported Efforts in Colombia and Bolivia*, Report to the Congress, November 1988, GAO/NSIAD-89-24, Washington DC: GAO, p. 63.

enforcement efforts, evaluated in the process of narcotic certification.[169] However, according to one official interviewed, coca growers in the Andes would not abandon their lucrative crop without fear of punishment because legal crops cannot make the profits of coca leaves.[170]

Although US alternative development projects are preferred by Andean governments to law enforcement programmes, the local population has remained sceptical. This may partly be because the failure of projects in the 1980s undermined the credibility of alternative development programmes. This section will examine both elements of the alternative development programme: first, crop substitution intended to reduce coca cultivation and provide for the immediate needs of the locals after eradication is carried out. Second, the social development projects attempt to empower local government and to construct the social infrastructure in order to establish the legal economic system that can function sufficiently with cultivation of alternative crops.

Crop Substitution   One aim of crop substitution is to provide assistance to eradicated areas: the other is to introduce legal crop cultivation to replace coca.[171] Crop substitution aims to cover the losses to farmers caused by eradication programmes and provide immediate assistance to support their lives. Also, they are expected to persuade coca farmers to abandon their coca bushes and shift to legal crops supplied by USAID, such as cacao, citrus fruits and macadamia nuts, thereby creating legal economic markets rather than illegal ones.

As a consequence of crop substitution, the amounts of licit crops produced and sold have increased, and there is development in agribusinesses. Recognising the opportunities to engage in legal economic activities with sufficient incomes, participation in alternative development has increased. In Peru, for example, licit crop production rose to 236 tonnes (valued at US $46 million), mainly from coffee and cacao.[172] This was regarded as a successful case from the US perspective and was achieved by a combination of factors: the loss of the coca market, alternative development opportunities and government efforts to control trafficking organisations.

After the crackdowns on the Medellín and Cali cartels of Colombia, the market for coca leaves declined. This brought a surplus of coca leaves and low prices. The prices of coca leaves are crucial for the coca farmers, and they began changing their products from coca to alternative crops provided by USAID. In Peru, the government's policy of shooting down aeroplanes suspected to be involved in narcotics trafficking reduced the demand for Peruvian coca leaves.[173] When the price

169 See chapter 3, section titled 'Diplomatic Impact', for the details of narcotics certification.

170 Interviews at the USAID on 27 May 2003; and Wisotsky, S., *Beyond the War on Drugs: Overcoming a Failed Public Policy*, 1990, New York: Prometheus Books, p. 49.

171 Interview at the USAID in Washington DC on 27 May 2003.

172 GAO, *Drug Control: Efforts to Develop Alternatives to Cultivating Illicit Crops in Colombia Have Made Little Progress and Face Serious Obstacles*, pp. 35–36.

173 Ibid., p. 6.

of coca leaves fell below US$1 per kilogram, farmers abandoned coca cultivation and shifted to legal crop cultivation.[174] In the Upper Huallaga Valley, the primary concern of most farmers is economic survival, and hence, whoever offers 'the best alternative and has the strength to impose their will' can lead the population.[175]

Crop substitution in Bolivia brought not only increases incomes from legal crops, but also the development of markets and industries. As a result of the Cochabamba project (1991–1997), the annual income of families involved in this project rose from $280 in 1993 to $520 in 1996.[176] The Chapare, by the end of fiscal year 2000, registered 67 agribusinesses and an estimated private sector investment of US$ 33.4 million.[177] Before the disruption caused by demonstrations against coca eradication, legal crops in the Chapare were estimated to amount to US $64 million.[178] Further, in Chimoré, alternative development projects empowered economic and political community development, and increased employment.[179] The existence of alternative development programmes in these areas led to social changes and reduced harassment by law enforcers and violence by drug traffickers.[180] This contributed to a much safer environment for farmers to engage.

Nevertheless, farmers remained sceptical about the US alternative development programme. In Bolivia, for example, there are several reports of vandalism against US alternative development project offices, and one of them was burnt down by coca growers in 2003.[181] There are four factors that have affected the alternative development programme negatively: the lack of financial resources, safety issues, failure of the market strategy and the lack of co-ordination within the agencies involved.

Although the US provides economic aid to the Andes, the economic development of Andean states is not a US priority. The United States prevents international aid being delivered to cocaine producing states if they have failed its narcotics

---

174 TNI, *Alternative Development and Eradication: A Failed Balance*, Drug and Democracy Programme, TNI Briefing Series, No. 2002/4, April 2002, Amsterdam: Transnational Institute, p. 11.

175 Youngers, C., 'The War in the Andes: The Military Role in US International Drug Policy', *Issues in International Drug Policy*, Issue Brief #2, 14 December 1990, Washington DC: Washington Office on Latin America, p. 20.

176 GAO, *Drug Control: Efforts to Develop Alternatives to Cultivating Illicit Crops in Colombia Have Made Little Progress and Face Serious Obstacles*, pp. 22–23.

177 24 producer and agro-processing businesses ($13.1 million); 12 service providers ($0.75 million); 16 producer associations ($14.3 million); and 12 hotel and tourism operations ($5.2 million). USAID, *Bolivia: Activity Data Sheet*, CBJ FY2002: Bolivia, http://www.usaid.gov/pubs/cbj2002/lac/bo/511-005.html (Accessed 4 July 2003).

178 Ibid.

179 'Emprenden actividades para el desarrollo económico de la región', *Nuevo Gran Angular*, February 2001.

180 McFarren, P., 'Bolivia Weeding Out Its Coca Trade', *Los Angeles Times*, 27 February 2000, http://www.mapinc.org/drugnews/v00/n279/a08.html?98661 (Accessed 11 April 2000).

181 Interview with an official at the Organisation of American States in Washington DC on 30 May 2003.

certification process. US influence on international organisations, such as the International Monetary Fund, makes it impossible for the Andean countries to get their funding proposals accepted. The lack of financial resources to perform drug control could lead the Andean states into a vicious circle of decertification and rejection of funding by international organisations. Discontinuation of funding also affects the sustainability of alternative development programmes and it is difficult for disrupted programmes to recover and achieve their goals. Consequently, during the 1980s, US alternative development projects carried out in Bolivia and Peru could not play their expected role in drug control.[182]

In Colombia, following its decertification in 1996 and 1997, the United States froze about US$ 1.5 billion in investment credits and loans from the Overseas Private Investment Corporation and the Export-Import Bank. The lack of funding caused by the sanction weakened the competitiveness of Colombian corporations in the markets, and led to the loss of potential sales at US$ 875 million.[183] This sanction made the Colombian government increase its law enforcement efforts against drug cartels, but at the cost of pressure on the growth of the legal economy that is significant if Colombia is to increase its capability against cocaine trafficking. If the United States is keen to see an improved legitimate economy in Colombia, the policy of economic sanctions is self-defeating.[184]

In the 1980s, the US attempt to carry out an alternative development programme in the Upper Huallaga Valley in Peru failed due to the hostile environment caused by guerrilla groups. This area is known both for its coca cultivation and the activities of guerrilla groups. Ensuring a safe environment in which to conduct alternative development programmes is crucial for the continuation and sustainability of the projects: more than in the case of eradication and interdiction programmes.[185] The projects in the Upper Huallaga Valley were curtailed because of the US approach to progress in the operation and the disruption by the guerrilla groups. As terrorist activities by the Sendero Luminoso and Tupac Amar Revolutionary Movement escalated in the mid-1980s, the projects were suspended.[186] Those engaged in alternative development projects were forced to leave to avoid threats to their lives. It was only in the early 1990s that the US government was able to resume the project following the successful anti-terrorist policy of the Peruvian government.[187]

In order to sustain legal crop cultivation, the marketability of commodities is essential. Alternative development programmes require long-term planning to maintain markets for alternative crops. However, the United States made a significant

182 GAO, *Drug Control: US-Supported Efforts in Colombia and Bolivia*, pp. 63–64; and GAO, *Drug Control: Efforts to Develop Alternatives to Cultivating Illicit Crops in Colombia Have Made Little Progress and Face Serious Obstacles*, pp. 7 and 22.

183 GAO, *Drug Control: US Counternarcotic Efforts in Colombia Face Continuing Challenges*, Report to Congressional Requesters, GAO/NSIAD-98-60, February 1998, Washington DC: General Accounting Office, p. 28.

184 GAO, *Drug Control: US-Supported Efforts in Colombia and Bolivia*, pp. 63–64.

185 See chapter 4 for successful alternative development programmes.

186 GAO, *Drug Control: Efforts to Develop Alternatives to Cultivating Illicit Crops in Colombia Have Made Little Progress and Face Serious Obstacles*, p. 6.

187 Ibid., p. 6.

error by failing to conduct market research and pursue a market strategy in an operation in the Upper Huallaga Valley in the 1980s. This left the strong impression that alternative crops would not bring sufficient earnings to farmers.[188] For example, coffee is one of the substitution crops, but major coffee producers, such as Colombia, have been facing annual losses of US $200–400 million since the 1989 collapse of the International Coffee Agreement.[189] As a consequence, USAID estimates that Bolivia and Peru have lost US $0.8–3 billion annually between 1996 and 2001 due to the eradication of coca fields.

USAID admits that, in the past, there were occasions when its programmes for introducing alternative crops to the region failed to consider the consequences for the market.[190] The result was a sharp decline in commodity prices and insufficient income for farmers to be able to support themselves. The problem was compounded by insufficient funding from international organisations to cover the losses made by the Andean states.[191] This experience has created scepticism about alternative development programmes and cultivation of legal crops among coca farmers. Therefore, it may become more difficult to persuade coca growers to participate in alternative development projects in the future.

Another shortcoming in the US alternative development programmes is the lack of co-ordination within US agencies. This hampered the progress of USAID projects. The lack of communication between law enforcement agencies and USAID has been pointed out repeatedly. USAID has been requesting information sharing on interdiction, eradication and alternative development, but there has been no solution.[192] According to a GAO report, 'The director of Bolivia's Alternative Development Regional Program, USAID and Bolivian alternative development agencies worked almost entirely apart from US and Bolivian counternarcotics enforcement agencies.'[193] Poor communication between officials in charge of alternative development and law enforcement teams at both the policy and operational levels undermined the projects USAID was working on. This forced the peasants to live without any immediate income that in turn led to hostility towards the government's drug control policies.[194]

The failures in co-ordinating eradication and alternative development programmes made Bolivia's drug control unsustainable. In Bolivia, there are high percentages of coca growers among farmers, and they have few alternative ways to make a living. Therefore, eradication of coca without aftercare by alternative development leaves them without livelihoods. There has been frustration and complaints over the way that

---

188 Ibid., p. 38.

189 The discontinuation of the International Coffee Agreement was decided due to the US insistence on fees and fair trade of commodities. Bagley, B.M., 'Dateline Drug Wars: Colombia: Support Package Strategy', *Foreign Policy*, No. 77, Winter 1989–1990, p. 159.

190 Interview at USAID in Washington DC on 29 May 2003.

191 'Estado Unidos no da nada a cambio de erradicar la coca', *El Diario*, 14 August 2003, http://www.eldiario.net/noticias/nt030814/3_09ecn.html (Accessed 14 August 2003).

192 Interview with an official at the USAID on 29 May 2003.

193 GAO, *Drug Control: Efforts to Develop Alternatives to Cultivating Illicit Crops in Colombia Have Made Little Progress and Face Serious Obstacles*, p. 27.

194 Ibid., p. 6.

the government carried out coca eradication. This is because the Bolivians consider that drug control policy is imposed by the Americans and ignores 'the needs of its people, or the country's economic, social and political circumstances'.[195] The anger of the coca growers is directed at their own government, at the United States and at those who participate in the project.[196] Those who have participated in US supported alternative development projects were threatened by the cocaine traffickers.[197] The escalation of the demonstrations and road blockades prevented the transportation of legal crops causing the losses of US $20 million in 2000.[198] The difficulty reaching the Chapare, as well as the attendant risks, has caused private sector investment and the export of legal products from the region to decline.

The losses caused by the demonstrations are not only the annual incomes of the farmers, but also the effort and money spent on the alternative development. The Cochabamba has established agro-industry through support from 15 years of alternative development efforts.[199] This success, according to a USAID official, is based on huge amounts of international funding poured into the region.[200] The Cochabamba has received more than the total sum spent on all other rural areas of Bolivia. Therefore, the alternative development programmes carried out to establish a legal economic system in the region is too costly to be a moral for other coca cultivating areas.[201] The US considers that the need to review its alternative development programmes is more cost-effective.[202]

In summary, crop substitution programmes were not received well by the local population, despite the fact that some projects led to positive economic returns to the region. This comes partly from the scepticism about alternative development among coca growers based on their experiences. In the early years, the United States failed to provide sustainable alternative development programmes because it was not willing to conduct alternative development programmes and lacked research for them. To support existing industries is as crucial as developing alternative crops. In order for coca farmers to earn reasonable sums from legal crops, market protection is required from the beginning. For example, Peruvian success in coca eradication in the 1990s was assisted by the deregulation of the market for alternative crops to ensure

---

195 'Conflict Flares in the Bolivian Tropics', *Drug Policy Briefing*, No. 2 January 2002, Amsterdam: Transnational Institute.

196 Interview with a USAID official on 29 May 2003.

197 GAO, *Drug Control: Efforts to Develop Alternatives to Cultivating Illicit Crops in Colombia Have Made Little Progress and Face Serious Obstacles*, p. 26.

198 USAID, *Bolivia: Activity Data Sheet*, CBJ FY2002; and 'Bolivia: Cocaleros destruyen centros de erradicación', *Noticias Paginadigital*, 4 April 2003, http://www.paginadegital.com. ar/articulos/2003seg/noticias10/blv4-4pl.asp (Accessed 4 July 2003).

199 'Alternative Development Promotes Competitive Agroindustry', *Nuevo Gran Angular*, September 2001, pp. 4–6.

200 Interview with an official at the USAID in Washington DC on 27 May 2003.

201 Ibid.

202 US Department of State, *Fact Sheets: USAID Supports Alternative Development in Bolivia and Peru*, 24 June 2002, http://usinfo.state.gov/topical/global/drugs/02062402.htm (Accessed 4 July 2003).

advantages to the new converts.[203] It is difficult for new comers to be competent in the market, so there should be protection for them. Considering the development of the legal economy in the Andes, the United States should have supported international agreements to protect producers as well as providing trade benefits by the Andean Trade Preference Act (ATPA).[204] This is because relying on bi-lateral trade benefits increases the dependency of the Andean economy on the US.

Social Development Programmes   Under the alternative development programme, USAID offers wide ranging programmes to support not only economic but also social development for a community, such as road building, health programmes and the provision of portable water.[205] The objectives in social development projects are improving social infrastructure and strengthening local government in order to ensure the maintenance of crop substitution. From past experiences in supporting alternative development programmes in Bolivia and Peru, the US government is aware that: 'effective alternative development demands a strong host government commitment to a comprehensive array of counternarcotics measures and years of sustained US assistance to support them.'[206] Weak government control over lands and low credibility of the government in the local population undermine operations, such as monitoring compliance with eradication agreements and discouraging illicit commercial activities.[207] In order to restore popular confidence in the authorities, local governments need sufficient ability to provide necessary services to the locals. Therefore, alternative development projects include building social infrastructures.

It is important to build social infrastructures in order to increase competitiveness in the market economy, with roads and paths and to provide services to the community through schools and hospitals. In the areas in which coca is cultivated, there are often no road networks for farmers to transport commercial crops such as bananas. Good roads would allow farmers to gain better prices by selling at non-local markets.[208] It is necessary to prepare the environment to support farmers' participation and competitiveness in legal markets if coca eradication is to be taken seriously. In Bolivia, for example, USAID introduced an electricity system designed to: 'expand the use of electricity for rural industry and export-related activities that would provide jobs and alleviate poverty, and improve the operational standards of rural electric distribution.'[209]

---

203 Tammen, 'The Drug War VS. Land Reform in Peru'; and Regional Inspector General/ San Salvador, *Audit of USAID-Financed Alternative Development Activities in Peru*, Audit Report No. 1-527-02-011-P, 15 May 2002, http://www.usaid.gov/oig/publivc/fy02rpts/1-527-02-011-p.pdf (Accessed 20 May 2003).

204 Department of State, *Fact Sheet: Andean Region Initiative*, 16 May 2001, http://www.state.gov/p/wha/rls/fs/2001/2980pf.htm (16 May 2003).

205 USAID, Data sheets in *Peru*, 2003, http://www.usaid.gov/country/lac/peru.pdf (Accessed 20 May 2003).

206 GAO, *Drug Control: Efforts to Develop Alternatives to Cultivating Illicit Crops in Colombia Have Made Little Progress and Face Serious Obstacles*, p. 2.

207 Ibid., p. 2.

208 Ibid., p. 40.

209 Ibid., p. 22.

Material changes in coca growing regions are not the only objective of development projects. They are also trying to re-educate the locals about the concept of cocaine. In 1995, when the US re-introduced the Alternative Development Programme (ADP) to the coca-growing Upper Huallaga River Valley in Peru, it found that the perception of cocaine in the area has changed: 'the percentage of the population recognizing drug production and consumption as damaging to society reached 94%.'[210] Between 1981 and 1994, a US development project, the Upper Huallaga Area Development (UHAD), experienced difficulties in continuing the operation due to the activities of guerrilla groups and the lack of popular support.[211] The change of perception is probably what the United States most longed for in order to pursue its war on drugs with popular support in the source countries. It is, in other words, the Americanisation of Peruvian cocaine culture.

Such development projects are approved by the Andean governments as well as the local population. The Bolivian President, Banzer, believed that 'development is the best weapon for combating poverty and getting the drug traffickers out of [Bolivia]', but without sufficient support from international donors, the Bolivian plan to control the cocaine trade could not be successful.[212] Despite the support from both authorities and the locals, drug control is a difficult project to make successful. The problems drug control faces are not only financial, but also co-ordination and communication among involved agencies.

According to Higgins, who studied the failure of a humanitarian mission of Southern Command (SouthCom) in Colombia, the failure was caused by a lack of communication and misunderstanding based on false assumptions.[213] His case study was on the Department of Defence's Humanitarian Civic Assistance (HCA) in Juanchaco, Colombia, between 1993 and 1994. The operation aimed to establish strategic bases to attack the Cali cartel, to introduce basic infrastructure to the village of Juanchaco and to improve the Colombia-US relationship and co-operation between the militaries. The result of the operation, however, was unsatisfactory. This was caused by the lack of communication, co-ordination and flexibility in and among involved agencies – SouthCom, US Embassy in Colombia and the Colombian Ministry of Defence. Consequently, the local population misunderstood the nature of operation and saw it not as development support, but as a military exercise.[214]

---

210 Ibid., pp. 35–36.

211 Through the ADP, the USAID 'rehabilitated 1,000 kilometres of roads and 46 bridges, stone-paved 21 kilometres of roads, supported 136 engineering studies, piloted 1 regional maintenance program, and provided 3 pools of heavy equipment. In addition, the project has supported about 1,000 small social infrastructure projects involving schools, potable water system, health posts, mini hydroelectric systems and other community improvements. As a result, the percentage of households with access to basic services in program areas increased from 16% to 51%.' Ibid., pp. 35–36.

212 ODCCP, 'Interview with His excellency President Hugo Banxar Suárez of Bolivia', *Update*, June 2000, p. 7.

213 Higgins, Jr., D.P., 'Personae Non Gratae: Misunderstanding a Humanitarian Mission at Juanchaco, Colombia', *Low Intensity Conflict & Law Enforcement*, Vol. 6, No. 2, Autumn 1997.

214 Ibid., p. 31.

Following the difficulties it encountered through the operation, SouthCom cancelled planned operations in Colombia for 1994 and 1995.[215]

Despite the lessons learned from the difficulties in the operation, the US side was convinced that its approach was the best way of handling the situation. On the other side, the Colombians felt that more consideration for their approach was necessary. It seems that what was missing was an opportunity for consultation among the involved parties and adjustments of their own rules to handle the situations. American officials were disappointed by the Colombians as they did not handle the matter as the Americans expected. Furthermore, some US agents may have needed to be more patient to show respect for the differences in their Colombian counterparts.

In addition to these weaknesses, alternative development programmes require large amounts of resources and patience before they show some results. Donors may need to understand that alternative development is a complex and gradual process. Whereas alternative development projects make progress only gradually, these projects are easily distracted by other elements of drug control policy. As the Bolivian case shows, several years' efforts may be damaged by one-year road blockades and this can turn some farmers back to growing coca. Further, the US pressure on the Peruvian government with its eradication targets and deadlines has undermined the effectiveness of progress in drug control by strengthening guerrilla groups in the state.[216]

Change in Andean Attitudes Toward Drug Control

The US government reported that the decline of coca cultivation in the Andes was the result of 'an effective program of eradication, alternative development, stricter drug laws, and an intense precursor chemical interdiction'.[217] This may indicate the active commitment of the Andean governments in drug control as well as the effectiveness of US operations. The decline of coca cultivation followed the active drug control policy launched by the Andean states, such as intensified Peruvian drug control in the mid-1990s, *Plan Dignity* of the Bolivian government in the late 1990s, and *Plan Colombia* by the Colombian government in 2000.

The Andean states have been submissive to the US drug control strategy in the Andes and accepted it in a passive manner. However, the Andean governments became more actively committed to drug control as the number of cocaine addicts increase in their countries. Their drug control programmes had one thing in common, the governments expected to receive international funding, particularly from the US, to carry them out. In the mid-1990s, the Bolivian government asked for about US $800 million international funding for the US $925 million Plan Dignity, a programme with

---

215 Ibid., p. 59.

216 'Peru: From Virtual Success to Realistic Policies?' *Drug Policy Briefing*, No. 3 April 2002, Amsterdam: Transnational Institute.

217 ONDCP, *ONDCP Fact Sheet: Bilateral Cooperation with Bolivia*, March 2002, http://www.whitehousedrugpolicy.gov/publications/international/factsht/bolivia.html (Accessed 16 May 2003).

almost the same objectives as the US.[218] To some extent, the Andean governments came to use the US policy to support their own narcotics control policies.

The change of attitudes in the Andes has been received positively by the US because the commitment of the host nations leads to progress in US drug control projects.[219] For example, the change in the Peruvian notion of coca cultivation and cocaine trafficking as its own problem increased the popular support for the US alternative development projects. This also leads to cost-effectiveness of a project as the sustainability of the alternative development projects depends on the commitment of the community concerned.[220] As a result of Plan Dignity, the Bolivian government eradicated 80% of its illicit coca fields by 2003.[221] In addition, coca cultivation in Bolivia has remained at a low level since 1999 due to the successful eradication efforts in the Chapare, Cochabamba.[222]

The US style drug control programme, Plan Dignity, was approved and supported by the US government. However, the Bolivian government has been challenged by its people.[223] There are continuous demonstrations and road blockades in the state. Bolivia lost its stability politically and economically. Following the previous president's resignation, Evo Morales, a leader of Chapare coca union, won the presidential election in 2005.[224] His policy supports coca cultivation for traditional use among the indigenous people, but it is against the production of cocaine. This policy was received with scepticism by the EU and the US, as they were unsure of

218 Document obtained at the Embassy of Bolivia in Brussels on 25 April 2002; and CICAD/OAS, *Substituting the Coca Economy: The Anti-Drug Strategy in Bolivia: An Evaluation of the Dignity Plan 1998-2002*, 2002, Washington DC: OAS, p. 9.

219 Carpenter, *Bad Neighbor Policy*, p. 26.

220 GAO, *Drug Control: Efforts to Develop Alternatives to Cultivating Illicit Crops in Colombia Have Made Little Progress and Face Serious Obstacles*, p. 39.

221 Associated Press, 'Bolivian Police Seize 5 Tons of Cocaine'.

222 Coca cultivation has moved to more remote areas where it is impossible to conduct crop substitution due to poor soil conditions and distance to the markets. CICAD/OAS, *Substituting the Coca Economy*, pp. 25–32; CICAD, *Cultivos de Coca en la Region Andina 1992-2002*, Obtained at the CICAD/OAS during the interview on 29 May 2003; and USAID, *Evaluation of Alternative Development Strategy in the Andes and Bolivia Program Challenge*, USAID-INL Briefings, 17 January 2003, PowerPoint Document, obtained during an interview at the USAID on 27 May 2003.

223 Gori, G., 'Bolivia's Cabinnet Resigns After Protests', *The Washington Post*, 18 February 2003, http://www.washingtonpost.com/ac2/wp-dyn/A26838-2003Feb18?language=printer (Accessed 7 March 2003); and Ziazo, A., 'Coca Farmers' Chief Could Lead Bolivia', *The Washington Post*, 11 July 2002, http://www.washingtonpost.com/wp-dyn/articles/A54044-2002Jul11.html (Accessed 11 July 2002).

224 In order to win the nation, President Sanchez de Lozada had to give up his salary, reform his cabinet, and eventually leave his office. However, the Bolivian economy did not make an acceptable improvement. Evo Morales, a leader of Coca Union, was elected as the President with a high support rate. Sanchez, M., 'Will the US Bend in Bolivia?' *The Washington Post*, 20 February 2003, http://www.washingtonpost.com/ac2/wp-dyn/A36581-2003Feb20?language=printer (Accessed 21 May 2003); 'Bolivia's new leader vows change', *BBC*, http://news.bbc.co.uk/1/hi/world/americas/4636190.stm (Accessed 19 August 2006).

the Morales administration's support of their drug control operations in Bolivia.[225] Sustaining drug control policy was a choice between popular support and US assistance and economic support.[226] As far as Bolivia is concerned, the war on drugs US style did more harm than good to society and the state. It is believed that Bolivia needs to pursue a different approach from the drug control programme that produces political, social and economic damage to the state, despite the pressure from the United States.[227] In reality, Bolivia may be unable to change its policy without the United States changing its approach to international cocaine control because opposing the US policy puts the Bolivian economy at risk.

Conclusion

Through the Andean Strategy, the United States has been tackling the cocaine trade from various angles, eradication of coca bushes, interdiction of cocaine loads, demolishing criminal groups and providing alternative crops and social infrastructures. Law enforcement operations (interdiction and eradication) are also expected to function as a deterrent, causing coca growers to withdraw from coca cultivation, and an incentive to shift their production to alternative crops provided by the alternative development projects. The logic is that the United States three-prong strategy may have the potential to reduce the Andean cocaine industry despite the fact that so far it has posed a danger of instability to the region. According to Beers, the three-prong strategy of the United States contributed to a reduction in coca cultivation in Peru and Bolivia 'dramatically'.[228] Success in eradicating coca in Bolivia and Peru was the result of the combined effects of alternative development, re-establishing government control over the region as well as forceful eradication efforts supported by the United States.

American policy, in rhetoric and in legislation, denied that drugs are a permanent problem that needs to be managed rather than eliminated. Such an approach to drugs has worsened the situation in various ways, and affects the community and the state.[229] Bolivia, in particular, has destroyed 80% of illicit coca with large economic

---

225 Interviews with EU and US officials in Brussels on 15 January 2003 and Washington DC on 27 May 2003 respectively. Gluesing, J., 'Is Coca the New Hemp?' *Spiegel Online*, 28 March 2006, http://www.spiegel.de/international/spiegel/0,1518,408364,00.html (Accessed on 13 March 2007).

226 The White House, *National Drug Control Strategy 2003*, p. 36; 'Bolivia requiere ayuda para salir de la crisis y pobreza', *El Diario*, 14 August 2003, http://www.eldiario.net/noticias/nt030814/3-07.html (Accessed 14 August 2003). Sanchez, 'Will the US Bend in Bolivia?'.

227 'Estados Unidos no da nada a cambio de erradicar la coca', *El Diario*, 14 August 2003, http://www.eldiario.net/noticias/nt030814/3-09ecn.html (Accessed 14 August 2003).

228 Beers, R., *Statement* before the Senate Armed Service Committee, 4 April 2000, http://www.state.gov/www/policy_remarks/2000/000404_beers_sasc.html (Accessed 5 May 2002); and Deal, M., *On the Record Briefing: Andean Region Initiative*, 16 May 2001, http://www.state.gov/g/inl/narc/rm/2001/may_aug/index.cmf?docid=2925 (Accessed 12 June 2002).

229 Peuter, P., 'The Limits of Supply-Side Drug Control', *The Milkin Institute Review*, First Quarter 2001.

sacrifices. The statistics of seizures and eradication do not indicate success because those eradicated fields tend to be replaced in remote areas and other states, such as Colombia. Consequently, total coca flow to the United States remains steady. The third element of the three-prong strategy, alternative development, used to be affected by the sanctions to the Andean countries, and did not fulfil its role as a 'safety net' for farmers who eradicated coca from their fields. Therefore, the US approach could not gain popular support or credibility in the Andes. The Andean governments, however, supported the US policy for the sake of economic support attached to the drug control aid.

The militarisation of the drug war has undermined civilian control of the militaries in the Andes and spread human rights violations through torture, disappearance and extrajudicial executions.[230] The military extended its authority to the private trial of those suspected of participation in the cocaine trade, and thereby some citizens were convicted without lawful trial in some states.[231] Instead of supporting democracy and protecting human rights, the US aid to counter-narcotics operations increased human rights violations through aerial spraying, military involvement and undermining democratic political systems in the Andes.[232] In this sense, US anti-drug operations may be more harmful to the Andean countries and their society than the cocaine trade *per se*.[233]

Also, the US war on drugs increased the dependency of Andean states on the US with certification, threatening the continuation of US aid. As Gerber and Jensen maintain: 'Drug control policy is simply another area in which the United States tries to force other nations to adopt its ideology.'[234] Hostile reactions from some concerned states and the increased tension between the Latin American states and the United States stemmed from the coercive manner of the United States to pursue its interests.[235]

It is said that the United States has transferred the costs of war on drugs to the producer side foreseeing social disruption and political and economic pressures at home.[236] The intention of the United States, however, is not as it appears to the rest of the world. The Americans believe they are pursuing their policy not only for

---

230 WOLA, *Going to the Source*, Section IV.

231 Freeman, L., *Troubling Patterns: The Mexican Military and the War on Drugs*, 2002, Washington DC: Latin American Working Group.

232 Salinas, C.M., 'Colombia and the Kaleidoscope of Violence', *US Foreign Policy in Focus*, 27 October 1997, Vol. 1, No. 8.

233 Acción Andina-Transnational Institute, *The Drug War in the Skies*.

234 Gerber, J., and Jensen, E.L., 'The Internationalization of US Policy on Illicit Drug Control', in Gerber, J., and Jensen, E. L. (eds), *Drug War American Style: The Internationalization of Failed Policy and Its Alternatives*, 2001, New York: Garland Publishing, p. 11.

235 Lee, *The White Labyrinth*, p. 2; and Hakim, P., 'The Three Temptations on Latin America' in Manwaring, M.G. (ed.), *Security and Civil-Military Relations in the New World Disorder: The Use of Armed Forces in the Americas*, September 1999, http://www.carlisle. army.mil/ssi/pubs/1999/newworld/newworld.pdf (16 May 2003), p. 25.

236 Tokatlián, 'National Security and Drugs', p. 135.

their own interests, but also for others interests.[237] The impression that the United States is coercive may come from the use of certification and sanctions as well as the way in which the United States handles the execution of policies. According to Bagley, 'One of the most glaring deficiencies of the US strategy is the tendency toward nonconsultative, unilateral decision-making in bilateral or multilateral affairs.'[238] The United States aims at its policy without any concern or warning to the host governments, particularly 'during electoral campaigns or after dramatic incidents'.[239]

Drug control does not work with a unilateral or bilateral approach, as the balloon effect in the Andes clearly indicates. Youngers argues: 'Effective policies to confront these problems which cross national boundaries must be seen as mutually beneficial and must be developed jointly, in co-operation and consultation by those most affected by the problems and potential solutions.'[240] In other words, the drug phenomenon is one that requires cooperation at every level, regional, state, and non-governmental. There is the need for regional policy co-ordination among the Andean states as well as among other Latin American states in order to maintain democracy and security in the region.[241] Such a project, however, requires huge commitment and enormous resources.[242] Large scale foreign aid, a so-called *Mini-Marshall Plan* has been suggested to tackle Latin American cocaine trade as 'the only feasible method' to solve the problem.[243] The plan, however, is operable only with large-scale multinational co-operation involving several developed countries.[244] Based on the concept of a mini-Marshall plan and the balanced approach of the three-prong strategy, the Colombian government developed a drug control programme called Plan Colombia.

---

237 Interview at US Mission to the European Union in Brussels on 25 April 2002.

238 Bagley, B.M., 'Colombia and the War on Drugs', *Foreign Affairs*, Vol. 67, No. 1, Fall 1988, p. 89.

239 Ibid., p. 89.

240 Youngers, C., 'A Fundamentally Flawed Strategy', p. 19.

241 Tokatlián, 'National Security and Drugs', p. 151.

242 Bagley, B.M., 'The New Hundred Years War? US National Security and the War on Drugs in Latin America', *Journal of Interamerican Studies and World Affairs*, Vol. 80, No. 1, Spring 1988, p. 180.

243 Perl, *88093: Drug Control*; Friman, H.R., *Narco Diplomacy: Exporting the US War on Drugs*, 1996, Ithaca: Cornell University Press, p. 117; and Bagley, B.M., 'The Use of Armed Forces in Drug Interdiction: The Strategic Context', in Manwaring, M.G. (ed.), *Security and Civil-Military Relations in the New World Disorder: The Use of Armed Forces in the Americas*, September 1999, http://www.carlisle.army.mil/ssi/pubs/1999/newworld/newworld.pdf (16 May 2003), p. 62.

244 Perl, *88093: Drug Control*, Friman, H.R., 'Narco Diplomacy', in Manwaring, M.G. (ed.), *Security and Civil-Military Relations in the New World Disorder*, p. 62.

Chapter 6

Plan Colombia:
An Attempt at Multinational Co-operation

Introduction

This chapter will analyse the way in which the United States and the European Union have worked together on Plan Colombia[1]. Plan Colombia is the first programme designed for drug control through multilateral co-operation. It is a programme with a multidimensional approach to drug control. It consists of various components to tackle not only cocaine trafficking but also drug related issues, such as poverty and the peace process with the guerrilla groups. Plan Colombia aims at an ideal approach, through a balance between law enforcement and economic and social development. The Colombian government expected the members of the international community, particularly the EU and the United States, to assist various projects within the overall programme.

As examined in chapters 4 and 5, the approaches of the United States and the EU to drug control are considerably different: the United States emphasises repressive law enforcement, whilst the EU emphasises development. Through the examination of their respective approaches to Plan Colombia and assistance provided to Colombia, this chapter will attempt to clarify differences between the two sides. Although the EU and the United States have been operating their drug control projects in Colombia and other Andean states, their projects have been independent from each other and based on bilateral co-operation with the recipient. However, both the EU and the United States recognise the role that transnational and multidimensional efforts can play in tackling cocaine trafficking in the Andes. A large-scale programme to combat various aspects of cocaine trafficking simultaneously is beyond the capacity of bilateral co-operation due to the cost and expertise required.

In order to analyse EU and US policy, this chapter will focus on the characteristics of the EU and the US approach to drug control in Colombia and also the way in which they contributed to multinational co-operation with the Colombian government. The investigation of EU and US approaches to Plan Colombia will be undertaken through three sections. Firstly, the emergence and characteristics of Plan Colombia will be examined. Despite the focus on the US and the EU role, it will be necessary to consider the background to the programme, as this affected the decision-making of the EU and the United States. Secondly, the US role in and its contributions to Plan Colombia will be analysed. The United States is the largest contributor and has

---

1   Plan Colombia concluded its first phase in 2003, and from 2004, the second phase has commenced.

played a key role. The US support for Plan Colombia emphasised law enforcement and provided military equipment; almost as an extension of its Andean strategy in Colombia. Thirdly, the EU approach and its commitment to Plan Colombia will be investigated. The EU was expected to play a financial and political role as large as the one of the United States. However, the EU contribution turned out to be a disappointment for Colombia. The EU has not been involved in Plan Colombia, although some EU member states assisted the programme on an individual basis. The EU has continued to provide development projects to Colombia outside Plan Colombia.

Plan Colombia

In this section, the political and diplomatic characteristics of Plan Colombia will be explored. This investigation intends to explain whether the characteristics and planning of the scheme influenced the decision-making of the EU and the US towards the Plan. The Colombian government's attempt to launch Plan Colombia was designed to involve the international community in its domestic drug control projects. The attempt to conduct Plan Colombia as a multinational programme, however, led the Colombian government into complex international politics. In order to illustrate the complexity of the situation surrounding the Plan, the following four issues will be investigated: the aim and objectives of Plan Colombia; the significance of international support; the process taken before the official proposal; and the initial reaction from the international community.

Plan Colombia is a US $7.5 billion 'Marshall-style Plan' for Colombia designed to bring peace to the country.[2] It was proposed by the Pastrana administration of Colombia in 1999 as an integrated plan to solve the Colombian problem of drug trafficking, civil war and poverty. Plan Colombia aimed to restore peace and strengthen the state through ten strategies developed by the Colombian government.[3] According to Godoy, this was because President Pastrana saw the solution to the Colombian situation in the peace process.[4] Hence, the goal of Plan Colombia was to establish peace with insurgent groups, principally the Revolutionary Armed Forces of Colombia (FARC) and the National Liberation Army (ELN).[5] The strategy included economic and social development as well as plans to control drug trafficking.[6] The central focus of the plan was on drug control supported by the United States.

---

2   Interview with an official at the Colombian Embassy in Brussels on 10 July 2002.

3   The plan consists of 10 elements: economic, finance and financial, peace, national defence, judicial and human rights, counter-narcotics, alternative development, social participation, human development and international-oriented strategy.

4   See Introduction of this book for a discussion of Andean cocaine trafficking.

5   Godoy, H., *Plan Colombia's Strategic Weaknesses*, a paper presented at the 2003 meeting of the Latin American Studies Association in Dallas, Texas, 27–29 March 2003, http://136.142.158.105/Lasa2003/GodoyHoracio.pdf   (Accessed   13   November   2003), pp. 4–10.

6   Colombian President, *Plan Colombia: Plan for Peace, Prosperity, and the Strengthening of the State*, 1999, Bogotá: Presidency of the Republic, http://www.usip.org/

The determination of Colombia to achieve drug control in the country was stated in the target of a 50% reduction of narcotics trafficking within 6 years.[7] The drug control strategy indicated the need to deal with guerrilla groups connected to the cocaine industry, and the aim of encouraging development. In this respect, Plan Colombia appears to tackle drug trafficking from several different aspects in order to ensure success – the parallel approach of law enforcement and development projects. In order to achieve these goals, Plan Colombia represents a drug control strategy with six objectives (including the fight against drug trafficking organisations and corruption, and reform of the judicial system),[8] accompanied by seven detailed targets, such as human rights protection, cocaine interdiction and crop eradication.[9] Through the various elements of Plan Colombia, President Pastrana tried to indicate that it was not only drug issues that mattered but also issues of public order and development.[10]

It was clear to the Pastrana administration that the plan would not work without international support because it was a costly, large-scale project and the nature of the cocaine industry required international attention.[11] Also, according to Carpenter, Pastrana considered Plan Colombia as a long-term project, which could last for up to 15–20 years, and estimated that 'as much as another $500 million a year was needed' to sustain the plan.[12] Consequently, the budget for Plan Colombia depended on potential international contributions: $3.5 billion out of $7.5 billion was to be generated from international donors.

According to a Colombian government source, the importance of attracting international commitment to Plan Colombia was reflected in the fact that the initial proposal was published in English not in Spanish.[13] The proposal for Plan

---

library/pa/colombia/adddoc/plan_colombia_101999.html (Accessed 31 October 2003).

7   Ibid.

8   The six objectives of the drug control strategy of Plan Colombia are: 1) to strengthen the fight against drug trafficking and dismantle the trafficking organisations through an integrated effort by the armed forces; 2) strengthen the judicial system and combat corruption; 3) neutralise the drug trade's financial system and seize its resources for the state; 4) neutralise and combat violent agents allied with the drug trade; 5) integrate national initiatives into regional and international efforts; and 6) strengthen and expand plans for alternative development in areas affected by drug trafficking.

9   The seven strategies presented are: 1) complimentary actions by the armed forces and the police; 2) human rights and democracy protection, including civil population against guerrilla groups; 3) air interdiction; 4) cocaine and chemical interdiction at sea and on rivers; 5) increased joint operations between the Colombian National Police and Army, and Colombia and the United States; 6) operations against laboratories and stockpiles; and 7) crop eradication.

10   Garrido, R.S., 'La Guerra Global Contra El terror, Plan Colombia, El IRA Y La Región Andino Amazonica: Wanted or Certified?' *Mamacoca*, http://www.mamacoca.org/ FSMT_sept_2003/es/abs/soberon_guerra_global_terror_abs_es.htm (Accessed 15 December 2003).

11   Interview with an official at the Colombian Embassy in Brussels on 10 July 2002.

12   Carpenter, T.G., 'Plan Colombia: The Drug War's New Morass', *CATO Policy Report*, Vol. 23, No. 5, September/October 2001.

13   Interview with an official at the Colombian Embassy in Brussels, 10 July 2002.

Colombia targeted the international community rather than Colombia.[14] The aim of this approach was to appeal to the international community with regard to its co-responsibility for international cocaine trafficking, and to urge other states and international organisations to engage in the Plan.[15] In order to increase compatibility with different actors' interests in Plan Colombia (particularly the United States and the EU), the Colombian government presented a multi-dimensional scheme.[16] Within the framework of Plan Colombia, the Colombian government expected the contributors to sponsor various projects to achieve different goals in the programme in accordance with each actor's priorities in drug control policies. However, the Colombian government could not propose concrete and precise projects for potential donors for support due to its uncertainty about the resources available for the projects.[17] Consequently, when Plan Colombia was publicised, the projects ready to be carried out were only those of law enforcement funded by the United States.

The official version is, therefore, known as the 'US backed' Plan Colombia due to the deep US involvement in drafting the plan. The original Plan Colombia presented by President Pastrana called the 'Marshall Plan for Colombia' (Plan Marshall para Colombia)[18] in 1998 was a plan to 'alleviate the poverty and inequality, particularly in rural areas'.[19] It was described as: 'the sum of educational, scientific, technical, cultural, economic, and political resources to help develop the [country's] existing capacities.'[20] The economic issues remained a significant element for the Colombian government because, as Codoy maintains, economic recovery 'was seen as a prerequisite' to bring peace to the country, although the majority of the proposal describes strategies for drug control.[21] For the execution of this plan, Colombia expected international support because of its inability to confront all its problems alone.

The original Plan Colombia, however, could not secure funding from the United States. The US Under Secretary of State Thomas Pickering suggested in 1998 that the United States would increase aid dramatically if Colombia revised some elements

---

14 Nagle, L.E., *The Search For Accountability and Transparency in Plan Colombia: Reforming Judicial Institution - Again*, May 2001, http://www.miami.edu/nsc/publication/IPCseries/pcacount.pdf (Accessed 13 November 2003), pp. 9–10; See also, Carrigan, A., 'A Foolish Drug War', *The New York Times*, 10 February 2001.

15 Interview with an official at the Colombian Embassy in Brussels, 10 July 2002.

16 Gaitán Pavía, P., Pard Gracía-Peña, R., and Manuel Osorio, J., *Communidad Internacional, conflicto armado y perspectivas de paz en Colombia*, 2002, http://www.ideaspaz.org/publicaciones/download/communidad_internacional_english.pdf (Accessed 30 January 2004), p. 31.

17 Interview with an official at the Colombian Embassy in Brussels, 10 July 2002.

18 There are several drafts of Plan Colombia, and the one presented to the United States in 1998 was entitled 'An Integrated Policy on Drugs for Peace'.

19 Vaicius, I., and Isacson, A., "Plan Colombia': The Debate in Congress', *International Policy Report*, December 2000, http://www.ciponline.org/colombia/aid/ipr1100.pdf (Accessed 29 October 2003), p. 1.

20 Godoy, *Plan Colombia's Strategic Weaknesses*, p. 5.

21 Ibid.

of the plan – namely drug control.[22] Over the possible projects and aid package for Plan Colombia, the Colombian government consulted the US government almost on a daily basis, after the US Congress approved the US$ 1.3 billion budget for the plan.[23] A US source revealed that even just before the plan was officially released meetings were taking place between Colombia and the United States to discuss the details.[24] With the encouragement of the United States, the emphasis was directed more to dismantling the connection between insurgency groups and drug trafficking with military involvement, rather than projects for economic development.[25]

According to Gentleman, the changes did not affect the goal and objectives of Plan Colombia; it was merely a change in the priorities.[26] Colombia was primarily aiming at establishing peace with insurgency groups: the United States, on the other hand, was aiming at cracking down on cocaine trafficking. Since the principal aims of Colombia and the United States differed, Colombia had to adjust its approaches to suit the US priorities. Colombia, however, considered that either approach could bring peace to the state as the activities of insurgency groups and the cocaine industry were closely connected. Without removing the insurgent groups from Colombia, it is impossible to wipe out the drug trafficking, and vice versa. As a Colombian source confirms, 'it is virtually impossible to separate the drug trafficking from the activities of Colombia's insurgent and paramilitary forces'.[27] However, it made a significant difference to the perceptions of international contributors.

Colombian expectations of international financial support were disappointed. Initially, the Colombian government expected to finance about two-thirds of the Plan's budget with contributions from the United States and the EU. The actual donations promised, however, were much less than anticipated, except from the United States. The US Congress approved US $1.3 billion (including $250–280 million for alternative development) whilst the EU offered only US $100 million for development and human rights protection programmes.[28] The total European

22 Vaicius *et al.*, "Plan Colombia': The Debate in Congress', p. 2.

23 Beers, R., *Testimony* before the Criminal Justice, Drug Policy, and Human Resources, Subcommittee of the House Committee on Government Reform, 12 October 2000, http:// www.state.gov/www/policy_remarks/2000/001012_beers_criminal.html (Accessed 6 March 2003).

24 Interview with officials of the US Department of State in Washington DC, on 27 May 2003.

25 Godoy, *Plan Colombia's Strategic Weaknesses*, pp. 12–14.

26 Gentleman, J.A., *The Regional Security Crisis in the Andes: Pattern of State Response*, July 2001, p. 11, http://www.carlise.army.mil/ssi/pubs/2001/andes/andes.pdf (Accessed 16 May 2003).

27 Interview with an official at the Colombian Embassy in Brussels on 10 July 2002; cited in Gaitán Pavía, P., Pard Gracía-Peña, R., and Manuel Osorio, J., *Communidad Internacional, conflicto armado y perspectivas de paz en Colombia*, 2002; http://www.ideaspaz.org/publicaciones/download/communidad_internacional_english.pdf (Accessed 30 January 2004), pp. 61–62.

28 According to Patten, the EU contribution was planned (excluding EUR 35 million of unprogrammable aid) as follows: EUR 105 million of programmable aid over the period 2000–2006 to be spent on the following sectors: social and economic development and

contribution, including all bilateral assistance by the member states, amounted to about US \$350 million. The resources offered to Colombia, however, were not provided as promised. According to the September report on Plan Colombia First Phase, the United States provided 91% of the sum offered to Colombia, while the rest of the world contributed only 44% of the promised amount.[29]

The reluctance of international donors[30] was triggered partially by the focus 'exclusively based on a strategy against narcotics' and the lack of a definitive plan for humanitarian and development issues.[31] Since the US-backed Plan had no resemblance to the old Pastrana version and focused only on drug control and counter-insurgency, the international community regarded it as a US military-oriented operation rather than a Colombian plan.[32] The strong emphasis on drug control, leading to reliance on the military, could not gain approval from the neighbouring states, such as Ecuador, Venezuela and Brazil.[33] Although supportive of the peace talks, the neighbouring states were seriously concerned about the spill over effects that may be caused by the repressive drug control measures. They feared that a large-scale drug control operation would increase problems at their border

---

combating poverty (EUR 40 million); alternative development (EUR 30 million); support for the reform of the judicial sector (EUR 25 million); support and promotion of human rights (EUR 10 million)'. Fithin, C., 'Plan Colombia', *Oxford Analytica*, 4 January 2001, http://www.ciaonet.org/pbei/oxan/oxa10020104.html (Accessed 14 November 2003); McDermott, J., 'Colombia frustrated by EU aid', *BBC*, 28 March 2001, http://news.bbc.co.uk/1/hi/world/americas/1246877.stm (Accessed 30 October 2003); Patten, C. on behalf of the Commission, 25 June 2001, *Official Journal of European Communities*, 20 December 2001, C364E; and Patten, C., on behalf of the Commission, 31 May 2001, *Official Journal of European Communities*, 13 November 2001, C318E/59, p. 59.

29 Deparmanento Nacional de Planeación, *Balance del Plan Colombia*, 17 September 2003, http://www.dnp/gov.co/ArchivosWeb/Direccion_Evaluacion_Gestion/Repor_y_Doc/Balance_Plan_Colombia.pdf (Accessed 29 October 2003), p. 31.

30 The sums other international donors agreed to contribute at the donor meeting in 2000 were: Japan \$170 million, Spain \$100 million, Italy \$10 million, Norway \$20 million, Germany \$10.5 million, the UK \$5 million. Fithin, op cit.

31 *Plan Colombia: A Plan for Peace or a Plan for War?* Statement made by social organisations, non-Governmental Organisations, and the Colombian Human Rights and Peace Movement, http://www.tni.org/drugs/research/plcoleu.htm (Accessed 15 December 2003); Penalva, C., *El Plan Colombia y Sus Implicaciones Internacionales*, http://www.ua.es/cultura/aipaz/docs/Plancol.ref (Accessed 20 January 2004); The actual text of Plan Colombia, see: President, *Plan Colombia: Plan for Peace, Prosperity, and the Strengthening of the State*, 1999, Bogotá: Presidency of the Republic, http://www.usip.org/library/pa/colombia/adddoc/plan_colombia_101999.html (Accessed 31 October 2003).

32 Observatorio para la Paz, 'Plan Colombia: Juego de Máscaras', *Mamacoca*, http://www.mamacoca.org/plancol_mascaras_es.htm (Accessed 21 November 2003).

33 Marguis, C., 'Ambitious Antidrug Plan for Colombia is Faltering', *New York Times*, 15 October 2000; Rohter, L., 'Latin Leaders Rebuff Call by Clinton on Colombia', *New York Times*, 2 September 2000; and Metcalfe, R., 'Plan Colombia under Scrutiny', *Radio Netherlands Wereldomroep*, 17 October 2000, http://www.rnw.nl/hotspots/html/colombia001017.html (Accessed 30 October 2003).

areas, such as the cocaine trade, violence and refugees.[34] There was suspicion that: 'The complexity of the Colombian crisis and its subsequent spill over effect in the Andean region may present an insurmountable obstacle, too large to be solved by the assistance given by European-led aid.'[35] Colombia's neighbours were not willing to form 'a tight circle around Colombia' to support drug control and handle all the problems stemming from Plan Colombia.[36]

Furthermore, the neighbouring states suspected Plan Colombia of being a project based on US desires and not those of Colombia.[37] The neighbouring states and the EU were not consulted or informed about the negotiation between Colombia and the United States until the official announcement of the scheme.[38] Such a close negotiation between the United States and Colombia, according to an EU official, was not looked on favourably by the Europeans or amongst other Latin American states.[39] They expressed the wish to the Colombian government for open international discussions on the plan if they were to be expected to give their support. There were suspicions, among the international donors, that Colombia only wanted the support of the United States judging by its decision-making process.[40]

There were also concerns about the share of international funding of the budget for Plan Colombia. In order to establish the credibility of the Plan, the Colombian government should have allocated it more of their own resources.[41] The high financial dependence on international sources for Plan Colombia allowed large donors, such as the United States, to influence the project strongly and push their own priorities.[42] For example, the strong presence of a military component in Plan Colombia created

---

34 By the end of 2000, the spillover of crimes such as violence, kidnapping and refugees had occurred in the neighbouring states, such as Ecuador, Brazil, Venezuela and Panama. Flynn, S., *US Support of Plan Colombia: Rethinking the Ends and Means*, May 2001, http://www.carlisle.army.mil/ssi/2001/pcussprt/pcussprt.pdf (Accessed 16 May 2003), p. 4; Arias Calderón, R., 'A View from Panama', in *Plan Colombia: Some Differing Perspectives*, July 2001, http://www.carlisle.army.mil/ssi/pubs/2001/pcdiffer.pdf (Accessed 16 May 2003), p. 33.

35 Roy, J., *European Perceptions of Plan Colombia: A Virtual Contribution to A Virtual War and Peace Plan?* May 2001, http://www.miami.edu/nsc/publications/IPCservice/PCEUROPE.PDF (Accessed 4 January 2004) pp. 21–22.

36 Flynn, *US Support of Plan Colombia*, p. 4; Arias Calderón, op cit., p. 33.

37 Garrido, 'La Guerra Global Contra El terror, Plan Colombia, El IRA Y La Región Andino Amazonica'.

38 Interviews with officials at the EU delegation in Washington DC and the CICAD of the OAS on 29 May 2003, at the Mexican Foreign Ministry on 16 June 2003.

39 Interview with an official at the EU delegation in Washington DC on 30 May 2003.

40 Ibid.

41 Buscaglia, E., and Ratliff, W., *War and Lack of Governance in Colombia: Narcos, Guerrillas, and US Policy*, 2001, http://www.hoover.stanford/edu/publications/epp/107/107. pdf (Accessed 11 July 2003). 70% of the National budget of 2001 was spent on the war on drugs and counter-insurgency (the budget is equivalent to 15% of GDP). Sarmiento Anzola, L., 'Plan Colombia, conflicto e intervención', *Mamacoca*, http://www.mamacoca.org/sarmiento_plan_conflicto.htm (Accessed 21 November 2003).

42 Arias Calderón, 'A View from Panama', p. 32.

alarm that it would help the US re-establish its military presence in Latin America.[43] Serrano argues that Plan Colombia was part of US intervention in Latin America, and US military support is not limited to Colombia. Neighbouring states, such as Peru and Bolivia have been receiving military training aid, and through Plan Colombia, the US intends to increase its military commitment to Venezuela and Ecuador under the name of regional security.[44] Such arguments, according to a Colombian official source, might have stemmed from the suspicion that Plan Colombia was drafted around US policy.[45]

The Colombian acceptance of military involvement was due in part to the outcome of the 2001 presidential election in which Alvaro Uribe, who promised to take radical action against drug trafficking and guerrilla groups, won the presidential office. The Uribe administration has carried out more 'aggressive' policies to control drugs.[46] Based on a belief in 'democratic security', that is to say that 'order is good for every one and can be achieved democratically',[47] Uribe pursued stronger military action against the leftist guerrilla group (FARC) as well as aerial eradication of coca fields to re-establish safety in the state.[48] Uribe emphasised the significance of this policy as a policy concerning soft (non-traditional) security issues.[49]

As for the lack of social and economic development programmes in Plan Colombia, it reflects the neglect of solutions for the 'real problems' of Colombia: weak government and inequality.[50] According to Nagle, the lack of development projects means that Plan Colombia lacks 'the right methodology and balance' to tackle the core problems.[51] Such an approach, failing to reflect the needs of local people, is symptomatic of the inappropriate drafting of the plan. From the perspective of the European Parliament, Plan Colombia is not 'the product of a process of dialogue amongst the various partners in society' because the local governments and

---

43 Garrido, 'La Guerra Global Contra El terror, Plan Colombia, El IRA Y La Región Andino Amazonica'.

44 Serrano, P., *Plan Colombia, la guerra sin limites*, 23 May 2002, http://www.rebelion. org/plancolombia/serrano230502.htm (Accessed 20 January 2004).

45 Interview with an official at the Colombian Embassy in Brussels on 10 July 2002.

46 Interview with an official at the ONDCP in Washington DC on 28 May 2003.

47 McLean, P., 'Who is Alvaro Uribe and How Did He Get Elected?', *Hemisphere Focus: 2001-2002*, 12 July 2002, http://www.ciaonet.org/pbei/csis/hem2001-2002/020712/ index.html (Accessed 13 November 2003).

48 Selsky, A., 'Colombia Vows to Down Drug Flights', *Associated Press*, 29 October 2003,   http://www.washingtonpost.com/ac2/wp-dyn/A36752-2003Oct29?language=printer (Accessed 30 October 2003).

49 'Uribe defends security policies', *BBC News*, 18 November 2004 http://news.bbc. co.uk/2/hi/americas/4021213.stm (Accessed 9 March 2007).

50 According to Nagle, the real problems of Colombia are: a weak government, inequality, an absence of citizen participation, institutional immorality and cultural corruption, and an ineffective legal system. Nagle, op cit., pp. 4–5.

51 Ibid.

Non Governmental Organisations (NGOs) were not involved in the project's design process.[52]

The negative response to Plan Colombia from the European Union was damaging to its desire for multinational co-operation in drug control. To the Colombian government, EU support had symbolic as well as practical meaning. EU participation in Plan Colombia had a particular significance to the success of the scheme. As Godoy maintains, the Pastrana government needed European support to prove that Plan Colombia was an integrated and multinational programme to deal with all drug related issues, not simply another US military drug control plan.[53] Colombia also needed EU support for economic and environmental affairs, in which the United States is less eager to contribute.[54] Furthermore, it is believed that the EU's experiences, resources, and expertise in the field can 'help to avoid any further deterioration in Colombia's security'.[55]

In the light of EU negativity, the Colombian government produced another proposal under Plan Colombia, which focused on development and human rights protection without the military component.[56] It became known as 'Plan Colombia: European version' since it was targeted almost exclusively on the EU.[57] This new proposal, however, could not overturn the initial European impression of Plan Colombia, and hence, had little influence over EU decision making about its contribution to the plan.[58] Consequently, the participation of the international community remains marginal, and support for Colombia retains two dimensions: one, national security led by the United States, and the other, non-violent measures preferred by the EU.[59]

In sum, Plan Colombia was the first attempt at a multinational project for Colombia. It was carried out with support from various international actors, although the amount of material support has been less than hoped for by the Colombian government. The Colombian government concluded that there were three benefits

---

52 *European Parliament Resolution on Plan Colombia and Support for the Peace Process in Colombia*, 1 February 2001, B5-0087/2001, http://www.narconews.com/euroresolution2001.html (Accessed 30 October 2003).

53 Godoy, *Plan Colombia's Strategic Weaknesses*, p. 3.

54 Gaitán Pavía, *et al.*, op cit., p. 21.

55 Ibid., p. 72.

56 President of Colombia, *Plan Colombia: Institutional Strengthening and Social Development 2000-2002*, July 2000, Bogotá: National Planning Department, http://www.tni.org/drugs/research/PlanColEurope.doc (Accessed 15 December 2003).

57 Interview with an official at the Colombian Embassy in Brussels on 10 July 2002.

58 See below for the detailed discussion. Officially, the European Union does not take any part in Plan Colombia.

59 Although the European Commission denies involvement in Plan Colombia, the support from the EU in the period of Plan Colombia is considered by the Colombian government to be more or less of the same value as EU participation would have been in Plan Colombia. Departamento Nacional de Planeación, *Plan Colombia Balance 1999-2003*, November 2003, http://www.dnp.gov/co/ArchivosWeb/Direccion_Evaluacion_Gestion/Report_y_Doc/Balance_Plan_Colombia.pdf (Accessed 15 January 2004), p. 7.

from the Plan.[60] It was easier for Colombia to establish bilateral co-operation than multinational, the latter requiring higher management skills.[61] The close association with the United States was re-established, after it had soured during the Samper administration.[62] In addition, the Colombian government claimed that invoking the concept of co-responsibility against universal challenges, such as drug trafficking and violation of human rights, was another benefit.[63] Although the Colombian attitude to the first phase of Plan Colombia remains positive, clear differences are identifiable between the approach of the EU and the military oriented approach of the United States. In the next section, the aspect to be examined will be the US perception of and commitment to Plan Colombia.

Plan Colombia and the United States

Plan Colombia was an almost ideal project for the United States because it matched US interests so closely.[64] The US priority in Colombia was clear, as General McCaffrey, former drug czar for the Clinton administration, maintains: 'The [number one] objective [for the United States] is the reduction in the supply of cocaine and heroin that is destroying the region and the American people.'[65] The reduction in the cocaine flow has been the main focus in US drug control policy and foreign policy toward Colombia.[66] Those two policies have been regarded as almost the equivalent of each other. Shifter analyses the relationship between them, as 'one has nearly become a proxy for the other'.[67] In a sense, the US relationship with Colombia has revolved around drug control policy.

The governance capability of the Colombian government administration, in the face of the drug trafficking problem, has also been a US concern. The maintenance of Colombian stability and that of other Andean states is important to the stability

---

   60 Departamento Nacional de Planeación, *Balance del Plan Colombia*, 17 September 2003, http://www.dnp/gov.co/ArchivosWeb/Direccion_Evaluacion_Gestion/Repor_y_Doc/Balance_Plan_Colombia.pdf (Accessed 29 October 2003), p. 30.

   61 Ibid.

   62 Godoy, *Plan Colombia's Strategic Weaknesses*, p. 4.

   63 Ibid., p. 30.

   64 GAO, *Drug Control: Narcotics Threat From Colombia Continues to Grow*, Report to Congressional Requesters, GAO/NSIAD-99-136, June 1999, Washington DC: GAO, p. 11.

   65 McCaffrey, B., *The Crisis in Colombia: What Are We Facing?* Testimony before the House Subcommittee on Criminal Justice, Drug Policy, and Human Resources of the Committee on Government Reform, 106th Congress, 15 February 2000, No. 106–151, Washington DC: US GPO, pp. 82–83.

   66 According to a report to the EU, the US has demanded the import of US agricultural products, such as cotton, potatoes, corn and grain to Colombia in exchange for support for Plan Colombia. *Colombia: European Union & Cauca Delegation*, http://www.paxchristi.net/PDF/LA4NL106.pdf (Accessed 31 October 2003).

   67 Shifter, M., *US Policy in the Andean Region*, http://www.ciaonet.org/wps/coj05/coj05.pdf (Accessed 13 November 2003), p. 10.

of the region.[68] According to Arnson, 'the threat posed to US interest was no longer focused primarily on narcotics entering the Untied States, but rather, on lawlessness, insecurity, and instability within Colombia itself.'[69] The United States came to regard its interests as being threatened not only by drug trafficking but also the Colombian government's inability to control it, which allowed the insurgency to grow stronger. Colombia could provoke instability in the Andean region, which includes states vulnerable to the activities of drug trafficking organisations, such as Bolivia and Peru.[70]

Economic interests play a significant role in US participation in Plan Colombia. As Jelsma argues, the United States has more interests in Colombia than simply cocaine: for example, oil production in northern Colombia.[71] US interests in Plan Colombia, according to Under-Secretary for Political Affairs, Grossman, are mainly economic and stem from the fact that Colombia supplies $3.6 billion in oil to the United States.[72] The oil fields of Colombia are located in areas controlled by insurgency groups, and therefore the growing influence of these groups is a serious concern to both the Colombian government and the United States. From the US perspective, supporting Colombia's drug control initiatives can contribute to the United States' fight against cocaine and protect its interests from insurgency groups.

The United States supplemented its repressive drug control approach with a large aid package.[73] The aid package was presented as assistance to Colombia in 'its efforts to confront the cocaine and heroin industries'.[74] The US strategy for Plan Colombia had five objectives, which aimed to tackle various issues related to drug trafficking and the reform of the Colombian government.[75] One of these objectives was to eradicate coca fields in southern Colombia where the FARC control the land.[76] This strategy targeting the production of drugs was also expected to be compatible with

---

68 Interviews with US officials at Department of State and ONDCP on 27 and 28 May 2003.

69 Arnson, C.J., *US Interests and Options in Colombia: An Alternative Framework*, http://www.ciaonet.org/wps/arc02/arc02.pdf (Accessed 13 November 2003), p. 22.

70 See chapter 2 for further information.

71 Van Rheenen, S., 'Plan Colombia Divides Europe and US', *Radio Netherlands Wereldomroep*, 1 March 2001, http://www.rnw.nl/hotspots/html/colombia010302.html (Accessed 30 October 2003).

72 Grossman, M., *US Support for Plan Colombia*, 31 August 2001, http://www.state. gov/g/inl/narc/rm/2001/may_aug/index.cfm?docid=4798 (Accessed 16 April 2003).

73 GAO, *Drug Control: Narcotics Threat From Colombia Continues to Grow*, p. 3.

74 Beers, R., *Statement* before the Senate Services Committee, 4 April 2000, http://www. state.gov/www/policy_remarks/2000/000404_beers_sasc.html (Accessed 5 May 2002).

75 The US $1.3 billion assistance in Plan Colombia targeted: 1) the disrupting and dismantling of drug-trafficking organisations; 2) the reduction of the availability of drugs through eradication and enforcement efforts; and 3) strengthening Colombian institutions to enable them to support a full range of counter-narcotics activities. GAO, *Drug Control: Narcotics Threat From Colombia Continues to Grow*, p. 3.

76 Hunter, C., and Brownfield, W.R., *US Assistance to Colombia*, Remarks at Special Briefing, Washington DC, 12 March 2001, http://www.state.gov/inl/narc/rm/2001/jan_apr/index.cfm?docid=1198 (Accessed 16 April 2003).

the fight against corruption, as well as strengthening and modernising the judicial system of Colombia.[77]

The US government described Plan Colombia as: '… a plan developed by the Colombian Government to address Colombian issues in Colombia.'[78] To some extent, the United States regarded it as a project based on the needs of Colombia. Nevertheless, it was a project that also reflected the interests of the United States due to its frequent discussion with Colombia. Plan Colombia was based on the idea that economic development, security and peace were directly linked, this appealed to the Americans who believed that the reduction of cocaine production would help to solve drug trafficking and the problem of insurgency groups.[79] According to a GAO report, a draft version of Plan Colombia was presented to the United States in 1998 and contained elements that parallel the US counter-narcotics strategy for the Andes.[80]

The United States expanded the programmes to assist neighbouring states affected by Plan Colombia in order to increase their capability to control drug trafficking.[81] In view of the transnational nature of drug trafficking, the US government recognised the need to need to provide assistance to the region. According to Brownfield, the Colombian issues need to be part of a 'regional approach' rather than treated in isolation.[82] Under the newly re-enforced regional focus, 33% of about US$ 900 million for the Andean Initiative was 'devoted to programs focused on alternative development and support for democratic institutions'.[83] This increased funds to

---

77 The US assistance in Plan Colombia is particularly targeting the following areas: strengthening and modernising Colombia's criminal justice system, more alternative development programmes, and human rights protection, counter measures against corruption, money laundering and kidnapping. Grossman, op cit.

78 Hunter *et al.*, *US Assistance to Colombia*.

79 Marcella, G., 'Plan Colombia: An Interim Assessment', *Hemisphere Focus: 2001-2002*, 25 January 2002, http://www.ciaonet.org/pbei/csis/hem2001-2002/020125/index.html (Accessed 13 November 2003); Vargas M.,R., *The New Global Era: Threats and impacts for Colombia*, December 2001, http://www.ciponline.org/colombia/121302.htm (Accessed 12 October 2003); Marguis, 'Ambitious Antidrug Plan for Colombia is Faltering'; and Rohter, 'Latin Leaders Rebuff Call by Clinton on Colombia'.

80 Those parallel elements listed are: eradication and interdiction to reduce illegal cocaine production, alternative development, legislation and institutional reforms to combat drug trafficking organisations, demand reduction programmes in Colombia, environmental actions and efforts to strengthen international co-operation against drug trafficking. GAO, *Drug Control: Narcotics Threat From Colombia Continues to Grow*, p. 11.

81 See chapter 6 for further information on the Andean Initiative. Interview with an official at Mission to the European Union in Brussels on 25 April 2002; and Romero, P., Written answer to a question submitted, *The Crisis in Colombia: What Are We Facing?* Hearing before the House Subcommittee on Criminal Justice, Drug Policy, and Human Resources of the Committee on Government Reform, 106th Congress, 15 February 2000, No. 106–151, Washington DC: US GPO, pp. 217–218.

82 Hunter, C., *et al.*, *US Assistance to Colombia*.

83 Mack, J., 'Plan Colombia and the Andean Regional Initiative', 28 June 2001, *Testimony* before the House International Relations Committee Subcommittee on the Western Hemisphere.

the Andean region in order to balance the counter-narcotics efforts in Colombia.[84] McCaffrey strongly believes that Plan Colombia worked and will result in 'a massive reduction in the production of drugs on Colombian soil and a comparable lowering of the level of violence'.[85] The former Under-Secretary of State, Thomas Pickering, has expressed the expectation to further regional commitment and multinational co-operation in drug control encouraged by Plan Colombia.[86]

US interests in Plan Colombia remained unchanged even after the change of administrations in both Colombia and the United States. The United States had additional interests towards Colombia after 11 September 2001 – the war on terrorism. The terrorist attacks changed the US foreign policy focus and merged drug control policy and counter-terrorist policy into one in Colombia.[87]. Also, the military involvement in Colombian drug control was limited in order to prevent the collapse of the peace negotiations between the Colombian government, the FARC and the ELN. The US emphasised the difference between their policies for drug control and counter-terrorism to reassure the guerrilla groups that the US commitment in Plan Colombia was purely for controlling cocaine.[88] The military was expected to liaise with anti-narcotics operations, not counter-insurgency groups.[89]

After 11 September, however, the United States has changed its focus. The connection between the insurgency groups and drug trafficking organisations became prioritised. In 2002, it announced a budget for counter-insurgency operations under the framework of Plan Colombia with certain restrictions placed on it. The budget allocated to support the Colombian National Police (CNP) and Colombian Army increased sharply between fiscal year 2002 and 2004.[90] In addition, the US government removed the restrictions on distribution of funding from military assistance in Plan

---

84 Interview with a US official at US Mission to the EU in Brussels on 25 April 2002.

85 McCaffrey, B.R., *The Drug Scourge as a Hemispheric Problem*, August 2001, http://www.arlisle.army.mil/ssi/pubs/2001/scrouge/scrouge.pdf (Accessed 9 October 2003).

86 Marguis, C., 'US Weighs Expanding Aid Plan to Colombia's Neighbours', *The Washington Post*, 4 December 2000.

87 Shifter, *US Policy in the Andean Region*, p. 10.

88 Marcella, 'Plan Colombia: An Interim Assessment'.

89 Valencia Tovar, A., 'A View from Bogotá', in *Plan Colombia: Some Differing Perspectives*, July 2001, http://www.carlisle.army.mil/ssi/pubs/2001/pcdiffer.pdf (Accessed 16 May 2003), pp. 21–22.

90 Fiscal year 2002 budget for CNP was $134,100,000 and for the Army, $104,000,000. But fiscal year 2003, CNP $130,950,000 and the Army received $147,050,000. In fiscal year 2004, CNP is expected to receive $147,496,000, and the Army $158,704,000. *Fiscal year 2004 Congressional Budget Justification*, p. 36, obtained during the interviews in Washington DC in May 2003.

Colombia for fiscal year 2004.[91] This allowed both counter-narcotics and counter-insurgency operations to benefit from the fund.[92]

US Backed Projects in Plan Colombia

The major programmes supported by the United States are categorised into three: support for law enforcement, aerial eradication, and alternative development. The eradication and alternative development projects were in the same package in the US policy because alternative development was regarded as a measure to prevent the peasants returning to illicit cultivation.[93] The projects on law enforcement and eradication were under severe criticism internationally due to the military involvement. The projects that influenced international participation will now be investigated.

Law Enforcement and Aerial Eradication   The supply of military equipment to the CNP and Colombian Army were the items on which the United States spent most of its $1.3 billion budget.[94] This was because Colombia did not have sufficient military and law enforcement units for coca eradication and the interdiction of cocaine.[95] The high expenditure on military equipment meant that not all the money was spent in Colombia but went towards defence spending within the United States. Accepting military aid is often a condition of the host state being granted other forms of aid. This is not new in US foreign policy.[96] For example, supplying helicopters for drug control will inject a few hundreds million dollars into the US military industry.[97] In

---

91 Until the removal of this restriction, military funding in Plan Colombia was provided only to counter-narcotics operations. If there is any insurgent involvement in cocaine trafficking, the funding could not be released because it was prohibited for it to be used against insurgency groups. Sanchez, M., 'Once Held at Arms Length, Colombia's Military Gets Bush's Embrace', *The Washington Post*, 6 February 2003, http://www.washingtonpost.com/ac2/wp-dyn/A36191-2003Feb6?language=printer (21 May 2003).

92 Interviews with officials at the ONDCP in Washington DC on 28 May 2003.

93 Interview with a Police General at the Colombian Embassy in London, 14 January 2002.

94 80% of the budget was allocated to military support including 60 Blackhawk helicopters. However, opposition inside the US government changed the plan to send re-built Huey II helicopters (costing $1.4 million a helicopter) rather than expensive Blackhawks ($14 million a helicopter). Lister, R., 'US commits to Colombia', *BBC*, 31 August 2000, http://news.bbc.co.uk/1/hi/world/americas/902035.stm (Accessed 20 October 2003); Vaicius, *et al.*, ''Plan Colombia': The Debate in Congress', p. 6; and Ballenger, *The Crisis in Colombia: What Are We Facing?* Testimony before the House Subcommittee on Criminal Justice, Drug Policy, and Human Resources of the Committee on Government Reform, 106th Congress, 15 February 2000, No. 106–151, Washington DC: US GPO, p. 76.

95 GAO, *Drug Control: Efforts to Develop Alternatives to Cultivating Illicit Crops in Colombia Have Made Little Progress and Face Serious Obstacles*, GAO-02-291, February 2002, Washington DC: US General Accounting Office, p. 13.

96 Sarmiento Anzola, 'Plan Colombia, conflicto e intervención'.

97 Manufacturing helicopters involves huge sums of money and the manufactures of Blackhawk and Huey compete to get the contract. Therefore, the provision of these helicopters

a sense, this project served US economic interests by increasing employment for US subcontractors and promoting US military industries.[98]

According to a Colombian government source, the equipment was a significant element in enabling Colombia to pursue its drug control policy since such equipment was otherwise unaffordable.[99] For example, the United States provided helicopters and fixed-wing aircraft, which are essential for policing and patrolling the vast territory of Colombia, particularly the areas with illicit coca fields. The lack of resources affected the ability of the CNP to conduct effective law enforcement, and for the Colombian government to execute its policy against the drug traffickers. The traffickers are known to possess more sophisticated weapons than the government, such as fixed wing aircraft and radar systems.[100] According to a Colombian police source, the technologies and equipment offered by the United States substantially improved the drug control capability of the CNP.[101]

Nevertheless, there is a serious fault in this programme. The US government did not take into account the resources necessary for Colombia to maintain the equipment. The helicopters could not be fully mobilised because of the shortage of spare parts and a lack of funding for maintenance. According to a US official source, such problems occurred because the US policy makers did not properly grasp the Colombian situation.[102] The supply of spare parts was organised based on calculations of the use of helicopters by the US army, which is considerably less than use by the Colombians. The lack of necessary parts made operations with the helicopters impossible.[103] Re-examining the situation, the US government reconsidered the quantity and frequency for parts to be supplied in order to increase their operability.[104]

Under the framework of law enforcement support, the United States also supported judicial reform. Judicial reform was considered a key project to strengthen democracy and local government and human rights protection, and also to achieve increased accountability of the Colombian government. The projects included increasing police presence in rural areas and *Casa de Justicia* (the mediation centre or judicial

---

can be compromised under the political conflicts in the US, and the host state may receive different equipment from what they originally agreed in the draft for the drug control project. Vaicius *et al.*, "Plan Colombia': The Debate in Congress', p. 6.

98 Interview with an official at the Department of State in Washington DC on 27 May 2003.

99 Interview with an official at the Colombian Embassy in Washington DC on 29 May 2003.

100 See chapter 2 of this book.

101 Interview with a police general at the Colombian Embassy in London on 14 January 2002.

102 Interview with an official at ONDCP in Washington DC on 28 May 2003.

103 Ford. J.T., *Drug Control: Challenges in Implementing Plan Colombia*, testimony 12 October 2000, GAO-01-76T, US General Accounting Office: Washington DC, pp. 6–22.

104 Interview with an official at the ONDCP in Washington DC on 28 May 2003; and Ford, *Drug Control: Challenges in Implementing Plan Colombia*, pp. 6–22.

centre).[105] Through the programme 180 municipalities in Southern Colombia came to enjoy government control through more police presence.[106] Before the programme, it was difficult for the Colombian government to provide sufficient services to the rural areas, so the control of the region had been in the hands of guerrilla groups and paramilitaries. The programme of *Casa de Justicia* also aimed at providing judicial and health services to rural areas, of which there are 32 in Colombia.[107]

Secondly, aerial eradication was one of the major repressive efforts of the United States in drug control and directly reflected US interests in the reduction of Colombian cocaine. According to Carpenter, the US ambassador to Colombia warned in 2001 that US aid and fumigation were inseparable.[108] Under the framework of Plan Colombia, the operations were executed in the southern region of Colombia, the departments of Putumayo and Caqueta.[109] The department of Putumayo is known for the concentration of coca cultivation, particularly in the Bajo Putumayo. Those regions register high rates of violence linked to the drug industry and the strong presence of the FARC and paramilitary groups.[110]

Aerial eradication is quick, and brings a clear result. According to Colombian official reports, coca cultivation in Colombia has been falling dramatically since 2000 as aerial eradication progresses, and Plan Colombia reduced coca production in Colombia by 37.5%.[111] The speed of eradication was remarkable. About a month from the start of the project, the Colombian government eradicated 20,000 hectares

---

105 This is a project operated by USAID, and Casa de Justicia offers various services, such as legal advice, police functions, consultation and health services.

106 Interview with an official at the Department of States in Washington DC on 27 May 2003.

107 Franco, A.A., *Testimony* before the House Appropriations Committee's Subcommittee on Foreign Operations US Assistance to Colombia and the Andean Region, 10 April 2002, http://www.state.gov/press/spe_test/testimony/2002/ty020410.html (Accessed 20 May 2003); *Colombia's House of Justice*, http://www.restorativejustice.org/rj3/Feature/2003/July/housesofjustice.htm (Accessed 17 February 2004); and US Department of States, 'Fact Sheet: The USAID/Colombia Casa de Justicis National Program', Washington File, 31 August 2000, http://usinfo.state.gov/regional/ar/colombia/fact3004.htm (Accessed 17 February 2000).

108 Uribe promised an end to fumigation when he was standing for the Presidential election. Carpenter, *Bad Neighbor Policy*, p. 145.

109 Isacson, A., and Olsen, J., *Just the Facts 2000-2001*, 2001, Latin American Working Group, pp. 30–32.

110 Viceprecidencia de la Republica de Colombia, *Panorama Actual del Putumayo*, May 2001, Bogotá, http://www.derechoshumanos.gov.co/observarotio/04_publicaciones/04_03_regiones/putumayo/violenci.htm (Accessed 26 January 2004).

111 With the efforts in Plan Colombia, coca cultivation dropped to 102.071 hectares. A 37.5% reduction in Colombian coca production has led to 21.8% reduction of world coca production. Departamento Nacional de Planeación, Hacia un Estado Comunitario: Primeros resultados del Plan Nacional de Desarrollo Seguridad Democrática, August 2003, Bogotá: Sinergia, http://www.dnp.gov/co/ArchivosWeb/Direccion_Evaluacion_Gestion/Report_y_Doc/Reportes_de_Evaluacion_N3.pdf (Accessed 15 January 2004), p3; and Departamento Nacional de Planeación, *Brindar Seguridad Democrática: Seguimiento a Resultados Tercer Trimestre 2003*, November 2003, http://www.dnp.gov/co/ArchivosWeb/Direccion_Evaluacion_Gestion/Report_y_Doc/Seguridad_democratica_3er_trimestre_2003.

in Putumayo.[112] By 2002, the United States had trained and equipped the Colombian counter-narcotics brigade, which destroyed 84,000 hectares of illicit coca fields.[113] *The Washington Post* reported a 93% decline in coca cultivation in Putumayo after their three-year operation.[114] Also, a US report expressed the hope of achieving a 50% cut in Colombian coca by 2005.[115]

The strength of aerial eradication lies not only in its speed, but also in the cost. Although the Colombian government sees manual and voluntary eradication as a principal solution in the fight against drug trafficking, the cost and risks are lower for fumigation.[116] According to a Colombian police source, despite the requirement for expensive equipment such as aeroplanes and helicopters, it costs less than manual eradication because the coca cultivation areas are protected by the guerrilla groups, and the police officers cannot avoid attacks from them during their operations.[117] Aerial eradication operation also face attacks from the guerrilla groups, and so they are escorted by police helicopter. The risks, however, are still lower in the operations from the air than on the ground.[118]

Despite those strengths, fumigation has brought some regrettable issues. A Colombian police official described three negative effects stemming from eradication.[119] Firstly, coca fields have not reduced commensurately with the efforts made in eradication. The satellite maps produced by the US government clearly indicate the move of coca fields toward the Pacific coast and the Amazonian jungle to avoid fumigation.[120] As noted by a US government source, the coca fields have

---

zip (Accessed 15 January 2004); and Departamento Nacional de Planeación, *Plan Colombia Balance 1999-2003*, p. 13.

112 Boucher, R., *Counternarcotics Cooperation with Colombia*, US Department of State Office of the Spokesman Press Statement, 19 January 2001, http://secretary.state.gov/www/ briefings/statements/2001/ps010119.html (Accessed 13 March 2001).

113 The brigade also destroyed 800 coca base laboratories and 21 cocaine-refining laboratories. Gutierrez, L., *Peace and Security in Colombia*, 20 June 2002, http://www.state. gov/p/wha/rls/rm/11297pf.htm (Accessed 16 May 2003).

114 Wilson, S., 'In Colombia, Coca Declines But the War Does Not', *The Washington Post*, 21 December 2003, http://www.washingtonpost.com/wp-dyn/articles/A17533-2003Dec20. html (Accessed 13 February 2004).

115 The US Department of State, *A Report to Congress on United States Policy Towards Colombia and Other Related Issues*, 3 February 2003, http://www.state.gov/p/wha/rls/rpt/ 17140pf.thm (Accessed 16 May 2003).

116 Deparmanento Nacional de Planeación, *Balance del Plan Colombia*, p. 5.

117 Interview with a police general at the Colombian Embassy in London on 14 January 2002.

118 There were 94 attacks against spray aeroplanes in 2003. Wilson, 'In Colombia, Coca Declines But the War Does Not'.

119 Interview with a police general at the Colombian Embassy in London on 14 January 2002.

120 Interview with an official at the ONDCP in Washington DC on 28 May 2003. In Putumayo, new coca fields that are smaller than 3 hectares have emerged since the beginning of Plan Colombia because fumigation targets fields that are larger than 3 hectares. 'Colombians bypass Plan Colombia', *Jane's Foreign Report*, 26 April 2001, http://groups/yahoo.com/ group/ColombiaUpdate/message/247 (Accessed 29 October 2003).

been removed to more and more remote areas, in which eradication is difficult because the helicopters are unable to reach there without refuelling – and those areas do not have any facility to refuel helicopters.[121] Conducting eradication in the remote areas is problematic enough, but afterwards, there is no way to offer alternative development projects due to the distance from the markets and the lack of basic social infrastructure.

Secondly, the guerrilla groups have become more active in response to eradication.[122] For example, in southern Colombia, the insurgency groups have increased their use of violence to protect their coca fields.[123] The involvement of the guerrilla groups in cocaine trafficking prior to eradication was a minor one designed to protect the peasants and coca fields. The increase in eradication projects between 1994 and 1998 in southern Colombia, however, changed their role to a more active one, such as taxing the peasants for their protection and punishing them if they did not obey the rules set by the guerrilla groups.[124] As Tinkner maintains, Plan Colombia has increased the tension in Colombia and could weaken the government rather than strengthen it.[125]

In Putumayo, one of the coca growing areas in southern Colombia, the influence of insurgency groups is stronger than that of the government. The FARC and paramilitaries divide the region, and those who do not follow the rules are punished.[126] Although there are police officers, the locals know that public order is not in the hands of the government. The lack of government capability and trust from citizens was reflected in the national poll. According to the poll in 2000 by the Colombian National Polling Centre, 46% of Colombians thought the most powerful person in the country was the FARC leader Manuel Marulanda, compared to only 10% for President Pastrana.[127] The rise of control by the insurgency groups reflects the decline of government authority over the areas. The government authorities lost popular support due to economic difficulties and instability caused by eradication. Carpenter argues that economic difficulties brought by eradication could trigger the eruption of anger from the peasants and induce frequent demonstrations backed by the guerrilla groups.[128]

---

121 Interview with an official at the ONDCP in Washington DC on 28 May 2003.

122 Interview with a police general at the Colombian Embassy in London on 14 January 2002.

123 *Colombia: European Union & Cauca Delegation.*

124 Interview with a police general at the Colombian Embassy in London on 14 January 2002.

125 Tinkner, A.B., 'Tensions Y Contradicciones en los Objectivos de la Política Exterior Estadounidense en Colombia: Consecuencias involuntarias de la política antinarcóticos de Estados Unidos en un Estado débil', *Revista Colombia Internacional*, No. 49/50, Parte II, http://www.lablaa.org/blaavirtual/colinter/arlene2.htm (Accessed 13 November 2003).

126 Webb, J., 'Dead Man Tells of Colombian Cocaine Culture', *Reuters*, 7 February 2004, http://www.washingtonpost.com/wp-dyn/articles/A21290-2004Feb7.html (Accessed 9 February 2004).

127 31% of Colombians participating in the poll said the most powerful actor in the country is the United States. Lister, op cit.

128 Carpenter, 'Plan Colombia: The Drug War's New Morass', p. 14.

Thirdly, the unemployment rate has increased as eradication progressed.[129] It has been caused by the loss of cocaine income and undelivered aid. As a USAID official admits, the progress of eradication is too rapid to be followed up by alternative development projects because they take a long time to establish and lack resources.[130] The fumigated areas and some surrounding areas have been experiencing difficulties in cultivation because fumigation destroyed everything. The peasants in Putumayo lost the means to support their families and themselves.[131] In addition, according to Isacson and Vaicius, the alternative development project[132] for palm hart and fish plantations in Putumayo conducted by the Colombian government projects, PLANET, was destroyed by fumigation.[133] The land became unsuitable for cultivation and failures in alternative development disrupted regional economic activities. Consequently, those who live in the fumigated areas were removed from their lands and had to search for jobs, resulting in the increase of internally displaced people.[134]

If the supply of aid had arrived in the aftermath of eradication, the peasants in the fumigated areas might have overcome the situation. The aid materials, however, did not reach the necessary areas. Those delays were caused by bureaucratic procedures and a malfunctioning transportation system as well as disagreements between the governments. In Putumayo, the delivery of alternative development and food aid was affected by an unsolved policy dispute between the US and Colombian government.[135] As a result, the peasants were left without any food or means to earn an income. The USAID claims that a great damage to the local economy was caused in the fumigated areas, but the Colombian national economy is unaffected.[136]

The chemical used in fumigation have affected the coca growing areas. The damage posed to the local communities by aerial fumigation was criticised by

---

129 Interview with a police general at the Colombian Embassy in London on 14 January 2002.

130 According to the Colombian alternative development agency PLANTE, alternative development projects were promoted in 28,485 hectares of Colombian territory between 1997 and 2001, compared with the fumigated areas of about 108,800 hectares in 2001 alone. Interview with an official at USAID in Washington DC on 27 May 2003; Comptroller General of Colombia, *Evaluation of Plan Colombia*, Third Report, July 2002, pp. 23–24.

131 Isacson, A., and Vaicius, I., 'Plan Colombia's 'Ground Zero'', *International Policy Report*, April 2000, http://www.ciponline.org/colombia/0401putu.pdf (Accessed 20 October 2003) pp. 10–12; and Salinas Abdala, Y., 'Plantearnientos de la Defensoría Frente al Programa de Erradicación Aérea de Cultivos Ilícitos con Glifosato', *Mamacoca*, 5 September 2003, http://www.mamacoca.org/FSMT_sept_2003/s/lat/Conversatorio_UROSARIO.htm (Accessed 21 November 2003).

132 For details of alternative development under Plan Colombia, see below; for the US alternative development projects in the past, see chapter 5.

133 Isacson, *et al.*, 'Plan Colombia's 'Ground Zero'', p. 13.

134 There are about 2 million internally displaced people in Colombia.

135 Haugaard, L., *Blunt Instrument: The United States' punitive fumigation program in Colombia*, November 2002, Washington DC: Latin American Working Group, pp. 5–6.

136 USAID, *Evolution of Alternative Development Strategy in the Andes and Bolivia Program Challenge*, USAID-INL Briefings, 17 January 2003, Powerpoint document obtained at the USAID during the interviews on 28 May 2003.

Salinas. There was a lack of research before the execution of aerial eradication as well as no investigation into the damage caused by the operation.[137] The effects of chemicals on human health have elicited international criticism. The US and Colombian governments are confident that the chemicals used for aerial eradication are safe for human beings and the environment, and consider European criticism as propaganda to create a hostile environment against aerial eradication.[138] The research by the Department of Nariño[139] to investigate the impacts of the chemical used in fumigation on the human body could not confirm cases of chemical related illness in the fumigated areas, although there were many complaints registered in the aftermath of aerial spraying.[140] The report, however, was received with scepticism due to the ambiguity of the research method.[141] An EU source maintains that opposition to aerial eradication was because one of the chemicals used[142] in the process is banned in the EU. A report to the EU indicates the negative impact of aerial spraying on human health and the environment.[143] It claims that: 'Washington's military-like interdiction efforts, such as aerial spraying of coca crops have not slowed the flow of drugs to the United Sates nor helped Colombia's economic development.'[144]

Alternative Development and the Issue of More Multinational Co-operation
Although the significance of economic support to coca growing regions has been

137 Salinas Abdala, 'Plantearnientos de la Defensoría Frente al Programa de Erradicación Aérea de Cultivos Ilícitos con Glifosato'.

138 Interview with an official at the Department of State in Washington DC on 27 May 2003; and Mack, J., *Testimony*, 28 June 2001.

139 Nariño is a town in Putumayo region targeted for aerial eradication.

140 After the operation, there were 1,000 complaints in the region, and 800 of them were filed as fumigation related complaints. The medical investigations for those who had complained did not state the cause of the illness as the chemical used for fumigation. Department of Nariño, Municipality of E Tablón de Gómez, *Final Report: A Study of the Health Complaints Related to Aerial Eradication in Colombia*, September 2001, Bogotá, http://ysenvasst.state.gov/bogota/wwwfapoe.pdf (Accessed 5 May 2002); and USINL, *Report on Issues related to the Aerial Eradication of Illicit Coca in Colombia*, September 2002, http://www.state.gov/g/inl/rls/rpt/aeicc/13242pf/htm (Accessed 16 May 2003).

141 During the investigation by the Department of Nariño, there were pressures from a doctor to nurses working in the regional hospital, and one doctor did not provide a report he said he would submit. Also some hospital records were not well filed and some records lack dates, so the research team concluded that they could not decide if those symptoms were cause by fumigation.

142 The chemical banned in the EU is Fusarium oxysporum. Also Carpenter argues that a chemical called 'Roundup' is used though it is not meant for direct contact on humans. *European Parliament Resolution on Plan Colombia*: and Carpenter, *Bad Neighbor Policy*, p. 163.

143 Interview with an official at the European Commission on July 2002; and van Rheenen, op cit.

144 Krause, A., 'EU Courting Latin America', *EUROPE*, August 2001, Issue No. 408, http://www.eurunion.org/magazine/0108/p12.htm (Accessed 31 October 2003); see also Vaicius, *et al.*, 'The 'War on Drugs' meets the 'War on Terror'', pp. 17–18.

reviewed, the emphasis on alternative development is still modest.[145] USAID is aiming at 30,000 hectares of voluntary eradication and the cultivation of alternative crops in Colombia in five years.[146] Voluntary eradication received more support from the local population than aerial eradication. Since the peasants prefer gradual and manual eradication rather than fumigation, reaching agreements to voluntarily eradicate illicit crops in exchange for help finding other income-producing opportunities was attractive to communities.[147] Although some communities participated in the project, its operation was not smooth.

The project of *Plan National de Desarrollo Alternativo* (PNDA – National Plan of Alternative Development), for example, was designed to provide economic support to those fields that had been eradicated. However, it was insufficient to secure the livelihoods of those who live in the eradicated areas.[148] USAID aimed to 'eliminate 900 hectares of coca, provide assistance to produce 1,200 hectares of licit crops or livestock, and provide assistance to 825 families' by voluntary eradication.[149] In the projects, PNDA is expected to provide immediate support to those who voluntarily eradicated coca and to encourage and negotiate with communities to participate in voluntary eradication.[150] Puerto Asís of Lower Putumayo agreed to participate in the alternative development project, but the food package delivery to substitute for

145 The USAID initially provided US $122.2 million under the framework of Plan Colombia. Since fiscal year 2003, the annual budget for alternative development has increased by about US $10 million to over $60 million. Franco, *Testimony*, 10 April 2002; and *Fiscal year 2004 Congressional Budget Justification*, p. 36.

146 In Bolivia and Peru, voluntary eradication contributed to the reduction of coca cultivation by 55% and 67% respectively. Leonard, C., *Implementing Plan Colombia: The US Role*, Testimony before the House Subcommittee on the Western Hemisphere of the Committee on International Relations, 106th Congress 2nd Session, 21 September 2000, No. 106-188, p. 32.

147 GAO, *Drug Control: Efforts to Develop Alternatives to Cultivating Illicit Crops in Colombia Have Made Little Progress and Face Serious Obstacles*, p. 9.

148 In order to operate PNDA, the US government assigned a US company to conduct the project rather than subcontracting Colombian companies due to the lack of confidence in Colombian institutions. In April 2001, using Plan Colombia funds, USAID awarded an $87.5 million, 5 year contract to Chemonics to oversee, administer, and carry out alternative development activities in the coca growing areas in the Putumayo and Caqueta departments. For Plan Colombia, the United States assigned over 300 civilian contractors to operate projects. GAO, *Drug Control: Efforts to Develop Alternatives to Cultivating Illicit Crops in Colombia Have Made Little Progress and Face Serious Obstacles*, pp. 9–15; Sarmiento Anzola, L., 'Plan Colombia, conflicto e intervención'; and Isacson *et al.*, 'Just the Facts 2001–2002', p. 3.

149 Cox, T.E., *Audit of the USAID/Colombia-Financed Coca Alternative Development Program Under the Plan Colombia Supplemental Appropriation*, Report No. 1-514-02-005-P, 16 January 2002, San Salvador: USAID, http://www.usaid.gov/oig/public/fy02rpts/1-514-02-005-P.pdf (Accessed 20 May 2003), p. 5.

150 GAO, *Drug Control: Efforts to Develop Alternatives to Cultivating Illicit Crops in Colombia Have Made Little Progress and Face Serious Obstacles*, p. 15.

their income had not arrived by February 2002, six months after the beginning of the project.[151]

In another case, the coca fields of a community that agreed to pursue voluntary eradication were fumigated. In Putumayo, the coca fields of project participants were sprayed despite the agreement to allow the peasants one year from the arrival of food aid to eradicate coca voluntarily.[152] It is uncertain how such an incident happened since, according to a US government source, the eradication took place after notice was given to the community.[153] Such incidents present a predicament for communities participating in eradication projects, because the peasants feel there is no sign of alternative development.[154]

Besides the management of the projects, there is a safety issue for those participating. The southern region of Colombia is under *de facto* control by the FARC and paramilitaries and the region is considered to unsafe for the alternative development agents to work in.[155] Metcalfe notes that alternative development projects face difficulties because guerrilla groups sabotage them.[156] A US report emphasises the significance of ensuring security based on post incidents, such as assassinations of development workers in Putumayo.[157] Some NGOs have pulled out of the region because the environment was too hostile. In 2001 alone, there were several kidnappings of development workers, and the assassinations of two Colombian development workers and several community leaders who collaborated in the eradication project. There were also death threats to those associated with the project.[158]

Considering the incidents in Putumayo, a GAO report concluded that certain conditions needed to be fulfilled for alternative development programmes to be successful. Namely, the government must control the project areas; there must be effective interdiction; and there must be co-ordination of eradication, interdiction and alternative development efforts.[159] The view on safety and public order has been supported internationally. Berg, a German alternative development worker, maintains that alternative development needs to be combined with other elements such as law enforcement, demand reduction and improvement of social infrastructure.[160] Vogel,

151 Vaicius *et al.*, 'The 'War on Drugs' meets the 'War on Terror'', pp. 6–7; and TNI, *Alternative Development and Eradication: A Filed Balance*, Drug and Democracy Programme, TNI Briefing Series, No. 2002/4, April 2002, Amsterdam: Transnational Institute, p. 13.

152 Haugaard, *Blunt Instrument*, pp. 5–6.

153 Interview with an official at ONDCP in Washington DC on 28 May 2003.

154 Isacson, *et al.*, 'Plan Colombia's 'Ground Zero'', pp. 13–14.

155 Vaicius, *et al.*, 'The 'War on Drugs' meets the 'War on Terror'', pp. 6–7.

156 Metcalfe, op cit.

157 Cox, *Audit of the USAID/Colombia-Financed Coca Alternative Development Program*, p. 4.

158 GAO, *Drug Control: Efforts to Develop Alternatives to Cultivating Illicit Crops in Colombia Have Made Little Progress and Face Serious Obstacles*, p. 13, p. 47.

159 Ibid., p. 12.

160 Berg, C., *Alternative Development as an Important Strategy within Development Oriented Drug Control*, presented at Senlis Council, the Vienna Civic Centre, 15 April 2003,

a European Commission official, also emphasises the importance of stability and order in the project areas.[161]

Although US law enforcement measures have been criticised by international actors, from the US perspective, the military component remains vital to ensure 'the necessary security' to operate in Colombia.[162] In regions with guerrilla groups and paramilitaries opposed to US backed projects, it may be necessary to protect project workers as well as to re-establish lawful government. Therefore, although the United States recognises the importance of economic and social development in Colombia, the budget allocated for military operations remained larger.[163]

However, there was scepticism about the US military oriented approach even in Congress.[164] The lack of a visible reduction in cocaine supplies over the past decades and the involvement of the US army in Colombian drug control and counter-insurgency have recalled the experience of the Vietnam War. Fears developed of a 'Vietnamisation' of Plan Colombia.[165] According to a US government source, the 'balanced approach' has generated substantial concerns in the United States: not only the balance between law enforcement and alternative development, but also between supply and demand reduction. The United States faces demands to re-think the balance between '[alternative development] and repressive law enforcement' or even to separate the two in drug control.[166] The United States may not abandon the military component in its drug control policy, but its approach to drug control became more flexible to take account of the balance between law enforcement and development projects in order to achieve effective operations.[167]

The US government took a more active role to persuade the international community to support the plan based on the logic that: 'Colombia's crisis ... requires simultaneous efforts to alter the military balance and address questions of exclusion and socio-economic need.'[168] Although the US contribution to Colombia heavily emphasised the military approach, it was concerned that a lack of political and economic support might weaken the Uribe government and make the peace process more difficult.[169] The United States tried to pull the international community together and encourage them to play a supplementary role in Plan Colombia. The determination and support of the United States was symbolised in a speech of Rand Beers, Assistant Secretary of International Narcotics and Law Enforcement, which states that the US has not only a budgetary but also a political role to play in Plan

---

http://www.senlis council.net/documents/christoph_berg_alternative_development (Accessed 17 July 2003).

161 Interview with K. Vogel at EU Commission in Brussels on 23 April 2003.

162 Vaicius, *et al.*, A., "Plan Colombia': The Debate in Congress', p. 3.

163 See above, the section on Plan Colombia.

164 Vaicius, *et al.*, "Plan Colombia': The Debate in Congress', p. 3.

165 Shifter, *US Policy in the Andean Region*, p. 11.

166 Interview with an official at the US Mission to the EU in Brussels, 25 April 2002; and TNI, *Alternative Development and Eradication*, p. 3.

167 Interview with an official at the US Mission to the EU in Brussels, 25 April 2002.

168 Emphasis in the original. Arnson, op cit., p. 27.

169 Ibid., p. 27.

Colombia.[170] By bringing international donors to support Bolivia and Peru, the US are committed to 'lending [its] political influence to engage European and Asian donor countries in the effort to buttress Latin American counternarcotics efforts'.[171]

The results from past experiences have also brought demands for more multinational involvement in drug control because, according to Senator Dodd, bilateral efforts may be insufficient and inadequate to tackle the problem.[172] Multinational co-operation did not seem to be important to the United States in the early 1990s. According to a GAO report, the United States regarded: 'multinational assistance as complementary to its programs, but ... basically, bilateral assistance mechanisms provide the necessary controls over the political, strategic, and economic interests of the United States.'[173] For the US, bilateral co-operation enables maximum influence to be exercised over other states. For example, bilateral aid provided by the USAID is 'tied aid' which reserves contracts for US companies.[174] According to a US official source, negotiations with multinational actors, particularly the Europeans, have not been for the US to exercise its influence.[175] The manner in which the Europeans deal with situations is different from that of the United States, and among the US officials there is curiosity as well as occasional frustration in negotiations with the European Union.[176]

It is, however, believed that the United States has 'a better opportunity to influence countries using bilateral assistance'.[177] The Colombian government was required to shift its emphasis according to the US policy focus. The Pastrana administration reformed a development plan for a drug control plan in 1998 to secure US funding. Then the Uribe administration adjusted the project from drug control and peace negotiation to drug control and counter-terrorism in order to co-ordinate with US foreign policy.[178] To the Colombian government, the change of US foreign policy emphasis and its repercussions on Plan Colombia were crucial. As Shifter maintains 'Colombia might find itself to be in a much more vulnerable position in the relationship with the US, and sustaining reforms and projects to solve its problems' after 11 September.[179]

---

170 Beers, R., *Statement*, 4 April 2000.

171 Ibid.

172 Dodd, C.J., *Statement*, 'Lack of International Support Will Cause Plan Colombia to Wither on the Vine', 1 November 2000, http://dodd.senate.gov/pceso/Speeches/106_00/1101.htm (31 October 2003).

173 GAO, *Drug Control: How Drug-Consuming Nations Are Organized For the War on Drugs*, January 1990, GAO/NSIAD-90-133, Washington DC: GAO, p. 9.

174 Beattie, A., 'US companies to be big gainers from Iraq outlay', *The Financial Times*, 18–19 October 2003, p. 4.

175 Interview with an official at the ONDCP in Washington DC on 27 May 2003.

176 Interview with officials at the US Department of State in Washington DC on 28 May 2003.

177 GAO, *Drug Control: How Drug-Consuming Nations Are Organized For the War on Drugs*, p. 9.

178 Shifter, *US Policy in the Andean Region*, p. 10.

179 Shifter, M., 'Ayuda a Colombia: razones y sinrasones', *Revista Cambio*, 27 October 2003, http://avanza.org.co/index.shtml?x=81 (Accessed 29 October 2003).

Concerning the operation of Plan Colombia, however, Dodd refers to the need for a larger role by the Organisations of American States (OAS), and for suggestions by regional and EU institutions to improve the plan, particularly in regard to humanitarian aid and development.[180] According to an EU source, some changes are evident in the US attitude symbolised by the apology made by a US official at an Inter-American Dialogue regarding Plan Colombia.[181] Although the United States has been criticised for its unilateral approach to drug control, there is increasing awareness of the significance of international support for its policy. This is because the US capability of quick decision-making and providing large sums of military aid was a double-edged sword to Plan Colombia.

Plan Colombia and the European Union

The European Union refused to contribute under the framework of Plan Colombia because it regarded it as a controversial scheme due to its policy on drug control. This section will investigate EU co-operation with Colombia by focusing on three issues. First, the reasons why the European Union declined to work with Plan Colombia will be explored. Second, the EU project to support Colombia will be examined. Although the EU does not participate in Plan Colombia, it assists peace building in Colombia through alternative development and social and political development projects. Third, the cost and benefits of the EU's non-military approach to drug control will be analysed.

The European Union and the Refusal of Plan Colombia

The European Union regards drug control as a shared responsibility and part of the self-interest of the international community.[182] Although the European Parliament recognises the importance of drug control in the Andes as 'a fundamental part of EU-Andean community dialogue',[183] it is not the dominant issue, as it is in the US-Colombian relationship.[184] EU support to Colombia is aimed 'at the root causes, and not just the symptoms of Colombia's years of conflict'.[185] Considering the cause of the Colombian problem, according to former EU Commissioner for External Affairs, Chris Patten, 'the biggest contribution' the European Union could make to Colombia

---

180 Dodd, op cit.

181 Interview with an official at the EU delegation to the United States in Washington DC on 28 May 2003.

182 Patten, C., *Colombia: an international commitment to peace*, speech at Meeting of the Support Group for the Peace Process in Colombia, Brussels, 30 April 2001, SPEECH/01/192, http://www.tni.org/drugs/research/patten.htm (Accessed 29 October 2003).

183 European Parliament, *Note on the Political and Economic Situation in Colombia*, p. 15.

184 Interview with an official at the European Commission in Brussels on 23 April 2002.

185 Patten, *Colombia: an international commitment to peace*.

'would be to curb drug demand, and stifle the numerous illegal activities related to illicit drug trafficking that fuel the Colombian conflict.'[186]

The main objectives of the EU support to Colombia, according to an EU officer, are the protection of human rights and building of peace and stability in the country.[187] In order to help to solve Colombia's problems, the European Union has chosen to support the peace process to overcome the endemic violence in Colombia inflicted by the insurgency groups and drug trafficking organisations.[188] A European Parliament resolution claims that this is because the use of violence by the insurgency groups and cocaine traffickers cause more of the human rights abuses in Colombia than cocaine per se.[189] Also, the EU believes that this approach will help to consolidate the Colombian government's efforts to bring a peace agreement with the guerrilla groups. In order to make the peace process 'irreversible', the EU supports long-term economic and development projects by working through international organisations.[190] EU Commissioner, Chris Patten, remarked that: 'This programme is a concrete expression of the EU's firm support for the peace process. We want to contribute to a wide national consensus in favour of peace.'[191] In short, the European Union supports the peace process but not Plan Colombia, although one of the goals of Plan Colombia is to restore peace in the country.

The main reason for the EU's refusal to support Plan Colombia is the military component, which the EU does not regard as an appropriate means for peace building or drug control. In other words, its preference for a non-military approach to drug control prevented it from approving Plan Colombia. A delegate of the European Parliament expert on Latin America, Paul Emile Dupret, told the Colombian press that the European Union could not support a plan consisting of a 63% military component.[192] The European Commission refused to be associated with plan

---

186 Patten, C., *The EU Commitment to Colombia*, Speech at Colombia-EU forum in Bogotá, Colombia, 12–13 May 2003, SPEECH/03/241, http://europa.eu.int/comm/external=relations/news/patten/sp03=241.htm (Accessed 29 October 2003).

187 Interview with an official at the European Commission in Brussels on 15 January 2003.

188 *Monthly Review: Human Rights and Democratisation*, October 2000, Brussels: European Commission, p. 7.

189 *European Parliament Resolution on Plan Colombia and Support for the Peace Process in Colombia*, 1 February 2001, B5-0087/2001, http://www.narconews.com/euroresolution2001.html (Accessed 30 October 2003).

190 The EU recommended that the Colombian government adopt structural reform policies for reducing inequalities, promoting social development and improving the standard of living, particularly in the countryside. *Monthly Review: Human Rights and Democratisation*, p. 7; and Krause, A., 'EU Courting Latin America', *EUROPE*, August 2001, Issue No. 408, http://www.eurunion.org/magazine/0108/p12.htm (Accessed 31 October 2003).

191 European Commission, *Peace Process in Colombia: Commission launches 'Peace Laboratory in the Magdalena Medio'*, 7 February 2002, IP/02/213, http://www.reliefweb.int/w/rwb.nsf/0/3d7963a94e62ffe8c1256b59004a367a?Open Document (Accessed 29 October 2003).

192 Also, he indicated that Colombia is not the priority of EU policy by saying that the EU is under economic restrictions and it would be very difficult to allocate part of the budget for Colombia. Gayón, O., 'Plan Colombia is a Dracula', *El Espectador*, 11 June 2000,

Colombia and even distanced itself from it because 'Plan Colombia remains a Colombian domestic issue'.[193]

Such EU opposition to Plan Colombia did not exist at the early stage of the Plan. Patten responded positively to a potential multinational co-operation opportunity in Plan Colombia and promised possible EU support.[194] Later, however, some member states, such as Belgium, France, Germany and Sweden, criticised Plan Colombia and refused to make any contribution under its framework. The view was that the anti-drug component would harm the peace process.[195] Although the Spanish presidency expressed its support for Plan Colombia, it did not have the support of all the EU member states.[196] Consequently, the European Union was unable to support Plan Colombia, and it was concluded as bilateral co-operation between Colombia and the United States.[197]

According to an EU source, the EU preference for a non-military approach stemmed from the belief that force is not the way to obtain development and peace.[198] The strengthening of the military would not bring peace in Colombia as has been proved by the history of Colombia. Worse, it was believed that this would aggravate problems in Colombia,[199] which would disrupt existing EU projects. The European Union was afraid that the military would prevent progress in the peace process and violate human rights.[200] Since the European Union is funding the projects to protect and promote human rights, approving military oriented-projects is seen to be controversial.[201] To avoid this, the EU pursued a peaceful approach through

---

http://www.elespectador.com/0006/11/genotici.htm#01, English translation on: http://www.narconews.com/europlan1.html (Accessed 31 October 2003).

193 Patten, C., on behalf of the Commission, 31 May 2001, *Official Journal of European Communities*, 13 November 2001, C318E/59, p. 59; and Lucas, C., *Parliamentary Questions - Oral Questions*, Reply to oral question, H-03/5/01, April 2001, http://www.carolinelucasmep.org/parliament/colombia=22032001.html (Accessed 29 October 2003).

194 Interview with an official at the Colombian Embassy in Brussels on 10 July 2003.

195 Oficina Internacional de Derechos Humanos Acción Colombia, *Plan Colombia: A Strategy Without End*, February 2000, Brussels: OIDHACO, http://www.tni.org/drugs/research/plcoleu.htm (Accessed 15 December 2003).

196 The document was published in Spanish only, and this is a very unusual practice for the EU. Also, for details of the analysis of the EU decision-making process over Plan Colombia and peace process, see articles by Roy. Roy, J., *Europe: Neither Plan Colombia nor Peace Process – From Good Intention to High Frustration*, North-South Center Working Paper Series, No. 11, January 2003, http://www.revistainterforum.com/english/pdf_en/WP11.pdf (Accessed 24 February 2004).

197 Interview with an official at the European Commission in Brussels on 8 July 2002.

198 Interview with an official at the European Commission in Brussels on 15 January 2003.

199 Oficina Internacional de Derechos Humanos Acción Colombia, *Plan Colombia*.

200 Valencia Tovar, A., 'A View from Bogotá', in *Plan Colombia: Some Differing Perspectives*, July 2001, http://www.carlisle.army.mil/ssi/pubs/2001/pcdiffer.pdf (Accessed 16 May 2003), pp. 21–22.

201 'European Parliament resolution', pp. 75–78.

social and economic development, such as land reform, the construction of social infrastructure, and manual eradication of coca plants.[202]

Another reason why the EU does not favour Plan Colombia is its approach to eradication. The EU aims to introduce alternative development projects and to support the establishment of political and social development in the coca growing regions. The fumigation programme of the United States aims to eradicate coca fields and can jeopardise the success of EU projects. It is believed among the Europeans that eradication needs to be pursued through voluntary and manual measures in order not to disturb the environment and agricultural activities in the region.[203] Aerial eradication by the United States damages not only coca bushes and the soil but also legal crops.[204] Failure to be able to harvest alternative crops devastates the lives of farmers.[205] The EU member states found that alternative development projects are less likely to be successful in regions under fumigation.[206]

Aware of opposition to Plan Colombia, the United States tried to encourage international participation, particularly by the EU as 80% of European cocaine comes from Colombia.[207] Wilhelm, the US Commander in chief of the Southern Command, claims that the European Union overly emphasises the US military contribution to Plan Colombia.[208] He claims the military component in Plan Colombia is merely 18% of the total project. Despite the large military contribution by the United States, Plan Colombia is not 'a $1.313 billion military strategy with a small social component' but 'a $7.513 billion peace strategy with a subordinate counterdrug component'.[209] For the Colombian government, the non-military support from the Europeans was crucial to the Plan since it was expected that European development projects would supplement US military support.

The original Plan Colombia did emphasise economic and social development projects.[210] The Colombian government had already commenced some alternative development projects through its own project, the National Alternative Development

202 Patten, *Colombia: an international commitment to peace*; van Rheenen, S., 'Plan Colombia Divides Europe and US', *Radio Netherlands Wereldomroep*, 1 March 2001, http://www.rnw.nl/hotspots/html/colombia010302.html (Accessed 30 October 2003); and European Parliament, *Note on the Political and Economic Situation in Colombia*, p. 15.

203 Capeda Ulloa, F., 'The European Union Contributes to the peace process in Colombia', *Nueva Mayoria*, 29 May 2001, http://www.nuevamayoria.com/english/analysis/cepeda/icepeda290501.htm (Accessed 31 October 2003).

204 *European Parliament Resolution on Plan Colombia*.

205 See section above on US drug control efforts in Plan Colombia.

206 See below for the details.

207 Grossman, M., *Joint Efforts for Colombia*, 24 June 2002, http://www.state.gov/p/11498pf.htm (Accessed 16 May 2003).

208 Wilhelm, C.E., 'A View from Washington', in *Plan Colombia: Some Differing Perspectives*, July 2001, http://www.carlisle.army.mil/ssi/pubs/2001/pcdiffer.pdf (Accessed 16 May 2003).

209 Ibid., p. 9.

210 See section on Plan Colombia above.

Plan (PLANTE),[211] based on the expectation that it would receive about $300 million from European donors.[212] The European Union, therefore, was presented with another version of Plan Colombia in 2000 at the donor meeting in Madrid.[213] This was known as the 'European version' of Plan Colombia and the focus of the plan was almost entirely on social and economic development programmes with popular participation, human rights, and peace negotiation with the FARC.[214] It reflected international criticism against the original Plan. It aimed to attract more states to support alternative development and human rights protection programmes.

Colombia expected the continuation of European support along with increased funding under the framework of Plan Colombia. The objectives of the European version of the Plan are consistent with the established priorities in past help to Colombia. The Colombian government focused on five key strategic issues in the Plan.[215] Those key issues included alternative development, the peace process, and strengthening the rule of law.[216] The EU also aimed to tackle poverty and promote economic development.[217] According to the *Multiannual Guidelines* of the European Union, the effectiveness of EU aid may deepen when it is integrated into the Colombian government's political and financial priorities.[218] The Europeans are aware of the necessity to co-ordinate their policies with the Colombian government in order to achieve maximum effect.

Considering the record of past co-operation between the European Union and the United States, the framework introduced in Plan Colombia for international participation appeared reasonable: the EU supported alternative development and the US supported drug control and law enforcement. As a Colombian government source maintains, both military and non-military aspects were considered to be necessary in Plan Colombia, hence, contributions were asked from suitable donors.[219] Colombia

---

211 UN Office on Drugs and Crime, *Support to operational capacities: Office of National Alternative Development Plan (PLANTE)*, http://www.unodc.org/unodc/en/alternative_ development_database_03.html (Accessed 12 March 2005).

212 GAO, *Drug Control: Efforts to Develop Alternatives to Cultivating Illicit Crops in Colombia Have Made Little Progress and Face Serious Obstacles*, p. 15.

213 Godoy, H., *Plan Colombia's Strategic Weaknesses*, a paper presented at the 2003 meeting of the Latin American Studies Association in Dallas, Texas, 27–29 March 2003, http://136.142.158.105/Lasa2003/GodoyHoracio.pdf (Accessed 13 November 2003), pp. 16–17.

214 President of Colombia, *Plan Colombia: Institutional Strengthening and Social Development 2000-2002*, July 2000, Bogotá: National Planning Department, http://www.tni. org/drugs/research/PlanColEurope.doc (Accessed 15 December 2003).

215 The European Commission, *Multiannual Guidelines for Community Aid: Colombia*, Brussels: The European Community, 12 November 1998, IB/1035/98-EN.

216 The Colombian government's five key strategic issues are: modernisation of the production apparatus, strengthening the rule of law, support for alternative development, flanking the peace process, and protecting the environment and conserving natural resources. The EU has focused on four key issues: tackling poverty and social exclusion, economic co-operation, human rights protection and protecting natural resources and environment.

217 Ibid.

218 Ibid.

219 Interview with an official at the Colombian Embassy in Brussels on 10 July 2002.

attempted to suggest international division of labour in its large-scale drug control programme.

At the donor conference, the EU member states assured 'full support' to the Colombian government and pledged $500–600 million.[220] In 2001, the European Parliament approved support to Colombia in order to restore peace and assist political and economic development.[221] However, the actual amount committed by the Europeans was only about half of the promised amount[222] because of scepticism stemming from the initial impression of Plan Colombia.[223] Some EU member states accused Spain of being too quick to approve Plan Colombia and agreeing US $100 million funding.[224] The accusation could have reflected the view of the EU presidency[225] at the time. The Swedish presidency stated clearly that the EU did not want to be a part of Plan Colombia. This is because it thought that the EU was expected to supplement and reconstruct what the US destroyed by military operations.[226]

There is international scepticism about the division of labour in Plan Colombia. According to the International Office of Human Rights – Acción Colombia (OIDHACO) – there are two parallel streams from an international perspective: the US donation to anti-drug operations, and the EU support for the reconstruction of Colombia and the peace process 'as a result of war'.[227] Such divided roles in Plan Colombia were not appreciated by the EU member states. Roy maintains that:

> [the Europeans] felt they were being asked to pay for what could be described as big 'incidentals', with some becoming even larger than the core projects, for example, some

---

220 *London Declaration: London meeting on international support for Colombia*, 10 July 2003, http://www.delcol.cec.eu.int/en/eu_and_colombia/news.htm (31 October 2003); and Grossman, *Joint Efforts for Colombia*.

221 *European Parliament resolution*, pp. 75–78.

222 A community contribution of EUR 140 million (EUR 105 million of programmable aid and EUR 35 million of non-programmable aid) were confirmed by the External Relation section of the Commission at the 30 April meeting, and also there was an announcement that a 'commitment of up to EUR 43 million will be made this year by the Commission.' Patten, C., on behalf of the Commission, 25 June 2001, *Official Journal of the European Communities*, 20 December 2001, C364E.

223 See above section regarding Plan Colombia for details; Grossman, *Joint Efforts for Colombia*.

224 Although some Europeans argue that Plan Colombia is a controversial programme pursuing both militarisation and demilitarisation, the Spanish government believes that the social development programmes in Plan Colombia are compatible with militarised drug control operations. Jelsma, M., 'Europe Rejects Plan Colombia', *The Progress Response*, Vol. 5, No. 5, 12 February 2001, http://www.tni.org/archives.jelsma/progress.htm (Accessed 31 October 2003); Penalva, C., *El Plan Colombia y Sus Implicaciones Internacionales*, http://www.ua.es/cultura/aipaz/docs/Plancol.ref (Accessed 20 January 2004), p. 11; and McCaffrey, B.R., *The Drug Scourge as a Hemispheric Problem*, August 2001, http://www.carlisle.army.mil/ssi/pubs/2001/scourge/scourge.pdf (Accessed 9 October 2003).

225 The EU presidency changes every six-months.

226 Jelsma, op cit.

227 Oficina Internacional de Derechos Humanos Acción Colombia, *Plan Colombia*.

of those construction projects where the original modest budget balloons to stratospheric highs. Moreover, additional European financial help would be needed once all the Colombian military hardware and munitions were exhausted and the last drop of blood of the last Colombian soldier was expended.[228]

European scepticism about the structure of projects in Plan Colombia and the sense of injustice made European support 'more political than material'.[229] Among the EU officials, the EU support to Plan Colombia is described as 'a virtual contribution to a virtual peace plan'.[230]

The European Projects to Support Colombia The Colombian effort to attract European funding was not in vain, although it failed to change the EU perception of Plan Colombia. According to a Colombian government source, there were increasingly positive responses from European governments as well as the European Union to the development projects.[231] EU sources emphasised that support to Colombia was not related to Plan Colombia.[232] Despite the reluctance of some member states towards some elements in Plan Colombia, it nevertheless presents an important opportunity for the European Union to consolidate its relationship with Colombia and the entire region of Latin America. According to Arias, if the EU was: 'effectively absent from the efforts to resolve the Colombian conflict … its efforts to maintain and develop its Latin American connection would be seriously damaged.'[233]

Alongside EU support, some member states are keen to support Colombia through bilateral relationships. Their contribution and approaches to Plan Colombia vary and some of them even support a military component in Plan Colombia, despite the EU non-military approach. The British government has been supportive of law enforcement projects in the Plan, providing military assistance to Colombia.[234] In other cases, individual state's particular interests lead them to assist Colombia, such as Spain. Providing support to Colombia was inevitable for Spain because of its political reasons, particularly to prove the ties between Spain and Latin America.[235] According to a Colombian official source, the German government has increased

228 Roy, J., *European Perceptions of Plan Colombia: A Virtual Contribution to A Virtual War and Peace Plan?* May 2001, http://www.miami.edu/nsc/publications/IPCservice/PCEUROPE.PDF (Accessed 4 January 2004) p. 4.

229 Godoy, *Plan Colombia's Strategic Weaknesses*, p. 3.

230 Roy, *European Perceptions of Plan Colombia*, p. 22.

231 Interview with an official at the Colombian Embassy in Brussels on 10 July 2002.

232 Interviews with officials at the European Commission in Brussels on 8 July 2002 and 15 January 2003.

233 Arias Calderón, 'A View from Panama', pp. 36–37.

234 According to *The Guardian*, the British Foreign Office Minister Bill Rammell does not think the military can provide a solution to the Colombian situation. The British government wants to keep a low profile in the military aspect although it is the second largest donor of military aid to Colombia. Interview with an official at the Colombian Embassy in Brussels on 10 July 2002; Pallister, D., Brodzinsky, S., and Bowcott, O., 'Secret aid poured into Colombian drug war', *The Guardian*, 9 July 2003, http://www.guardian.co.uk/international/story/0,3604,994219,00.html (Accessed 13 February 2004).

235 Arias Calderón, 'A View from Panama', pp. 36–37.

alternative development assistance after the launch of Plan Colombia, although it has insisted upon the separation of its projects from the Plan.[236] Germany was supporting development projects in Colombia even before Plan Colombia. Also, the Belgian government offered to fund some projects through the European Union and direct funding to NGOs in Colombia because of its aim of decentralised support.[237]

The EU member states' responses to Plan Colombia were various and occasionally contradictory. The European Union exposed its complexity and weakness in decision-making – the EU policy is influenced by the EU Presidency and the interests of member states. According to a Colombian government source, discrepancies between EU policies and those of individual member states made negotiation difficult, and frequent presidency changes caused delay in the negotiation and operation of projects.[238] The length of time required for decision-making also prevented the European Union from aiding the peace process despite its strong support for the Colombian government's policies.[239] Such differences among the member states and the EU were a cause of ambiguity in the EU attitude to the Plan, and led to frustration on the part of the US and Colombia.[240] Penalva opines that this is just a reflection of the EU's multiple personality as a regional organisation.[241]

Despite its rejection of Plan Colombia, the EU firmly supported the peace process. Although the member states have different approaches, the common aim of the European Union is to support the Colombian government to achieve its goals for peace building.[242] In order to assist Colombia, the EU focuses on supporting grassroots peace movements and NGOs, in a 'bottom-up' approach.

The difficulty with this approach is the way support is provided to the NGOs. In some cases, they are regarded as a violation of sovereignty by the Colombian government. According to a Colombian government source, although the European Union has a policy of discussing how funds should be spent under a co-operative project, in some cases, no notice was given to the government.[243] For example, the Belgian government offered to support Colombian NGOs through co-operation with Belgian NGOs. There was, however, no information given to Colombia except the amount earmarked for the project.[244]

---

236 Interview with an official at the Colombian Embassy in Brussels on 10 July 2002.

237 Ibid.

238 Although the EU officials interviewed assured the author that the process of changing the presidency has little affect on the negotiation and operation of projects, it seems to cause delays. Ibid.

239 Godoy, *Plan Colombia's Strategic Weaknesses*, p. 3.

240 Penalva, op cit.; and Arenas Garcia, P.J., Statement at *Comision Quinta Camara de Representantes, Reunion del Parlamento Europeo*, Bogotá, DC, 21 February 2002, http://www.mamacoca.org.foro%20legal/comision_v_minutes_reunion.htm (Accessed 21 November 2003).

241 Penalva, op cit., p. 5.

242 Interviews with officials at the European Commission in Brussels on 23–25 April, 8–10 July 2002 and 15 January 2003.

243 Interview at the Colombian Embassy in Brussels on 10 July 2002.

244 The Belgian government indicated the sums earmarked for the projects to support Colombian NGOs. When the Colombian government later enquired after the projects, it found

The Peace Laboratory in the Magdalena Medio has been a major project of the European Union in Colombia.[245] The region of Magdalena Medio has been an active operational front for the FARC and the ELN for nearly three decades, and later the AUC (a paramilitary group), due to its rich natural resources, such as oil.[246] Therefore, the main aim of the project was to establish peace with the insurgency groups in the region rather than undertake drug control.[247] However, it had an indirect impact on reducing cocaine production through weakening the influence of the insurgency groups in the region. The European Union intended to pursue economic and social development to strengthen local communities.[248] The EU aimed at: 'building the program's sustainability and mitigating risks by shifting the focus of decision making and leadership from [the Corporation Development and Peace of the Magdalena Medio (CDPMM)] to local and regional institutions…'[249] Alternative development and the promotion of popular participation were important elements in the EU project to encourage the local economy.[250] The Peace Laboratory project contained over 300 projects with 80% funding from the European Community by 2003.[251] Following the success of the Peace Laboratory, the European Union extended

---

that Belgium had already executed them without further notice being given. Ibid.

245 Those projects include human rights protection and education projects conducted by the Department of European Union Humanitarian Aid (ECHO), and there are 14 projects with funding between 0.5–8 million euros. European Commission Delegation to Colombia, *Cooperación no reembolsable*, http://www.delcol.cec.eu.int/en/eu_and_colombia/proyects. htm (Accessed 25 February 2004).

246 Viceprecidencia de la Republica de Colombia, *Panorama Actual del Magdalena Medio*, May 2001, Bogotá, http://www.derechoshumanos.gov.co/observarotio/04_ publicaciones/04_03_regiones/magdalenamedio/cap2.htm (Accessed 21 January 2004); and Weinberg, B., *Special Report: Cimitarra Valley*, Colombia, 4 September 2003, http:// colombia.indymedia.org/news/2003/09/5565.php (Accessed 29 October 2003).

247 The Magdalena Medio has been known for illegal trade, such as petrol and gold to finance insurgency groups. Interview with an official at the Colombian Embassy in Brussels on 10 July 2002; Interview with an official at the European Commission in Brussels on 15 January 2003; and Viceprecidencia de la Republica de Colombia, *Panorama Actual del Magdalena Medio*.

248 According to Chris Patten, the European package to support the Colombian 'Peace Laboratory' is to improve structural weakness through the programmes on 'the reform of the administration of justice, the promotion of integrated agricultural reform and the planning and delivery of sound environmental policies.' Also, it contained projects to fight against violence and human rights violations in the country and voluntary manual eradication of illicit crops and mapping of the state terrain for drug control. Patten, *Colombia: an international commitment to peace*; and The European Commission, *Peace Process in Colombia*.

249 World Bank, 'Colombia: Development and Peace in the Magdalena Medio Region', *En Breve*, July 2002, No. 5, p. 3.

250 Weinberg, *Special Report*; Patten, *The EU Commitment to Colombia*; and European Commission, *Peace Process in Colombia*.

251 There are 308 projects in 13 municipalities, which cost over 80 thousand million pesos. Over 80% of resources come from the European Commission, of which over 20% is supported by Germany in the Magdalena Medio. Castrillón, G., 'El Mundo del Padre de

its support to three surrounding regions of the Magdalena Medio for the creation of Peace Laboratories.[252]

Alternative development projects require stability and support from the local community.[253] In order to reduce the risk of failure, it is necessary to examine the conditions of the host community and potential risks and successes. There are three reasons the Peace Laboratory in the Magdalena Medio appealed to the Europeans. Firstly, according to an EU source, it satisfied the criteria regarded to be necessary for the reasonable success of the project: popular participation.[254] Since the Peace Laboratory commenced as a regional project managed by a Colombian NGO, it clarified the 'ownership' of the project.[255] In other words, the Magdalena Medio project is a 'demand driven' project that was planned and operated to meet the needs of the local population.[256] It has been regarded as an advantage that the European Union can work directly at the grassroots level and with NGOs.[257]

Secondly, the Peace Laboratory project in the Magdalena Medio has been managed by local organisations that enjoy high credibility and accountability from the local population based on their previous work. The EU entrusted CDPMM with the operation of the programme.[258] According to an EU official, it was desirable for the European Commission to fund a project based on well-established local organisations since the budget was limited.[259] Also, the involvement of local agencies will be an advantage, enabling access to local knowledge and contacts as well as developing the capability of local institutions to manage local issues. It may reduce tension with the locals created by the arrival of foreigners, and increase the potential for effective operations.

Roux', *Cromos*, 11 August 2003, No. 4, 461, http://www.cromos.com.co/4461/actualidad1-1.htm (Accessed 15 January 2004).

252 The EU will continue to support Magdalena Medio for Peace Laboratory, and also three other places, Norte de Santander, Oriente Antioqueño, and Macizo Colombiano will be granted the project of Peace Laboratory supported by the EU. The new project has 34.8 million euros, and from European and national compensation, 7.4 million euros. The EU also contributes to the negotiation with the FARC and the ELN. 'Colombia cumplir sus compromisos, dice C. Patten', *El Tiempo*, 18 January 2004; and The EU Delegation to Colombia, *La CE confirma interés en un segundo laboratorio de paz en Colombia*, 15 May 2003, http://www.delcol.cec. eu.int/es/novedades/boletin_32.htm (Accessed 15 January 2004).

253 See chapter 4 of this book for the details.

254 The EU evaluated the legitimacy of the project and its execution from the aspects of security, sustainability, risks and management. Interview with an official at the European Commission in Brussels on 15 January 2003.

255 The ownership of a project has been regarded as an important issue by the EU, and the EU only supports projects proposed by the recipients. In the case of Colombia, the EU supports NGOs through funding projects proposed and carried out by them. Those projects need to be derived from Colombian initiatives, not imposed by the EU.

256 Lucas, *Parliamentary Questions*.

257 Interview at the European Commission on 15 January 2003; and European Commission, *Peace Process in Colombia*.

258 Ibid.

259 The budget for the Peace Laboratory was only 30 million euros. Interview with an official at the European Commission in Brussels on 15 January 2003.

Thirdly, the European Union has valued the possibility of rapid progress in a project. The Peace Laboratory was already established as a project by the Colombian government when the EU decided to support it.[260] It was estimated to be capable of making rapid progress.[261] Also, the Peace Laboratory project had established local acceptance.[262] It was considered that the Peace Laboratory offered fewer obstacles to the approach of the European Union.

The Peace Laboratory required the EU to take a risk in executing the project.[263] Alternative development projects had faced predicaments in the past. For example, US fumigation had damaged alternative crops. As Weinberg reports, the farmers' legal crops were damaged because they were planted near to the coca and the chemical drifted away from its target.[264] In April 2002, according to a US official source, there were allegations by the EU that their sites were fumigated by the United States.[265]

In relation to their alleged US fumigation, there was a lack of communication between the European Union and the United States in operating their own projects. Some of the US officials maintain that despite official statements of EU-US co-operation of drug related matters there is little co-operation between them in practice, particularly in supply reduction efforts.[266] The European Union does not provide sufficient information on its projects whilst the United States supplies clear indications of the next fumigation sites to avoid colliding with EU projects.[267] Although there are meetings between the United States and the European Union on Colombian affairs, it has not led them to co-operate or promote their own projects.

One of the reasons for the lack of communication between the United States and the European Union could be strong distrust. The Europeans express fierce opposition to the US approach.[268] According to a European Commission official, the Europeans oppose US operations, but the United States supports the EU operations whilst differing with them over their approach.[269]

---

260 The Peace Laboratory was a well-established project by 2002 launched by the Colombian authorities and an NGO with funding from Ecopetrol and the World Bank to protect the oil pipeline and ensure security in the region from the guerrilla groups and paramilitaries. The European Commission, *Peace Process in Colombia*.

261 Interview at the European Commission on 15 January 2003; World Bank, op cit., p. 3; and Kenety, B., 'EU to aid Magdalena Medio', *Inter Press Service*, 27 April 2001, http:// groups.yahoo.com/group/ColombiaUpdate/message/247 (Accessed 29 October 2003).

262 Interview at the European Commission on 15 January 2003.

263 Ibid.

264 Weinberg, *Special Report*.

265 Interview with an official at the US Mission to the European Union in Brussels on 25 April 2002.

266 Ibid.; and the US Department of State in Washington DC on 27 May 2003.

267 According to the US Department of State official, the EU has provided a map of an entire department as its project site without any explanation, which was inappropriate for US operational planning to schedule its project for June 2003. A similar incident occurred in April 2002. Interviews at the US Mission to the European Union on 25 April 2002; and the US Department of State in Washington DC on 27 May 2003.

268 Interviews with several officials at the European Commission on 23–24 April and 8 July 2002 and 15 January 2003.

269 Interview at the European Commission on 8 July 2002.

Non-Military Approaches and Security

Regarding EU alternative development programmes, the non-military approach of the Europeans has gradually been accepted among the Colombian local population. Furthermore, alternative development projects are considered to encourage positive interaction among the actors in a community. According to a report on German alternative development projects, the farmers are willing to participate in alternative development and convert their coca fields to organic coffee plantation without any coercion, although this took a long time.[270] García and Sarmiento argue that the development projects can serve as an intermediary between paramilitaries, guerrillas, peasants and local and national governments.[271] Alternative development has been considered to serve two purposes: one is development and the other is drug control.[272] As an EU official emphasises, the EU approach is a holistic approach to solve Colombian problems through alternative development.[273]

The development projects, however, require stability in the project area. Private violence has been a predicament for progress in alternative development.[274] Also, there are necessary pre-conditions for effective operation. According to the Feldafing Declaration signed at an international conference of alternative development agents:

> Alternative Development has often succeeded in eliminating illicit drug crops whilst at the same time, improving the living conditions within the project area. The chances of success are particularly high where specific political and economic framework conditions are fulfilled and law enforcement measures are considered as a complementary element whose implementation was made dependent on clearly defined conditions closely co-ordinated with the results of Alternative Development.[275]

In other words, the capability of national and local governments can be important in alternative development projects. According to García and Sarmiento, a lack of

---

270 The German alternative development workers recognised the change in farmers' attitudes after 12 months from the start of the project. *Colombia: Cultivation and Marketing of Organically Grown Coffee*, Document from the Colombian Embassy in Brussels on 16 November 2001.

271 They produced a report of alternative development projects in different areas. The projects investigated are in: Magdalena Medio, Oriente Antioqueño, la Sierra Nevada de Santa Marta and Valle. García, A., and Sarmiento, A., *Programas Regionales de Desarrollo Y Paz: Casos de capital social y desarrollo institucional*, 6 August 2002, PNUD: Bogotá, pp. 49–51.

272 Berg, C., *Alternative Development as an Important Strategy within Development Oriented Drug Control*, presented at Senlis Council, the Vienna Civic Centre, 15 April 2003, http://www.senlis council.net/documents/christoph_berg_alternative_development (Accessed 17 July 2003).

273 Interview with an official at EU delegation in the United States in Washington DC on 30 May 2003.

274 García, *et al.*, A., *Programas Regionales de Desarrollo Y Paz*, pp. 49–51.

275 *Feldafing Declaration*, January 2002, http://www.alternative-development.net/downloads/dec/declaration/pdf (Accessed 17 July 2003).

government in a region can facilitate private violence: strengthening national and local government would help sustainable development projects.[276] Considering law enforcement and public order, it may be necessary on occasion for the European Union to support the Colombian government with forces.

It appears, as an EU official in the United States claims, that the European Union lacks understanding of security in drug control, and excludes this element from its policy.[277] EU operations focused on social and economic issues are valuable efforts, and need to be strengthened.[278] However, the European Union seems to disregard security issues in the name of a non-military approach. Security is an essential element for social and economic development and needs to be addressed even in development support.

Alternative development projects may not be accepted by those who benefit from the cocaine industry. Conducting operations in regions controlled by insurgency groups may involve risks to safety.[279]As an EU official admits, armed groups in regions may require law enforcement forces to establish public order.[280] Some officials argue that the lack of an EU military capability is the reason why the European Union is not keen on the protection of project sites; whilst others argue from the EU principle of non-use of the military.[281] According to a Commission official, in order to ensure the safety of development workers, it is necessary to make a clear distinction between EU and US projects.[282] This is because the development workers for EU projects can be vulnerable to attacks due to the lack of military capability by the European Union.

Although there are weaknesses in the security and law enforcement spheres, there are strengths in the EU approach. The majority of the American population seems to be unaware of drug control measures conducted through development programmes and their success in reducing cocaine production.[283] An EU official calls for wider publicity for EU projects, and for increased recognition of the advantages of such an approach. To prove the lack of international awareness of the role of the

---

276 García, *et al.*, op cit., pp. 49–51.

277 Interview with an official at the EU delegation to the United States in Washington DC on 30 May 2003.

278 Ibid.

279 In July 2001, a lawyer working for Peace Laboratory in the Magdalena Medio was killed. Red de hermandad y solidaridad con Colombia, *Asesinada Otra Líder de DH en el Sur de Bolívar*, 1 July 2001, http://www.xarcaneta.org/tsurdebolivar/colsitjulio2.htm (Accessed 15 January 2004).

280 Interview with an official at the European Commission in Brussels on 8 July 2002.

281 Interviews with officials at the European Commission, the European Council and the US Mission to the European Union, the US Department of State, the ONDCP on 23–25 April, 8–11 July 2002 and 15 January, 27–29 May 2003.

282 Interview with an official at the European Commission in Brussels on 8 July 2002.

283 Interview with an official at the EU delegation to the United States in Washington DC on 30 May 2003.

development projects in drug control, a member of a human rights protection group recalls no knowledge of EU projects in Colombia and other Andean states.[284]

Conclusion

Plan Colombia for the United States was a project to pursue its drug control operations in Colombia with maximum benefit. It allowed the United States to extend its commitment to the war on terrorism after 11 September. Plan Colombia enabled the United States to pursue its interests in the manner it preferred: focused on law enforcement and fumigation with alternative development playing a supportive role. Although the United States maintains its militarised approach, the emphasis on alternative development has been increased.

However, several problems exist in co-ordination efforts between eradication and alternative development, such as delays in the arrival of alternative development support, which undermines the credibility of the operation. The lack of communication between and among US government institutions has also been a concern. A GAO report recommended that: 'the Departments work together in determing [sic] Colombia's future needs and identifying the necessary training, spare parts, or other assistance needed, regardless of which Department originally provided the equipment.'[285] Co-ordination and co-operation among the US government institutions may increase the efficiency of the US backed projects, and also it could establish trust by the Colombians.

There are calls to review past efforts and reconsider US strategy to make for more effective drug control policy through broader regional approaches and the wider participation of political actors. According to Gonzáles, the approach is incompetent in demand reduction and, considering the failure of the war on drugs, it is necessary to review the concept and definition of anti-drug policies.[286] Drug control cannot bring satisfactory results through a project targeting one country, and therefore it may be necessary to aim at the entire region through several projects operated in parallel and make: 'eradication and interdiction not ends in themselves but benefits that result from resolution of broader social and economic troubles.'[287] According to the critiques, alternative development projects function with more efficiency when political actors of various levels[288] are involved in project design as well as

---

284 Interview with an official of the Latin American Working Group in Washington DC on 29 May 2003.

285 Ford, *Drug Control: Challenges Implementing Plan Colombia*, p. 27.

286 Gonzáles Posso, D., and Rodoríguez Salazsar, A., *Colombia: Crónica de un Debate No Concluido Contra Proyecto de Armas Biológicas: en defensa de los derechos humanos y la biodiversidad*, 16 de abril de 2001, http://www.mamacoca.org/gonzalez_cronica_debate_ es.htm (Accessed 21 November 2003).

287 Sanchez, M., 'When the War on Drugs Is Too Narrow', *The Washington Post*, 16 May 2003, http://www.washingtonpost.com/ac2/wp-dyn?pagename=article&node=&contentId=A 60008-2003May15&notFound=true (21 May 2003).

288 Such as local governments and community leaders in the target region, NGOs and neighbouring state governments.

operation to reflect the needs of the target community and to increase transparency in the process.[289]

The military-oriented approach of the United States has been criticised because it violates human rights. It is important to consider the peasant's life after eradication, and pacify guerrilla groups and drug traffickers through a non-military approach. Simultaneously, economic development requires stability and public order, and hence, the eradication of coca through alternative development would not exist without order in the society. In this sense, it requires the application of both law enforcement and economic and social development projects in a well-balanced manner. The United States is still seeking an effective balance.

The European Union regards drug control in Plan Colombia from a moral perspective. The militarised drug law enforcement projects in Plan Colombia held the European Union back from making a commitment. The European Union opposed the military components of Plan Colombia, based on its belief that the military is an inappropriate means for effective drug control. Consequently, the European Union has decided to contribute to drug control in Colombia indirectly through the Peace Process with alternative development and grassroots support projects. Although the European Union promised full support to Colombia, the projects and resources actually provided by the European Union were only about half of the offered amount. As an EU official recalls, the approach of Plan Colombia was contrary to European ideas, and if the presentation had been different, the Europeans could have assisted Colombia with more generous resources.[290]

In order to support Colombia, the European Union launched a project to create a peace zone to weaken the insurgency groups and encourage legal crop cultivation. Its non-military approach has helped to promote voluntary eradication. However, the issues of safety and security related to the project's operation have remained unsolved.

Despite some weaknesses in alternative development projects operated in a non-militarised manner, they can offer more than social and economic development and drug control to the target region. They can provide a place for interaction among different actors in the community and work as a mediator for a peaceful settlement and the reduction of illicit cultivation. However, alternative development as a drug control policy has made no impact on the Americans. It may be because the results of EU projects are not clear and the EU projects have a very low profile.[291] As an EU official admits, the European efforts are not sufficient to make visible changes which can appeal internationally and demonstrate that there is another means to tackle drug trafficking.

---

289 Vaicius, *et al.*, 'The 'War on Drugs' meets the 'War on Terror'', pp. 17–18; *European Parliament Resolution*.

290 Interview with an official at the EU delegation to the United States in Washington DC on 30 May 2003.

291 It is very difficult (if not impossible) to find details of EU projects in public documents of the EU.

The EU opposition to the US approach, however, could undermine the principle of international co-operation for the EU.[292] The EU emphasis on regional co-operation and co-operation through multinational organisations would require US involvement at certain levels to establish sustainable and effective projects.[293]

Over all, Plan Colombia presented an opportunity for multinational co-operation against the cocaine trafficking through a multi-faceted approach. At the same time, it has illustrated the differences between the US and the EU attitude to drug control operations. Those differences are not merely over policies on drug control, but also the way in which they execute their policy. As for the policies, the European Union seeks to promote economic and social development based on local demands. The EU approach in drug control has not changed since the 1980s because, according to an EU source, a non-military approach is the best way for drug control in Colombia.[294]

The United States, on the contrary, emphasises a law enforcement oriented approach with the use of the military to control drugs, and grants funds based on US interests. Although US projects are determined by purchases of commodities from the United States and the employment of US subcontractors, the Colombian government regards the assistance provided by the United States as satisfactory for the operation of Plan Colombia. Also, the United States has shifted its emphasis on alternative development due to international critiques against the US approach and its awareness of the significance of the development aspect in drug control.

The clear US stand point on drug control makes Colombia and US negotiations to obtain US assistance for Plan Colombia easier. Despite international critiques on the strong US influence over Plan Colombia, both Colombia and the United States increased their co-operation: for Colombia, it was financial and material support necessary for the execution of Plan Colombia, and for the United States, drug control operations on a larger scale.

With the European Union, the negotiation was more difficult for the Colombian government. This is because negotiating with the European Union is more complex than ordinary bilateral relationships because there are two relationships in the process: one is the relationship between Colombia and the European Union and the other is between the European Union's member states. The EU had to find the approach its member states can agree, as there were various views on Plan Colombia.

Those differences between the United States and the European Union have long existed, but became clearer under the proposed framework of Plan Colombia. Although the EU side emphasised the shared goal of cocaine supply reduction from projects undertaken in Colombia, their approaches to drug control remained parallel.

---

292 GAO, *Drug Control: How Drug-Consuming Nations Are Organized for the War on Drugs*, January 1990, GAO/NSIAD-90-133, Washington DC: GAO, pp. 8–9.

293 *European Parliament Resolution*.

294 Interview with an official at the European Commission in Brussels on 15 January 2003; and GAO, *Drug Control: How Drug-Consuming Nations Are Organized For the War on Drugs*, p. 4.

Conclusion

It is inevitable that the EU and the United States adopt different drug control policies towards the Andes, because their policies are based on how they conceptualise cocaine trafficking. An actor evaluates and determines whether cocaine trafficking is a threat through the process of securitisation. The way in which an actor securitises the threat of cocaine trafficking depends on the perception of the damage it posed to the actor. Each actor may focus on different harms caused by cocaine trafficking because these harms will not be uniform. The harms caused by cocaine trafficking undermine state functions and the identity of the state. As a result, there are different levels of securitisation in relation to cocaine trafficking: some actors may regard it as a national security threat, and others may consider it a societal security threat. Consequently, the way in which actors securitise cocaine trafficking becomes a determinant of their approach to drug control.

Drug control policies, however, are determined not only by the process of securitisation but also by the actor's capabilities and its sense of self-image in the international community. The United States, as a superpower, sees itself as having the role of an international policeman and a special responsibility for preserving the *status quo*. Its huge coercive capabilities have led it to pursue a particular form of drug control policy. In contrast, the EU, with its complex structure and more limited capabilities has pursued a more consensual approach to drug control.

Regarding cocaine trafficking, the European Union and the United States agree on two points: one is that cocaine trafficking is a security threat and second that international co-operation is essential for drug control. However, in order to achieve the fundamental goal of reducing cocaine production in the Andes, the EU and US take almost parallel approaches. In order to clarify the implications of the securitisation of cocaine trafficking and policy making, this chapter will be divided into three sections. First, it will analyse the societal threat of cocaine trafficking to the EU and the way in which development policy is seen as a solution. Second, how the US securitised cocaine trafficking as a national security threat and follows a law enforcement approach towards the source countries. Third, it will consider the possibility of more effective drug control through multinational co-operation.

The European Union: A Societal Threat and Economic Development

The EU regards cocaine trafficking as a societal threat that damages its social fabric and moral values. From an EU perspective, cocaine trafficking is regarded as a societal threat that affects both the well being of its member states and potentially their national and European identity. This is partly because the EU regards cocaine as a substance of temptation that some people cannot resist: the focus is the weakness in human nature rather than the danger of cocaine. To some extent, drug consumption is seen as an 'enemy within'. Cocaine is treated as a security threat in the sense that cocaine is an illegal substance incompatible with European moral values, and consequently, with its identity. There is the potential that cocaine trafficking could affect the identities of the EU member states through the increasing use of cocaine and the expanding cocaine market. If the EU chose not to criminalise the cocaine trade, this would have implications for its definition of 'self' from a social constructivist's point of view. Therefore, by defining cocaine as a threat, the EU tries to protect its society from the spread of cocaine problems. In this respect, two of the most significant impacts of cocaine trafficking for the EU member states are health issues and the movement of illegal immigrants into Europe. Moreover, these two issues have complex linkages to economic, political and diplomatic issues.[1]

In respect of health, the rapid increase of cocaine consumption and addiction, and the spread of infectious sexual diseases, such as HIV, was alarming in the 1990s. The costs of health care for the member states increased rapidly as the numbers of drug addicts increased. This does not mean that cocaine was the only cause of increasing health costs. The EU member states have larger numbers of heroin addicts, and in Europe heroin is a more serious concern than cocaine. Cocaine worsened the situation by increasing the number of poly drug users.

The EU member states treat drug users as 'sick people' who need treatment and rehabilitation, rather than treating them as criminals. From an EU perspective, there are always some people who lack self-control or who make a mistake of using cocaine and become addicted.[2] They are not criminals except in the sense that they are using illegal substances. There is a growing acceptance within the EU that what they need is treatment rather than punishment. To some extent, the users of illicit substances are one of the features in a society that acknowledges the weakness of human nature. The EU approach is to try to contain the cocaine business. Whilst the EU member states pay lip service to the UN conventions of a drug free society, in reality it is harm reduction that informs policy.

Another EU concern in relation to cocaine trafficking is the involvement of immigrants, particularly illicit ones. It is perceived that cocaine trafficking can provide economic means to those who do not have access to the legal economy in the European Union. The EU fears that the cocaine trade could support the settlement of illegal immigrants and create instability in local communities through the isolation of particular ethnic groups, and lead to hostility against them.[3] This is because the cocaine trade is contrary to the moral values of the EU members. The increase in the number of cocaine dealers leads to competition in the European cocaine market, and accompanying violence. In communities with high cocaine trafficking rates, safety, moral values and health are at stake.

The way the EU securitised cocaine trafficking does not require external policies to control the flow of cocaine. A social problem is a domestic matter of the EU member states, and therefore it remains an internal issue to the EU. Therefore, the

---

1   See chapter 2 above.

2   Interviews with officials at the European Commission in Brussels on 8 July 2002, and 15 January 2003.

3   Interview with officials at the European Commission in Brussels on 15 January 2003.

EU does not prioritise supply reduction in the source countries, unlike the United States. The EU focuses on demand reduction to reduce the number of addicts that are costly to its member states' health systems. As a consequence, drug control is not the dominant component for the EU in its relationship with Andean states. Rather, it sees cocaine production as part of the justification for the assistance the EU gives to Andean countries.[4]

EU involvement in drug control in the Andean states stems from two factors. One is its sense of responsibility as a member of the international community, and the other is the difficulty in controlling the movement of cocaine and traffickers within the EU. This approach of 'shared responsibility', based on a moral obligation reflects the EU belief that cocaine trafficking is an international issue, and that co-operation within the community is necessary to control it. This is the way the EU identifies itself as a member of the international community and associates with it. From Realist and Neo-Realist perspectives, an international organisation like the EU cannot be accepted as a political actor in international relationships. However, the EU tries to identify itself as an actor capable of pursuing external policies and to be recognised as a member of the international community. Treating the international community's interests as synonymous with its own, however, is not sufficient to generate sponsorship from the EU member states to execute substantial drug control operations in the Andes.

The weaknesses in EU projects are that they need to be sponsored by the member states due to the lack of resources at the EU level. It does not mean that they do not value co-operation. On the contrary, the EU member states recognise the significance of international co-operation to tackle cross-border crimes. However, being a regional organisation limits the ability of the EU to make decisions on its policies because of its need to reflect the member states' interests and preferences in its policies. Also, EU policies are influenced by the process of its political and economic integration. The EU member states are not yet fully prepared to make policies of political and legal matters because the EU was established as an economic organisation.

Due to the organisational nature of the EU, economic projects are preferred as drug control policy towards the Andes. This stems from the freedom of movement adopted by the EU. Since adopting the policy of freedom of movement of people within the EU, it is considered to be more difficult for the member states to control the movement of illegal immigrants and cocaine once they have entered into European territory. Therefore, the EU focuses on tackling the root causes of illegal immigration by improving economic conditions in their home countries.[5] This comes from the assumption that the reason why these immigrants came to the EU is to achieve better living standards. Supporting economic and social development in the cocaine producing countries could help people to leave cocaine production and stay in their countries. The Andean cocaine industry is one of the key businesses in employing people and generating foreign currency. In order to curb this industry, it is necessary to provide alternative economic development.

---

4   Interview with an official at the European Commission in Brussels on 24 April 2002.

5   Interviews with officials at the European Commission in Brussels on 8 July 2002, and 15 January 2003.

The policy of alternative development in the Andean states is not easy because of the complex nature of the problem. According to the EU understanding of the situation in the Andean states, cocaine trafficking is a major cause of their political, economic and social problems. The cocaine trade expanded in the Andean states because these governments have a weak control over their territories and insufficiently developed economic and political institutions. Therefore, in order to introduce sustainable alternative economic development, the EU needs to support the reform of political and judicial systems and social infrastructures. The EU believes that drug control operations should take a holistic approach to deal with not only cocaine trafficking but also other connected issues and problems.

EU drug control policy towards the Andean region therefore focuses on economic, social and political development in the coca growing areas through alternative development programmes.[6] In its programme, the EU is trying to achieve the improvement of social infrastructure, the strengthening of local government, and the introduction of legal economic projects to wean these areas from coca dependence. This is because in order to access markets for legal crops and be competitive, the coca growing areas require basic infrastructures, such as roads and irrigation systems, which the national and local government cannot afford to provide. Through these projects, the EU is trying to re-establish confidence in communities and the credibility of local government.

The EU approach to drug control is operable only in certain conditions, since the EU cannot deploy the military to protect its projects. Therefore the EU requires stability and popular support for its projects. However in most coca growing areas in the Andes, the stability required for alternative development projects cannot really be expected due to armed traffickers and insurgency groups. Therefore, as Vogel claims, the EU can conduct alternative development to reduce coca only in Bolivia, but it is unable to do it in Colombia and Peru where traffickers and insurgency groups are actively involved in cocaine trafficking.[7] Despite the EU policy of a non-military approach to drug control, there are those who believe that armed protection is required for the success (and continuation) of alternative development. Hence, the EU ability to contribute to drug control is limited.

On the other hand, the strength of the EU is that it can have several potential donors for long-term projects. Various member states can sponsor the continuation of one project by funding different periods of the project. Alternative development projects require long-term commitment, substantial resources and markets for crops introduced by the projects. This is because the growth of economic and political systems is slow and the management and sustainability of the project is the key to consolidating legal crop cultivation. The programme does not reduce cocaine immediately, but it can make a gradual contribution over a period of time. The slow progress means that each project takes a considerable time to complete, so states may be deterred from supporting such a project, as it is difficult to see the progress. However, in order to succeed in drug control, it is necessary for the Andean

6   See chapters 4 and 6 above.
7   Interview with K.H. Vogel, at the European Commission in Brussels on 23 April 2002.

governments to regain sovereignty over their territories. Therefore, support to a project by multiple sponsors is desirable.

Considering the needs of the Andean states and EU assumptions about cocaine trafficking, the EU approach to Colombia was justifiable. EU support focuses on human rights protection and the prevention of terrorism supported by narco-dollars, as well as the establishment of peace in the region of Magdalena Medio.[8] The EU works towards peace building in the Magdalena Medio because the conduct of alternative development programmes requires a stable environment. Therefore, supporting a peace settlement between the Colombian government and insurgency groups, particularly the FARC, is a priority for the EU. This programme seems to be a marginal operation for drug control under Plan Colombia. However, it can fit well into the scheme by securing a safe ground for the farming of alternative crops, and it can support the eradication of coca fields, thereby tackling the nexus between cocaine trafficking and insurgency groups.

The EU initially refused to participate in Plan Colombia. It was concerned about the repercussions of associating with a US-led drug control project, which are not always accepted by local people because of the militarisation of the projects.[9] The EU feared for the safety of their personnel and worried that the progress of their projects might be jeopardised if they co-operated with the US. Through the past support provided for the Andean states, the EU has earned a reputation of pursuing economic approaches to drug control, and assisting the development of these states. The EU believes that this is one of the reasons why EU projects rarely faced attacks by local residents. The lack of protection for alternative development personnel in the EU has made it prudent to be less confrontational.

The reluctance of the EU commitment to coercive drug control comes not only from an imperative to protect its personnel and projects but also from its nature as a multinational organisation. The EU was established as an organisation for economic co-operation, and therefore it has a military capability that only began in 1999, but it lacks the capability to make rapid decision in a crisis. In order to make a foreign policy decision, the EU requires unanimity among its member states. This can slow or even halt the progress of some projects, and make it difficult to react swiftly. On the other hand, the EU demonstrates strength in its capacity to co-ordinate policies and encourage co-operation. Through its policy co-ordination, it can undertake wide-ranging development projects over a long period of time.

What the EU aims to achieve through its alternative development programmes in the Andes is to improve economic conditions by introducing legal economic means to coca growing areas. At the same time, it also intends to re-educate local people on moral values, respect for law and order, obligation to (and trust in) the community, supporting local government to provide social services. This is an attempt to reconstruct social knowledge about cocaine trafficking and society in the Andes by exporting EU moral values. The drug control policies carried out in Andean states are based on its understanding of the nature of cocaine trafficking. For the choice of operation, however, the EU is cautious not to get involved in areas where they

---

8   See chapter 6 above.
9   See chapters 5 and 6 above.

may conflict with the interests of cocaine cartels and insurgency groups. This stems from its inability to protect the project sites from attacks. Therefore, the EU tries to maintain the reputation that its projects are economically driven and non-coercive in order to avoid the risk of attack.

The United States: A National Security Threat and Law Enforcement

In the United States, cocaine trafficking is treated as a foreign threat that undermines the economy and the country's moral values. From the US perspective, cocaine trafficking is a national security threat from Latin America that affects its values and identity. Cocaine is perceived as a foreign enemy invading the United States. In addition, the US distrusts the ability of Andean countries to control drugs and this has partly justified its interventionist approach. For the United States, it could be said that cocaine trafficking is a hybrid of traditional and non-traditional security threats because cocaine trafficking affects both its identity and the quality of its functions as a state, but it is a harm caused by a foreign enemy. In this sense, supply reduction for the United States is equal to waging a war against Latin American cocaine cartels. The difference between the EU and US perceptions of cocaine trafficking is that the US emphasises the foreign origin of cocaine whilst the EU emphasises domestic consumption of cocaine.

The US regards cocaine as a social 'evil' that harms the nation.[10] Cocaine spreads sexual diseases, such as HIV/AIDS, it costs the US economy an estimated $100 billion and affects the social fabric and America's moral values. Americans have a zero-tolerance attitude to the harm cocaine causes in their community.[11] Drug traffickers and addicts are referred to as 'enemies' in the war on drugs, and need to be captured and punished. The war on drugs targets ethnic minorities, particularly black people who use crack and Hispanics who deal in crack cocaine. The US is concerned about traffickers bringing cocaine into its territory, as well as the instability of the Andean region caused by narco-dollars. The Andean region is regarded as particularly vulnerable to the spread of insurgency conflicts from one country to another. The US is concerned because of its proximity, dominance in the region, and close relationships with many Latin American states.[12]

In the war on drugs, the way the United States protects its homeland is to try to prevent the 'enemy' entering its territory. This is the concept behind supply reduction by eradicating coca fields and the interdiction of cocaine supply. The capitalist economy is based on the interactions of supply and demand. However, the United States has taken the view that if there were no supply there would be no demand. This reverses the idea of capitalism: which holds that where there is demand, supply will arise to meet it. Therefore, the US government has emphasised

---

10 Interview with an official at the ONDCP in Washington DC on 28 May 2003.

11 Interview with an official at the United States Mission to the European Union in Brussels on 25 April 2002.

12 Interview with an official at the Department of State in Washington DC on 27 May 2003.

law enforcement operations and supply reduction in the source countries.[13] Law enforcement operations are executed with expanded authority, and less attention than Europe pays to human rights. This is because human rights and sovereignty of Andean states are a secondary concern for the United States in a 'war situation'. Coca bushes were eradicated in the Andean countries and cocaine was interdicted in the transit states, both measures were intended to reduce the cocaine reaching US territory.

To stop the supply from source countries, the agreement of the host states to US drug control operations is necessary. In order to secure agreements with the Andean states, the US uses its political and economic influence through economic aid and trade benefits and annual narcotics certification. The Andean states that co-operate with US drug control policy are guaranteed large sums of aid and trade preferences. Those who do not comply are sanctioned by the withdrawal and reduction of aid. In view of the political and economic weakness of the Andean states, the US government can exercise considerable influence over their decision making.

Co-operation between the United States and the Andean states is determined by US preference rather than the needs of the host states. From the US perspective, this operation style is beneficial for both sides as the recipient of the aid can obtain equipment and expertise on drug control, whilst it enables the US to pursue its own goals in producer states. The US has exported its law enforcement agents and equipment regardless of the readiness of the host states. The delivery of aid is dependent on the decision of the US Congress rather than that of the host state. Therefore, the United States deployed the military to Bolivia without the Bolivian government's acceptance. The pursuit of such a policy does not receive support from local residents. The US drug control operation is equivalent to a military operation to those who live in the Andes. This image, particularly, was created in the 1980s under the Reagan and Bush administrations. Thereafter, this image is always associated with the US drug control policy when it is referred to the international community.

Although military operations in drug control evoke negative aspects, such as human rights abuses, militarised law enforcement is an essential means to control and prevent cocaine trafficking. This is because it is important to impress on society the consequences of violating laws and to punish criminals. In respect of cocaine trafficking, personnel may need to arm themselves for protection against violent attacks by armed traffickers. The military approach of the United States enables it to use force to demolish cocaine production sites and coca fields that are protected by armed traffickers.

The United States is willing to co-operate and to provide military operations for drug control whenever it has an opportunity. Therefore, it was keen to participate in Plan Colombia. After three decades of failure in drug control, the US is aware of the importance of a multidimensional approach to drug control and the limits of bi-lateral co-operation. The US discussed the plan and agreed to provide support in accordance with US interests and priorities. This led Plan Colombia in a different direction from what the Colombian government intended, but secured the funding of $1.3 billion from the United States.

---

13 See chapters 5 and 6 above.

Alongside its militarised operations, the US has been operating alternative development programmes. This is an indication that the US is aware of the need for an economic alternative to cocaine production, although this type of operation is not where the United States places its emphasis. The US government is not prepared to wait several years for the results. Such hastiness in the US government is not suitable for development projects. Consequently, the agency in charge of alternative development, USAID, is always under pressure from budget cuts and halting operations. Without the constant supply of resources for the long-term, alternative development may struggle to produce a functioning local economic system and enable local government to manage legal crop cultivation. In addition, the reputation of coercive military operations left a strong impression in Andean states, so it is difficult to change people's perception about US operations. Alternative development projects that do not have any military component are still regarded as coercive operations and face a lack of support from local communities. Due to prejudice in the Andean states against US operations and inadequate management of the projects, alternative development programmes have been a failure for the United States.

The perception of US drug control stems from the projects the United States conducted as well as the way it pursued them. The problem is that the US falls in the Realist camp in respect of its drug control policies, and therefore pursues its operations in a selfish way irrespective of the host states' sovereignty and international law. In Plan Colombia, the United States redirected the plan closer to its own interests, and assumed that the international community would accept it. This is because the economic and political influence of the United States allows it to pursue drug control in a coercive manner in the Andes. However, the strong emphasis on US interests and decisive operations in the Andean region have drawn international criticism, and made the EU unwilling to co-operate in the original Plan Colombia initiatives.

The United States ignores the repercussions of its drug control policy and its reputation on decision-making on other members of the international community. The US media report on Plan Colombia, however, made generating an international contribution to Plan Colombia difficult. The US announcement of a large military budget for Plan Colombia gave the impression to the international community that this was another US military project. With its large contribution to Plan Colombia, the US expected to encourage other members of the international community to participate in this Colombian drug control scheme. However, the US announcement prevented multinational co-operation. Other states were sceptical of the US role in the programme, and were reluctant to participate.

The aim of US drug control operations is to destroy cocaine cartels abroad and eliminate cocaine from its own territory. For the United States, cocaine trafficking is a non-traditional national security threat because cocaine cartels are not a state threatening its physical existence. However, it is a foreign enemy attacking its values and well-being. Hence, the response of the United States has been through militarised law enforcement operations, which are similar to the way it would react to traditional security threats. The United States sees itself as the 'global policeman' enforcing the law on cocaine traffickers for the good of the international community.[14] Plan Colombia was an opportunity for the United States to conduct its law enforcement policy without being criticised for a coercive and inadequate approach. Also it was an opportunity for it to appear 'multilateralist' in drug control. But the United States was not aware was that there was strong opposition to its policy, and the project was mostly associated with its militarised law enforcement. Despite the international criticism of militarised law enforcement operations, the strength of the United States is its capability for quick decision-making in a crisis and the decisive deployment of force. Also, the US's enormous resources enabled it to make a substantial contribution to Plan Colombia. It cannot be denied that the United States has devoted more resources to tackling drug trafficking than any other state since the 1980s, and it has great capability to conduct military operations.

A Possibility for Multinational Supply Reduction Project

Drug control policies adopted by the EU and the United States have not achieved their goal to reduce cocaine production in the Andes, although they are making some progress. The EU's alternative development programmes have introduced legal crops to substitute coca cultivation, and strengthened local government. However, it is questionable whether coca growers give up cultivation when their incomes reach a certain level. Generating income from legal crops is more difficult than obtaining an income from cocaine because of the competition in the market. Therefore, a USAID official claims that the coca growers continue coca cultivation in order to spread risks.[15] In order to eliminate poverty by alternative crops, the Andean farmers need protected markets until they become competitive in the global economy. This, however, conflicts with the interests of EU domestic producers and those who have already been granted trade preference.[16] After contributing substantial sums to development projects, states may refuse further 'sacrifices' for Andean states. The weakness of alternative development projects is the lack of an income guarantee, and the lack of power to impose legal crop cultivation.

On the other hand, US law enforcement operations weaken cocaine trafficking networks and encourage people to uphold law and order in the community. Law enforcement has two aims: one is to punish cocaine traffickers and make seizures of cocaine; and the other is to deter people from entering the cocaine trade. However, in order to pursue punishment and deterrence, law enforcement agents and government authorities need to be prepared for the risks of attacks from armed cocaine traffickers.

---

14 Interview with an official at the Department of State in Washington DC on 27 May 2003.

15 Interview with an official at the USAID in Washington DC on 27 May 2003.

16 For example, the EU offers bananas as one of the priority crops, but the European banana market is dominated by Caribbean producers. Due to the ties between some EU member states and the Caribbean, changing market quotas causes oppositions from both the member states and the Caribbean. 'Banana war exposes old trade divisions', *BBC*, 5 March 1999, http://news.bbc.co.uk/1/hi/business/the_economy/290981.stm (Accessed 24 March 2005); and 'The Economy Banana trade war looms', *BBC*, 12 January 1999, http://news.bbc. co.uk/1/hi/business/the_economy/253705.stm (Accessed 24 March 2005).

In addition, law enforcement operations can show the consequences of becoming involved in cocaine trafficking to the community, but it does not provide any alternative way of living, unlike economic projects.

Considering these facts, supply reduction in the Andean states requires a large programme of wide-ranging projects that need to be followed in parallel. This is because of the very nature of the cocaine problem in the Andes. Firstly, coca leaves (but not cocaine) are in the life of indigenous people, and policies should be supported to turn the coca leaves into legal products, such as teas.[17] Secondly, the cocaine industry impacts deeply on the economic, political and social spheres, and has partly grown from the weakness of the government authorities. In order to weaken the cocaine industry, a drug control scheme should tackle two elements simultaneously: one is the cocaine trafficking network and the other is the strengthening of the government. This is the equivalent of balancing law enforcement operations and alternative development programmes.

However, tackling multiple problems related to cocaine trafficking in one project is impossible to achieve by bi-lateral co-operation due to the costs involved. In order to conduct such an operation, it is necessary to divide tasks among the capable members of the international community through multinational co-operation, as the Colombian government attempted in Plan Colombia. In this manner, each participant of the project can pursue its prioritised policy with co-ordination and co-operation with other participants. For example, the EU conducts alternative development whilst the United States operates law enforcement.

This division of tasks is possible because of various perceptions of threats posed by cocaine trafficking. Cocaine trafficking affects the weakest point of each state, and every state experiences the impact in various degrees.[18] Therefore, the elements each actor regards as threats and problems posed by cocaine trafficking are equally important to the control of the flow of cocaine. The analysis of EU and US drug control policy leads to the fact that these actors employ solutions that they can operate most comfortably. In other words, participants playing to their strengths in a co-ordinated manner can achieve a common goal to reduce cocaine production.

The difficulty in multinational co-operation against cocaine trafficking is that each participant has a different perception of the threat posed by cocaine trafficking. Therefore, they may not agree to co-operate with each other, as was the case with the EU and the United States in Plan Colombia. A drug control programme consisting of various components to cover several aspects of the problem may be possible because of the various ways actors securitise cocaine trafficking. But, such programmes are difficult to realise because of the differences in how the actors see the threat. The actors can refuse to co-operate because they do not share the other side's understanding of cocaine trafficking. If the participants of a multinational drug control co-operation could commit themselves to controlling drugs and accept working with those who have different points of view, a project like Plan Colombia might work.

.

---

17 This is one of the reasons why Bolivia's Coca Union leader Evo Morales won his presidential election.

18 See chapter 1 above.

Bibliography

Abbate, L., 'La Caccia al tesoro della mafia', *Polizia di Stato*, http://www.poliziadistato. it/pds/primapagina/parliamo_di/caccia_tesoro_mafia.htm (Accessed 20 February 2005).

Abruzzerse, R., 'Coca-leaf production in the countries of the Andean subregion', *Bulletin on Narcotics*, 1989, Issue 1, http://www.undcp.org/adhoc/bulletin/1989/ bulletin_1989-01-01_page008.html.

Abt Associates Inc., *What America's Users Spend on Illegal Drugs 1988-2000*, December 2001, http://www.whitehousedrugpolicy.gov/publications/pdf/ american_users_spend_2002.pdf.

Acción Andina-Transnational Institute, *The Drug War in the Skies The US Air Bridge Denial Strategy: The Success of A Failure*, 1999, Cochabamba: TNI.

Adler, E., 'The Emergence of Cooperation: National Epistemic Communities and the International Evolution of Idea of Nuclear Arms Control', *International Organization*, Vol. 46, No. 2, 1992.

Adler, E., 'Seizing the Middle Ground', *European Journal of International Relations*, Vol. 3, No. 3, September 1997.

Advisory Council on the Misuse of Drugs, *Report: AIDS and Drug Misuse Part 1*, 1988, London: Her Majesty's Stationary Office.

Agencia, 'Huyen tres 'narcos' justo antes de que la Audiencia Nacional les condene por un alijo de 1991', *El Mundo*, 20 June 2003, http://www.elmundo. es/elmundo/2003/06/19/sociedad/1056019909.html (Accessed 1 March 2005).

Anderson, B., *Imagined Communities: Reflections on the Origins and Spread of Nationalism*, 1989, London: Verso Press.

Anderson, M. and den Boer, M. (eds), *Policing Across National Boundaries*, 1994, London: Pinter.

Andreas, P.R., Bertram, E.C., and Sharpe, K.E., 'Dead-end Drug Wars', *Foreign Affairs*, Winter 1991-1992, No. 85.

Andreas, P., 'When Policies Collide', in Friman, H.R. and Andreas, P., *The Illicit Global Economy & State Power*, 1999, New York: Rowman & Littlefield Publishers, Inc.

Andreas, P., *Free Market Reform and Drug Market Prohibition: US Policies at Cross-Purposes in Latin America*, 1995, http://www.lindesmith.org/news (Accessed 7 July 1999).

Anthony, R., *Farmgate-to-Street Model of Narcotics Trafficking*, paper presented at Roundtable entitled Business Practices of Narcotics Trafficking Enterprises, at the Library of Congress on 29 January 2003, http://www.loc.gov/rr/frd/Drug_ conference/pdf-files/Farmgate-to-Street-Model-of-Narcotics-Trafficking.pdf.

Arenas Garcia, P.J., *Statement* at Comision Quinta Camara de Representantes, Reunion del Parlamento Europeo, Bogotá, DC, 21 February 2002, http://www.

mamacoca.org.foro%20legal/comision_v_minutes_reunion.htm   (Accessed   21 November 2003).

Arias Calderón, R., 'A View from Panama', in *Plan Colombia: Some Differing Perspectives*, July 2001, http://www.carlisle.army.mil/ssi/pubs/2001/pcdiffer.pdf (Accessed 16 May 2003).

Arnson, C.J., *US interests and Options in Colombia: An Alternative Framework*, http://www.ciaonet.org/wps/arc02/arc02.pdf (Accessed 13 November 2003).

Ashley, R., *Cocaine: Its History, Uses and Effects*, 1975, New York: St. Martin's Press.

Ashton, R., *This is Heroin*, 2002, London: Sanctuary.

Associated Press, 'Farmers block key road in Bolivia to protest eradication of coca', *CNN*, 17 April 2000, http://www.cnn.com/2000/WORLD/americas/04/17/bolivia.protests.ap/index.html (Accessed 17 April 2000).

Associated Press, 'Former Mexican governor said negotiating surrender in drug case', *CNN* News, 20 February 2000, http://www.cnn.com/2000/WORLD/americas/02/20/bc.mexico.fugativegov.ap/index.html.

Astorga, L., 'Cocaine in Mexico: a prelude to 'los Narcos'', in Gootenberg, P. (ed), *Cocaine: Global Histories*, 1999, London: Routledge.

Atkins, A., *European Drug-Control Policy and the Andean Region, Narcotics and Development Discussion Paper 6*, 1993, London: Catholic Institute of International Relations.

Audit Commission, *Health Data Briefings: 2 Drug Treatment Services*, October 2007 http://www.audit-commission.gov.uk/Health/Downloads/HealthDataBriefing_DrugTreatmentServices1.pdf (Accessed 19 October 2007).

Axelrod, R., *The Evolution of Cooperation*, 1984, New York: Basic Books Inc.

Axelrod, R., *The Complexity of Cooperation: Agent-Based Model of Competition and Collaboration*, 1997, Princeton: Princeton University Press.

Ayoob, M., *The Third World Security Predicament: State-Making, Regional Conflict, and the International System*, Boulder, OC: Lynne Reinner, 1995.

Bagley, B.M., 'Colombia and the War on Drugs', *Foreign Affairs*, Vol. 67, No. 1, Fall 1988.

Bagley, B.M., 'The New Hundred Years War? US National Security and the War on Drugs in Latin America', *Journal of Interamerican Studies and World Affairs*, Vol. 80, No. 1, Spring 1988.

Bagley, B.M., 'Dateline Drug Wars: Colombia: The Wrong Strategy', *Foreign Policy*, No. 77, Winter 1989–90.

Bagley, B.M., 'The Use of Armed Forces in Drug Interdiction: The Strategic Context', in Manwaring, M.G. (ed.), *Security and Civil-Military Relations in the New World Disorder: The Use of Armed Forces in the Americas*, September 1999, http://www.carlisle.army.mil/ssi/pubs/1999/newworld/newworld.pdf   (Accessed 16 May 2003).

Bagley, B.M. and Walker III, W.O. (eds), *Drug Trafficking in the Americas*, 1996, Miami: North South Center Press.

Balassa, B., 'The Process of Industrial Development and Alternative Development Strategies', *Essays in International Finance*, No. 141, December 1980, Princeton: Princeton University Press.

Baldwin, D. (ed), *Neo-Realism and Neo-Liberalism: The Contemporary Debate*, 1993, New York: Columbia University Press.

Ball, N., *Security and Economy in the Third World*, 1988, Princeton: Princeton University Press.

Ballenger, 'The Crisis in Colombia: What Are We Facing?' *Testimony* before the House Subcommittee on Criminal Justice, Drug Policy, and Human Resources of the Committee on Government Reform, 106th Congress, 15 February 2000, No. 106-151, Washington DC: US GPO.

Balloni, A., Bisi, R., Forlivesi, A., Mazzucato, F., and Sette, R., 'The Infiltration of Organised Crime in the Emilia-Romagna Region: Possible Interpretations for a New Social Defence', in Viano, E.C. (ed.), *Global Organized Crime and International Security*, 1999, Aldershot: Ashgate.

Barker, R., *Political Legitimacy and the State*, 1990, Oxford: Clarendon Press.

Barkin, D., 'Rural Development Effects', in Downing, T.E., Hecht, S.B., Pearson, H.A., and Garcia-Downing, C. (eds), *Development or Destruction: The Conversion of Tropical Forest to Pasture in Latin America*, 1992, Colorado: Westview Press.

Baum, D., *Smoke and Mirrors: The War on Drugs and the Politics of Failure*, 1997, Boston: Little Brown.

Bean, P. and Pearson, Y., 'Crack and Cocaine Use in Nottingham 1989/90 and 1991/92', in Mott, J. (ed.), *Crack and Cocaine in England and Wales*, 1992, RPU Paper 70, London: Home Office.

Bean, P. (ed.), *Crack and Cocaine: Supply and Use*, 1993, London: Macmillan.

Bean, P., 'Cocaine and Crack: The Promotion of an Epidemic', in Bean, P. (ed.), *Crack and Cocaine: Supply and Use*, 1993, London: Macmillan.

Beattie, A., 'US companies to be big gainers from Iraq outlay', *The Financial Times*, 18–19 October 2003.

Becchi, A., 'Italy: Mafia-dominated Drug Market?' in Dorn, N., Jepsen, J., and Savona, E. (eds), *European Drug Policies and Enforcement*, 1996, London: Macmillan.

Beers, R., *Statement* before the Senate Armed Service Committee, 4 April 2000, http://www.state.gov/www/policy_remarks/2000/000404_beers_sasc.html (Accessed 5 May 2002).

Beers, R., *Testimony* before the Criminal Justice, Drug Policy, and Human Resources, Subcommittee of the House Committee on Government Reform, 12 October 2000, http://www.state.gov/www/policy_remarks/2000/001012_beers_criminal. html (Accessed 6 March 2003).

Beetham, D., *The Legitimation of Power*, 1991, London: Macmillan.

Bell, D., 'Crime as an American Way of Life', *Antioch Review*, June 1953.

Bentham, M., *The Politics of Drug Control*, 1998, New York: St Martin's Press.

Berg, C., *Alternative Development as an Important Strategy within Development Oriented Drug Control*, presented at Senlis Council, the Vienna Civic Centre, 15 April 2003, http://www.senlis council.net/documents/christoph_berg_alternative_ development (Accessed 17 July 2003).

Bewley-Taylor, B.D., Fazey, C.S.J. with Boekhout van Solinge, T., 'The Mechanism and Dynamics of the UN System for International Drug Control', *Forward*

Thinking on Drugs: A Release Initiative, 14 March 2003, http://www.forward-thinking-on-drugs.org/review1-print.html (Accessed on 9 January 2005).

Bewley-Taylor, D.R., *The United States and International Drug Control*, 1909–1997, 1999, London: Pinter.

Bigo, D., 'The European Internal Security Field: States and Rivalries in a Newly Developing Area of Police Intervention', in Anderson, M. and den Boer, M. (eds), *Policing Across National Boundaries*, 1994, London: Pinter.

Bigo, D., 'Security and Immigration: Toward a Critique of the Governability of Unease', *Alternatives*, Vol. 27, Special Issue, February 2002.

Billings, D.B., and Blee, K.M., *The Road to Poverty: The Making of Wealth and Hardship in Apparachia*, 2000, Cambridge: Cambridge University Press.

Bilmes, J., *Discourse and Behavior*, 1986, New York: Plenum Press.

Blickman, T., 'The Rothschilds of the Mafia on Aruba', *Transnational Organized Crime*, Vol. 3, No. 2, Summer 1997.

Blueston, K., and Blickman, T., 'Lessons to Learn', *The World Today*, Vol. 54, No. 6, June 1998, http://www.lindesmith.org/news/news.html (Accessed 5 November 1999).

Bockma, H., 'Distributing Heroin to addicts is pointless (interview with J. P. Grund)', *International Journal on Drug Policy*, Vol. 3, No. 4, 1992.

Boekhout van Solinge, T., *Drugs and Decision-Making in the European Union*, 2002, Amsterdam: CEDRO/Mets en Schilt.

Bogusz, B. and King, M., 'Controlling Drug Trafficking in Central Europe: The Impact of EU Policies in the Czech Republic, Hungary and Lithuania', in Edwards, A. and Gill, P. (eds), *Transnational Organised Crime: Perspectives on Global Security*, 2003, Oxford: Routledge.

Booth, K., 'Security and Emancipation', *Review of International Studies*, Vol. 17, No. 4, October 1991.

Booth, K., 'Security in anarchy: Utopian Realism in theory and practice', *International Affairs*, Vol. 67, No. 3, July 1991.

Booth, K., 'Human Wrongs and International Relations', *International Affairs*, Vol. 71, No. 1, 1995.

Boucher, R., 'Colombian Rebel Connection to Mexican drug Cartel', *US Department of State Office of the Spokesman Press Statement*, 29 November 2000, http://secretary.state.gov/www/briefings/statements/2000/ps001129.html.

Boucher, R., 'Counternarcotics Cooperation with Colombia', *US Department of State Office of the Spokesman Press Statement*, 19 January 2001, http://secretary.state.gov/www/briefings/statements/2001/ps010119.html (Accessed 13 March 2001).

Boulding, K.E., *The Image*, 1956, Ann Arbour: University of Michigan Press.

Bouley, Jr., E.E., 'The Drug War in Latin America: Ten Years in a Quagmire', in Gerber, J., and Jensen, E.L. (eds), *Drug War American Style: The Internationalization of Failed Policy and Its Alternatives*, 2001, New York: Garland Publishing.

Bramley-Harker, E., *Sizing the UK Market for Illicit Drugs*, 2001, RDS Occasional Paper 74, London: Home Office.

Brecher, E.M., *Licit and Illicit Drugs*, 1972, Boston: Little, Brown.

Brian, K., Parker, H., and Bottomley, T., *Evolving Crack Cocaine Careers: News Users, Quitters and Long Term Combination Drug Use in N.W. England*, 1998, Manchester: University of Manchester Press.

Briquet, J-L., 'The Hidden Aspect of Democracy', *Nuove Effemeridi*, No. 50, 2000/ II.

Brodzinsky, S., and Bowcott, O., 'Secret aid poured into Colombian drug war', *The Guardian*, 9 July 2003, http://www.guardian.co.uk/international/ story/0,3604,994219,00.html (Accessed 13 February 2004).

Brooke, J., 'Bogotá Journal: A Captain in the Drug War Wants to Call it Off', *The New York Times*, 8 July 1994.

Brownfield, W.R., *On the Record Briefing: Andean Region Initiative*, 16 May 2001, http://www.state.gov/g/inl/narc/rm/2001/may_aug/index.cmf?docid=2925 (Accessed 12 June 2002).

Brownstein, H.H., *The Rise and Fall of a Violent Crime Wave: Crack Cocaine and the Social Construction of a Crime Problem*, 1996, New York: Criminal Justice Press.

Builta, J., 'Mexico faces corruption, crime, drug trafficking and political intrigue', *Criminal Organizations*, Vol. 10, No. 4, Summer 1997, http://www.acsp.uic.edu/ iasoc.crime_org/vol10_4/art_4v.htm.

Bull, H., *The Anarchic Society*, 1977, Basingstoke: Macmillan.

Bullington, B. and Block, A.A., 'A Trojan horse: Anti-communism and the war on drugs', *Contemporary Crises*, No. 14, 1990.

Bullington, B., 'All About Eve: The Many Faces of United States Drug Policy', in Pearce, F., and Woodiwiss, M. (eds) *Global Crime Connection*, 1993, London: Macmillan.

Burchell, G., Gordon, C., and Miller, P. (eds), *The Foucault Effect: Studies in Governmentality*, 1991, Chicago: University of Chicago Press.

Bureau of International Narcotics and Law Enforcement Affairs, *Drug Control Fact Sheet – Colombia*, 3 March 1998, http://www.state.gov/www/global/narcotics_ law/1997_narc_report/fs_colombia.html.

Bureau for International Narcotics and Law Enforcement Affairs, *Fact Sheet: FY 2003 Narcotics Certification Process*, 31 January 2003, http://www.state.gov/g/ inl/rls/fs/17010.htm (Accessed 20 February 2005).

Buscaglia, E., and Ratliff, W., *War and Lack of Governance in Colombia: Narcos, Guerrillas, and US Policy*, 2001, http://www.hoover.stanford/edu/publications/ epp/107/107.pdf (Accessed 11 July 2003).

Buzan, B., *People, States and Fear: An Agenda For International Security Studies In The Post-Cold War Era*, 1991, London: Harvester Wheatsheaf.

Buzan, B., 'From International System to International Society: Structural Realism and Regime Theory Meet English School', *International Organization*, Vol. 47, No. 3, Summer 1993.

Buzan, B., Wæver, O., and de Wilde, J., *Security: A New Framework For Analysis*, 1998, London: Lynne Rienner.

Camera dei Deputati, *Conoscere Le Mafie Costruire La Legalita'*, http://www. camera.it/_bicamerali/antimafia/sportello/dossier/dossier1_4.html (Accessed 20 February 2005).

Camiller, J.A. and Falk, J., *The End of Sovereignty?* 1992, Aldershot: Edward Elgar.

Campbell, D., *Writing Security: United States Foreign Policy and the Politics of Identity*, Manchester: Manchester University Press.

Capeda Ulloa, F., 'The European Union Contributes to the peace process in Colombia', *Nueva Mayoria*, 29 May 2001, http://www.nuevamayoria.com/english/analysis/cepeda/icepeda290501.htm (Accessed 31 October 2003).

Carbajol, C., 'Psychosis Produced by Nasal Aspiration of Cocaine Hydrochloride', in Jeri, F.R. (ed.), *Cocaina 1980*, 1980, Lima: Pacific Press.

Carneiro, L., *Report: Transnational Organised Crime*, PE 301.417, RRI435185EN. doc, 15 March 2001, Luxembourg: Office for Official Publications of the European Communities.

Carpenter, T.G., 'Plan Colombia: The Drug War's New Morass', *CATO Policy Report*, Vol. 23, No. 5, September/October 2001.

Carpenter, T.G., and Channing Rouse, R., 'Perilous Panacea: The Military in the Drug War', *CATO Policy Analysis*, No. 128, 15 February 1990, http://www.cato.org/pubs.pas.pa128.html (20 May 2003).

Carpenter, T.G., *Bad Neighbor Policy: Washington's futile war on drugs in Latin America*, 2003, New York: Palgrave Macmillan.

Carr, E.H., *Twenty Year's Crisis 1919-1939: An Introduction to the Study of International Relations*, 2001, Basingstoke: Palgrave Macmillan.

Carrigan, A., 'A Foolish Drug War', *The New York Times*, 10 February 2001.

Casteel, S.W., DEA *Testimony*, Narco-Terrorism: International Drug Trafficking and Terrorism – a Dangerous Mix, before the Senate Committee on the Judiciary, 20 May 2003, http://www.usdoj.gov/dea/pubs/cngrtest/ct052003p.html (Accessed 20 February 2005).

Castillo, F., *Los Jinetes de la Cocaína*, 2001, chapter 3, http://www.derechos.org/nizkor/colombia/libros/jinetes/cap3.html (Accessed 28 September 2004).

Castrillón, G., 'El Mundo del Padre de Roux', *Cromos*, 11 August 2003, No. 4, No. 461, http://www.cromos.com.co/4461/actualidad1-1.htm (Accessed 15 January 2004).

Caulkins, J., Rydell, P. and Schwabe, W.L., and Chisea, J., *Mandatory minimum drug sentences: Throwing away the key or the taxpayers' money?* 1997, Santa Monica, CA: RAND.

Chalk, P., *Non-Military Security and Global Order: The Impact of Extremism, Violence and Chaos on National and International Security*, 2000, London: Macmillan.

Chaiken, J.M., and Chaiken, M.R., 'Drugs and Predatory Crime', in Tonry, M and Wilson, J.Q. (eds), *Drug and Crime: Crime and Justice A Review of Research*, Vol. 73, 1990, Chicago: The University of Chicago Press.

Chepesiuk, R., 'The Colombian Drug Connection: its source, distribution and impact', *Journal of Defense & Diplomacy*, April 1998.

Chomsky, N., *Rogue States: The Rule of Force in World Affairs*, 2000, Cambridge, MA: South End Press.

Chomsky, N., *The Drug War*, http://www.mega.nu:8080/ampp/drugtext/ial5.html (Accessed 18 February 2004).

Christie, N., and Bruun, K., *Der Nuetzliche Feind: Die Drogenpolitik und ihre Nutzniesser*, 1991, Bielefeld: AJZ Verlag.

Ciba Fundation, *Cocaine: Scientific and Social Dimensions*, Ciba Fundation Symposium 166, 1992, West Sussex: John Wiley & Sons.

CICAD, *Cultivos de Coca en la Region Andina 1992-2002*, Obtained at CICAD during the interview on 29 May 2003.

CICAD/OAS, *Substituting the Coca Economy: The Anti-Drug Strategy in Bolivia: An Evaluation of the Dignity Plan 1998-2002*, 2002, Washington DC: OAS.

Clark, I., *Globalisation and International Relations Theory*, 1999, Oxford: Oxford University Press.

Claudio, A., 'United States-Colombia Extradition Treaty: Failure of a Security Strategy', *Military Review*, December 1991.

Clawson, P.L., and Lee III, R.W., *The Andean Cocaine Industry*, 1998, New York: St Martin's Griffin.

Clinton, W.J., *A National Security Strategy for a New Century*, Washington DC: The White House, October 1998.

Clutterbuck, R., *Drug, Crime and Corruption*, 1995, New York: New York University Press.

CNN, '6 more convictions overturned in LAPD corruption scandal', *CNN*, 23 March 2000, http://archives.cnn.com/2000/US/03/23/lapd.probe/.

CNN, *Alejandro Bernal Madrigal: Reputed Drug Lord*, http://edition.cnn.com/interactive/specials/0008/colombia.key/bernal.html (Accessed 18 January 2005).

Coffin, P., 'Coca Eradication', *Foreign Policy in Focus*, Vol. 3, No. 29, October 1998, http://www.lindesmith.org/news/news.html (Accessed 5 November 1999).

Colombian President, *Plan Colombia: Plan for Peace, Prosperity, and the Strengthening of the State*, 1999, Bogotá: Presidency of the Republic, http://www.usip.org/library/pa/colombia/adddoc/plan_colombia_101999.html (Accessed 31 October 2003).

Committee for a Safe Society, *Defining Organized Crime*, 6 April 1996, http://www.alternatives.com/crime2.html (Accessed 6 May 1999).

Comptroller General of Colombia, *Evaluation of Plan Colombia*, Third Report, July 2002.

Connolly, W. (ed.), *Legitimacy and the State*, 1984, Oxford: Basil Blackwell.

Constantine, T.A., DEA *Congressional Testimony* before the Subcommittee on Western Hemisphere House International Relations Committee, 7 March 1996, http://www.druglibrary.org/schaffer/dea/pubs/cngrtest/ct960307.htm (Accessed 14 April 2000).

Constantine, T.A., DEA *Congressional Testimony* Regarding Drug Trafficking in Mexico, before the Senate Committee on Banking, Housing, and Urban Affairs, 26 March 1996, http://www.usdoj.gov/dea/pubs/cngrtest/ct960328.htm (Accessed 6 June 1999).

Constantine, T.A., *Congressional Testimony, National Drug Control Strategy and Drug Interdiction*, Before the Senate Caucus on International Narcotics Control, and The House Subcommittee on Coast Guard and Maritime Transportation, 12 September 1996, http://www.usdoj.gov/dea/pubs/cngrtest/ct960912.htm (Accessed 13 December 1998).

Constantine, T.A., DEA *Congressional Testimony* Regarding Cooperation with
    Mexico, before the National Security, International Affairs and Criminal Justice
    Subcommittee of House Government Reform and Oversight Committee, 25
    February 1997, http://www.usdoj.gov/dea/pubs/cngrtest/ct970225.htm (Accessed
    8 June 1999).

Constantine, T.A., DEA *Congressional Testimony*, International Organized Crime
    Syndicates and their impact on the United States, Before the Senate Foreign
    Relations Committee, Subcommittee on the Western Hemisphere, Peace Crops,
    Narcotics, and Terrorism, 26 February 1998, http://www.usdoj.gov/dea/pubs/
    cngrtest/ct980226.htm (Accessed 20 February 2005).

Constantine, T.A., DEA *Congressional Testimony* before the Senate Drug Caucus, 24
    February 1999, http://www.usdoj.gov/dea/pubs/cngrtest/ct022499.htm (Accessed
    20 February 2005).

Conzáles Posso, D., and Rodoríguez Salazsar, A., *Colombia: Crónica de un Debate
    No Concluido Contra Proyecto de Armas Biológicas: en defensa de los derechos
    humanos y la biodiversidad*, 16 de abril de 2001, http://www.mamacoca.org/
    gonzalez_cronica_debate_es.htm (Accessed 21 November 2003).

Coomber, R. (ed.), *The Control of Drugs and Drug Users: Reason or Reaction?*
    1998, Amsterdam: Harwood Academic Publishers.

Cooperation Group to Combat Drug Abuse and Illicit Trafficking in Drugs (Pompidou
    Group), *Multi-City Study: Drug misuse trends in thirteen European Cities*, 1994,
    Strasbourg: Council of Europe Press.

*Coordination and Cooperation Mechanism on Drugs Between The EU, Latin
    America and the Caribbean: Annual Report 2000–2001*, Obtained during an
    interview in Brussels.

Cornes, R., and Sandler, T., *The Theory of Externalities, Public Goods, and Club
    Goods*, 1996, Cambridge: Cambridge University Press.

Corruption and Drugs in Colombia: Democracy at Risk, A Staff Report to the
    Committee of Foreign Relations US Senate, February 1996, Washington DC:
    GPO.

Council of Europe, *Convention on Laundering, Search, Seizure and Confiscation
    of the Proceeds from Crime*, Strasbourg, 8.XI.1990, http://conventions.coe.int/
    treaty/en/Treaties/Html/141.htm (Accessed 20 February 2005).

Council Regulation (EC) No 2501/2001 of 10 December 2001, http://europa.eu.int/
    comm/external_relations/andean/doc/gspreg01_en.pdf (Accessed 25 August
    2002).

Council Regulation (EEC) No 302/93 of 8 February 1993, Official Journal L 036,
    12/02/1993 P. 0001 – 0008, http://europa.eu.int/smartapi/cgi/sga_doc?smartapi!
    celexapi!prod!CELEXnumdoc&lg=en&numdoc=31993R0302&model=guichett
    (Accessed 3 March 2005).

Country Strategy Paper: Colombia 2001-2006, http://europa.eu.int/comm/external_
    relations/colombia/csp/02_06en.pdf (Accessed 26 June 2003).

Cox, R., *Production, Power, and World Order: Social forces in the making of history*,
    1987, New York: Columbia University Press.

Cox, T.E., *Audit of the USAID/Colombia-Financed Coca Alternative Development
    Program Under the Plan Colombia Supplemental Appropriation*, Report No. 1-

514-02-005-P, 16 January 2002, San Salvador: USAID, http://www.usaid.gov/oig/public/fy02rpts/1-514-02-005-P.pdf (Accessed 20 May 2003).

Crandall, R., *Driven by Drugs: U.S. Policy Toward Colombia*, 2002, Boulder: Lynne Rienner.

Cressy, D., 'Methodological Problems in the Study of Organized Crime as a Social Problem', 1967, *Annuals of the American Academy of Political and Social Science*, Vol. 374.

Dalby, S., *Creating the Second Cold War: The Discourse of Politics*, 1990, New York: Guilford.

Davidson, D., 'Actions, reasons, and causes', *Journal of Philosophy*, Vol. 60, 1963.

Davison, P., 'Escobar's hand seen in Bogota bomb atrocity', *The Independent*, 1 February 1993.

De Franco, M., and Godoy, R., 'The Economic Consequences of Cocaine Production in Bolivia: Historical, Local and Macroeconomic Perspectives', *Journal of Latin American Studies*, Vol. 24, 1992.

De Kort, M., 'Doctors, diplomats, and businessmen: conflicting interests in the Netherlands and Dutch East Indies, 1860-1950', in Gootenberg, P. (ed.), *Cocaine: Global Histories*, 1999, London: Routledge.

DEA Intelligence Division, *The Drug Trade in Colombia: A Threat Assessment*, March 2002, DEA-02006, http://www.usdoj.gov/dea/pubs/intel/02006/indexp.html (Accessed 16 May 2003).

DEA, *The South American Cocaine Trade: An 'Industry' in Transition*, June 1996, http://www.usdoj.gov/dea/pubs/intel/cocaine.htm (Accessed 28 February 2002).

DEA, 'Cocaine: Trafficking by Colombian and Mexican Organizations', in *Drug Trafficking in the United States*, September 2001, http://www.dea.gov/pubs/intel/01020/index.html#cocaine.

DEA, 'Head of One of the World's Largest Cocaine Transportation Organizations Extradited to the United States', *News Release: Immediate Release*, 30 October 2001, http://www.usdoj.gov/dea/pubs/pressrel/pr103001.html (Accessed 18 January 2005).

DEA, *DEA Staffing & Budget*, http://www.usdoj.gov/dea/agency/staffing.htm (Accessed 4 March 2005).

DEA, *Drug Intelligence Brief: Changing Dynamics of Cocaine Production in the Andean Region*, June 2002, http://www.usdoj.gov/dea/pubs/omte;/02033/02033p.html (Accessed 16 May 2003).

Deal, M., *On the Record Briefing: Andean Region Initiative*, 16 May 2001, http://www.state.gov/g/inl/narc/rm/2001/may_aug/index.cmf?docid=2925 (Accessed 12 June 2002).

Dean, A., Carvell, A., Green, A., Pickering, H., and Stimson, G.V., 'Crack and Cocaine Use in Britain in 1990: First National Report', in Mott, J. (ed.), *Crack and Cocaine in England and Wales*, 1992, RPU Paper 70, London: Home Office.

Declaration of Rio de Janeiro, 29 June 1999, http://europa.eu.int/comm/external_relations/andean/doc/rio_prio06_00.htm (Accessed 17 October 2002).

Della Porta, D., and Vannucci, A., 'The resources of corruption: some reflections from the Italian case', *Crime, Law & Social Change*, Vol. 27, Nos 3–4, 1997.

Dennis, R.J., 'The economics of legalizing drugs', *The Atlantic*, Vol. 266, 1990, p. 128.

Departamento Nacional de Planeación, *Balance del Plan Colombia*, 17 September 2003, http://www.dnp/gov.co/ArchivosWeb/Direccion_Evaluacion_Gestion/ Repor_y_Doc/Balance_Plan_Colombia.pdf (Accessed 29 October 2003).

Departamento Nacional de Planeación, *Brindar Seguridad Democrática: Seguimiento a Resultados Tercer Trimestre 2003*, November 2003, http://www.dnp.gov/ co/ArchivosWeb/Direccion_Evaluacion_Gestion/Report_y_Doc/Seguridad_ democratica_3er_trimestre_2003.zip (Accessed 15 January 2004).

Departamento Nacional de Planeación, *Plan Colombia Balance 1999-2003*, November 2003, http://www.dnp.gov/co/ArchivosWeb/Direccion_Evaluacion_ Gestion/Report_y_Doc/Balance_Plan_Colombia.pdf (Accessed 15 January 2004).

Department of Nariño, Municipality of E Tablón de Gómez, *Final Report: A Study of the Health Complaints Related to Aerial Eradication in Colombia*, September 2001, Bogotá, http://ysenvasst.state.gov/bogota/wwwfapoe.pdf (Accessed 5 May 2002).

Department of State Office of Press Secretary, *Fact Sheet: Andean Region Initiative*, 23 May 2002, http://www.state.gov/p/wha/rls/fs/8980.htm (16 May 2003).

Department of State, *Fact Sheet: Andean Region Initiative*, 16 May 2001, http:// www.state.gov/p/wha/rls/fs/2001/2980pf.htm (16 May 2003).

Desch, M.C., 'Culture Crash: Assessing the Importance of Ideas in Security Studies', *International Security*, Vol. 23, No. 1, Summer 1998.

Deutsch, K., *The Analysis of International Relations*, 1968, Englewood Cliffs, N.J.: Prentice Hall, Inc.

DeYoung, K., 'Clinton Pledges To Keep U.S. Out Of Colombia War; Visit Highlights Anti-Drug Support', *The Washington Post*, 31 August 2000.

DeYoung, K., 'Colombia to Get Fewer, Stronger Helicopters; White House Modifies Anti-Drug Aid in Face of Criticism From GAO, Congress', *The Washington Post*, 13 October 2000.

Dictionary of English Language, 4th edition, 2000, Boston: Houghton Mifflin.

Dillon, S., 'In Letter From Hiding, Mexican Governor Charges Political Plot', *The New York Times*, 7 April 1999, http://www.nytimes.com/library/world/americas/ 040799mexico-governor.html (Accessed 8 April 1999).

Dillon, S., 'Tijuana Official Says Slaying Shows Traffickers' Power', *The New York Times*, 29 February 2000, http://www.nytimes.com/yr/mo/day/news/world/ tijuana-slaying.html (Accessed 1 March 2000).

Directive 2001/97/EC of the European Parliament and of the Council of 4 December 2001 amending Council Directive 91/308/EEC on prevention of the use of the financial system for the purpose of money laundering - Commission Declaration, *Official Journal, L 344*, 28/12/2001 P. 0076 – 0082, http://europa.eu.int/smartapi/ cgi/sga_doc?smartapi!celexapi!prod!CELEXnumdoc&lg=EN&numdoc=32001 L0097&model=guichett (Accessed 20 February 2005).

Dodd, C.J., *Statement*, 'Lack of International Support Will Cause Plan Colombia to Wither on the Vine', 1 November 2000, http://dodd.senate.gov/pceso/ Speeches/106_00/1101.htm (31 October 2003).

Dorn, N., 'Borderline Criminology: External Drug Policies of the EU', in Dorn, N., Jepsen, J., and Savona, E. (eds), *European Drug Policies and Enforcement*, 1996, London: Macmillan.

Dorn, N., (ed.) *Regulating European Drug Problems: Administrative Measures and Civil Law in the Control of Drug Trafficking, Nuisance and Use*, 1999, London: Kluwer Law International.

Dorn, N. and South, N., 'Drug Market and Law Enforcement', *The British Journal of Criminology*, Vol. 30, No. 2, 1990.

Dorn, N. and South, N., 'After Mr Bennett and Mr Bush: US Foreign Policy and the Prospects for Drug Control', in Pearce, F. and Woodiwiss, M. (eds) *Global Crime Connections: Dynamics and Control*, 1993, London: Macmillan.

Dorn, N., and South, N., *Global Crime Connection*, 1993, London: Macmillan.

Dorn, N., Jepsen, J., and Savona, E. (eds), *European Drug Policies and Enforcement*, 1996, London: Macmillan.

Dorn, N., Murji, K., and South, N., *Traffickers: Drug Markets and Law Enforcement*, 1992, London: Routledge.

Dorn, N., Oette, L., and White, S., 'Drug Importation and the Bifurcation of Risk: Capitalization, Cut Outs and Organized Crime', *The British Journal of Criminology*, Vol. 38, No. 4, Autumn 1998.

Dorner, P., and Felstenhaousen, H., 'Agrarian reforms and employment - the Colombian case', Land Tenure Centre, University of Wisconsin, *LTC Reprint*, No.66, 1970.

Doyle, M., *Ways of War and Peace*, 1997, New York: MIT Press.

Drugs and Community Safety: The Strategic Challenge, Report of a Local Government Forum Conference held on 10 December 1997, 1998, London: HMSO.

DrugScope, *United Kingdom: Drug Situation 2000*, 2000, REITOX REF/2000, http://www.emcdda.org/multimedia/publications/national_reports/NRuk_2000. PDF (Accessed 14 March 2003).

Dudley, S., 'Colombia sets negotiations with a second rebel group', *The Washington Post*, 26 April 2000, http://www.washingtonpost.com/wp-dyn/articles/A14228-2000Apr25.html (Accessed 28 April 2000).

Dudley, S., 'Battle Brews Over Plan Colombia; U.S.-Backed Program to Eradicate Drug Crops Faces Gathering Opposition', *The Washington Post*, 20 September 2000.

Duque Gómez, D., 'El Presidente debe ser juzgado', *Colombia Analítica*, 14 June 2001, http://colombia.analitica.com/politica/3171552.asp?frameactive=0 (Accessed 20 February 2005).

Durkheim, E., *The Rules of Sociological Method*, 1964, New York: Free Press.

Duster, D., 'Pattern, Purpose, and Race in the Drug War: The Crisis of Credibility in Criminal Justice', in Reinarman, C., and Levine, H.G. (eds) *Crack in America: Demon Drugs and Social Justice*, 1997, Berkeley: University of California Press.

Dziedzic, M.J., 'The transnational drug trade and regional security', *Survival*, Vol. XXXI, No. 6, November/December 1989.

Edmunds, M., Hough, M., Urguía, T.N., *Tackling Local Drug Markets*, 1996, Crime Detection and Prevention Series Paper 80, London: Home Office.

Edwards, A. and Gill, P. (eds), *Transnational Organised Crime: Perspectives on Global Security*, 2003, Oxford: Routledge.

EFE, 'Desmantelan una red de tráfico de cocaíina distribuida en locales de lujo', *El Mundo*, 26 February 2001, http://www.elmundo.es/elmundo/2001/02/26/sociedad/983201993.html (Accessed 1 March 2005).

EFE, 'Los Quince acuerdan ampliar su lucha contra el blanqueo de dinero', *El Mundo*, 16 October 2001, http://www.elmundo.es/elmundo/2001/10/16/enespecial/1003245309.html (Accessed 1 March 2005).

EFE, 'El abogado Pablo Vioque pide que testifique Liaño en el juicio al que se le someterá por narcotráfico', *El Mundo*, 14 January 2003, http://www.elmundo.es/elmundo/2003/01/13/sociedad/1042486158.html (Accessed 1 March 2005).

EFE, 'La policía desarticula un grupo dedicado a lavar dinero procedente del narcotráfico', *El Mundo*, 17 September 2003, http://www.elmundo.es/elmundo/2003/09/16/madrid/1063713774.html (Accessed 1 March 2005).

Elster, J., *Explaining Technical Change*, 1983, Cambridge: Cambridge University Press.

European Monitoring Centre for Drug and Drug Abuse (EMCDDA), *Euro-Ibero American Seminar: Cooperation on Drugs and Drug Addiction Policies (Conference Proceedings)*, 1999, Luxembourg: Office for Official Publications of the European Communities.

EMCDDA, 'Annual report on drugs in the EU – 2000: Problem Drug Use – Changing Trends', *News Release*, No. 5/2000 – 11 October 2000, Lisbon: EMCDDA.

EMCDDA, *Annual Report on the State of the Drugs Problem in the European Union 2000*, Luxembourg: Office for Official Publications of the European Communities.

EMCDDA, *Annual Report on the State of the Drugs Problem in the European Union 2001*, Luxembourg: Office for Official Publications of the European Communities.

EMCDDA, *Annual Report 2003: The State of the Drugs Problem in the European Union and Norway*, 2003, Luxembourg: Office for Official Publications of the European Communities.

EMCDDA, 'Table Markets-6. Quantities of cocaine seized (kgs). Part (ii) 1985 to 2002', *Statistical Bulletin 2004*, http://stats04.emcdda.eu.int/index.cfm?fuseaction=public.Content&nNodeID=5362 (Accessed 3 March 2005).

EMCDDA, *About the EMCDDA*, http://www.emcdda.eu.int/index.cfm?fuseaction=public.Content&nNodeID=373&sLanguageISO=EN (Accessed 3 March 2005).

EMCDDA, *National and EU drug strategies and policies*, http://www.emcdda.eu.int/index.cfm?fuseaction=public.Content&nNodeID=2176&sLanguageISO=EN (Accessed 3 March 2005).

Erickson, P.G., Adlaf, E.M., Murray, G.F., and Smart, R.G., *The Steel Drug: Cocaine in Perspective*, 1987, Lexington, Mass: Heath.

Estievenart, G. (ed.), *Policies and Strategies to Combat Drugs in Europe*, 1995, Martinus Nijhoff Publishers: London.

Estievenart, G., *The Agencies of the European Community: European Centre for Drugs and Drug Addiction*, http://europa.eu.int/agencies/emcdda/index_en.htm (Accessed 3 March 2005).

EU-Rio group: Santiago Declaration/Xth institutionalised ministerial meeting, 28 March 2001, http://europa.eu.int/comm/external_relations/andean/intro/santiago28_03_01.htm (Accessed 15 February 2003).

Europa Press, "El Negro' era el 'delegado' del cártel de Bogotá en España y ponía precio a la cocaína', *El Mundo*, 8 March 2002, http://www.elmundo.es/elmundo/2002/03/07/espana/1015518180.html (Accessed 1 March 2005).

European Commission Delegation to Colombia, *Cooperación no reembolsable*, http://www.delcol.cec.eu.int/en/eu_and_colombia/proyects.htm (Accessed 25 February 2004).

European Commission, *Multiannual Guidelines for Community Aid: Colombia, Brussels: The European Community*, 12 November 1998, IB/1035/98-EN.

European Commission, Peace Process in Colombia: Commission launches 'Peace Laboratory in the Magdalena Medio', 7 February 2002, IP/02/213, http://www.reliefweb.int/w/rwb.nsf/0/3d7963a94e62ffe8c1256b59004a367a?OpenDocument (Accessed 29 October 2003).

European Community Support for the Fight Against Drugs in Bolivia, http://europa.eu.int/comm/external_relations/bolivia/intro/drugs.htm (Accessed 23 March 2002).

European Council, *A Secure Europe in the Better World: European Security Strategy*, 12 December 2003, Brussels: European Union, http://consilium.europa.eu/uedocs/cmsUpload/78367.pdf (Accessed 15 October 2007).

European Parliament Resolution on Plan Colombia and Support for the Peace Process in Colombia, 1 February 2001, B5-0087/2001, http://www.narconews.com/euroresolution2001.html (Accessed 30 October 2003).

European Parliament, *Note on the Political and Economic Situation in Colombia and its Relations with the European Union*, PE 313.371, 8 May 2002, Luxembourg: The European Community.

Evaluation of EU development aid to ALA states: Phase III – Synthesis Report (Final Report), 15 March 1999, European Commission Joint Relex Service For the Management of Community and to Non-Member Countries.

Evans, P.B., 'Transnational Linkages and the Economic Role of the States: An Analysis of Developing and Industrialized Nations in the Post-World War II Period', in Evans, P.B., Rueschemeyer, D., and Skocpol, T. (eds), *Bringing the State Back In*, 1985, Cambridge: Cambridge University Press.

Evans, P.B., Rueschemeyer, D., and Skocpol, T. (eds), *Bringing the State Back In*, 1985, Cambridge: Cambridge University Press.

Evans, P.B., Rueschemeyer, D., and Skocpol, T., 'The Post-World War II Period', in Evans, P.B., Rueschemeyer, D., and Skocpol, T. (eds), *Bringing the State Back In*, 1985, Cambridge: Cambridge University Press,

Ewald, F., 'Insurance and Risk', in Burchell, G., Gordin, C., and Miller, P. (eds), *The Foucault Effect: Studies in Governmental Rationality*, Chicago: University of Chicago Press.

Faaland, J., and Parkinson, J.R., *The Political Economy of Development*, 1986, London: Frances Pinter.

Fagan, J., 'Intoxication and Aggression', in Tonry, M., and Wilson, J.Q. (eds), *Drugs and Crime: Crime and Justice: A Review of Research*, 1990, Chicago: The University of Chicago Press.

Fahrenkrug, H., 'Drug Control in a Federal System: Zurich, Switzerland', in Dorn, N., Jepsen, J., and Savona, E., *European Drug Policies and Enforcement*, 1996, London: Macmillan.

Farrell, G., Mansur, K., and Tullis, M., 'Cocaine and Heroin in Europe 1983-1993: A Cross-National Comparison of Trafficking and Prices', *The British Journal of Criminology*, 1996, Vol. 36, No. 2, Spring, p. 275.

Farthing, L., 'Social Impacts Associated with Antidrug Law 1008', in Léons, M.B., and Sanabria, H. (eds), *Coca, Cocaine and the Bolivian Reality*, 1997, New York: State University of New York Press.

Federal Bureau of Prisons, *Substance Abuse and Treatment Programs in the Federal Bureau of Prisons: Report to Congress*, January 1999, Washington DC: U.S. Department of Justice.

Feldafing Declaration, January 2002, http://www.alternative-development.net/downloads/dec/declaration/pdf (Accessed 17 July 2003).

Fellon, M., 'Bush Turns to Military Aid to Stanch Narcotics Flow', *Congressional Quarterly Weekly Report*, 9 September 1989.

Fijnaut, C., 'Organized Crime: A Comparison Between the United States of America and Western Europe', *The British Journal of Criminology*, Vol. 30, No. 3, 1990.

Findlay, M., *The Globalisation of Crime: Understanding Transitional Relationships in Context*, 1999, Cambridge: Cambridge University Press.

Fiscal year 2004 Congressional Budget Justification, obtained during the interviews in Washington DC in May 2003.

Fithin, C., 'Plan Colombia', *Oxford Analytica*, 4 January 2001, http://www.ciaonet.org/pbei/oxan/oxa10020104.html (Accessed 14 November 2003).

Flynn, S., *US Support of Plan Colombia: Rethinking the Ends and Means*, May 2001, http://www.carlisle.army.mil/ssi/2001/pcussprt/pcussprt.pdf (Accessed 16 May 2003).

Ford, J.T., *Drug Control: DoD Allocates Fewer Assets to Drug Control Efforts*, Testimony before the Subcommittee on Criminal Justice, Drug Control and Human Resources, Committee on Government Reform, House of Representatives, 27 January 2000, GAO/T-NSIAD-00-77.

Ford. J.T., *Drug Control: Challenges in Implementing Plan Colombia*, Testimony, 12 October 2000, GAO-01-76T, Washington DC: US General Accounting Office.

Foucault, M., *The Archaeology of Knowledge and Discourse on Language*, 1972, New York: Pantheon Books.

Franco, A.A., *Testimony* before the House Appropriations Committee on Foreign Operations US Assistance to Colombia and the Andean Region, 10 April 2002, http://www.state.gov/press/spe_test/testimony/2002/ty020410.html (Accessed 20 May 2003).

Freeman, L., *Troubling Patterns: The Mexican Military and the War on Drugs*, 2002, Washington DC: Latin American Working Group.

Freemantle, B., *The Octopus: Europe in the Grip of Organised Crime*, 1995, Orion: London.

Friedman, A., 'Inquiry into BCCI 'tip-off' to drug dealers', *Financial Times*, 28 October 1991.

Friedman, A., and Waters, R., 'US indicts BCCI officials on drug money charges', *Financial Times*, 6 September 1991.

Friedmann, J., *Empowerment: The Politics of Alternative Development*, 1992, Oxford: Blackwell.

Friman, H.R., *NarcoDiplomacy: Exporting the US War on Drugs*, 1996, Ithaca: Cornell University Press.

Friman, H.R., 'Germany and the transformations of cocaine, 1880-1920', in Gootenberg, P. (ed.), *Cocaine: Global Histories*, 1999, London: Routledge.

Friman, H.R., 'Narco Diplomacy', in Manwaring, M.G. (ed.), *Security and Civil-Military Relations in the New World Disorder: The Use of Armed Forces in the Americas*, September 1999, http://www.carlisle.army.mil/ssi/pubs/1999/newworld/newworld.pdf (16 May 2003).

Fiorentini, G. and Peltzman, S. (eds), *The Economics of Organised Crime*, 1995, Cambridge: Cambridge University Press.

Frontline: When Cops Go Bad, original air date 16 October 1990, http://www.pbs.org/wgbh/pages/frontline/shows/drugs/archive/copsgobad.html (Accessed 18 October 2002).

Fukumi, S., *National Security Threat in the Changing World: The Case of Andean Cocaine Trafficking*, MPhil Thesis at the University of Birmingham, UK, 2001.

Gaitán Pavía, P., Pard Gracía-Peña, R., and Manuel Osorio, J., *Communidad Internacional, conflicto armado y perspectivas de paz en Colombia*, 2002, http://www.ideaspaz.org/publicaciones/download/communidad_internacional_english.pdf (Accessed 30 January 2004).

Gamarra, E.A., 'US-Bolivia Counternarcotics Efforts During the Paz Zamora Administration: 1989-1992', in Bagley, B.M. and Walker III, W.O. (eds), *Drug Trafficking in the Americas*, 1996, Miami: North South Center Press.

Gambetta, D. and Reuter, P., 'Conspiracy among the many: the mafia in legitimate industry', in Fiorentini, G. and Peltzman, S. (eds), *The Economics of Organised Crime*, 1995, Cambridge: Cambridge University Press.

GAO, *Drug Control: US-Supported Efforts in Colombia and Bolivia, Report to the Congress*, November 1988, GAO/NSIAD-89-24, Washington DC: GAO.

GAO, *Drug Control: How Drug-Consuming Nations Are Organized for the War on Drugs*, January 1990, GAO/NSIAD-90-133, Washington DC: GAO.

GAO, *Drugs: International Efforts to Attack a Global Problem*, June 1993, Report to the Chairman and Ranking Minority Members, Committee on Foreign Affairs, House of Representatives, GAO/NSIAD-93-165, Washington DC: GAO.

GAO, *Drug Control: US Antidrug Efforts in Peru's Upper Huallaga Valley*, December 1994, GAO/NSIAD-95-11, Washington DC: GAO.

GAO, *Drug Control: US Counternarcotic Efforts in Colombia Face Continuing Challenges*, Report to Congressional Requesters, GAO/NSIAD-98-60, February 1998, Washington DC: GAO.

GAO, *Report to the Honorable Charles B. Rangel, House of Representatives, Law Enforcement: Information on Drug-Related Police Corruption*, May 1998, GAO/GGD-98-111, Washington DC: GAO.

GAO, *Drug Control: INS and Customs Can Do More To Prevent Drug-Related Employee Corruption*, March 1999, GAO/GGD-99-31, Washington DC: GAO.

GAO, *Drug Control: Narcotics Threat From Colombia Continues to Grow, Report to Congressional Requesters*, GAO/NSIAD-99-136, June 1999, Washington DC: GAO.

GAO, *Drug Control: DEA's Strategies and Operations in the 1990s*, GAO/GGD-99-108, July 1999, Washington DC: GAO.

GAO, *Drug Control: Efforts to Develop Alternatives to Cultivating Illicit Crops in Colombia Have Made Little Progress and Face Serious Obstacles*, GAO-02-291, February 2002, Washington DC: GAO.

García Argañarás, F., 'The Drug War at the Supply End', *Latin American Perspectives*, Issue 96, Vol. 24, No. 5, September 1997.

García, A., and Sarmiento, A., *Programas Regionales de Desarrollo Y Paz: Casos de capital social y desarrollo institucional*, 6 August 2002, PNUD: Bogotá.

García-Altés, A., Ma Ollé, J., Antoñanzas, F., and Colom, J., 'The social cost of illegal drug consumption in Spain', *Addiction*, Vol. 97, No. 9, September 2002.

Garrido, R.S., 'La Guerra Global Contra El terror, Plan Colombia, El IRA Y La Región Andino Amazonica: Wanted or Certified?' *Mamacoca*, http://www.mamacoca.org/FSMT_sept_2003/es/abs/soberon_guerra_global_terror_abs_es.htm (Accessed 15 December 2003).

Gayón, O., 'Plan Colombia is a Dracula', *El Espectador*, 11 June 2000, http://www.elespectador.com/0006/11/genotici.htm#01 (Accessed 12 June 2000).

Gelbard, R., *Press Briefing by Robert Gelbard, Assistant Secretary of State for International Narcotics Matters; Richard Newcombe, Assistant Secretary of the Treasury, Office of Foreign Assets Control; George Ward, Acting Assistant Secretary of State for International Organizations; and Richard Clarke, Senior Director, Global and Multinational Affairs, NSC*, The White House: Washington, DC, 22 October 1995, http://www.pub.whiltehouse.gov/uri-res/I2R?urn:pdi://oma.eop.gov.us/1995/10/23/6.text.1 (Accessed 18 November 2000).

Gelbard, R.S., *U.S. Counternarcotics Policy Toward Colombia, Statement to the House Committee on International relations*, 11 September 1996, http://www.fas.org/irp/congress/1996_hr/h960911g.htm (Accessed 18 November 2000).

Gellner, E., *Nations and Nationalism*, 1983, Oxford: Blackwell.

Gerber, J., and Jensen, E.L. (eds), *Drug War American Style: The Internationalization of Failed Policy and Its Alternatives*, 2001, New York: Garland Publishing.

Gerber, J., and Jensen, E.L., 'The Internationalization of US Policy on Illicit Drug Control', in Gerber, J., and Jensen, E.L. (eds), *Drug War American Style: The Internationalization of Failed Policy and Its Alternatives*, 2001, New York: Garland Publishing, p. 11.

Getler, W., 'A Major Bank Accused by U.S. Of Laundering Cocaine Profits', *International Herald Tribune*, 12 October 1988.

Geuileman, J.A., *The Regional Security Crisis in the Andes: Pattern of State Response*, July 2001, p. 11, http://www.carlise.army.mil/ssi/pubs/2001/andes/andes.pdf (Accessed 16 May 2003).

Gillard, M.S. and Flynn, L., 'Corruption squad under fire', *The Guardian*, 4 March 2000, http://www.guardian.co.uk/Archive/Article/0,4273,3970352,00.html (Accessed 20 July 2003).

Gilpin, R., 'Politics of International Economic Relations', *International Organizations*, Vol. 25, 1971.

Gilpin, R., *War and Change in World Politics*, 1981, Cambridge: Cambridge University Press.

Gilpin, R., *The Political Economy of International Relations*, 1987, Princeton: Princeton University Press.

Glasser, I., and Siegel, L., 'When Constitutional Rights Seem Too Extravagant to Endure: The Crack Scare's Impact on Civil Rights and Liberties', in Reinarman, C., and Levine, H. G. (eds), *Crack in America: Demon Drugs and Social Justice*, 1997, Berkeley: University of California Press.

Global Security Org, *Operation Selva Verde*, http://www.globalsecurity.org/military/tps/selva_verde.htm (Accessed 18 January 2005).

Goddard, D., *Easy Money*, 1978, New York: Farrar.

Godoy, H., *Plan Colombia's Strategic Weaknesses*, a paper presented at the 2003 meeting of the Latin American Studies Association in Dallas, Texas, 27–29 March 2003, http://136.142.158.105/Lasa2003/GodoyHoracio.pdf (Accessed 13 November 2003).

Godson, R. and Williams, P., 'Strengthening Cooperation Against Transnational Crime', *Survival*, Vol. 40, No. 3, 1998.

Golden, T., 'Mexican Tale of Absolute Drug Corruption', *The New York Times*, 9 January 2000, http://www.nytimes.com/library/world/americas/010900mexico-us-drugs.html (Accessed 10 January 2000).

Goldstein, P., 'The drug/violence nexus: A tripartite conceptual framework', *Journal of Drug Issues*, Vol. 14, 1985.

Goldstein, P., Brownstein, H.H., Ryan, P.J., and Bellucci, P.A., 'Crack and homicide in New York City, 1988: A conceptually based event analysis', *Contemporary Drug Problem*, Vol. 16, 1989.

Gonzalez, S., *DEA Statement* before the US House of representatives Committee on Government Reform Subcommittee on Criminal Justice, Drug policy, and Human Resources, 15 April 2003, http://www.usdoj.gov/dea/pubs/cngrtest/ct041503.html (Accessed 28 May 2004).

Gootenberg, P., 'Reluctance or resistance? Constructing cocaine (prohibitions) in Peru, 1910-1950', in Gootenberg, P. (ed.), *Cocaine: Global Histories*, 1999, London: Routledge.

Gori, G., 'Bolivia's Cabinet Resigns After Protests', *The Washington Post*, 18 February 2003, http://www.washingtonpost.com/ac2/wp-dyn/A26838-2003Feb18?language=printer (Accessed 7 March 2003).

Gould, K., Weinberg, A., and Schnaiberg, A., 'Natural Resource Use in a Transnational Treadmill: International Agreements, National Citizenship Practices, and

Sustainable Development', *Humboldt Journal of Social Relations*, Vol. 21, No. 1, 1995.

Gourevitch, P., 'The Second Image reversed: The International Sources of Domestic Politics', *International Organization*, Vol. 32, No. 4, Autumn, 1978.

Gray, C., 'Global Security and Economic Wellbeing: A Strategic Perspective', *Political Studies*, Vol. 42, No. 1, 1994.

Gray, J.P., *Why Our Drug Laws Have Failed and What We Can Do About It: A Judicial Indictment of the War on Drugs*, 2001, Philadelphia: Temple University Press.

Green, P., *Drugs, Trafficking and Criminal Policy*, 1998, Winchester: Waterside Press.

Gregorie, D., *Frontline: Drug Wars Interview*, http://www.pbs.org/wgbh/pages/ frontline/shows/drugs/interviews/gregorie.html (Accessed 6 August 2004).

Grosse, R.E., *Drugs and Money: Laundering Latin America's Cocaine Dollars*, 2001, Westport: Praeger.

Grossman, M., *Remarks to EU/IDB Conference on Colombia*, 30 April 2001, http:// www.state.gov/g/inl/narc/index.htm (Accessed 17 November 2003).

Grossman, M., *US Support for Plan Colombia*, 31 August 2001, http://www.state. gov/g/inl/narc/rm/2001/may_aug/index.cfm?docid=4798 (Accessed 16 April 2003).

Grossman, M., *Joint Efforts for Colombia*, 24 June 2002, http://www.state.gov/ p/11498pf.htm (Accessed 16 May 2003).

Guardian Staffs and Agencies, 'Colombian President vows to retake rebel land', *The Guardian*, 21 February 2002, http://www.guardian.co.uk/colombia/ story/0,11502,653729,00.html (Accessed 11 July 2004).

Gumble, A., 'Bush appoints moral crusader to fight drugs', *The Independent*, 1 May 2001.

Gusheko, J., 'Colombia Asks Help in Protecting Judges', *The Washington Post*, 30 August 1989.

Gutierrez, L., *Peace and Security in Colombia*, 20 June 2002, http://www.state.gov/ p/wha/rls/rm/11297pf.htm (Accessed 16 May 2003).

Haas, E.B., 'Why Collaborate?: Issue-Linkage and International Regime', *World Politics*, Vol. 32, No. 3, April 1980.

Haasen, C., and Krausz, M., 'Myths versus Evidence with Respect to Cocaine and Crack: Learning from the US Experience,' *European Addiction Research*, Vol. 7, No. 4, 2001.

Haftendorn, H., 'The Security Puzzle: Theory-building and Discipline-building in International Security', *International Security Quarterly*, Vol. 35, No. 1, 1991.

Haggard, S., and Simmons, B.A., 'Theories of International Regimes', *International Organization*, Vol. 41, No. 3, Summer 1987.

Hakim, P., 'The Three Temptations on Latin America', in Manwaring, M.G. (ed.), *Security and Civil-Military Relations in the New World Disorder: The Use of Armed Forces in the Americas*, September 1999, http://www.carlisle.army.mil/ ssi/pubs/1999/newworld/newworld.pdf (16 May 2003).

Hakim, P., *US Drug Certification Process Is in Serious Need of Reform*, http://www. foreignpolicy-infocus.org (Accessed 20 February 2005).

Hak-Su, K., *A drug-free Asia is an essential condition for sustainable economic and social development*, the paper presented at the International Congress in Pursuit of a Drug-free ASEAN 2015: Sharing the vision, leading the change, 11 October 2000, http://www.unescap.org/esid/hds/drug/drugfree.htm (Accessed 31 May 2004).

Harsanyi, J., 'Measurement of social power, opportunity costs and the theory of two-person bargaining games', *Behavioral Science*, Vol. 7, No. 1, 1962.

Hart, R., *Drugs and its impact on crime: Europe's response*, 526th Wilton Park Conference, 6–8 April 1998, http://www.wiltonpark.org.uk/conference/reports/wp536report.html (Accessed 25 August 2002).

Hartley-Brewer, J., 'Police held in drug case', *The Guardian*, 25 September 1999, http://www.guardian.co.uk/Archive/Article/0,4273,3905553,00.html (Accessed 28 June 2003).

Hartnoll, R., Avico, U., Ingold, F., Lange, K., Lenke, L., O'Hare, A., and de Roij-Motshagen, A., 'A multi-city study of drug misuse in Europe', *Bulletin on Narcotics*, Vol. XLI, Nos 1/2.

Harvey, C., Jacobs, J., Lamb, G., and Schaffer, B., *Rural Employment and Administration in the Third World: Development Methods and Alternative Strategies*, 1979, Farnborough: Saxon House.

Hasenclever, A., Mayer, P., and Rittberger, V., 'Interests, Power, Knowledge: The Study of International Regimes, *Meschon International Studies Review*, Vol. 40, No. 2, October 1996.

Haugaard, L., *Blunt Instrument: The United States' punitive fumigation program in Colombia*, November 2002, Washington DC: Latin American Working Group.

Heidensohn, F., *Crime and Society*, 1989, London: Macmillan Education.

Henman, A., 'Cocaine Futures', in Henman, A., Lewis, R., and Malyon, T., *Big Deal: The Politics of the Illicit Drug Business*, 1985, London: Pluto Press.

Henman, A., Lewis, R., and Malyon, T., *Big Deal: The Politics of the Illicit Drug Business*, 1985, London: Pluto Press.

Henry, S., *The Hidden Economy: The Context and Control of Borderline Crime*, 1978, Oxford: Martin Robertson.

Herrera, H.A., 'Kidnapping Policy During the Drug War Era: Ethical and Legal Implications', *Low Intensity Conflict & Law Enforcement*, Vol. 5, No. 3, Winter 1996.

Herz, J.H., 'Idealist Internationalism and the Security Dilemma', *World Politics*, Vol. 2, No. 2, 1950.

Higgins, Jr., D.P., 'Personae Non Gratae: Misunderstanding a Humanitarian Mission at Juanchaco, Colombia', *Low Intensity Conflict & Law Enforcement*, Vol. 6, No. 2, Autumn 1997.

Hinton, H.L., *Drug Control: Counternarcotics Efforts in Colombia Face Continuing Challenges*, Testimony before the Committee on International Relations, House of Representatives, 26 February 1998, GAO/T-NSIAD-98-103, Washington DC: GPO.

Hinton, Jr., H.L., *Drug Control: Observation on US Counternarcotics Activities*, Testimony before the Subcommittee on Western Hemisphere, Peace Corps, Narcotics, and Terrorism, Committee on Foreign Relations; and the Caucus on

International Narcotics Control, US Senate, 16 September 1998, GAO/T-NSIAD-98-249, Washington DC: GAO.

Hirsch, F., *The Social Limits to Growth*, 1976, Cambridge: Harvard University Press.

HM Customs and Excise Annual Report, cm. 2352, October 1993, London: HMSO.

Hodgson, M., 'Troops close on in Colombia's rebel heaven', *The Guardian*, 12 January 2002, http://www.guardian.co.uk/international/story/0,3604,631544,00.html (Accessed 11 July 2004).

Hodgson, M., 'Colombian rebels pose as soldiers to kidnap state MPs', *The Guardian*, 12 April 2002, http://www.guardian.co.uk/international/story/0,3604,683118,00.html (Accessed 11 July 2004).

Holmberg, A.R., and Dobyns, H.F., 'Case Study: The Cornell Program in Vicos, Peru', in Wharton, C.R. (ed.), *Subsistence Agriculture and Economic Development*, 1969, Chicago: Aldine Press.

Holsti, K., *The State, War, and the State of War*, 1996, Cambridge: Cambridge University Press.

Home Affairs Committee, *Misuse of Hard Drugs*, interim report, 1985, London: HMSO.

Home Affairs Committee, *Drug Trafficking and Related Serious Crimes Vol. II; Minutes of Evidences and Appendices*, HC 370-II, 1989, London: HMSO.

Home Affairs Select Committee, *Third Report: The Government's Drugs Policy: Is It Working?* 9 May 2002, http://www.publications.parliament.uk/po/cm200102/cmselect/cmhaff/318/31808.htm (Accessed 28 June 2004).

Honey, M., 'CIA and rebels linked to Colombian cocaine cartel', *The Times*, 30 June 1988.

Hopf, T., 'The Promise of Constructivism in International Relations Theory', *International Security*, Vol. 23, No. 1, Summer 1998.

Hopkins, N., 'Crack dealers threaten more cities with violence', *The Guardian*, 25 June 2002.

Hopkins, N., 'Growing impact of drug from abroad', *The Guardian*, 25 June 2002, http://www.guardian.co.uk/drugs/Story/0,2763,743343,00.html (Accessed 3 May 2003).

Hosenball, M., and Klaidman, D., 'A Deadly Mix of Drugs and Firepower', *Newsweek*, April 19, 1999.

House of Commons, *Home Affairs Committee, Session 1988-89*, Seventh Report, Drug Trafficking and Related Serious Crime, Vol. 1, 1989, London: HMSO.

Human Rights Watch, *Bolivia Under Pressure: Human Rights Violation and Coca Eradication*, Vol. 8, No. 4, 1996, http://www.hrw.org/hrw/summaries/s.bolivia965.html (Accessed 25 April 1999).

Hunt, D.E., 'Drugs and Sensual Crimes: Drugs dealings and prostitution', in Tonry, M. and Wilson, J.Q. (eds), *Drug and Crime: Crime and Justice A Review of Research*, Vol. 73, 1990, Chicago: The University of Chicago Press.

Hunter, C., and Brownfield, W.R., *US Assistance to Colombia*, Remarks at Special Briefing, Washington DC, 12 March 2001, http://www.state.gov/inl/narc/rm/2001/jan_apr/index.cfm?docid=1198 (Accessed 16 April 2003).

Hurrell, A., 'Security in Latin America', *International Affairs*, Vol. 74, No. 3, July 1998.

Hutchins, E., 'The Social Organisation of Distributed Cognition', in Resnick, L., Levine, J., and Teasley, S. (eds), *Perspectives on Socially Shaped Cognition*, 1991, Washington DC: American Psychological Association.

Hutchinson, A., *DEA and Doctors: Cooperation for the Public Good*, Speech at American Pain Society, 14 March 2002, http://www.usdoj.gov/dea/speeches/s031402.html (Accessed 3 March 2003).

Ianni, F.A.J., 'Formal and Social Organization in an Organized Crime 'Family': A Case Study', *University of Florida Law Review*, Vol. 24, 1971.

INCB, *The International Narcotics Board Annual Report 2001*, 2002, New York: UN Official Publications.

Interpol, *Cocaine*, http://www.interpol.org/Public/Drugs/cocaine/default.asp (Accessed 3 March 2005).

Interpol, *Heroin*, http://www.interpol.int/Public/Drugs/heroin/default.asp (Accessed 3 March 2005).

Isacson, A., and Olsen, J., *Just the Facts 2000-2001*, 2001, Washington DC: Latin American Working Group.

Isacson, A., and Vaicius, I., 'Plan Colombia's 'Ground Zero'', *International Policy Report*, April 2000, http://www.ciponline.org/colombia/0401putu.pdf (Accessed 20 October 2003).

Isikoff, M., 'Colombia's Drug King Becoming Entrenched', *The Washington Post*, 8 January 1989.

Isikoff, M., 'DEA in Bolivia: Guerrilla Warfare', *The Washington Post*, 16 January 1989.

Isikoff, M., 'Suspected Planes May Become Targets', *The Washington Post*, 17 September 1989.

Isikoff, M., 'Bolivia Offers Non-Extradition Deal to Traffickers', *The Washington Post*, 19 July 1991.

Islam, F., 'Class A capitalism', *The Observer*, 21 April 2002.

Istituzione di una Commissione parlamentare d'inchiesta sul fenomeno della mafia e delle altre associazioni criminali similari, *LEGGE 1o ottobre 1996*, n. 509, http://www.camera.it/_bicamerali/antimafia/legge.htm (Accessed 20 February 2005).

Jackson, R., (ed.) *Sovereignty at the Millennium*, 1999, Oxford: Blackwell.

Jackson, R., 'Sovereignty in World Politics: a Glance at the Conceptual and Historical Landscape', in Jackson, R. (ed.), *Sovereignty at the Millennium*, 1999, Oxford: Blackwell.

James, A., *Sovereign Statehood*, 1986, London: Allen & Unwin.

Jamieson, A., *The Modern Mafia: Its Role and Record*, Conflict Studies 224, 1989, London: Centre for Security and Conflict Studies.

Jeffery, C.G., 'Drug Control in the United Kingdom', in Phillipson, R.V. (ed.), *Modern Trends in Drug Dependence and Alcoholism*, 1970, London: Butterworths.

Jelsma, M., 'Europe Rejects Plan Colombia', *The Progress Response*, Vol. 5, No. 5, 12 February 2001, http://www.tni.org/archives.jelsma/progress.htm (Accessed 31 October 2003).

Jepperson, R.L., Wendt, A., and Katzenstein, P.J., 'Norms, Identity, and Culture in National Security', in Katzenstein, P.J. (ed.), *The Culture of National Security: Norms and Identity in World Politics*, 1996, New York: Columbia University Press.

Jepsen, J., 'Copenhagen: A War on Socially Marginal People', in Dorn, N., Jepsen, J., and Savona, E. (eds), *European Drug Policies and Enforcement*, 1996, London: Macmillan.

Jervis, R., *Perception and Misperception in International Relations*, 1976, Princeton: Princeton University Press.

Jervis, R., 'Realism, Neo liberalism, and Cooperation', *International Security*, Vol. 24, No. 1, Summer 1999.

Jiménez, J.B., 'Cocaine, Informality, and the Urban Economy in La Paz, Bolivia', in Partes, A., Castells, M., and Benton, L.A. (ed.), *The Informal Economy: Studies in Advanced and Less Developed Countries*, 1989, Baltimore: The Johns Hopkins University Press.

Johnson, B.D., Hamid, A., Sanabria, H., 'Emerging Models of Crack Distribution', in Mieczkowski, T. (ed.), *Drugs, Crime, and Social Policy: Research, Issues, and Concerns*, 1992, Boston: Allyn and Bacon.

Joint Action Plan, http://europa.eu.int/comm/external_relations/us/action_plan/2. global_challenges.htm (Accessed 20 February 2005).

Jordan, A., and Taylor Jr., W., *American National Security*, 1981, Baltimore: The Johns Hopkins University Press.

Jordan, D.C., *Drug Politics: Dirty Money and Democracy*, 1999, Norman: University of Oklahoma Press.

Kaldor, M., *New and Old Wars: Organized Violence in a Global Era*, 2002, London: Polity Press.

Karch, S.B., 'Japan and the cocaine industry of Southeast Asia, 1864-1944', in Gootenberg, P. (ed.), *Cocaine: Global Histories*, 1999, London: Routledge.

Katzenstein, P.J., *Cultural Norms and National Security: Police and Military in Postwar Japan*, 1996, Ithaca, NY: Cornell University Press.

Katzenstein, P.J. (ed.), *The Culture of National Security: Norms and Identity in World Politics*, 1996, New York: Columbia University Press.

Keeley, J.H., 'Toward a Foucaldian Analysis of International Regimes', *International Organization*, Vol. 44, No. 1., Autumn 1992.

Kelly, R.J., 'The Nature of Organized Crime and Its Operations', in Edelhertz, H. (ed.), *Major Issue in Organized Crime Control, Symposium Proceedings*, 25–26 September 1986, Washington DC: US Government Printing Office.

Kendall, S., 'Violence mars road to Colombia elections', *Financial Times*, 9 March 1994.

Kendall, S., 'Bogota counts cost of crackdown', *Financial Times*, 30 August 1999.

Keohane, R.O., 'The Demand for International Regimes', *International Organization*, Vol. 36, No. 2, Spring 1982.

Keohane, R.O., *After Hegemony: Cooperation and Discord in the World Political Economy*, 1984, Princeton: Princeton University Press.

Keohane, R. (ed.), *Neorealism and its Critics*, 1986, New York: Columbia University Press.

Keohane, R.O., 'International Institutions: Two Approaches', *International Studies Quarterly*, Vol. 32, No. 4, December 1988.

Keohane, R.O., and Milner, H.V. (eds), *Internationalization and Domestic Politics*, 1996, Cambridge: Cambridge University Press.

Keohane, R., and Nye, J.S., *Power and Interdependence: World Politics in Transition*, 1977, Boston: Little, Brown.

Kindleberger, C.P., *The World in Depression 1929-1939*, 1973, London: Penguin.

Kissinger, H.A., *A World Restored: From Castlereagh, Metternich and the Restoration of Peace, 1812-1822*, 1957, Boston: Houghton Mifflin.

Klein, B., *Strategic Studies and World Order: The Global Politics of Deterrence*, 1994, Cambridge: Cambridge University Press.

Kline, D., 'How to Lose the Coke War', *Atlantic Monthly*, May 1987.

Kolodziej, E.A., 'What is Security and Security Studies?' *Arms Control*, Vol. 13, No. 1, April 1992.

Koppel, T., 'Illegal Drugs, Mexico, and NAFTA: Rise in Illegal Drugs Entering U.S. From Mexico', *ABC*, 6 May 1997, http://more.abcnews.go.com/onair/nightline_new/transcripts/ntl0506.html (Accessed 20 February 2005).

Korczak, D., *Epidemiology of Cocaine in Europe*, Cocaine: proceedings of the scientific meeting, Luxembourg, 14–16 January 1987, 1988, Luxembourg: Commission of the European Communities.

Krasner, S., 'Transforming International Regimes: What the Third World Wants and Why', *International Studies Quarterly*, Vol. 25, No. 1, March 1981.

Krasner, S. (ed.), *International Regimes*, 1983, London: Cornell University Press.

Krasner, S.D., 'Structural causes and regime consequences: regimes as intervening variables', in Krasner, S.D. (ed.), *International Regime*, 1983, London: Cornell University Press.

Krasner, S., *Structural Conflict: The Third World Against Global Liberalism*, 1985, Los Angeles: University of California Press.

Krause, A., 'EU Courting Latin America', *EUROPE*, August 2001, Issue No. 408, http://www.eurunion.org/magazine/0108/p12.htm (Accessed 31 October 2003).

Krause, K. and Williams, M. (ed.), *Critical Security Studies: Concept and Cases*, 1997, London: UCL Press.

Krausse, H., 'FBI Director Says Drugs, Terrorism To Force New Balance of Law, Liberty', *Austin American Statesman*, 11 February 1989.

Kubálková, V., Onuf, N., and Kowert,P. (eds), *International Relations in a Constructed World*, 1998, London: M.E. Sharpe.

La Comisión Europea, *Consejo de la Unión Europea: Proyectos propuestos por los Estados miembros y la Comisión*, 6008/01, Bruselas, 8 de febrero de 2000.

La Paz 4839 Cable Text for the meeting between the Bolivian President Jorge Quiroga and the US President George W. Bush during Quiroga's visit to the United States, Meeting on 6 December 2002, FOIA 200201357, http://jeremybigwood.net/FOIAs/US2Tuto/images/US-Tuto-1.jpg (Accessed 4 July 2003).

La Procuraduría General de la República, *Boletín*, No. 333/99, 15 October 1999, http://wwwpgr.gob.mx/cmsocial/bol99/oct/b0033399.htm (Accessed 18 January 2005).

Lane, C., Waller, D., Larmer, B., and Latel, P., 'The Newest War', *Newsweek*, 13 January 1992.

Lazare, D., 'Drugs & Money', *NACLA: Report on the Americas*, Vol. XXX, No. 6, May/June 1997.

Lea, J., *Organised Crime, the State and the Legitimate Economy*, http://www.bunker8.pwp.blueyonder.co.uk/orgcrim/3806.htm (Accessed 30 July 2004).

Ledwith, W.E., *DEA Testimony* before the House Government Reform Committee, Subcommittee on Criminal Justice, Drug Policy and Human Resources, 15 February 2000, http://www.usdoj.gov/dea/pubs/cngrtest/ct021500.htm (Accessed 14 August 2003).

Ledwith, W., *Counter-narcotics in Mexico*, Testimony before the Subcommittee on Criminal Justice, Drug Policy, and Human Resources, 29 February, 2000, http://www.usdoj.gov/dea/pubs/cngrtest/ct022900.html (Accessed 20 February 2005).

Lee III, R.W., 'Why the US Cannot Stop South American Cocaine', *Orbis*, Vol. 32, No. 4, Fall 1988.

Lee III, R., 'Dimensions of the South American Cocaine Industry', *Journal of Interamerican Studies and World Affairs*, Vol. 30, Nos 2&3, 1988.

Lee III, R, *Cocaine Production in the Andes*, Hearing before the Select Committee on Narcotics Abuse and Control, House of Representatives, 101st Congress, 1st Session, 7 June 1989, Washington DC: GPO.

Lee III, R.W., 'The Latin American Drug Connection', *Foreign Policy*, 1989.

Lee III, R.W., *The White Labyrinth: Cocaine & Political Power*, 1989, New Jersey: Transaction Publishers.

Lee III, R.W., 'Global Reach: The Threat of International Drug Trafficking', *Current History*, Vol. 94, No. 592, May 1995.

Lee, M., 'London: 'Community Damage Limitation' through Policing?' in Dorn, N., Jepsen, J., and Savona, E. (eds), *European Drug Policies and Enforcement*, 1996, London: Macmillan.

Lee, R. and Clawson, P., *Crop Substitution in the Andes*, December 1993, Washington DC: ONDCP.

Lee, R.W., 'Why the US Cannot Stop South American Cocaine', *Orbis*, Vol. 32, No. 4, Fall 1988.

Lee, R.W., 'Policy Brief: Making the Most of Colombia's Drug Negotiations', *Orbis*, Vol. 35, No. 2, Spring 1991.

Leonard, C., *Implementing Plan Colombia: The US Role*, Testimony before the House Subcommittee on the Western Hemisphere of the Committee on International Relations, 106th Congress 2nd Session, 21 September 2000, Nos. 106-188.

Léons, M.B. and Sanabria, H. (eds), *Coca, Cocaine, and the Bolivian Reality*, 1997, New York: State University of New York Press.

Lewis, R., 'European Market in Cocaine', *Contemporary Crises*, Vol. 13, 1989.

Liddy, G., *Will: The Autobiography of G. Gordon Liddy*, 1980, New York: St Martin's Press.

Linklater, A., *Beyond Realism and Marxism: Critical Theory and International Relations*, 1990, Basingstoke: Macmillan.

Linklater, A., 'The Achievement of Critical Theory', in Smith, S., Booth, K., and Zalewski, M. (eds), *International Theory: Positivism and Beyond*, 1996, Cambridge: Cambridge University Press.

Lipschutz, R.D. (ed.) *On Security*, 1995, New York: Columbia University Press.

Lipset, S.M., 'Social Conflict, Legitimacy, and Democracy', in Connolly, W. (ed.), *Legitimacy and the State*, 1984, Oxford: Basil Blackwell.

Lister, R., 'US commits to Colombia', *BBC*, 31 August 2000, http://news.bbc.co.uk/l/hi/world/americas/902035.stm (Accessed 20 October 2003).

London Declaration: London meeting on international support for Colombia, 10 July 2003, http://www.delcol.cec.eu.int/en/eu_and_colombia/news.htm (31 October 2003).

Lowry, S.T., 'Bargaining and contract theory in law and economics', in Samuels, W.J. (ed.), *The Economy as a System of Power*, 1979, New Brunswick, NJ: Transaction Books.

Lucas, C., *Parliamentary Questions - Oral Questions, Reply to oral question*, H-03/5/01, April 2001, http://www.carolinelucasmep.org/parliament/colombia=22032001.html (Accessed 29 October 2003).

Ludford, S., *EU Money Laundering Rules - Tough Implementation Needed*, 'We'll Make Europe Work for You', 18 October 2001, http://www.sarahludfordmep.org.uk/news/306.html (Accessed 20 February 2005).

Lupsha, P.A., 'Transnational Organized Crime versus the Nation-State', *Transnational Organized Crime*, Vol. 2, No. 1, Spring 1996.

Lyman, M., *Business Principles of Modern Narcotics Trafficking Operations*, paper presented at Roundtable entitled Business Practices of Narcotics Trafficking Enterprises, at the Library of Congress on 29 January 2003, http://www.loc.gov/rr/frd/Drug_conference/pdf-files/Business-Principles-of-Modern-Narcotics-Trafficking-Operations.pdf (Accessed 28 September 2004).

Mabry, D.J., 'Andean Drug Trafficking and the Military Option', *Military Review*, March 1990.

MacCoun, R.J. and Reuter, P., *Drug War Heresies: Learning from Other Vices, Times, and Places*, 2001, Cambridge: Cambridge University Press.

Machiavelli, N., *The Prince*, Skinner, Q. (ed.), 1988, Cambridge: Cambridge University Press.

Mack, J.A., with Kerner, H-J., *The Crime Industry*, 1975, Farnborough: Saxon House.

Mack, J., *Plan Colombia and the Andean Regional Initiative*, 28 June 2001, Testimony before the House International Relations Committee Subcommittee on the Western Hemisphere.

Mack, J., *Testimony*, 28 June 2001, http://www.state.gov/g/inl/narc/rm/2001/may_aug/index.cfm?docid=3847 (Accessed 16 April 2003).

Magruder, J.S., *One Man's Guide to Watergate*, 1974, London: Hodder & Stoughton.

Malamud-Goti, J., *Smoke and Mirrors: The Paradox of the Drug Wars*, 1992, Oxford: Westview Press.

Mann, M., *The Source of Social Power: A History of Power from the Beginning to AD 1760*, 1986, Cambridge: Cambridge University Press.

Manners, I., 'Normative Power Europe: a contradiction in terms?' *Journal of Common Market Studies*, Vol. 40, No. 2, 2002.

Mansback R.W., and Vasquez, J.A., *In Search of Theory: A New Paradigm for Global Politics*, 1981, New York: Columbia University Press.

Mansfield, D. and Sage, C. 'Drug Crop Producing Countries: A Development Perspective', in Coomber, R. (ed.), *The Control of Drugs and Drug Users: Reason or Reaction?* 1998, Amsterdam: Harwood Academic Publishers.

Manski, C.F., Pepper, J.V., and Petrie, C.V., *Informing America's Policy on Illegal Drugs: What We Don't Know Keeps Hurting Us*, 2001, Washington DC: National Academy Press.

Manwaring, M.G., 'National Security Implications of Drug Trafficking for the USA and Colombia', *Small Wars and Insurgencies*, Vol. 5, No. 3, Winter 1994.

Manwaring, M.G. (ed.), *Security and Civil-Military Relations in the New World Disorder: The Use of Armed Forces in the Americas*, September 1999, http://www.carlisle.army.mil/ssi/pubs/1999/newworld/newworld.pdf (Accessed 16 May 2003).Marcella, G., 'Plan Colombia: An Interim Assessment', *Hemisphere Focus: 2001-2002*, 25 January 2002, http://www.ciaonet.org/pbei/csis/hem2001-2002/020125/index.html (Accessed 13 November 2003).

Marelli, F., 'Falcone, Borsellino and the Difficult Antimafia Struggle', *OC Newsletter*, May issue 2002, http://members.lycos.co.uk/ocnewsletter/SGOC0502/Francesco.html (Accessed 23 June 2002).

Marguis, C., 'Ambitious Antidrug Plan for Colombia is Faltering', *New York Times*, 15 October 2000.

Marguis, C., 'US Weights Expanding Aid Plan to Colombia's Neighbours', *The Washington Post*, 4 December 2000.

Mariano H. Ospina, *Petitioner v. United States of America*, No. 90-6719, October Term, 1990, http://www.usdoj.gov/osg/briefs/1990/sg900324.txt (Accessed 20 February 2003).

Marlts, M.D., 'On Defining 'Organized Crime': The Development of a Definition and a Typology', *Crime and Delinquency*, Vol. 22, No. 3, July 1976.

Marquis, 'Tough Conservative Picked for Drug Czar', *New York Times*, 26 April 2001.

Marshall, C., *The Last Circle*, 1994, http://www.lycaeum.org/books/books/last_circle/circle!.htm (Accessed 20 February 2005).

Marshall, D., *DEA Congressional Testimony*, US Law Enforcement Response to Money Laundering Activities in Mexico, before the Subcommittee on General Oversight and Investigation of the Committee on Banking and Financial Services, 5 September 1996, http://www.usdoj.gov/dea/pubs/cngrtest/ct960906.htm (Accessed 2 December 2003).

Marshall, D., *DEA Congressional Testimony* before the Subcommittee on National Security, International Affairs and Criminal Justice, 9 July 1997, http://www.usdoj/dea/pubs/cngrtest/ct970709.htm (Accessed 29 October 1999).

Marshall, D.R., *DEA Testimony* before Committee on Government Reform Subcommittee on Criminal Justice, Drug Policy and Human Resources, 2 March 2001, http://www.ict.org.il/documents/documentdet.cfm?docid=61 (Accessed 15 August 2003).

Mathews, J.T., 'Redefining Security', *Foreign Affairs*, Vol. 68, No. 2, 1989.

Matthew, R.A., and Shanbaugh, G.E., 'Sex, Drugs, and Heavy Metal: Transnational Threats and National Vulnerabilities', *Security Dialogue*, Vol. 29, No. 2, June 1998.

Matthews, W., 'Special Report: U.S. Southern Command', *Army Times*, Vol. 13, No. 52.

Maynard, A., 'The economics of drug use and abuse', in Ciba Fundation, *Cocaine: Scientific and social dimensions, Ciba Fundation Symposium*, 1992, West Sussex: John Wiley and Sons.

McAllister, W.B., *Drug Diplomacy in the Twentieth Century: An International History*, 2000, London: Routledge.

McCaffrey, B., *The Crisis in Colombia: What Are We Facing?* Testimony before the House Subcommittee on Criminal Justice, Drug Policy, and Human Resources of the Committee on Government Reform, 106th Congress, 15 February 2000, Nos 106–151, Washington DC: GPO.

McCaffrey, B.R., *The Drug Scourge as a Hemispheric Problem*, August 2001, http://www.arlisle.army.mil/ssi/pubs/2001/scrouge/scrouge.pdf (Accessed 9 October 2003).

McCaughan, M., 'Cartel profits fuel a corrupt Colombian boom', *The Guardian*, 26 February 1992.

McFarren, P., 'Bolivia Weeding Out Its Coca Trade', *Los Angeles Times*, 27 February 2000, http://www.mapinc.org/drugnews/v00/n279/a08.html?98661 (Accessed 11 April 2000).

McKernan, V., 'The Real War on Drugs', *Newsweek*, 21 September 1992, p. 14.

McLean, P., 'Who is Alvaro Uribe and How Did He Get Elected?', *Hemisphere Focus: 2001-2002*, 12 July 2002, http://www.ciaonet.org/pbei/csis/hem2001-2002/020712/index.html (Accessed 13 November 2003).

McSweeney, B., *Security, Identity and Interests: A Sociology of International Relations*, 1999, Cambridge: Cambridge University Press.

Mearshheimer, J., 'Back to the Future: Instability After the Cold War', *International Security*, Vol. 15, No. 1, 1990.

Meikle, J., 'Drug injectors still sharing equipment', *The Guardian*, 20 December 2003, http://society.guardian.co.uk/drugsandalcohol/story/0,8150,1110697,00.html (Accessed on 3 March 2005).

Menzel, S.H., *Fire in the Andes: US Foreign Policy and Cocaine Politics in Bolivia and Peru*, 1996, Maryland: University Press of America.

Menzel, S.H., *Cocaine Quagmire: implementing the US anti-drug policy in the north Andes – Colombia*, 1997, Maryland: University Press of America.

Mercer, J., 'Anarchy and Identity', *International Organization*, Vol. 49, No. 2, Spring 1995.

Metcalfe, R., 'Plan Colombia under Scrutiny', *Radio Netherlands Wereldomroep*, 17 October 2000, http://www.rnw.nl/hotspots/html/colombia001017.html (Accessed 30 October 2003).

Meyer, J.W., Frank, D.J., Hironaka, A., Schofer, E., Brandon Tuma, N., 'The Structure of a World Environmental Regime, 1870-1990', *International Organization*, Vol. 51, No. 4, Autumn 1997.

Mieczkowski, T., *Drugs, Crime, and Social Policy: Research, Issues, and Concerns*, 1992, Boston: Allyn and Bacon.

Milner, H. and Keohane, R., 'Internationalization and Domestic Politics: Introduction' in Keohane, R.D. and Milner, H.V. (eds), *Internationalization and Domestic Politics*, 1996, Cambridge: Cambridge University Press.

Ministerio de Sanidad Y Consumo, *HIV and AIDS in Spain 2001*, 2002, Madrid: Ministerio de Sanidad Y Consumo Centro de Puvlicaciones.

Minutes of the Fourth High-Level Meeting of Drug Expert of the Andean Community and the EU, 29-30 March 2000, Brussels, 12 April 2000, 7688/00.

Mishan, E.J., 'Narcotics: The Problem and the Solution', *Political Quarterly*, Vol. 61, No. 4, 1990.

Mitsilegas, V., Monar, J., and Rees, W., *The European Union and Internal Security: Guardian of People?* 2003, Basingstoke: Palgrave Macmillan.

Mohammed, A., 'US, Colombia Near Agreement on Anti-Drug Fights', *Reuters*, 15 July 2003, http://www.washingtonpost.com/wp-dyn/articles/A61589-2003Jul15. html (16 July 2003).

Monthly Review: Human Rights and Democratisation, October 2000, Brussels: European Commission.

Moore, M., 'Organized Crime as a Bussiness Enterprise', in Edelhertz, H. (ed.), *Major Issue in Organized Crime Control, Symposium Proceedings*, 25–26 September 1986, Washington DC: GPO.

Moore, M., 'Supply Reduction and Drug Law Enforcement', in Tonry, M and Wilson, J.Q. (eds) *Drug and Crime: Crime and Justice A Review of Research*, Vol. 73, 1990, Chicago: The University of Chicago.

Moore, M., 'Mexican Seeks Ex-Governor on Drug Charges', *The Washington Post*, 8 April 1999, http://www.washingtonpost.com/wp-srv/inatl/longterm/mexico/ mexico.htm (Accessed 8 April 1999).

Moore, M., 'Hostility Violence Threaten Rights Defenders in Mexico', *The Washington Post*, 26 December 1999, http://www.washingtonpost.com/wp-srv/ Wplate/1999-12/26/1411-122699-idx.html (Accessed 20 February 2004).

Moore, M., 'Mexican Stunned by Killing of Police Chief', *The Washington Post*, 29 February 2000, http://www.washingtonpost.com/wp-srv/Wplate/2000-02/29/0791-022900-idx.html (Accessed 29 February 2000).

Morales, E., *Cocaine: White Gold Rush in Peru*, 1989, Tucson: The University of Arizona Press.

Morgan, H.W., *Drugs in America: A Social History, 1800-1980*, 1981, New York: Syracuse University Press.

Morgan, J.P., and Zimmer, L., 'The Social Pharmacology of Smokeable Cocaine: Not All It's Cracked Up to Be', in Reinarman, C., and Levine, H.G. (eds), *Crack in America: Demon Drugs and Social Justice*, 1997, Berkeley: University of California Press.

Morgenthau, *Politics Among Nations: The Struggle for Power and Peace*, 1972, New York: Knopf.

Mott, J. (ed.), *Crack and Cocaine in England and Wales*, 1992, RPU Paper 70, London: Home Office.

Multiannual Guidlines For Community Aid Colombia, IB/1035/98-EN, 12 November 1998, Brussels: European Commission.

Munch, R., *Politics and Dependency in the Third World: The Case of Latin America*, 1984, London: Zed.

Musto, D.F., *The American Disease: Origins of Narcotic Control*, 1987, Oxford: Oxford University Press.

Musto, D.F., 'Cocaine's history, especially the American experience', in Ciba Fundation, *Cocaine: Scientific and Social Dimensions*, Ciba Fundation Symposium 166, 1992, West Sussex: John Wiley & Sons.

Nacional de Desarrollo Seguridad Democrática, August 2003, Bogotá: Sinergia, http://www.dnp.gov/co/ArchivosWeb/Direccion_Evaluacion_Gestion/Report_y_ Doc/Reportes_de_Evaluacion_N3.pdf (Accessed 15 January 2004).

Nadelmann, E.A., 'Global prohibition regimes: the evolution of norms in international society', *International Organizations*, Vol. 44, No. 4, 1990.

Nagle, L.E., *The Search For Accountability and Transparency in Plan Colombia: Reforming Judicial Institution* - Again, May 2001, http://www.miami.edu/nsc/ publication/IPCseries/pcacount.pdf (Accessed 13 November 2003).

National Commission on Marijuana and Drug Abuse, *Second Report: Drug Use in America: Problem in Perspective*, 1973, Washington, DC: GPO.

National Criminal Intelligence Services, *UK Threat Assessment of Serious and Organised Crime 2003*, http://www.ncis.co.uk/downloads/CADT_Org_Imm_ Crime.pdf (Accessed 20 March 2005).

National Research Council, (eds) Manski, C.F., Pepper, J.V., and Petrie, C.V., *Informing America's Policy on Illegal Drugs: What We Don't Know Keeps Hurting Us*, 2001, Washington DC: National Academy Press.

Naylor, R.T., *Wages of Crime: Black Markets, Illegal Finance, and the Underworld Economy*, 2002, Ithaca: Cornell University Press.

Neaigus, A., Friedman, S.R., Goldstein, M., Zldefonso, G., Curtis, R., and Jose, B., 'Using Dyadic Data for a Network Analysis of HIV Infection and Risk Behavior Among Injecting Drug Users', in Needle, R.H., Coyle, S.L., Genser, S.G., and Trotter II, R.T. (eds), *Social Networks, Drug Abuse, and HIV Transmission, Research Monograph*, Number 151, 1995, http://www.nida.nih.gov/pdf/ monographs/151.pdf.

Needle, R.H., Coyle, S.L., Genser, S.G., and Trotter II, R.T. (eds), *Social Networks, Drug Abuse, and HIV Transmission, Research Monograph*, Number 151, 1995, http://www.nida.nih.gov/pdf/monographs/151.pdf (Accessed 20 February 2005).

Neibuhr, R., *The Structure of Nations and Empire*, 1959, New York: Scribner's.

Neufeld, M., 'Reflexibility and International Relations Theory', in *Beyond Positivism: Critical Reflections on International Relations*, 1994, Boulder, CO: Lynne Rienner.

New York County Lawyer's Association, *Report and Recommendation of the Drug Policy Task Force*, 1996 (October), New York: New York County Lawyer's Association.

Newell, J.L., *Corruption mitigating policies in Italy*, a paper presented at 53rd PSA Annual Conference at the University of Leicester, 15–17 April 2003, http://www. psa.ac.uk/cps/2003/James%20Newell.pdf (Accessed 31 May 2004).

Nordland, R. and Contreras, J., 'Where Cocaine Is King', *Newsweek*, 29 February 1988.

NPR, 'Corruption at the Gates', *All Things Considered*, 12–13 September 2002, http://www.npr.org/programs/atc/features/2002/sept/border_corruption/ (Accessed 28 May 2003).

NTA, *Drug-related deaths*, http://www.nta.nhs.uk/programme/drd2.htm (Accessed 20 February 2005).

Observatorio para la Paz, 'Plan Colombia: Juego de Máscaras', *Mamacoca*, http://www.mamacoca.org/plancol_mascaras_es.htm (Accessed 21 November 2003).

ODCCP, 'Interview with His excellency President Hugo Banxar Suárez of Bolivia', *Update*, June 2000.

Office for National Statistics, *Diagnosed HIV-infected patients: by probable routes of HIV infection and region of residence when last seen for care in 2001: Regional Trend 37*, http://www.statistics.gov.uk/STATBASE/ssdataset.asp?vlink=5933 (Accessed on 2 March 2005.

Office for National Statistics, *Diagnosed HIV-infected patients: by probable routes of HIV infection and region of residence when last seen for care in 2002: Regional Trend 38*, http://www.statistics.gov.uk/STATBASE/ssdataset.asp?vlink=7762 (Accessed on 2 March 2005).

Office of National Drug Control Policy, *National Drug Control Strategy*, 1989, Washington, DC: GPO.

Office of the Attorney General, *Drug Trafficking – A Report to the President of the United States*, 1989, Washington, DC: The White House.

Office of the Press Secretary, *Andean Regional Initiative*, 23 March 2002, Washington DC: The White House, http://www.state.gov/p/wha/rls/fs/8980.htm (Accessed 18 March 2005).

Oficina Internacional de Derechos Humanos Acción Colombia, *Plan Colombia: A Strategy Without End*, February 2000, Brussels: OIDHACO, http://www.tni.org/drugs/research/plcoleu.htm (Accessed 15 December 2003).

OIDT, *Italy: Drug Situation 2000*, 2000, REITOX REF/2000, http://www.emcdda.org/multimedia/publications/national_reports/NRitaly_report_2000.PDF (Accessed 14 March 2003).

Olkon, S., 'Well-known Miami lawyer released while waiting for trial on money-laundering, obstruction charges', *The Miami Herald*, 20 February 2005, http://www.miami.com/mld/miamiherald/news/breaking_news/11016577.htm (Accessed 20 February 2005).

Olson, M. Jr., *The Logic of Collective Action: Public Goods and the Theory of Groups*, 1965, Cambridge: Cambridge University Press.

ONDCP, *The National Drug Control Strategy 1996*, Washington DC: GPO.

ONDCP, *The National Drug Control Strategy 1997*, http://www.ncjrs.org/htm/dea.htm (Accessed 15 August 2003).

ONDCP, *The Price of Illicit Drugs: 1981 through the Second Quarter of 2000*, October 2001, Washington, DC: Abt Associates Inc., http://www.whitehousedrugpolicy.gov/publications/pdf/price_illicit.pdf (Accessed 20 February 2005).

ONDCP, *ONDCP Fact Sheet: Bilateral Cooperation with Bolivia*, March 2002, http://www.whitehousedrugpolicy.gov/publications/international/factsht/bolivia. html (Accessed 16 May 2003).

ONDCP, *2002 Annual Assessment of Cocaine Movement*, March 2003, ONDCP-03-01, Washington DC: ONDCP.

ONDCP, *National Drug Control Strategy 2003*, 2003, Washington DC: GPO.

Onuf, N., 'Constructivism: A User's Manual', in Kubálková, V., Onuf, N. and Kowert, P. (eds), *International Relations in a Constructed World*, 1998, London: M.E. Sharpe.

Outcome of Proceedings of Working Party on Latin America, 10196/94, ill/JF/mn, Brussels, 19 October 1994.

Oye, K.A., *Cooperation under Anarchy*, 1986, Princeton: Princeton University Press.

Painter, J., 'Drugs may fund Bolivian campaign', *Independent*, 6 May 1989.

Painter, J., *Bolivia and Coca: A Study in Dependency*, 1994, London: Lynne Rienner.

Paoli, L., Güller, N., and Palidda, S., *Pilot Project to Describe and Analyse Local Drug Markets: First Phase Final Report: Illegal Drug Markets in Frankfurt and Milan*, 2000, European Monitoring Centre for Drug and Drug Abuse Scientific Report, EMCDDA/EPI/CT.99.EP.06/2000, Lisbon: European Monitoring Centre for Drug and Drug Abuse.

Parker, H., and Bottomley, T., *Crack Cocaine and Drugs – Crime Careers*, 1996, London: Home Office.

Parker, III, W., *Testimony*, 20 April 1999, http://financialservices.house.gov/banking/42099par.htm (Accessed 20 February 2005).

Partes, A., Castells, M., and Benton, L.A. (eds), *The Informal Economy: Studies in Advanced and Less Developed Countries*, 1989, Baltimore: The Johns Hopkins University Press.

Passas, N., 'Globalization and Transnational Crime: Effects of Criminologenic Asymmetries', *Transnational Criminal Organization*, 1998, Vol. 4, Nos 3&4, Autumn/Winter.

Patten, C., *A Common Foreign Policy for Europe: relations with Latin America*, 9 November 2000, SPEECH/00/427, http://europa.eu.int/comm/external_relations/news/patten/speech_00_427.htm (Accessed 28 October 2001).

Patten, C., *3rd meeting of the Support Group of the Peace Process: Colombia: A European contribution to peace*, 30 April 2001, http://europa.eu.int/comm/externall_relations/colombia/3msg/template_copy(1).htm (Accessed 28 March 2005).

Patten, C., *Colombia: an international commitment to peace*, speech at Meeting of the Support Group for the Peace Process in Colombia, Brussels, 30 April 2001, SPEECH/01/192, http://www.tni.org/drugs/research/patten.htm (Accessed 29 October 2003).

Patten, C., *Colombian international commitment to peace*, 30 April 2001, http://europa. eu.int/comm/external_relations/news/patten/speech_01_192.htm (Accessed 25 August 2002).

Patten, C., *Statement on Transatlantic Relations*, 16 May 2001, Strasbourg, SPEECH/01/223.

Patten, C., on behalf of the Commission, 31 May 2001, *Official Journal of European Communities*, 13 November 2001, C318E/59.

Patten, C. on behalf of the Commission, 25 June 2001, *Official Journal of European Communities*, 20 December 2001, C364E.

Patten, C., *The EU Commitment to Colombia*, Speech at Colombia-EU forum in Bogotá, Colombia, 12–13 May 2003, SPEECH/03/241, http://europa.eu.int/comm/external=relations/news/patten/sp03=241.htm (Accessed 29 October 2003).

Pearce, F., and Woodiwiss, M. (eds) *Global Crime Connections: Dynamics and Control*, 1993, London: Macmillan.

Pearson, G., Mirza, H.S., and Phillips, S., 'Cocaine in Context: Finding from a South London Inner-City Drug Survey', in Bean, P. (ed.), *Crack and Cocaine: Supply and Use*, 1993, London: Macmillan.

Penalva, C., *El Plan Colombia y Sus Implicaciones Internacionales*, http://www.ua.es/cultura/aipaz/docs/Plancol.ref (Accessed 20 January 2004).

Perl, R.F., 'Clinton's Foreign Drug Policy', *Journal of Interamerican Studies and World Affairs*, Vol. 35, No. 4, Winter 1993–1994.

Perl, R.F., *Drugs and Foreign Policy*, 1994, San Francisco: Westview Press.

Perl, R.F., *88093: Drug Control: International Policy and Options Update*, 7 January 1997, Washington DC: Department of State.

Perl, R.F., *Drug Control: International Policy and Approaches*, CRS Issue Brief IB88093, 7 April 2003, http://www.house.gov/htbin/crsprodget?/ib/IB88093 (Accessed 20 February 2005).

Peuter, P., 'The Limits of Supply-Side Drug Control', *The Milkin Institute Review*, First Quarter 2001.

Philpott, D., 'Westphalia, Authority, and International Society', in Jackson, R. (ed.), *Sovereignty at the Millennium*, 1999, Oxford: Blackwell.

Pickering, T.R., *Testimony* at Joint Hearing on Supplemental Request for Plan Colombia before the Senate Subcommittee on Foreign Operations, Export Financing, and Related Programs; Defense; and Military Construction, Committee on Appropriations, 106 Congress, 2nd Session, 24 February 2000, http://frwebgae.access.gpo.gov/cgi-bin/getdoc.cgi?dbname=106_senate_heringsedocid=f:63941.pdf (Accessed 28 October 2003).

Pitts, P., 'Fighting Drugs at the Source', *Proceedings*, July 1994.

Plan Colombia: A Plan for Peace or a Plan for War? Statement made by social organisations, non-Governmental Organisations, and the Colombian Human Rights and Peace Movement, http://www.tni.org/drugs/research/plcoleu.htm (Accessed 15 December 2003).

Plan nacional sobre drogas, *Spain: Drug Situation 2000*, 2000, REITOX REF/2000, http://www.emcdda.org/multimedia/publications/national_reports/NRspain_2000.PDF (Accessed 20 February 2001).

Powell, R., 'Anarchy in international relations theory: The neorealist-neoliberal debate', *International Organization*, Vol. 48, 1994.

PRAEDAC: Potencialidades de los Productos Forestales No Maderables en el Tropico de Cochabamba, Publicación No RN-002/2001, Agosto 2001, Cochabamba: Comision Europa.

President of Colombia, *Plan Colombia: Institutional Strengthening and Social Development 2000-2002*, July 2000, Bogotá: National Planning Department, http://www.tni.org/drugs/research/PlanColEurope.doc (Accessed 15 December 2003).

President, *Plan Colombia: Plan for Peace, Prosperity, and the Strengthening of the State*, 1999, Bogotá: Presidency of the Republic, http://www.usip.org/library/pa/colombia/adddoc/plan_colombia_101999.html (Accessed 31 October 2003).

Programa de Apoyo a la Estrategia de Desarrollo Alternativo en el Chapare – PRAEDAC, http://europa.eu.int/comm/external_relations/bolivia/intro/praedac.htm (23 March 2002).

Puchala, D.J., and Hopkins, R.F., 'International regimes: Lesson from inductive analysis', in Krasner, S.D. (ed.), *International Regimes*, 1983, London: Cornell University Press.

Pujalte, C., *Remarks* in Caucus on International Narcotics Control of The United States, The Congressional Research Service, 8 May 1987, Washington DC: GPO.

Putman, 'Diplomacy and Domestic Politics: The Logic of Two-Level Games', *International Organizations*, Vol. 42, No. 3, Summer 1988.

Rabasa, A., and Chalk, P., *Colombian Labyrinth*, 2001, Pittsburgh: RAND.

Reagan, R., *National Security Directive 221*, Narcotics and National Security, 8 April 1986.

Reagan, R., *Presidential Statement* of 14 October 1982.

Record of the third meeting on precursors and chemical frequently used for the illicit manufacture of narcotic drugs or psychotropic substances, 28 March 2000, http://europa.eu.int/comm/external_relations/andean/doc/lima.htm; EUR-Lex Document 295A1230 (10); and OJL 324 30.12.1995 (Accessed 20 February 2003).

Red de hermandad y solidaridad con Colombia, *Asesinada Otra Líder de DH en el Sur de Bolívar*, 1 July 2001, http://www.xarcaneta.org/tsurdebolivar/colsitjulio2.htm (Accessed 15 January 2004).

Regional Inspector General/ San Salvador, *Audit of USAID-Financed Alternative Development Activities in Peru*, Audit Report No. 1-527-02-011-P, 15 May 2002, http://www.usaid.gov/oig/publivc/fy02rpts/1-527-02-011-p.pdf (Accessed 20 May 2003).

Reinarman, C., and Levine, H.G., *Crack in America: Demon Drugs and Social Justice*, 1997, Berkeley: University of California Press.

Reinarman, C., and Levine, H.G., 'Crack in Context: America's Latest Demon Drug', in Reinarman, C., and Levine, H.G. (eds), *Crack in America: Demon Drugs and Social Justice*, 1997, Berkeley: University of California Press.

Resa-Nestares, C., 'Transnational Organised Crime in Spain: Structural Factors Explaining its Penetration', in Viano, E.C. (ed.), *Global Organized Crime and International Security*, 1999, Aldershot: Ashgate.

Reuter, 'Mexico Drug money-laundering operation had U.S., Russian ties', *CNN News*, 20 February 2000, http://www.cnn.com/2000/WORLD/americas/02/28/mexico.drugs.reut/index.html (Accessed 20 February 2000).

Reuter, P., 'The Limits and Consequences of US Foreign Drug Control Efforts', *The Annals*, No. 521, May 1992.

Reuter, P., *Do Middle Markets for Drugs Constitute an Attractive Target for Enforcement?*, paper presented at Roundtable entitled Business Practices of Narcotics Trafficking Enterprises, at the Library of Congress on January 29, 2003, http://www.loc.gov/rr/frd/Drug_conference/pdf-files/Do-Middle-Markets-for-Drugs-Constitute-an-Attractive-Target-for-Enforcement.pdf (Accessed 20 February 2004).

Reuter, P., *et al.*, *Sealing the Borders: The Effect of Increased Military Participation in Drug Interdiction*, RAND Report, R-3594-USDP, January 1988, Santa Monica, CA: RAND Corporation.

Reuters, 'Mexico finds cocaine in joint operation with U.S.', *ABC News*, 7 December 1999, http://abcnews.go.com/wire/World/reuters19991207_201.html (Accessed 8 December 1999).

Rhodes, W., Langenbahn, S., Kling, R., and Scheiman, P., *What America's Users Spend on Illegal Drugs, 1988-1995*, 29 September 1997, Washington DC: ONDCP, http://www.whitehousedrugpolicy.gov/publications/drugfact/retail/contents.html (Accessed 20 February 2003).

Rhodes, W., Layne, M., Johnston, P., and Hozik, L., *What America's Users Spend on Illegal Drugs 1988-1998, December 2000*, Washington D.C.: ONDCP, http://www.whitehousedrugpolicy.gov/publications/drugfact/american_users_spend/section1.html (Accessed 20 February 2003).

Richards, J.R., *Transnational Criminal Organization, Cybercrime, and Money Laundering*, 1999, Boca Raton: CRC Press.

Riley, K.J., *Snow Job? The War Against International Cocaine Trafficking*, 1996, New Jersey: Transaction Publishers.

Rittberger, V. (ed.), with the assistance of P. Mayer, *Regime Theory and International Relations*, 1993, Oxford: Clarendon Press.

Robinson, L., 'An inferno next door', *Newsweek*, 24 February 1997.

Robinson, S., 'US narcotics agents knew of drug links', *Daily Telegraph*, 6 September 1991.

Rohter, L., 'Colombia Agree to Turn Over Territory to Another Rebel Group', *The New York Times*, 26 April 2000, http://www.nytimes.com/library/world/americas/042600colombia-rebels.html (Accessed 26 April 2000).

Rohter, L., 'Latin Leaders Rebuff Call by Clinton on Colombia', *New York Times*, 2 September 2000.

Roldán, M., 'Colombia: cocaine and the 'miracle' of modernity in Medellín', in Gootenberg, P. (ed.), *Cocaine: Global Histories*, 1999, London: Routledge.

Rome Declaration on Relations Between the European Community and the Rio Group, pp. 91/90, Brussels, 20 December 1990.

Romero, P., *Written answer to a question submitted*, The Crisis in Colombia: What Are We Facing? Hearing before the House Subcommittee on Criminal Justice,

Drug Policy, and Human Resources of the Committee on Government Reform, 106th Congress, 15 February 2000, Nos 106–151, Washington DC: GPO.

Roosevelt, M., 'The war against the war on drugs', *Time Magazine*, 1 May 2001.

Rosenau, J.N., *The Scientific Study of Foreign Policy*, 1971, New York: The Free Press.

Ross, T., 'Blow to Colombia as tape links parties to Cali drug cartel', *The Guardian*, 28 June 1994.

Ross, T., 'Colombian judges court death', *Independent*, 18 November 1991.

Ross, T., 'Colombian rebels launch pre-election attacks', *The Guardian*, 23 February 1994.

Rostow, W.W., *The Stages of Economic Growth*, 1963, Cambridge: Cambridge University Press.

Rothenberg, R.B., Woodhouse, D.C., Potterat, J.J., Muth, S.Q., Darrow, W.W., and Klovdahl, A.S., 'Social Networks in Disease Transmission: The Colorado Springs Study', in Needle, R.H., Coyle, S.L., Genser, S.G., and Trotter II, R.T. (eds), *Social Networks, Drug Abuse, and HIV Transmission, Research Monograph*, Number 151, 1995, http://www.nida.nih.gov/pdf/monographs/151.pdf (Accessed 20 February 2003).

Roy, J., *Europe: Neither Plan Colombia nor Peace Process – From Good Intention to High Frustration*, North-South Center Working Paper Series, No. 11, January 2003, http://www.revistainterforum.com/english/pdf_en/WP11.pdf (Accessed 24 February 2004).

Roy, J., *European Perceptions of Plan Colombia: A Virtual Contribution to A Virtual War and Peace Plan?* May 2001, http://www.miami.edu/nsc/publications/IPCservice/PCEUROPE.PDF (Accessed 4 January 2004).

Rubin, J.P., *Peru's Coca Reduction Efforts*, US Department of State Office of the Spokesman Press Statement, 12 January 2000.

Ruggie, J.G., 'International Regimes, Transactions, and Change: Embedded Liberalism in the Postwar Economic Order', *International Organization*, Vol. 36, No. 2, Spring 1982.

Ruggie, J.G., 'International Response to Technology: Concepts and trends', *International Organization*, Vol. 29, No. 3, Summer 1975.

Ruggiero, V. and South, N., *Eurodrugs: drug use, markets and trafficking in Europe*, 1995, London: Routledge.

Ruggiero, V., 'The *Camorra*: 'Clean' Capital and Organised Crime', in Pearce, F. and Woodiwiss, M. (eds), *Global Crime Connection*, 1993, London: Macmillan.

Russett, B.M., *Power and Community in World Politics*, 1974, San Francisco: W.H. Freeman & Co.

Rydell, P. and Everingham, S., *The cost of cocaine control*, 1994, Santa Monica, CA: RAND.

Saffer, H., and Chaloupka, F., 'The demand for illicit drugs', *Economic Inquiry*, Vol. 38, No. 3, July 1999.

Salias, C.M., 'Colombia and the Kaleidoscope of Violence', *US Foreign Policy in Focus*, Vol. 1, No. 18, 27 October 1997, http://www.igc.apc.org (Accessed 20 February 2000).

Salinas Abdala, Y., 'Plantearnientos de la Defensoría Frente al Programa de Erradicación Aérea de Cultivos Ilícitos con Glifosato', *Mamacoca*, 5 September 2003, http://www.mamacoca.org/FSMT_sept_2003/s/lat/Conversatorio_UROSARIO.htm (Accessed 21 November 2003).

Salinas, C.M., 'Colombia and the Kaleidoscope of Violence', *US Foreign Policy in Focus*, 27 October 1997, Vol. 1, No. 8.

Samuels, W.J. (ed.), *The Economy as a System of Power*, 1979, New Brunswick, NJ: Transaction Books.

Sanabria, H., *The Coca Boom and Rural Social Change in Bolivia*, 1993, Michigan: The University of Michigan Press.

Sanchez, M., 'Once Held at Arms Length, Colombia's Military Gets Bush's Embrace', *The Washington Post*, 6 February 2003, http://www.washingtonpost.com/ac2/wp-dyn/A36191-2003Feb6?language=printer (Accessed 21 May 2003).

Sanchez, M., 'Will the US Bend in Bolivia?' *The Washington Post*, 20 February 2003, http://www.washingtonpost.com/ac2/wp-dyn/A36581-2003Feb20?language=printer (Accessed 21 May 2003).

Sanchez, M., 'When the War on Drugs Is Too Narrow', *The Washington Post*, 16 May 2003, http://www.washingtonpost.com/ac2/wp-dyn?pagename=article&node=&contentId=A60008-2003May15&notFound=true (Accessed 21 May 2003).

Sarkesian, S.C., Williams, J.A., and Cimbala, S.J., *U.S. National Security: Policymakers, Processes, and Politics*, Third Edition, 2002, London: Lynne Rienner.

Sarmiento Anzola, L., 'Plan Colombia, conflicto e intervención', *Mamacoca*, http://www.mamacoca.org/sarmiento_plan_conflicto.htm (Accessed 21 November 2003).

Savona, E., 'Money Laundering, the Developed Countries and Drug Control: the New Agenda', in Dorn, N., Jepsen, J., and Savona, E. (eds), *European Drug Policies and Enforcement*, 1996, London: Macmillan, p. 216.

Savona, E.U. (ed.), *Responding to Money Laundering: International Perspectives*, 1997, Amsterdam: Harwood Academic Publishers.

Savona, E.U., and De Feo, M.A., 'International Money Laundering Trends and Prevention/Control', in Savona, E.U. (ed), *Responding to Money Laundering: International Perspectives*, 1997, Amsterdam: Harwood Academic Publisher.

Schaar, J.H., 'Legitimacy in the Modern State', in Connolly, W. (ed.), *Legitimacy and the State*, 1984, Oxford: Basil Blackwell.

Schmid, A.P., 'The Links between Transnational Organized Crime and Terrorist Crimes', *Transnational Organized Crime*, Vol. 2, No. 4, Winter 1996.

Schneider, A., and Copeland, P., 'With little fanfare, US goes to war', *The Washington Times*, 5 July 1992.

Schulz, D.E., *The United States and Latin America: Shaping an Elusive Future*, March 2000, http://www.carlisle.army.mil/ssi/pubs/2000/uslatin/uslatin.pdf (Accessed 16 May 2003).

Scot, P.D., and Marshall, J., *Cocaine Politics: Drugs, Armies, and the CIA in Central America*, 1991, Berkeley, CA: University of California Press.

Selsky, A., 'Colombia Vows to Down Drug Flights', *Associated Press*, 29 October 2003, http://www.washingtonpost.com/ac2/wp-dyn/A36752-2003Oct29?languag e=printer (Accessed 30 October 2003).

Sensación de debilidad', *Siglo 21*, March 1991.

Serrano, P., *Plan Colombia, la guerra sin limites*, 23 May 2002, http://www.rebelion. org/plancolombia/serrano230502.htm (Accessed 20 January 2004).

Shannon, E., 'Attacking the Source', *The Time*, 28 August 1989.

Shapiro, H., 'Where Does All the Snow Go? The Prevalence and Pattern of Cocaine and Crack Use in Britain', in Bean, P. (ed.), *Crack and Cocaine: Supply and Use*, 1993, London: Macmillan.

Shapiro, B., 'How the War on Crime Imprisons America', 1996, *The Nation*, Vol. 262.

Sheridan, B.E., 'DoD's Restructured Counterdrug Policy', *Defense Issues*, Vol. 9, No. 21, 1994.

Sherwell, P., 'Liechtenstein 'a magnet for money launderers'', *Telegraph*, 23 January 2000, http://www.telegraph.co.uk/htmlContent.jhtml?html=%2Farchive%2F200 0%2F01%2Fwliech21html (Accessed 21 February 2005).

Shifter, M., 'Ayuda a Colombia: razones y sinrasones', *Revista Cambio*, 27 October 2003, http://avanza.org.co/index.shtml?x=81 (Accessed 29 October 2003).

Shifter, M., *US Policy in the Andean Region*, http://www.ciaonet.org/wps/coj05/ coj05.pdf (Accessed 13 November 2003).

Siebert, R., 'Living Under Siege: In Memory of Francesca Morvillo', *OC Newsletter*, May issue 2002, http://members.lycos.co.uk/ocnewsletter/SGOC0502/Renate. html (Accessed 23 June 2002).

Sierra Bedoya, Z.A., 'Fabio Ochoa busca recursos para evitar cadena perpetua', *El Colombiano*, 15 August 2003, http://www/elcolombiano.com/ historicod/200308/20030815/nnh001.htm (Accessed 18 January 2005).

Simons, P.E., 'US Narcotics Control Initiative in Colombia', *Testimony* before the Senate Drug Caucus, 3 June 2003, http://www.state.gov/g/inl/rls/rm21203.htm (Accessed 19 August 2003).

Simons, P., *Briefing* on the President's FY 2003 Narcotics Certification Determinations, 31 January 2003, http://www.state.gov/g/inl/rls/rm/17110.htm (Accessed: 11 September 2003).

Simpson, A., *The Literature of Police Corruption*, 1977, New York: John Jay Press.

Sjöstedt, G., Spector, B.I., and Zartman, I. W., 'The Dynamics of Regime-building Negotiations', in Spector, B.I., Sjöstedt, G., and Zartman, I.W. (eds), *Negotiating International Regimes: Lessons Learned from the United Nations Conference on Environment and Development*, 1994, London: Graham & Trotman Ltd.

Skol, M., *Cocaine Production in the Andes*, Hearing before the Select Committee on Narcotics Abuse and Control, House of Representatives 101st Congress, 1st session, 7 June 1989, Washington: GPO.

Smith, A., *The Wealth of Nations*, [1776] 1993, Oxford: Oxford University Press.

Smith Jr., D.C., 'Some Things That May Be More Important to Understand About Organized Crime Than Cosa Nostra', *University of Florida Law Review*, Vol. 24, No. 1, Fall 1971.

Smith, Jr., D.C., 'Paragons, Pariahs, and Pirates: A Spectrum-Based Theory of Enterprise', *Crime and Delinquency*, Vol. 26, July 1980.

Smith, K., *European Union Foreign Policy in a Changing World*, 2003, Oxford: Polity Press.

Smith, M., 'Peru Calls for US to Join Tougher Anti-Coca Effort', *The Washington Post*, 5 August 1988.

Smith, S., Booth, K., and Zalewski, M. (eds), *International Theory: Positivism and Beyond*, 1996, Cambridge: Cambridge University Press.

Somer, T., 'Armenian Terrorism and the Narcotic Traffic', in *International Terrorism and the Drug Connection*, 1984, Ankara: Ankara University Press.

Sosa, A.J. and Dallanegra Pedraza, L., *El Groupe de Los Ocho y el Futuro de America Latina*, http://www.amersus.org.ar/PolInt/GrupoRio.htm (Accessed 4 January 2005).

Spanier, J., *Games Nations Play: Analyzing International Politics*, 1972, London: Nelson.

Spector, B.I., Sjöstedt, G., and Zartman, I.W. (eds), *Negotiating International Regimes: Lessons Learned from the United Nations Conference on Environment and Development*, 1994, London: Graham & Trotman Ltd.

Spedding, A.L., 'Cocataki, Taki-Coca: Trade, Traffic, and Organized Peasant Resistance in the Yungas of La Paz', in Léons, M.B. and Sanabria, H. (eds), *Coca, Cocaine, and the Bolivian Reality*, 1997, New York: State University of New York Press.

Spedding, A.L., 'The Coca Field as a Total Social Fact', in Léons, M.B. and Sanabria, H. (eds), *Coca, Cocaine and the Bolivian Reality*, 1997, New York: State University of New York Press.

Spillane, J.F., 'Making modern drugs: the manufacture, sale, and control of cocaine in the United States, 1880-1920', in Gootenberg, P. (ed.), *Cocaine: Global Histories*, 1999, London: Routledge.

Stares, P.B., *Global Habit: The Drug Problem in a Borderless World*, 1996, Washington, DC: Brookings Institution.

Starita, J., 'Drug Dealers Pay in Jail, Out of Wallet', *Miami Herald*, 18 October 1982, section A.

State v. Hernando Ospina, 798 F.2d 1579 (1986).

Stein, A., 'Coordination and collaboration: regimes in an anarchic world', in Krasner, S.D. (ed.), *International Regimes*, 1983, London: Cornell University Press.

Stenson, K., 'Beyond histories of the present', *Economy and Society*, Vol. 27, No. 4, 1998.

Sterling, E., 'Comment'; in *Frontline: Snitch*, air date 12 January 1999, http://www.pbs.org/wgbh/pages/frontline/shows/snitch/etc/script.html (Accessed 20 February 2003).

Steve, 'Drug Wars: Interview Steve', *Frontline*, http://www.pbs.org/wgbh/pages/frontline/shows/drugs/interviews/steve.html.

Stevenson, R., 'Winning the War on Drugs: To Legalise or Not?' *Hobart Paper*, No. 124, 1994, London: The Institute of Economic Affairs.

Stille, A., 'All the Prime Minister's Men', *The Independent*, 24 September 1995.

Strange, S., *States and Markets*, 1988, London: Pinter.

Strange, S., *The Retreat of the State: the Diffusion of Power in the World Economy*, 1996, Cambridge: Cambridge University Press.

Strange, S., *Mad Money*, 1998, Manchester: Manchester University Press.

Streatfield, D., *Cocaine: An Unauthorised Biography*, 2001, London: Virgin Publisher.

Sullivan, J.P., 'Third Generation Street Gangs: Turf, Cartel, and Net Worriers', *Transnational Organized Crime*, Vol. 3, No. 3, Autumn 1997.

Sullivan, K., 'Tijuana Gang Figure Held After Slaying of Journalist', *The Washington Post*, 26 June 2004, http://www.washingtonpost.com/wp-dyn/articles/A6989-2004Jun25.html (Accessed 28 June 2004).

Tabata, S., *Kokusai-hou shin-kou (Jou)*, 1990, Toushin-do: Tokyo.

Tackling Drugs, Out of crime, into treatment, http://www.drugs.gov.uk/WorkPage/DrugInterventionsProgramme/Otherstakeholder/CJIP_ForTheCourts.pdf (Accessed 20 February 2005).

Tajfel, H., *Social identity and intergroup relations*, 1982, Cambridge: Cambridge University Press.

Tammen, M.S., 'The Drug War VS. Land Reform in Peru', *Cato Policy Analysis*, No. 156, 10 July 1991, http://www.cato.org/pubs/pas/pa-156.html (Accessed 20 May 2003).

Tandy, K.P., *United States Efforts to Combat Money Laundering and Terrorist Financing*, Before the US Senate Caucus on International Narcotics Control, 4 March 2004.

Taylor, C., Testimony at Joint hearing before Congress, *International Terrorism, Insurgency, and Drug Trafficking: Narcotic Trafficking, Terrorism, and Political Insurgency*, 14 May 1985, United States Senate, Committee on the Judiciary and Committee on Foreign Relations.

Taylor, R., 'Rebels Kidnap Colombian Presidential Candidate', *The Guardian*, 25 February 2002, http://www.guardian.co.uk/informer/story/0,1191,657897,00.html (Accessed 20 February 2002).

Terriff, T., Croft, S., James, L., Morgan, P.M., *Security Studies Today*, 1999, Polity Press: Cambridge.

Text: Rep. Gilman Urges European Cooperation in Drug Control Efforts, 21 February 2001, http://usinfo.state.gov/topical/global/drugs/01022310.htm (Accessed 8 May 2002).

The Andean countries benefit from the EU's 'Drugs' Generalised System of Preferences (GSP), http://europa.eu.int/comm/external_relations/andean/intro/index.htm (Accessed 25 August 2002).

The Bureau of International Narcotics and Law Enforcement Affairs, *International Narcotics Control Strategy Report 1998*, http://www.state.gov/www/global.narcotics_law/1998_narc_report/samer98.html (Accessed 28 January 2000).

The Bureau for International Narcotics and Law Enforcement Affairs, *International Narcotics Control Strategy 2002*, March 2003, http://www.state.gov/g/inl/rls/nrcrpt/2002/html/17944.htm (Accessed 12 August 2003).

The Commission on Narcotic Drugs, *World drug situation with regard to drug trafficking: report to the Secretariat, the United Nations, Economic and Social Council*, Vienna: The United Nations.

The EU Delegation to Colombia, *La CE confirma interés en un segundo laboratorio de paz en Colombia*, 15 May 2003, http://www.delcol.cec.eu.int/es/novedades/boletin_32.htm (Accessed 15 January 2004).

The EU's priorities for future drugs cooperation in Latin America, 6838/98 DG H II, Brussels, 12 March 1998.

The European Commission, *Conclusions of the Second Institutionalized Ministerial Meeting Between the European Community and the Rio Group*, Held in Santiago de Chile no 28 and 29 May 1992, 7111/92 (Press 108), Santiago, 29 May 1992.

The European Commission, *COM (1997) 670 final*, Luxembourg: Office for Official Publications of the European Communities.

The European Commission, *Andean Community: Indicative Multiannual Guidelines*, 12 March 1998, Brussels, IB/1038/98.

The European Commission, *COM (1999) 239 final*, Luxembourg: Office for Official Publications of the European Communities.

The European Commission, *Rural Development Policy and Strategic Framework: Bolivia Pilot Study*, October 2000, http://europa.eu.int/comm/development/rurpol/outputs/bolivia/bolivia.pdf (Accessed 12 January 2002).

The European Commission, *The EU and Latin America: The Present Situation and Prospects for Close Partnership 1996-2000*, pp. 10–14, http://europa.eu.int/comm/dg1b/pol_proentations/den_com95945.htm (Accessed 28 October 2001).

The European Commission, *Communication from the Commission on Conflict Prevention, COM (2001) 211 final*, 11 April 2001, Brussels.

The European Commission, *3ʳᵈ meeting of the Support Group of the peace process: Donor's concluding statement*, 30 April 2001, http://europa.eu.int/comm/external_relations/colombia/3msg/concl_state.htm (Accessed 20 February 2003).

The European Commission, *AL-Investment*, http://europa.eu.int/comm/europeaid/projects/al-invest/index_en.htm (Accessed 25 August 2002).

The European Commission, *The EU international policy on drugs*, July 2003, http://europa.eu.int/cgi-bin/etal.pl (Accessed 9 January 2005).

The European Commission, *A Secure Europe in a Better World: European Security Strategy*, 12 December 2003, Brussels: The European Community.

The European Council, *Community Regulation (EC) No. 2046/97 of the Council*, 13 October 1997.

The European Council, *Economic and Financial Affairs Budget*, 26 November 2001, Press: 424, No. 14157/01.

The European Council, *Economic and Financial Affairs Budget*, 11 December 2002, Press: 390, No. 15373/02.

The European Council, *Economic and Financial Affairs Budget*, 24 November 2003, Press: 331, No. 14939/03.

The European Council, *Economic and Financial Affairs Budget*, 26 November 2004, Press: 322, No. 14617/04.

The European Union, *A Secure Europe in a Better World: European Security Strategy*, 12 December 2003, Brussels.

The European Union, *Schengen Treaty Free Movement of Persons within the European Union*, http://europa.en.int/en/agenda/shengen.html (Accessed 3 November 2004).

The General Secretariat, 'Cocaine: European 'drug of the year' ', 1989, *International Criminal Policy Review*, May–June.

The International Institution of Strategic Studies, *The Military Balance 2002-2003*, 2002, Oxford: Oxford University Press.

The National Treatment Agency for Substance Misuse, *National Programme Funding*, 18 October 2004, http://wwwnta.nhs.uk/programme/national/funding_intro.htm (Accessed 20 February 2005).

The United Kingdom Harm Reduction Alliance, *Submission to The Home Affairs Select Committee on the Government's drug policy*, July 2001, http://www.ukhra.org/statements/select_committee.html (Accessed on 2 March 2005).

The United Nations Charter.

The United Nations Convention against Transnational Organized Crime and its Protocols, 2000, http://www.unodc.org/unodc/en/crime_cicp_convention.html (Accessed 1 June 2004).

The United Nations, *United Nations Convention against Illicit Traffic in Narcotic Drugs and Psychotropic Substances*, 1988.

The US Department of State, *A Report to Congress on United States Policy Towards Colombia and Other Related Issues*, 3 February 2003, http://www.state.gov/p/wha/rls/rpt/17140pf.thm (Accessed 16 May 2003).

The US National Security Council, *U.S. National Security Strategy: Prevent Our Enemies From Threatening Us, Our Allies, and Our Friends with Weapons of Mass Destruction*, June 2001, http://www.state.gov/r/pa/ei/wh/15425.htm.

The US National Security Council, *The National Security Strategy of the United States of America*, September 2002, Washington DC: The White House, http://www.whitehouse.gov/nsc/nss.html (Accessed 28 February 2003).

The US Office of National Drug Control Policy, *President's National Drug Control Strategy*, March 2004, http://www.whitehousedrugpolicy.gov/publications/policy/ndcs04/message.html (Accessed 31 May 2004).

The White House, *A National Security Strategy of Engagement and Enlargement*, February 1995.

The White House, *National Drug Control Strategy 2002*, February 2002, Washington DC: Government Printing Office.

Thomas, G.B., *Balance in Theory But Not in Practice: Exploring the Continued Emphasis on Supply Reduction in Canada's National Drug Control Policy*, http://www.johnhoward.ca/document/drugs/forum/1.htm (Accessed 31 May 2004).

Thompson, T., 'Corrupt police split reward cash with fake informants', *The Observer*, 17 December 2000.

Thompson, T., 'Deadly cargo', *The Observer*, 21 April 2002.

Thompson, T., 'Hull is Britain's new drug capital', *The Observer*, 12 May 2002.

Tinkner, A.B., 'Tensions Y Contradicciones en los Objectivos de la Política Exterior Estadounidense en Colombia: Consecuencias involuntarias de la política antinarcóticos de Estados Unidos en un Estado débil', *Revista Colombia Internacional*, No. 49/50, Parte II, http://www.lablaa.org/blaavirtual/colinter/arlene2.htm (Accessed 13 November 2003).

TNI, *Alternative Development and Eradication: A Filed Balance, Drug and Democracy Programme*, TNI Briefing Series, No. 2002/4, April 2002, Amsterdam: Transnational Institute.

Tokatlián, J.G., 'National Security and Drugs: Their Impact on Colombian-US Relations', *Journal of Interamerican Studies and World Affairs*, Vol. 30, No. 1, Spring 1988.

Tonry, M. and Wilson, J.Q. (eds), *Drugs and Crime: Crime and Justice: A Review of Research*, 1990, Chicago: The University of Chicago Press.

Toro, M.C., *Mexico's 'War' on Drugs*, 1995, Lynne Rienner: London.

Transparency International, *Transparency International Corruption Perceptions Index 2004*, 2004, Berlin: Transparency International.

Transparency International, *Transparency International Global Corruption Barometer 2004*, 2004, Berlin: Transparency International.

Treaste, J.B., 'US Gives Wrong Equipment to Fight Drugs, Bogota Says', *New York Times*, 12 September 1989.

Treaster, J., 'Jamaica, Close US Ally, Does Little to Halt Drugs', *New York Times*, 10 September 1984.

Trimbos-institut, *The Netherlands: Drug Situation 2000*, 2000, REITOX REF/2000, http://www.emcdda.org/multimedia/publications/national_reports/ NRnetherlands_2000.PDF (Accessed 14 March 2003).

Tuckman, J., 'Mexican town falls victim to its own drug trade', *The Guardian*, 30 March 2000, http://www.newsunlimited.co.uk/international/story/0,3604,153554,00. html (Accessed 20 February 2003).

Tullis, L., *Unintended Consequences: illegal drugs & drug policies in nine countries*, 1995, Colorado: Lynne Rienner.

Turenne-Sjolander, C., and Cox. W., *Beyond Positivism: Critical Reflections on International Relations*, 1994, Boulder, CO: Lynne Rienner.

UK National Criminal Intelligence Services, *United Kingdom Threat Assessment of Serious and Organised Crime 2003*, 6.8, http://www.ncis.ao.uk/ulta/2003/ threat06.asp (Accessed 22 February 2005).

Ullman, R., 'Redefining Security', *International Security*, Vol. 8, Summer 1983.

UN Office for Drug Control and Crime Prevention, *The United Nations Convention against Transnational Organized Crime*, 2000, http://www.unodc.org/palermo/ convmain.html (Accessed 1 June 2004).

UN Office for Drug Control, *World Drug Report*, 1997, http://www.unodc.org/ adhoc/world_drug_report_1997/CH4/4.6.pdf (Accessed 21 February 2005).

UN Office on Drugs and Crime, 'Is the international community meeting its drug control targets?' *Update 2003*, http://www.unodc.org/unodc/en/newsletter_2003- 03-31_1_page004.html (Accessed 31 May 2004).

UN Office on Drugs and Crime, *An Overview of the UN Conventions and the International Standards Concerning Anti-Money Laundering Legislation*, February 2004, http://www.imolin.org/Overview.pdf (Accessed 1 June 2004).

UN Office on Drugs and Crime, *Support to operational capacities: Office of National Alternative Development Plan (PLANTE)*, http://www.unodc.org/unodc/en/ alternative_development_database_03.html (Accessed 12 March 2005).

UNDCP, *Technical Series Report No. 6, Economic and Social Consequences of Drug Abuse and Illicit Trafficking*, 1998, New York: UNDCP.

United Nations Drug Control Policy, *Report on the Economic and Social consequences of drug abuse and illicit trafficking*, 1997, New York: United Nations Drug Control Policy.

United Nations Drug Control Policy, *World Drug Report 1997*, 1997, Oxford: Oxford University Press.

United Nations Drug Control Policy, *World Drug Report 2000*, 2000, Oxford: Oxford University Press.

United Nations Drug Control Policy, *Global Illicit Drug Trend 2001*, 2001, New York: United Nations Drug Control Policy.

UNODC, *Global Illicit Drug Trends 2003*, 2003, Vienna: UNODC.

UNODCCP, *Global Illicit Trends, 1999*, New York: UNODCCP.

US Commission on National Security, *Seeking a National Strategy: A Concert for Preserving Security and Promoting Freedom*, 2000, www.nssg.gov/PhaseII.pdf.

US Department of Justice, *Audit report: Asset forfeiture program - Annual financial statement*, 1995, Washington DC: US Department of Justice.

US Department of State, *International Narcotics Control Strategy Report 1985*, 1985, Washington, DC: US Department of State.

US Department of State, *International Narcotics Control Strategy Report 1995*, March 1996, http://www.hri.org/docs/USSD-INCSR/95/OtherUSG/DEA.html (Accessed 15 August 2003).

US Department of State, *International Narcotics Control Strategy Report 1999*, March 2000, http://www.state.gov/g/inl/rls/nrcrpt/1999/903.htm (Accessed 15 August 2003).

US Department of States, 'Fact Sheet: The USAID/Colombia Casa de Justicis National Program', *Washington File*, 31 August 2000, http://usinfo.state.gov/regional/ar/colombia/fact3004.htm (Accessed 17 February 2000).

US Department of State, *Fact Sheets: USAID Supports Alternative Development in Bolivia and Peru*, 24 June 2002, http://usinfo.state.gov/topical/global/drugs/02062402.htm (Accessed 4 July 2003).

US Department of State, *International Narcotics Control Strategy 2002*, March 2003, http://www.state.gov/g/inl/rls/nrcrpt/2002/html/17944.htm (Accessed 14 August 2003).

US Drug Enforcement Agency, *Fact 2: A balanced approach of prevention, enforcement, and treatment is the key in the fight against drugs*, http://www.usdoj.gov/dea/demand/speakout/02so.htm (Accessed 31 May 2004).

US General Accounting Office, *Border Control: Drug Interdiction and Related Activities Along the Southwestern US Border*, GAO/GGD-88-124FS, September 1988, Washington DC: GAO.

US General Accounting Office, *Drug Control: US-Supported Efforts in Colombia and Bolivia*, Report to the Congress, November 1988, Washington DC: GAO.

US General Accounting Office, *US-Mexican Border: Issue and Challenge Confronting the US and Mexico*, GAO/NSIAD-99-190, July 1999, Washington DC: GAO.

USAID, *Bolivia: Activity Data Sheet, CBJ FY2002: Bolivia*, http://www.usaid.gov/pubs/cbj2002/lac/bo/511-005.html (Accessed 4 July 2003).

USAID, *Data sheets in Peru*, 2003, http://www.usaid.gov/country/lac/peru.pdf (Accessed 20 May 2003).

USAID, *Evaluation of Alternative Development Strategy in the Andes and Bolivia Program Challenge*, USAID-INL Briefings, 17 January 2003, PowerPoint Document, obtained during an interview at USAID on 28 May 2003.

USINL, *Report on Issues related to the Aerial Eradication of Illicit Coca in Colombia*, September 2002, http://www.state.gov/g/inl/rls/rpt/aeicc/13242pf/htm (Accessed 16 May 2003).

Vaicius, I., and Isacson, A., 'The 'War on Drugs' meets the 'War on Terror'', *International Policy Report*, February 2003.

Vaicius, I., and Isacson, A., ''Plan Colombia': The Debate in Congress', *International Policy Report*, December 2000, http://www.ciponline.org/colombia/aid/ipr1100.pdf (Accessed 29 October 2003).

Valencia Tovar, A., 'A View from Bogotá', *Plan Colombia: Some Differing Perspectives*, July 2001, http://www.carlisle.army.mil/ssi/pubs/2001/pcdiffer.pdf (Accessed 16 May 2003).

Van Creveld, M., *The Transformation of War*, 1991, Free Press: New York.

Van de Velde, J.R., 'The Growth of Criminal Organizations and Insurgent Groups Abroad due to International Drug Trafficking', *Low Intensity Conflict & Law Enforcement*, Vol. 5, No. 3, Winter 1996.

van Doorn, J., 'Drug Trafficking networks in Europe', *European Journal on Criminal Policy and Research*, 1993, Vol. 1, No. 2, p. 101.

van Duyne, 'Organized crime, corruption and power', *Crime, Law & Social Change*, Vol. 26, No. 3, 1997.

van Rheenen, S., 'Plan Colombia Divides Europe and US', *Radio Netherlands Wereldomroep*, 1 March 2001, http://www.rnw.nl/hotspots/html/colombia010302.html (Accessed 30 October 2003).

Vargas M.R., *The New Global Era: Threats and Impacts for Colombia*, December 2001, http://www.ciponline.org/colombia/121302.htm (Accessed 12 October 2003).

Viano, E.C. (ed.), *Global Organized Crime and International Security*, 1999, Aldershot: Ashgate.

Viceprecidencia de la Republica de Colombia, *Panorama Actual del Magdalena Medio*, May 2001, Bogotá, http://www.derechoshumanos.gov.co/observarotio/04_publicaciones/04_03_regiones/magdalenamedio/cap2.htm (Accessed 21 January 2004).

Viceprecidencia de la Republica de Colombia, *Panorama Actual del Putumayo*, May 2001, Bogotá, http://www.derechoshumanos.gov.co/observarotio/04_publicaciones/04_03_regiones/putumayo/violenci.htm (Accessed 26 January 2004).

Wæver, O., 'Securitization and Desecuritization', in Lipschutz, R.D. (ed.), *On Security*, 1995, New York: Columbia University Press.

Wæver, O., Buzan, B., Kelstrup, M., and Lemaite, P., with Carlton, D., *Identity, Migration and the New Security Agenda in Europe*, 1993, London: Pinter.

Wagstaff, A. and Maynard, A., *Economic aspects of the illicit drug market and drug enforcement policies in the UK*, Home Office Research Study 95, 1988, London: HMSO.

Walfers, A., *Discord and Collaboration: Essays on International Politics*, 1962, Baltimore.

Walker III, W.O., 'US Narcotics Foreign Policy in the Twentieth Century: An Analytical Overview', in Perl, R.F. (ed.), *Drugs and Foreign Policy*, 1994, San Francisco: Westview Press.

Wallerstein, I., *The Politics of World Economy: The States, the movements and the civilizations*, 1984, Cambridge: Cambridge University Press.

Walt, S.M., 'The Renaissance of Security Studies', *International Studies Quarterly*, 1991, Vol. 35, No. 2.

Walters, J.P., *Fact Sheet: Drug Treatment in the Criminal Justice System*, March 2001, Washington DC: ONDCP, p. 2, http://www.whitehousedrugpolicy.gov/publications/factsht/treatment/index.html (Accessed 20 February 2005).

Waltz, K., *Man, the State and War: A Theoretical Analysis*, 1959, New York: Columbia University Press.

Waltz, K., *Theory of International Politics*, 1979, New York: McGraw-Hill.

Wankel, H.D., *DEA Congressional Testimony*, Money Laundering by Drug Trafficking Organizations, before the House Banking and Financial Committee, 20 February 1996, http://www.usdoj.gov/dea/pubs/cngrtest/ct960228.htm (Accessed 20 February 2003).

Washimi, K., *ODA (The reality of ODA projects)*, 1989, Tokyo: Iwanami.

Washington Office on Latin America, *Drug, Democracy and Human Rights: US Law Enforcement Overview 2002: Colombia*, http://www.wola.org/publications/ddhr_law_enforcement_overview_colombia.htm (Accessed 18 January 2005).

Weale, A., *The New Politics of Pollution*, 1992, Manchester: Manchester University Press.

Webb, J., 'Dead Man Tells of Colombian Cocaine Culture', *Reuters*, 7 February 2004, http://www.washingtonpost.com/wp-dyn/articles/A21290-2004Feb7.html (Accessed 9 February 2004).

Weinberg, B., *Special Report: Cimitarra Valley, Colombia*, 4 September 2003, http://colombia.indymedia.org/news/2003/09/5565.php (Accessed 29 October 2003).

Weiner, T., and Golden, T., 'Bill to Combat Drug Traffic Caught in Lobbying Battle', *New York Times*, 4 November 1999, http://www.nytimes.com/library/world/americas/110499drug_sanctions.html (Accessed 4 November 1999).

Weisman, A., 'The Cocaine Conundrum', *Los Angeles Times Magazine*, 24 September 1995, http://www.worldcom.nl/tni/drugs/links/lt950924.htm (Accessed 15 May1998).

Wendt, A., *A Social Theory of International Politics*, 1999, Cambridge: Cambridge University Press.

Westrate, D., 'Remarks', in *Caucus on International Narcotics Control of the United States Senate*, The Congressional Research Service, 8 May 1987, Washington DC: GPO.

Wharton, C.R. (ed.), *Subsistence Agriculture and Economic Development*, 1969, Aldine Press.

White House, *National Drug Control Strategy*, September 1989.

White House Office of Press Secretary, *Statement by the Press Secretary: Annual Presidential Determinations of Major Illicit Drug-Producing and Drug-Transit Countries*, White House Press Release, 31 January 2003, http://www.state.gov/g/inl/rls/prsrl/17092.htm.

White, B., Little, R., and Smith, M. (ed.), *Issues in World Politics* (Second Edition), 2001, Basingstoke: Palgrave Macmillan.

Wight, M., *Power Politics*, 1995, Leicester: Leicester University Press.

Wight, M., *Systems of State*, in Bull, H. (ed.), Leicester: Leicester University Press.

Wilhelm, C.E., 'A View from Washington', *Plan Colombia: Some Differing Perspectives*, July 2001, http://www.carlisle.army.mil/ssi/pubs/2001/pcdiffer.pdf (Accessed 16 May 2003).

Williams, J., *Waging the War on Drugs in Bolivia*, 20 February 1997, Washington DC: Washington Office on Latin America.

Williams, P., 'Transnational Criminal Organisation and International Security', *Survival*, Vol. 36, No. 1, Spring 1994.

Williams, P., and Black, S., 'Transnational Threat: Drug Trafficking and Weapons Proliferation', *Contemporary Security Policy*, Vol. 15, No. 1, April 1994.

Williams, P., and Savona, E.U., *The United Nations and Transnational Organized Crime*, 1996, Frank Cass: London.

Williams, P., 'Transnational Crime and Corruption', in White, B., Little, R., and Smith, M. (eds) *Issues in World Politics* (Second Edition), 2001, Basingstoke: Palgrave Macmillan.

Williams, T., *The Cocaine Kids: The Inside Story of a Teenage Drug Ring*, 1992, Cambridge, Mass.: Perseus Books.

Wilson, G.C., 'Chaney Pledges Wider War on Drugs', *The Washington Post*, 19 September 1989.

Wilson, S., 'In Colombia, Coca Declines But the War Does Not', *The Washington Post*, 21 December 2003, http://www.washingtonpost.com/wp-dyn/articles/A17533-2003Dec20.html (Accessed 13 February 2004).

Wisotsky, S., *Beyond the War on Drugs: Overcoming a Failed Public Policy*, 1990, New York: Prometheus Books.

WOLA, *Clear and Present Dangers: The US Military and the War on Drugs in the Andes*, 1991, Washington DC: WOLA.

WOLA, *Going to the Source: Results and Prospects for the War on Drugs in the Andes*, WOLA Policy Brief, 7 June 1991, http://www.lindesmith.org/news/news.html (Accessed 20 November 1999).

Woodiwiss, M., *Crime, Crusades and Corruption: Prohibitions in the United States, 1900-1987*, 1988, London: Pinter Publisher.

Woodiwiss, M., 'Crime's Global Reach', in Pearce, F. and Woodiwiss, M. (eds), *Global Crime Connections: Dynamics and Control*, 1993, London: Macmillan.

Worden, R.E., Bynum, T.S., and Frank, J., 'Police Crackdowns on Drug Abuse and Trafficking', MacKenzie, D.L. and Uchida, C.D. (eds), *Drugs and Crime: Evaluating Public Policy Initiatives*, 1994, Thousand Oaks, CA: Sage.

World Bank, 'Colombia: Development and Peace in the Magdalena Medio Region', *En Breve*, July 2002, No. 5.

Young, O., *International Cooperation: Building Regimes for Natural Resources and the Environment*, 1989, Ithaca: Cornell University Press.

Young, O., *Resource Regimes: National Resources and Social Institutions*, 1982, Berkley: University of California Press.

Young, O. (ed.), *The Effectiveness of International Environmental Regimes*, 1999, Cambridge: The MIT Press.

Young, O.R., 'Regime Dynamics: The Rise and Fall of International Regimes', *International Organization*, Vol. 36, No. 2, Spring 1982, p. 277.

Young, O.R., 'Regime dynamics: the rise and fall of international regimes' in Krasner, S.D. (ed.), *International Regimes*, 1983, London: Cornell University Press.

Young, O.R., 'Regime Effectiveness: Taking Stock', in Young, O.R. (ed.), *The Effectiveness of International Environmental Regimes*, 1999, Cambridge: The MIT Press.

Young, O.R., and Levy, H.A., 'The Effectiveness of International Environmental Regimes', in Young, O.R. (ed.), *The Effectiveness of International Environmental Regimes*, 1999, Cambridge: The MIT Press.

Youngers, C., 'The War in the Andes: The Military Role in US International Drug Policy', *Issues in International Drug Policy*, Issue Brief #2, 14 December 1990, Washington DC: Washington Office on Latin America.

Youngers, C., 'A Fundamentally Flawed Strategy: The US 'War on Drugs' in Bolivia', *Issue in International Drug Policy*, Issue Brief #4, 18 September 1991, Washington DC: Washington Office on Latin America.

Youngers, C., 'Coca Eradication Efforts in Colombia', *WOLA Briefing Series: Issues in International Drug Policy*, 2 June 1997, http://www.worldcom.nl/tni/drugs/links/guaiare.htm (Accessed 20 February 2003).

Zackrison, J.L. and Bradley, E., 'Colombian Sovereignty Under Siege', *Strategic Forum*, No. 112, May 1997, Institution for National Strategic Studies.

Zaitch, D., *Trafficking Cocaine: Colombian Drug Entrepreneurs in the Netherlands*, 2002, The Hague: Kluwer Law International.

Zalewski, M. and Enloe, C., 'Question about Identity', in Booth, K., and Smith, S. (eds), *International Relations Theory Today*, 1995, Cambridge: Polity Press.

Zengerle, P., 'Defendant vanishes in Miami lawyer's drug trial', *Reuters*, 17 July 1998.

Ziazo, A., 'Coca Farmers' Chief Could Lead Bolivia', *The Washington Post*, 11 July 2002, http://www.washingtonpost.com/wp-dyn/articles/A54044-2002Jul11.html (Accessed 11 July 2002).

Zimring, F.E., and Hawkins, G., *The Search for Rational Drug Control*, 1992, Cambridge: Cambridge University Press.

Zobel, R.W., *An Overview of the United States Sentence Guidelines*, from the public lecture organised by ACPF, UNAFEI, and JCPS on 10 February 1999 at the Ministry of Justice, Japan, http://www.acpf.org/Activities/Activities(Homepage3)/public%20lecture1999/SentenceGuidelines.html (Accessed 20 February 2005).

'7. Mafia, 1982-1988', *LutherBlissett.net*, http://www.lutherblissett.net/archive/078-08_it.html (Accessed 20 February 2005).

'All this and drugs', *The Economist*, 13 June 1998.

'Alternative Development Promotes Competitive Agroindustry', *Nuevo Gran Angular*, September 2001.

'Antidrug idea: more tests in U.S.', *The Miami Herald*, 28 November 2002, http://www. miami.com/mld/miamiherald/news/columnists/andres_oppenheimer/4622170. htm?template=contentModules/printstory.jsp (Accessed 1 November 2002).

'Bánzer sets record eradication target', *Latin American Weekly Report*, 1 June 1999.

'Bolivia requiere ayuda para salir de la crisis y pobreza', *El Diario*, 14 August 2003, http://www.eldiario.net/noticias/nt030814/3-07.html (Accessed 14 August 2003).

'Bolivia Seizes 2 Tons of Cocaine Meant for Spain', *Reuters*, 2 August 2003, http:// www.washingtonpost.com/wp-dyn/articles/A13626-2003Aug1.html (Accessed 4 August 2003).

'Bolivia seizes 5 Tons of Cocaine in Record Bust', *Reuters*, 3 August 2003, http:// www.washingtonpost.com/wp-dyn/articles/A16638-2003Aug3.html (Accessed 4 August 2003).

'Bolivia: Cocaleros destruyen centros de erradicación', *Noticias Paginadigital*, 4 April 2003, http://www.paginadegital.com.ar/articulos/2003seg/noticias10/blv4-4pl.asp (Accessed 4 July 2003).

'Bolivian Police Seize 2 Tons of Cocaine', *Associated Press*, 1 August 2003, http:// www.washingtonpost.com/wp-dyn/articles/A13626-2003Aug1.html (Accessed 4 August 2003).

'Cali Cartel: Do they really run the business?' *Latin American Regional Report: Andean group*, 29 June 1995.

'Colombia cumplir sus compromisos, dice C. Patten', *El Tiempo*, 18 January 2004.

Colombia: Cultivation and Marketing of Organically Grown Coffee, Document obtained at the Colombian Embassy in Brussels on 16 November 2001.

Colombia: European Union & Cauca Delegation, http://www.paxchristi.net/PDF/ LA4NL106.pdf (Accessed 31 October 2003).

'Colombia frustrated by EU aid', *BBC*, 28 March 2001, http://news.bbc.co.uk/1/hi/ world/americas/1246877.stm (Accessed 30 October 2003).

Colombia's House of Justice, http://www.restorativejustice.org/rj3/Feature/2003/ July/housesofjustice.htm (Accessed 17 February 2004).

'Colombian drug flights 'to resume'', *BBC*, 5 August 2003, http://news.bbc.co.uk/2/ low/americas/3127125.stm (Accessed 19 August 2003).

'Colombians bypass Plan Colombia', *Jane's Foreign Report*, 26 April 2001, http:// groups/yahoo.com/group/ColombiaUpdate/message/247 (Accessed 29 October 2003).

'Colombian poll win 'bought' by drug cartel', *Daily Telegraph*, 15 March 1994.

'Con un pie en avión de la DEA', *PostNuke*, 6 November 2004, http://www. diariooccidente.com.co/printarticle4939.html (Accessed 20 February 2003).

'Conflict Flares in the Bolivian Tropics', *Drug Policy Briefing*, No. 2 January 2002, Amsterdam: Transnational Institute.

'Council Regulation (EC) No 3294/94 of 22 December 1994', *Official Journal L 341*, 30/12/1994 P. 0007 – 0007, http://europa.eu.int/smartapi/cgi/sga_doc?sma

rtapi!celexapi!prod!CELEXnumdoc&lg=en&numdoc=31994R3294&model=gu ichett (Accessed 3 March 2005).

'Estado Unidos no da nada a cambio de erradicar la coca', *El Diario*, 14 August 2003, http://www.eldiario.net/noticias/nt030814/3_09ecn.html (Accessed 14 August 2003).

'EU to aid Magdalena Medio', *Inter Press Service*, 27 April 2001, http://groups. yahoo.com/group/ColombiaUpdate/message/247 (Accessed 29 October 2003).

'Exactly what impact do drug exports have on the Colombian economy?' *Latin American Regional Report: Andean groups report*, 29 June 1995.

'Golpe contra las redes de lavados de activos al servicio del narcotrafico', *El Espectador*, 16 January 2002, http://www.mindefensa.gov.co/prensa/temas/ narcotrafico (Accessed 18 January 2005).

'Growers dismayed by 5-year strategy', *Latin American Regional Group - Andean Group*, 27 January 1998.

'It's all in the price,' *The Economist*, 8 June 2002.

'NAO report links money-launderings to gambling', *VNU Network*, 14 January 2005, http://www.pcmag.co.uk/print/bf/1139158 (Accessed 21 February 2005).

'Peru: From Virtual Success to Realistic Policies?' *Drug Policy Briefing*, No. 3 April 2002, Amsterdam: Transnational Institute.

'Supreme Court Justice Lashes Student Challenging Drug Tests', *Boston Globe*, 20 March 2002, http://www.phs.bgsm.edu/sshp/rwj/GranteeResources/Newsreports/ 02march.htm.

'Text: DEA's Marchall Testifies on Law Enforcement Aspects of Plan Colombia', *Washington File*, 20 February 2001, http://usinfo.state.gov/regional/ar/colombia/ plan28c.htm (Accessed 18 January 2005).

'Text: U.S. and Colombia Authorities Deal Major Blow to Drug Traffickers', *Washington File*, 13 October 1999, http://www.fas.org/irp/news/1999/10/D13_ drugs20_usia.htm (Accessed 18 January 2005).

'Uribe defends security policies', *BBC News*, 18 November 2004 http://news.bbc. co.uk/2/hi/americas/4021213.stm (Accessed 9 March 2007).

'US Pressure forces minister to quit', *Latin American Andean Group Report*, 4 April 2000.

'US troops expelled', *International Herald Tribune*, 24 July 1992.

Appendix

List of Interviewees

The interviewees are listed in chronological order starting from the earliest interview to take place.

1. Police General, Embassy of Colombia, London, 14 January 2002.
2. Official in charge of Narcotics matters, Embassy of Mexico, Brussels, 15 January 2002.
3. K.H. Vogel, the European Commission, Brussels, 23 April 2002.
4. Official in charge of Andean Affairs, European Commission, Brussels, 24 April 2002.
5. Counsellor for Narcotics Affairs, US Mission to the European Union, Brussels, 25 April 2002.
6. Official in Andean Affairs, the European Commission, Brussels, 8 July 2002.
7. Official in charge of Alternative Development programmes, the European Commission, Brussels, 9 July 2002.
8. Official in charge of narcotics matters, Embassy of Colombia, Brussels, 10 July 2002.
9. J. Vos, European Council, Brussels, 11 July 2002.
10. Colombian Desk officer, the European Commission, Brussels, 15 January 2003.
11. EU Desk officer, the US Department of State, Washington DC, 27 May 2003.
12. Colombian Desk officer, the US Department of State, Washington DC, 27 May 2003.
13. Mexican Desk officer, Office of National Drug Control Policy, Washington DC, 28 May 2003.
14. Colombian Desk officer, Office of National Drug Control Policy, Washington DC, 28 May 2003.
15. Envoy of Coast Guard, Office of National Drug Control Policy, Washington DC, 28 May 2003.
16. Envoy of Drug Enforcement Agency, Office of National Drug Control Policy, Washington DC, 28 May 2003.
17. Attaché (Counterdrug Issues), Embassy of Mexico, Washington DC, 29 May 2003.
18. Lisa Hagaard, Latin America Working Group, Washington DC, 29 May 2003.
19. Official in charge of narcotics matters, Embassy of Colombia, Washington DC, 30 May 2003.
20. Manager of Alternative Development Unit, Inter-American Drug Abuse

Control Commission, The Organization of American States, Washington DC, 30 May 2003.

21. Eduardo Héctor Moguel Flores, Mexican Ministry of Foreign Affairs, Mexico City, 16 June 2003.

22. Official in charge of Latin American matters, the European Union Delegate to the United States of America, Washington DC, 30 July 2003.

Index

Due Date	Date Returned
NOV 1 6 2009	NOV 1 7 2009

www.library.humber.ca